BANKING REGULATION AND GLOBALIZATION

Banking Regulation and Globalization

ANDREAS BUSCH

OXFORD
UNIVERSITY PRESS

Great Clarendon Street, Oxford ox2 6DP

Oxford University Press is a department of the University of Oxford.
It furthers the University's objective of excellence in research, scholarship,
and education by publishing worldwide in

Oxford New York

Auckland Cape Town Dar es Salaam Hong Kong Karachi
Kuala Lumpur Madrid Melbourne Mexico City Nairobi
New Delhi Shanghai Taipei Toronto

With offices in

Argentina Austria Brazil Chile Czech Republic France Greece
Guatemala Hungary Italy Japan Poland Portugal Singapore
South Korea Switzerland Thailand Turkey Ukraine Vietnam

Oxford is a registered trade mark of Oxford University Press
in the UK and in certain other countries

Published in the United States
by Oxford University Press Inc., New York

British Library Cataloguing in Publication Data
Data available
Library of Congress Cataloging in Publication Data
Data available

Typeset by SPI Publisher Services Ltd, Pondicherry, India
Printed in Great Britain
on acid-free paper by
the MPG Books Group

ISBN 978–0–19–921881–3

1 3 5 7 9 10 8 6 4 2

Contents

Foreword   ix
List of Figures   xi
List of Tables   xi

1. Introduction: Globalization and State Capacity   1
   1.1. The Central Question   5
   1.2. Theoretical Approaches   7
   1.3. Theory and Reality   11
   1.4. The Design of the Study   12
   1.5. The Plan of the Book   20

2. The State and the Regulation of the Banking Sector   23
   2.1. Why the Banking Sector is Special   23
   2.2. State Regulation of the Banking Sector   26
   2.3. The Challenges of Last Three Decades   28

3. The United States: Deadlock Through Fragmentation   33
   3.1. Historical Background   34
      3.1.1. The Establishment of the Banking System   34
      3.1.2. Development of State Regulation   37
      3.1.3. The Political Context Until 1970   42
   3.2. The Challenges   43
   3.3. The Policy Network   45
      3.3.1. The American Banking Industry   45
      3.3.2. The Regulatory Agencies   49
      3.3.3. The Legal Framework   55
   3.4. The Battle for Reform   55
      3.4.1. The First Phase of Deregulation   57
      3.4.2. Legislative Deadlock and Administrative Action   59
      3.4.3. Legislative Re-Regulation   64
      3.4.4. Ratified Deregulation   66
   3.5. Characteristics of the Policy Field   67
      3.5.1. High Politicization   67
      3.5.2. Confrontational and Legalistic Policy Approaches   68
      3.5.3. Variety of Players   69

3.5.4. Circumventing Deadlock at the Administrative
        and Judicial Level   72
3.6. Summary: The American Case   72

4. The Federal Republic of Germany: Keeping the State at
    Arm's Length   75
4.1. The Historical Background   76
      4.1.1. The Establishment of the Banking System   76
      4.1.2. The Emergence of State Regulation   82
      4.1.3. Key Aspects of the Policy Field Until 1970   85
4.2. New Challenges Facing Bank Regulators   87
      4.2.1. Liberalization and Depositor Protection   87
      4.2.2. Left- and Right-Wing Critiques of the
              "Power of the Banks"   89
4.3. The Policy Network   91
      4.3.1. The German Banking Industry   91
      4.3.2. The Regulatory Agencies   95
      4.3.3. The Legal Framework   97
4.4. The Calm After the Storm: Continuity Rather than
      Fundamental Change   99
      4.4.1. The Herstatt Crisis and its Consequences   100
      4.4.2. Gradual Europeanization: Further Amendments
              to the KWG   111
4.5. Characteristics of the Policy Field   113
      4.5.1. Integration and Consultation   113
      4.5.2. Successful Policy-Outcomes   115
      4.5.3. Ongoing Debate about the "Power of the Banks"   117
      4.5.4. Institutional Continuity   118
4.6. Summary: The German Case   120

5. The United Kingdom: Late Codification, Early Reform   123
5.1. Historical Background   124
      5.1.1. Creation of the Banking System   124
      5.1.2. The Development of State Regulation   128
      5.1.3. The Policy Field Until 1970   130
5.2. New Challenges for Bank Regulators   131
5.3. The Policy Network   133
      5.3.1. The British Banking Industry   133
      5.3.2. The Regulatory Agencies   135
      5.3.3. The Legislative Process   139

5.4. The Interaction Between Crisis and Reform 141
    5.4.1. The Secondary Banking Crisis and Codification 141
    5.4.2. Johnson Matthey Bankers and Reform of the
            Regulation System 146
    5.4.3. BCCI and Barings Bank: Impulses for
            Fundamental Reform 149
5.5. Characteristics of the Policy Field 156
    5.5.1. Changes in the Style of Regulation 156
    5.5.2. Reactive Policy-making 158
    5.5.3. The Weak Role of Parliament 159
    5.5.4. The Easy Implementation of Fundamental Reform 160
5.6. Summary: The British Case 160

6. Switzerland: High Risks, Joint Responsibilities 163
6.1. The Historical Background 164
    6.1.1. Formation of the Banking System 164
    6.1.2. The Development of State Regulation 169
    6.1.3. The Policy Field Until 1970 175
6.2. New Challenges for Bank Regulators 176
6.3. The Policy Network 177
    6.3.1. The Swiss Banking Industry 177
    6.3.2. The Regulatory Agencies 185
    6.3.3. The Legislative Framework 188
6.4. Liberal Consensus and Partial Politicization 190
    6.4.1. The "Chiasso Scandal" and the Politicization of
            Banking Issues 190
    6.4.2. Banking Problems in the 1990s 200
6.5. Characteristics of the Policy Field 206
    6.5.1. Consensual Approach 206
    6.5.2. Strong Self-Regulation 208
    6.5.3. "Autonomous Convergence" 208
    6.5.4. Specific Domestic Problems 209
6.6. Summary: The Swiss Case 209

7. State and Banking Regulation in Comparative Perspective 213
7.1. Policy Networks in Comparison 213
    7.1.1. Industry and Interest Groups 213
    7.1.2. The Executive Branch 215
    7.1.3. The Legislative Branch 216
    7.1.4. The Need for Reform and Policy Outcomes 218

7.2. Political Systems in Comparison   219
7.3. "Anglo-Saxon" and "Rhenish" Capitalism in Comparison   224

8. Conclusion: National Institutions as Filters of Globalization   227
8.1. Convergence or Divergence?   228
8.2. History, Institutions, and Path Dependence   234
8.3. The Case of the Missing Model   238
8.4. Conclusion   241

Postscriptum: The 2007/8 Subprime Mortgage Crisis and
Banking Regulation   245

Bibliography   257
Index   279

Foreword

Does globalization erode the nation state's capacity to act? Are nation states forced to change their policies even if this goes against the democratic will of their electorates? How does government action change under conditions of globalization? Questions like these have not only featured highly in political debates in recent years, but also in academic discourse.

This book seeks to contribute to that debate, both theoretically and empirically. The general question it addresses is whether globalization leads to policy convergence—a central, but contested topic in the debate, as theoretical arguments can be advanced both in favour of and against the likelihood of such a development. The book seeks to contribute to an answer by concentrating on a specific policy area and analysing that in detail across four countries and a twenty-five-year period. Its results cannot claim to answer the above general question comprehensively, but it is hoped that they contribute, together with similar studies of other countries and policy areas, towards the emergence of a detailed picture of the conditions nation states act under at the beginning of the twenty-first century.

Like most academic work, this book could not have been written without the help of numerous other people—who are, however, not responsible for my remaining errors in fact or judgement. My first debt of gratitude is to the many employees and representatives of the various supervisory agencies, ministries, industry associations, parliaments, and parliamentary support services that I interviewed and who granted me insight into their work as well as providing information. To all interview partners outside academia I promised—as is usual—complete anonymity, but the following list provides an overview of institutions and organizations I had contact with.

In the United States, I received help and information from the Board of Governors of the Federal Reserve System, the Federal Deposit Insurance Corporation, the Office of the Comptroller of the Currency, the Conference of State Bank Supervisors, the Senate Banking Committee, the House of Representatives Banking Committee, the American Bankers Association, and the Independent Bankers Association of America. In the United Kingdom, I found support at the Bank of England, H. M. Treasury, the Financial Services Authority, the British Bankers Association, and the House of Lords. In Switzerland, the Swiss National Bank, the Swiss Federal Banking Commission, the Swiss Bankers Association, and the Council of States provided information and help. And in Germany, interviews were conducted at the

Bundesbank, the Federal Banking Supervisory Office (now part of the Federal Financial Supervisory Office), the Federal Ministry of Finance, the Association of German Banks, the German Savings Bank Association, the Association of German Public Sector Banks, the National Association of German Cooperative Banks, and with members of the German Bundestag.

I am also grateful to a number of academic institutions that supported me in my work by offering hospitality and/or access to resources. In particular, I want to thank the Center for European Studies as well as the Widener Library and the Kennedy School of Government at Harvard University, the Institute of Political Science at Berne University, the Library of the Institute for World Economy of the University of Kiel, the Parliamentary Archive of the German Bundestag, and the Library of the London School of Economics. A special note of thanks goes to the Institute for Political Science at the University of Heidelberg; and at the University of Oxford, I am grateful to Nuffield College, St. Antony's College, and Hertford College as well as, in particular, the Department of Politics and International Relations for providing support for my research.

Personal thanks for help at various stages of the project go to Klaus Armingeon, Ernst Baltensperger, Klaus von Beyme, Sir George Blunden, Mark Bovens, Lord Burns, William Coleman, Abby Collins, Pepper Culpepper, Anne Deighton, John Flemming †, Robert Glauber, Charles Goodhart, Peter Hall, Maximilian Hall, Paul 't Hart, Friedrich Heinemann, David Hine, Christine Hirszowicz, Hans Hirter, Werner Jann, Reimut Jochimsen †, Peter J. Katzenstein, Dietmar K. R. Klein, Stephan Leibfried, Robert Litan, Wolfgang Merkel, David Miliband, Sofía Pérez, B. Guy Peters, Paul Pierson, Brian Quinn, Wolfgang Reinicke, Manfred G. Schmidt, Byron Shafer, Jürg Steiner, Bent Sofus Tranøy, Raymond Vernon †, Steven Vogel, Vincent Wright †, and Reimut Zohlnhöfer.

Research support over the years is gratefully acknowledged from Martin Höpner, Tobias Jakobi, Tobias Lenz, Alexander Petring, and Julia Spitze; thanks also to Alexander Clarkson who drafted the English versions of the case studies that had originally been written in German, and to Greg Jennings and Ross Wackett who provided excellent IT support.

At Oxford University Press, Dominic Byatt provided untiring and friendly support for the book, even if I stretched his patience somewhat. The delays were due to the arrival of Benedict, a joyful event that transformed Veronika's and my life. To him, who will never know a world without globalization, this book is dedicated.

Oxford/Bremen
February 2008   Andreas Busch

List of Figures

1.1. Publications per year on globalization, 1985–2004   5

2.1. The liberalization of capital movements, 1973–95   29

2.2. Growth of cross-border bank credits and loans, 1972–92 (in bn. US dollars)   30

3.1. Conflict formation in the financial sector by the end of the nineteenth century   42

3.2. Bank insolvencies per year, 1934–99   44

3.3. Overlapping jurisdiction in the regulation of different types of banks   54

4.1. External shocks and domestic reactions in banking regulation policy, 1973–99   112

8.1. Typology of possible policy outcomes   229

List of Tables

1.1. Political and economic characteristics of the countries covered   18

2.1. Costs of banking crises in per cent of GDP   31

3.1. Number of American retail banks, 1934–93   46

3.2. Indicators of American retail banks, 1979–94   47

3.3. US federal banking supervision agencies and their responsibilities   53

3.4. Selection of important American banking laws   58

4.1. Banking industry sectoral market share, 1957–97   92

6.1. Banking employment as share of total workforce (in per cent, 1994)   164

6.2. Market share of Swiss bank groups, 1880   167

6.3. Market share of Swiss banking sectors (by balance sheet), 1930–98 (in per cent)   178

6.4. Number of institutions in each banking sector, 1973–98   179

7.1. State banking regulation: The case studies in comparison   220

1

Introduction: Globalization and State Capacity

Does globalization erode the nation state's capacity to act? Are nation states forced to converge in their policies even if these should not correspond to the democratically expressed will of their electorates? How does government action change under conditions of globalization? Questions like these have featured highly not only in public political discussions in recent years, but also in academic discourse, prompting a multiplicity of contributions to a debate that is still ongoing. This book aims to make a further contribution to this debate by focusing on a specific policy area and tracing and analysing developments there comparatively across four countries and an extended period of time. Its results make no claim to provide a general answer to the questions above; however, it is hoped that—taken together with those of similar studies in different policy areas, countries, and time spans—they may contribute to the mosaic that will ultimately give us a differentiated picture of the conditions under which politics, governments, and states act at the beginning of the twenty-first century.

The questions at stake are of central importance to the academic disciplines of comparative political science and comparative public policy, but they also touch the heart of modern democratic statehood as it has developed since the Second World War. The territorially based, democratically legitimated state that took on the tasks of welfare provision and provision for macroeconomic stability sees its capabilities potentially eroded—crucial capabilities such as the one for resource extraction to finance the wide-ranging responsibilities which also contribute centrally to its legitimacy. The concept of the "modern" or "Westphalian" state that had been crystallized by scholars such as Max Weber and Otto Hintze in the early twentieth century had emerged (above all in Europe) since the seventeenth century.[1] It conceived of the nation state as "an alliance of the people into a unit capable of action" (Hintze 1970: 485), whose central characteristic was sovereignty, defined by Hintze as "independence

---

[1] More precisely: since the Westphalian Peace which in 1648 ended the Thirty Years War. On a "History of Statehood" see the comprehensive study by Reinhard (1999).

from the outside and a monopoly of power within" (ibid.: 478).[2] This def-inition, however, no longer complies with the realities of statehood in the developed liberal democracies of today. Pluralist and corporatist develop-ments have exacerbated the trend towards differentiation within the state, and increasing trans- and supranational linkages have replaced sovereignty with interdependence. As a consequence, the "post-war settlement" of the "golden age" is being challenged, as states struggle to find resources in the face of tax competition, set binding rules under conditions of increasing inter- and supranational legal norms, and provide material security for their citizens while losing influence on business decision-making (Leibfried and Zürn 2005; Hurrelmann et al. 2007).[3] While the lowering and even abolition of tariff barriers has enabled states and their citizens to enjoy the fruits of growing welfare through increased economic exchange, the lowering and abolition of the borders of statehood that go with it may also have altered the situation for states and citizens alike, increasing vulnerability to outside influences beyond their control. Unable to protect its citizens, the state's legitimacy may be threatened in the medium and long run. But decoupling from the economic integration that has been growing over the last couple of decades and that has now literally spread around the globe would be no less costly economically and politically—if it were feasible at all.

Much of the public and academic debate around these issues is linked to the term "globalization". It has undergone an amazing career over the last two decades. There hardly seems to exist a facet of public life that cannot be linked to this term: be it domestic conflicts regarding the need for political reforms and the necessity of redesigning social security systems; structural economic change and the shift of economic power to the emerging economies of South and Southeast Asia; debates about the fairness of global trade or its increasing de-materialization; the threat to cultural diversity presented by global media power and tourism—all that is mentioned in one breath with "globalization", even if that link is often more one of mashing things together than providing proper explanation.

Given how often it is used, it may not be surprising that the term is also contentious. Some have called it a "key concept" for analysing the present social and political condition, while to others it seems a myth; and yet again others ask for the justification of talking of "globalization" when developments and change in reality vary quite a lot around the globe.

---

[2] All translations from German, except where otherwise indicated, are by the author.

[3] It should be noted that most of the literature in the debate referenced here focuses on the challenges to the state from outside. Challenges from within that emerge through developments of the welfare state undermining the rule of law (Grimm 1990) or changes in administrative practices that blur state accountability (Schuppert 1999) are far less integrated into the general debate on changing statehood.

We might also not be surprised to find that there is no agreement on the definition of what constitutes globalization. Some examples may serve to illustrate that:

- "Globalization, simply put, denotes the expanding scale, growing magnitude, speeding up and deepening impact of transcontinental flows and patterns of social interaction." (Held and McGrew 2002: 1)
- "[G]lobalisation means the partial erasure of the distinctions separating national currency areas and national systems of financial regulation." (Strange 1995: 294)
- "Globalisation of industry refers to an evolving pattern of crossborder activities of firms involving international investment, trade and collaboration for purposes of product development, production and sourcing, and marketing. These international activities enable firms to enter new markets, exploit their technological and organisational advantages, and reduce business costs and risks. Underlying the international expansion of firms, and in part driven by it, are technological advances, the liberalisation of markets and increased mobility of production factors." (OECD 1996: 9)
- "Globalization refers to a world in which, after allowing for exchange rate and default risk, there is a single international rate of interest." (Brittan 1996)
- "A social process in which the constraints of geography on social and cultural arrangements recede and in which people become increasingly aware that they are receding." (Waters 1995: 3)
- Globalization is "action at distance". (Giddens 1994: 4)

Globalization, we can conclude, is no clearly defined concept, and, as the aforementioned examples demonstrate, its use in that long debate has varied from concentration on specifically economic phenomena to very general social effects on a global scale. Beyond the very general insight that globalization denotes a continuing process of accelerated and deepened economic, but also general social, interaction on a global scale between formerly politically independent units (from which mutual influence follows), little agreement exists concerning the characteristics of globalization. Whether it constitutes a process of a historically new quality or not; whether states caused it or whether markets are the dominant actors; whether the economic, the social, or the political sphere is the main area of concern; whether it is a development to be applauded or to be contested—all these questions remained unanswered.

While this may initially be a cause for puzzlement to the uninitiated, the lack of a generally accepted definition can also be regarded as a precondition for the astonishing success and the career of the term globalization. For it allows countless actors and positions a common, if vague, point of reference. Throughout academia, scholars from a huge variety of subjects have therefore contributed to the debate on globalization, especially from the areas of

- international relations (e.g. Holm and Sorensen 1995; Clark 1999; Lawson 2002),
- comparative political economy (e.g. Berger and Dore 1996; Garrett 1998; Hays 2003),
- international political economy (e.g. Strange 1986; Schirm 2002; Rupert and Solomon 2006),
- political theory (e.g. Gray 1998; Kagarlitsky and Clarke 1999; Pensky 2005),
- sociology (e.g. Waters 1995; Goldthorpe 2002; Savage et al. 2005), and
- economics (e.g. Rodrik 1997; Aharoni and Nachum 2000; Glyn 2006).

The astonishing productivity of this debate[4] has produced a remarkable output of printed matter from this academic growth industry. As Figure 1.1 demonstrates, book and article publications discussing globalization show a steep upwards trend over the last 15 years, and only recently seem to stabilize on a high level—at (according to the database used) about 1,000–1,200 publications per year.[5]

Predecessors to this great globalization debate can be found in a number of areas.[6] Sociological theories of differentiation and modernization have argued, starting with Comte and Durkheim in the nineteenth century, that the processes of individualization, secularization, and rationalization would ultimately move societies into a unitary direction; discussions in international relations theory have acknowledged for some time that "interdependence" (Cooper 1968; Keohane and Nye 1977) would bid the model of nation states as key actors in international relations goodbye and that new transnational actors such as multinational corporations would contribute to the creation of "turbulence" (Rosenau 1990); and lastly, scholars in both international

---

[4] The list put forward here aims to give only a few landmark studies and is exhaustive with regard to neither authors nor subjects. Besides the various facets of the social sciences, philosophers, geographers, lawyers, management theorists, and historians have also contributed to the discussion of globalization (see the references in Busch 2000: 23ff.).

[5] The figure is derived from data of three bibliographic databases which were queried for the title words "globalisation", and "globalization", respectively. They are the *International Bibliography of the Social Sciences* (IBSS) as well as the databases "WorldCat" (books) and "ArticleFirst" (journal articles) of the Library of Congress. Originally conducted in August 2001, the dataset was updated in September 2005 for the years ranging from 2001 to 2004.

[6] I have made this argument in greater detail in Busch (2000: 25ff.) which also provides data on empirical indicators of globalization. See also Busch (2007*b*).

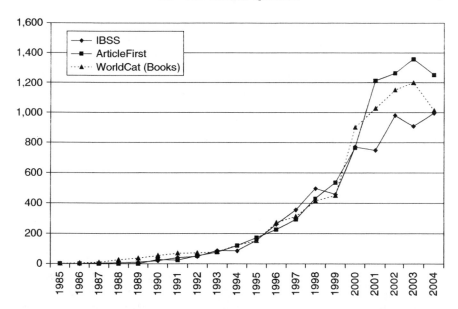

Figure 1.1. Publications per year on globalization, 1985–2004

relations and comparative government have debated the relationship between domestic and foreign policy and concluded that, rather than imposing an artificial separation between the two fields, both the "domestic sources of foreign policy" (Rosenau 1967) and the "international sources of domestic politics" (Gourevitch 1978) need to be analysed.

1.1 THE CENTRAL QUESTION

Given the multiplicity of inputs that have contributed to it, and the great variety of subjects and intellectual traditions, the diversity of the globalization debate mentioned above becomes perhaps less surprising. It also now becomes clearer why very different associations to this term exist, and that it must seem doubtful whether a common definition of it can ever be agreed on. In the past, a number of attempts have been made to categorize the contributions and thus facilitate a more structured debate. But here again, no general agreement could be found either: positions were grouped into the categories hyperglobalist, sceptic, and transformationalist (Held et al. 1999); liberal, sceptic and moderate (Busch 2000); liberal, social democratic, and rejectionist (Sally 2000); and globalist and sceptic (Held and McGrew 2000).[7] A common thread running through these different classifications, however, is that the main dividing line separating positions is the question whether globalization is perceived as an event that fundamentally alters the conditions states act under or not. It is this question—does globalization diminish the nation state's capacity to act?—that has been identified as the central focus of the whole debate by a number of authors (Berger 2000: 52; Gourevitch 2002: 313; Zürn 2002: 240) and is thus a consensus that has been emerging in this multifaceted debate in recent years. But whether this capacity to act is indeed under threat (and what consequences this would have for the self-conception of democratic governance) is again contested.

Those who see the state's capacity to act threatened by globalization emphasize that conditions for economic policy have changed substantially over the course of the last three decades. After the Second World War, controls over movements of currency and goods had allowed the state to siphon off rents from capital owners to finance public and welfare state spending (Scharpf 1996). After the breakdown of the Bretton Woods system of fixed exchange rates and the demise of currency controls, however, states lost command over the setting of domestic interest rates to the international financial markets and had to yield to their "tyranny" (Eichengreen 1997). In the sphere of fiscal policy, the state's room for manoeuvre was also strongly curtailed, since globalization enforced a shift of taxation from the (highly mobile) factor, capital, to the (less mobile) factor, labour. As a consequence, it was argued, states were faced with the unpalatable choice between either running permanent public deficits or facing a decline in international competitiveness due to excessive labour costs. Deregulation and transnationalization further reduced the capacity for active state policy, and in terms of welfare state measures, globalization would lead to cut-throat competition and a "race to the bottom". Consequently, authors arguing for this position spoke of the "erosion" of the nation state (Hilpert 1994), its "retreat" (Strange 1996), or even its "end" (Ohmae 1995).

The line of argument advanced by supporters of the "globalism" thesis was, however, contested by a string of authors and from a variety of perspectives. Some pointed out that markets required a strong regulatory state in order to function well, and that therefore the demise of the state was neither likely nor in the interest of the markets (Boyer and Drache 1996). Besides this more theoretical argument, authors of a more empirical persuasion also

---

[7] The semantics are sometimes puzzling here, since the frequently used term "sceptic" can refer to both the consequences of globalization (especially as far as state capacity is concerned) and to the validity of the globalization hypothesis. On the importance of discourse in the globalization debate see also Hay and Rosamond (2002).

questioned the decline scenarios of the globalists. They emphasized that the development over the last decades was not as unique as claimed, and that global economic integration was at a similar level at the beginning of the twentieth century (Hirst and Thompson 1996). A number of studies also questioned whether the restriction of state capacity was quite as drastic as sometimes stated: they found that tax competition between states, caused by globalization and international capital mobility, were not quite as pronounced and negative as expected, and that therefore neither were the consequences for welfare systems. Rather, it was argued, these systems demonstrated a remark-able degree of resilience and a capacity for adaptation, and party political preferences for taxation and redistribution could still be implemented (Garrett 1998; Swank 2002). Furthermore it could be shown that the costs of welfare state interventions in the economy through taxation were often balanced by positive externalities such as a high level of social stability and a well-trained workforce—and that these advantages were also recognized and appreciated by the owners of highly mobile capital. As a consequence, authors from this group have tended to see state capacity in a more positive light, spoken of "new tasks" for the state (Sassen 1998) and declared the thesis of the powerless state a "myth" (Weiss 1998).

1.2 THEORETICAL APPROACHES

But in order to analyse globalization beyond the merely descriptive, a theoret-ical basis is needed from which the relationship between increasing globaliza-tion and the effect this has on state capacity can be modelled. Contributions to the debate are often defective in this respect, implicitly making assumptions about theoretical relationships, but not discussing them openly. Basically, two theoretical approaches can be used in this context, both ultimately resting on different strands of economic theory. However, they lead to opposite predic-tions regarding the reactions of developed industrial societies to the challenges of increasing economic integration. One predicts a trend towards policy con-vergence, the other a scenario of stable or even increasing diversity of policies. State capacity (understood here mainly as policy self-determination) would be expected to shrink under the former scenario, while it would not be affected in the latter.

Theoretical considerations postulating a trend of convergence of state action are rooted, on the one hand, in the theory of international trade, and on the other hand, in theories of interjurisdictional or intergovernmental competition. The first approach builds on the factor-proportion theorem (also known as the *Heckscher–Ohlin* theorem) and posits a relationship between a country's factor endowment and the structure of its foreign trade linked to differences in comparative costs. According to this, a country will tend to export goods with whose production factor it is relatively abundantly endowed, while it will tend to import such goods whose production factors are relatively scarce at home. The reason is that a relative abundance in capital will cause the capital-abundant country to produce capital-intensive goods more cheaply than a labour-abundant country. Building on this standard economic theory, Ronald Rogowski some time ago developed a political science model to explain the emergence of societal cleavages (Rogowski 1989). Starting from rather simple assumptions about the domestic political process[8] and with the help of the *Stolper–Samuelson* theorem,[9] Rogowski was able to put forward hypotheses about the effects of increasing economic openness in order to explain the different political developments, coalitions, and cleavages in late nineteenth-century Britain, Germany, and the United States. In work done collaboratively with Jeffry Frieden, Rogowski undertook a—plausible—extension of this model to the process of globalization (Frieden and Rogowski 1996). The authors strove to explain the policy preferences of the relevant domestic actors, the policies carried out, and the development of national political institutions, claiming that the power of an interest group to assert its preferences varies with its mobility—or rather that of its factor of production. An interest group that can more credibly threaten to *exit* will increase its negotiation power and will thus have its preferences implemented into policy. Globalization will therefore lead to government policy adapting to the interests of capital owners (the most mobile factor of production), and since this adaptation will take place everywhere, policy convergence is the result.

The second approach focuses on government action under conditions of competition and arrives at similar conclusions.[10] The fundamental assumption is that governments compete for mobile capital (which looks for the highest net yield). This leads to an equalization of net yields across countries

---

[8] Rogowski (1987: 1123) merely makes two—rather undemanding—assumptions:

1. Those who profit from change will try to push it, while the losers will try to stop or delay it.
2. Citizens who benefit materially now or in the future are able to extend their political influence.

[9] This theorem also comes from the theory of international trade and is concerned with questions of gains and losses from free trade and protectionism. It posits that the owners of (compared to other countries) domestically *scarce* factors of production will *profit* from *protectionism*, while they will lose from free trade. Conversely, the owners of domestically *abundant* factors will *profit* from *free trade*, while they stand to lose from a protectionist trade regime (cf. Rogowski 1987: 1122).

[10] Kenyon (1997) provides an overview of theories of interjurisdictional competition.

and tax competition between states trying to provide the best business environment.[11] The degree of competition depends on the mobility of all factors of production. But it is not only the extent of taxation that influences yield expectations of capital—labour, social, and environmental regulations also play a part in this competition. Since regulations impose costs, firms will try to minimize such costs. Therefore (and with the same logic as in the case of taxation) equalization will be the result in these areas as well. Which direction this competitive equalization between states will take—a "race to the bottom" with a downward spiral of regulatory intensity and a convergence on the smallest common denominator, or a "race to the top" with escalating regulation as a consequence of competition—depends on a variety of factors and is not relevant in the present context.[12]

In conclusion we can say that while the models outlined in the preceding paragraphs differ with respect to their precise mechanisms, they posit the same effect of growing economic integration on domestic policy: either through a change in the domestic balance of power or through direct change in government policy, a convergence of policies and institutions will result from the change in external economic circumstances.

Quite the contrary development as the consequence of external change is what other theoretical approaches would lead us to expect, which focus on the stability of specific national characteristics. According to these theories (which give special emphasis to differences in policy styles, the resilience of institutional arrangements, and the path dependence of decisions more generally), continued or even increased diversity of policy outputs and institutional structures will be the likely result.

One of the first analyses to take such a perspective was probably Andrew Shonfield's book on "Modern Capitalism" (Shonfield 1965). Shonfield explained in his extensive empirical analysis the differences in economic policy between the United States, France, Britain, and the Federal Republic of Germany primarily with reference to the different attitudes with which national political and economic actors approached the economy. These attitudes, Shonfield stated, were largely based on culturally specific orientations deeply rooted in the national history. While differences between them were often small and diffuse, over time they amounted to a significant order of magnitude.

---

[11] See the survey of the respective literature provided by Schulze and Ursprung (1999).

[12] See for this the seminal work by Vogel (1986). Illustrations of the (in Vogel's terms) "Delaware effect" (race to the bottom) and "California effect" (race to the top) in different international attempts at cooperation can be found in Genschel and Plümper (1997), who also outline the conditions under which each of the two is likely.

Translating these diffuse differences into more manageable variables in the area of policy-making and policy implementation has been the merit of the concept of national "policy styles" (Richardson, Gustafsson, and Jordan 1982; see also Vogel 1986). These national policy styles differ on the one hand on the dimension of problem-solving, and on the other hand with respect to the relationship between government and the other actors in the decision-making process. While the former can be either anticipatory or reactive, the latter can be consensual or impositional (Richardson 1982: 13). These distinctions result in a typology of national policy styles which have (in addition to institutional factors) a significant influence on policy. Attitudes and orientations, more generally cognitive aspects and "ideas", thus play a significant role in the nationally specific approaches and implementations of policy.[13]

Especially implementation is an area in which national policy styles show great perseverance, as studies of public administration have shown:

Policy styles and policy networks in public administration are firmly rooted in nationally specific legal, political and administrative institutions which are the result of long historical processes and show great stability over time. Most of these institutions are linked to each other in one way or another which further stabilizes them.

(Waarden 1993: 206)

Institutional stability is therefore high and cannot be easily changed through shifts in political power:

[T]o portray political institutions simply as an equilibrium solution to the conflicting interests of current actors is probably a mistake. Institutions are not simply reflections of current exogenous forces or micro-behavior and motives. They embed historical experience into rules, routines, and forms that persist beyond the historical moment and condition.   (March and Olsen 1989: 167f.)

Under conditions of such stability we would also expect increases in international integration to induce no major changes, with respect to both institutions and policy content: "Given this strong rootedness, these institutions are not easily changed and with them national regulatory styles.", (Waarden 1995: 362).

The most general and perhaps theoretically most sophisticated form of this argument can be found in the concept of path dependence which is derived from the transaction cost and institutional school of economics.[14] This

---

[13] On the role of ideas in policy-making see, e.g. Braun and Busch (1999).

[14] An overview is Williamson (1994). Douglass North describes the attractiveness of the concept of path dependence as follows: "The promise of this approach is that it extends the most constructive building blocks of neoclassical theory—both the scarcity/competition postulate and incentives as the driving force—but modifies that theory by incorporating incomplete

approach describes how processes can over time (through positive returns to scale, network externalities, and feedback effects) achieve highly stable equilibria (*lock-in*) where the cost of fundamental change is prohibitively high and such change, accordingly, very rare. Economic models of that ilk have in the past been used to explain technological developments and decisions about the location of industries,[15] and have recently been successfully applied to political science topics, with a special focus on the dynamics that increasing returns to scale and self-reinforcing processes have on social interaction.[16] Political decisions, according to this line of argument, carry a substantial historical legacy which consists of past political investments and decisions that severely limit choice in the present. By raising the cost of path change, this also contributes to the stability of the originally chosen path. In addition, the disproportionate importance of changes at an early stage is being emphasized, as is the existence of "critical junctures".[17] Seen from such a perspective, one would expect states to further pursue their historically developed paths even under conditions of increasing international integration, thus leading not to convergence, but to constant and perhaps even increasing diversity of political and policy decisions.

1.3 THEORY AND REALITY

As the previous sections have demonstrated, expectations both of convergence and of diversity in the debate about globalization and its effects can put convincing and coherent theoretical models forward in their favour. There is thus no solution to be found for the dispute on the theoretical level alone, and empirical studies have to try to resolve the issue.

It is, however, no simple task for empirical studies to adjudicate between the rival approaches. One reason is that the globalization debate began to focus

information and subjective models of *reality* and the increasing returns characteristic of institutions" (North 1990: 112).

[15] Cf. Arthur (1989); Krugman (1991).   [16] Cf. Pierson (2004).

[17] Some examples from prominent political science contributions may serve to illustrate these mechanisms. The work of Stein Rokkan (2000) about the comparison of European societies, for example, demonstrates that small differences in starting positions can yield substantial differences over longer periods of time, while Putnam (esp. 1993: 179–81) shows the same for the comparative study of sub-national units. The importance of critical junctures and the stability of structures once they have been established is also evident in the development of European party systems. While fundamental social cleavages initially triggered the founding of political parties, the ensuing development is marked by inertia which impeded the emergence of new parties and caused a "freezing" of the party systems along the cleavages of the early twentieth century (Lipset and Rokkan 1967).

on empirical testing only after some time. An initial wave of the literature—that popularized the term and put it on the academic agenda—took up relatively crude stances on globalization that today seem exaggerated both with respect to the positive (e.g. Ohmae 1990) and negative (e.g. Strange 1986) consequences of globalization. It was followed with some delay by a second wave which focused on the collection of empirical facts, which then allowed to critically examine the claims of the first wave (such as Hirst and Thompson 1996; Beisheim et al. 1999). Building on these data, a third wave of the literature then undertook the task of testing the claims of the existing theoretical positions and explaining in more detail the consequences of globalization. A host of detailed sectoral studies were undertaken by a variety of authors looking mostly at welfare state, macroeconomic, and regulatory policies, generally in comparative perspective. Results often pointed in the direction of "common challenges and diverse responses" (thus the title of Scharpf and Schmidt 2000), and so far provide little support for the strong convergence hypothesis which assumes that all countries will react in the same way. However, the results of these many studies are often complex and support neither of the two rival hypotheses fully, which indicates that the discussion is far from over. A recent survey of the field (Heichel, Pape, and Sommerer 2005) concludes that results vary strongly according to policy area, countries, and time period considered, and that it is often difficult to clearly categorize a process of convergence or diversity.

This book aims to make a contribution to this third wave of globalization literature by providing a detailed analysis of a specific policy area across four countries and an extended time span. It makes no claim to provide an answer to the questions of the globalization literature *pars pro toto*, but hopes that eventually a fourth wave of the literature will succeed in synthesizing the wealth of empirical material that emerged over recent years into a comprehensive and coherent picture of the globalization process. The following section explains the reasoning behind the choice of the policy area, provides case studies, and describes the period of investigation for this book.

1.4 THE DESIGN OF THE STUDY

There are a number of reasons that make the area of regulatory policy particularly interesting for testing hypotheses about globalization.[18] Regulatory

---

[18] On typologizing policies see, classically, Lowi (1964), who distinguishes between distributive, regulatory, and redistributive policies (he later adds constituent policy). Klaus von Beyme (1998: 5–7) forgoes this extension, but adds restrictive and extensive policy as well as protective

policy has received much attention in the last decade or so, and analysing it has been described by some scholars as the "leading edge of public policy-making in Europe" (Majone 1996: 47). More important, however (and a main reason for that recent interest), seems the fact that regulatory policy has over the last decades been replacing older forms of state intervention that were more geared towards distribution or redistribution and linked to the concept of the Keynesian welfare state (ibid. 54–6). This change of focus has had many reasons that cannot be explored here any further. But for the purpose of the present investigation, the area of regulatory policy has a number of specific advantages.

On the one hand, regulatory policy produces few costs—compared to dis-tributive policy and state-spending programmes—as the production of laws and rules is generally not very expensive. Similarly, monitoring compliance with these rules also requires little financial commitment, especially since these costs can often be imposed onto the regulated sector of the economy. As a result, regulatory policy will be largely unaffected by budgetary problems of a state, and if the latter vary across a group of states that are under investigation, the analysis will consequently not be distorted by this variation.[19]

Distributive policies are also more easily affected by inertia and path depen-dence, resulting in changes of course only having an effect in the medium term (Beisheim and Walter 1997). Regulatory policy is comparatively more "flex-ible", which should result in quicker reaction to changes in the environment. Pressure for policy convergence should therefore more quickly result in policy changes here than in other policy areas.

The concrete policy area of choice for this study is the field of banking regulation. In her path-breaking book about the comparative evolution of vocational training in four countries, Kathleen Thelen (2004: xi) apologizes that some of her readers might not find this "the most scintillating of topics", but hopes to convince them that the subject holds many valuable insights for political economy and comparative politics generally. The same, I would hope, applies to the field of banking regulation. While it may not seem to promise the most riveting of reads, it is, as I argue in the following section, very well suited to the analysis of the question at hand.

Past excursions by political scientists into this field have included both single-country case studies and comparative endeavours. In the former cat-egory, studies like those of Reinicke (1995) or Khademian (1996) have

policy, thus creating a sixfold typology. In his study, a regulatory sphere (characterized by sparing use of financial resources) is distinguished from a distributive sphere.

[19] Budgetary problems can not only arise in absolute terms, but can also be self-imposed, as the so-called Stability and Growth Pact in the European Union as well as its predecessor, the "Maastricht criteria" for membership in the European Monetary Union, illustrate.

dissected in great detail the intricate manoeuvres that take place when trying to substantially alter the regulatory balance in a policy area that is of great (not least material) importance to big financial interests and consumers alike. As readers of this book will come to appreciate after reading Chapter 3, it is probably no coincidence that it was the case of the United States that inspired the analyses of both books. Comparative analyses of the field include the studies by Pauly (1988) on "Banking Politics on the Pacific Rim" (tracing the domestic politics of opening banking markets across four countries) and the book by Coleman (1996) that analyses the impact of domestic politics on financial market regulation in North America and the European Union. Both studies are thus close to the concerns of this book in that they link domestic banking policy to developments in international banking markets, but predate it in fieldwork and analysis by ten to fifteen years.

During that time, financial markets have made further progress towards integration and globalization. Today one can argue that hardly anywhere else is reality so close to the idea of a 24/7-integrated global market.[20] Banks play a central role in this market, and it is the nature of the goods they trade that exposes them, in particular, to globalization, for they trade intangible assets like risk, time, and promises to pay (Baecker 1991) which have been very strongly affected by technological developments in computerization and telecommunications in the last decades. The emergence of new, "derivative" financial instruments[21] that have been facilitated by these technological developments has influenced discussions about changed risk structures on financial markets, especially since the trading volume of derivatives exploded in the span of only a few years.[22] The question of how these new risks could best be hedged in and handled put the issue of regulation very much on the agenda.

But the focus of this book is not on financial markets as a whole. Rather, it is specifically on the banking sector, for a number of reasons. On the one hand, financial markets fall into various sub-sectors (such as insurance, stock markets, and banking) which are regulated in quite different ways, requiring

---

[20] See, e.g. the respective assessments by Underhill (1991), Simmons (1999: 36), or Genschel and Plümper (1999: 255). See also Section 2.3 of this book.

[21] This class of financial instruments includes so-called options, forwards, swaps, futures, and warrants. They are named derivatives because their value is derived from the value of some underlying variable, the so-called base. This base could be the price of a share or any other commodity, but just as well a price index, a specific interest rate, or an exchange rate. The value of the base at any given point in time determines the value of the derivative instrument. Derivatives largely developed in order to make increased market volatility and market risks tradeable and thus make them easier to handle.

[22] For empirical data on this, see, e.g. Beisheim et al. (1999), Busch (2000), or World Bank (2007: 30ff.).

a choice to be made. Analysis of the banking sector is particularly attractive as it has a number of characteristics that emphasize its political and macro-economic importance.[23] The regulation of the banking sector is therefore an important political topic in practically all countries, while that is much less the case in other financial sectors where important markets exist in only a few countries. But above all, banking systems have historically developed very differently in different countries (Pohl 1994). It has been argued that different trajectories of industrialization are the main determining factor for this (Gerschenkron 1966), and that industrial policy found greatly differing opportunities for intervention as a consequence (Zysman 1983). The same diagnosis is true for the sphere of state banking regulation: here as well, follow-ing from nationally specific experiences, very different solutions to the super-vision of the banking sector were developed, not least in institutional terms (Pecchioli 1987). Banking regulation as a policy area is thus characterized by a combination of high pressure for globalization and greatly differing national starting positions in both banking systems and state regulatory mechanisms. It is thus an excellent test case for theories of convergence through globalization.

For research into causal mechanisms in political science, different approaches exist. One focuses primarily on maximizing the number of obser-vations, most often by collecting data on as many countries as possible— a strategy suggested by Lijphart to escape the "many variables, small N" dilemma (Lijphart 1971: 686). Such a strategy will investigate correlations between macro-level statistical data and thus have to forgo causal investiga-tions for individual cases. Since the interest in this book is above all one in the precise country-level processes, this is not a strategy suitable for the research question followed here. In addition, the dominance of said research approach has been mentioned critically in the past as a cause for the shortcomings in globalization-related research (cf. Beisheim and Walter 1997: 176; Bernauer 2000: 66).

The present study focuses instead on detailed case studies that will yield insights about the processes in individual countries. However, such an approach also comes at a cost, and that is a lower level of generalizability. But that trade-off between detailed knowledge and generalizability is the result of a conscious choice in research design. In choosing the United States, the United Kingdom, the Federal Republic of Germany, and Switzerland as cases, the book follows a "most similar systems" design in which countries have to display similarity in as many variables as possible in order to best isolate the variables causing differences in outcomes.[24] All four cases are

---

[23] Chapter 2 unfolds this argument in greater detail.
[24] Cf. Przeworski and Teune (1970: 51–3); Teune (1990: 45).

highly developed industrial democracies which have liberalized their capital markets at a comparatively early stage and have not pursued selective credit regulation policies as an instrument of economic policy.[25] In addition, they display considerable variation with respect to "classical" institutional variables in the political system (such as presidentialism versus parliamentarism; federalism versus centralism; two party versus multiparty systems; the presence or absence of constitutional judicial review; party political dominance; and European Union membership).

In addition to these political system-level variations, the countries covered also differ with respect to economic system-level variables. In this area, the past decade and a half has seen a number of contributions aimed at classifying different market economy systems (e.g. Porter 1990, Albert 1993, Soskice 1999, Hall and Soskice 2001*b*, Amable 2003).[26] The differences that this research has identified in the area of financial systems is of particular interest to the present study. While "liberal market economies" (LMEs)[27] have been characterized as "capital market dominated", "coordinated market economies" (CMEs) are "credit oriented".[28] The former are less risk-averse, but more short-term in outlook, resulting in looser relations between capital owners and firms (and a lower propensity to invest in intangible assets such as quality, R&D, and worker retraining); the latter take a more long-term view (with ensuing more stable relations between firms and capital owners), resulting in higher investments in intangible assests, but limiting firms' flexibility and access to capital (especially for small and medium enterprises). These brief remarks should suffice to point out the interrelations between the various dimensions of economic systems mentioned above. And they should make clear why changes in one part of the system can be expected to influence other parts through feedback effects—an aspect particularly important in the

---

[25] Countries which pursued such policies faced special problems when switching from protective credit allocation regimes to open and liberal models (see the studies on Sweden by Tranøy 2001 and on Spain by Pérez 2001); these could potentially have influenced the respective outcomes this study is particularly interested in.

[26] Although the approaches in the works cited vary substantially, nearly all draw the main line of distinction between the "Anglo-Saxon" countries and the rest. See in addition the contributions by De Jong (1995); Moerland (1995); Rhodes and Apeldoorn (1997).

[27] The terminology underlying Soskice's (1999; 2001*a*) analyses is largely being used for this area in the remainder of this study, both because it is particularly well-founded (it distinguishes four dimensions: the financial system; the system of labour relations; the worker training system; and the relations among firms), and because it has become widely accepted.

[28] To give an empirical example: in 1987, 99 per cent of the 400 biggest firms in the United States were listed on the stock market, while the average in the European Community was only 54 per cent (Moerland 1995: 18). Additional empirical information and a description of the different economic logics of action arising from these differences can be found in Canals (1997: chapter 2, esp. 43ff.).

context of the globalization debate. For it has been argued (by those who expect economic system differences to have a greater impact than political system differences) that the deregulated "Anglo-Saxon" model will be more stable and thus come to dominate the (mainly continental European) coordinated economies (Hollingsworth, Schmitter, and Streeck 1994; Streeck 1995; Dettling 1999).

Table 1.1 on the following page summarizes the countries' characteristics. It shows that we can separate the country sample along three axes:

1. *"Liberal"* (United States, United Kingdom) versus *"coordinated"* (Germany, Switzerland) market economies.[29] The members of each group match with respect to economic variables (type of market economy; type of financial system; type of banking system), but they differ in the majority of the political variables (type of political system; relationship between upper and lower chamber; EU membership and existence of judicial review). It is only on the party system variable that they agree within each group.[30]

2. *EU members* (Germany, United Kingdom) versus *non-EU members* (United States, Switzerland). Here group members differ in economic system variables, while with respect to political system variables we find both agreement (type of political system; relationship between upper and lower chambers; EU membership) and disagreement (party system; dominant party; existence of judicial review). This also separates the parliamentary (United Kingdom, Germany) from the presidential (United States, Switzerland) systems.[31]

3. Grouping the United Kingdom with Switzerland against the United States and Germany is the last possible pairing, and it correlates to Lijphart's "ideal types" and those in between. The distance between the ideal *consensus democracy* Switzerland and the ideal *Westminster democracy* United Kingdom is evident from the fact that they differ on all political (and economic) system variables save the absence of judicial review. It is interesting, however, that also the "in betweens", Germany and United States, only match on two variables (presence of federalism and judicial review) and differ on all other economic and political variables.

---

[29] In Albert's (1993) terminology, this would be "Anglo-Saxon" versus "Rhenish" capitalism.

[30] Since the differentiation between LMEs and CMEs also includes the characteristics of the system of interest representation, that matches, too. See the data in Lijphart (1999: 177).

[31] For the classification of Switzerland as presidential (since the executive cannot be dismissed by Parliament) see Steffani (1992) and Beyme (1999: 29, 53).

Table 1.1. Political and economic characteristics of the countries covered

	USA	GB	D	CH
Political system	Presidential	Parliamentary	Parliamentary	Presidential
Relationship upper and lower chamber	Symmetric	Asymmetric	Asymmetric	Symmetric
Constitutional Court	Yes	No	Yes	No
Territorial organization	Federal	Unitary	Federal	Federal
Dominant party, 1950–94 (Schmidt 1996)	Conservative	Conservative	Centrist	Liberal
Party system	Two party system	Two party system	Multiparty system	Multiparty system
EU member	No	Yes	Yes	No
Type of economy (Soskice 1999)	Liberal market economy (LME)	LME	Coordinated market economy (CME)	CME
Type of financial system (Cox 1986)	Capital market oriented	Capital market oriented	Credit oriented	Credit oriented
Type of banking system (Pohl 1994)	Separated banking system (political regulation)	Separated banking system (historical development)	Universal banking system	Universal banking system

The group of four selected countries thus shows a lot of variance despite the comparatively small number of cases observed. And with reference to the debate about the relative importance of political and economic system variables it will be interesting to see which of the two will prove more important in this study.

The period of investigation of the present study is the time from 1974 to 1999. It covers thus twenty-five years—a time sufficiently long to analyse banking regulation policy in detail in the countries covered. But the period is, above all, chosen for the events that happened in it: its starting point is a fundamental change in the global exchange rate system, namely the switch from fixed exchange rates (under the Bretton Woods system) to floating exchange rates. This altered parameters on world financial markets substantially, increasing both opportunities and risks, and thus constituted a major challenge to state regulation. One consequence was the setting up of the *Basle Committee* which attempted to coordinate regulation on the international level.[32] After many years of negotiations, 1988 eventually saw the agreement on the *Basle Accord* which contained regulations on banks' own capital requirements. In 1999, consultations started to bring about a "Basle II" agreement which would reshape and re-focus regulations, mainly through introducing risk-weighted measures, constituting a "regime change" (Goodhart, Hofmann, and Segoviano 2004: 613). Negotiations lasted until 2004 (with the Committee releasing a revised version of the new accord in November 2006), and implementation is still in the future in many countries.[33] In addition, 1999 saw the start of the third stage of European currency union with the introduction of the common currency, the Euro, which (besides many other things) has prompted cross-border bank mergers in the Eurozone. Whether the higher level of banking market integration introduced by these mergers, and the existence of a common currency will eventually lead to more common and unified banking regulation and supervision (either in the form of a common regulator or in the form of a harmonization of national supervisory regimes) remains to be seen. Both the start of the Basle II process and the introduction of the Euro, however, point to the fact that 1999 marks a substantial change. The period after that is best left to some future study analysing the processes once they will have run their course. The period of investigation covered in the present study therefore ends in 1999.

---

[32] A good analysis of that process can be found in Kapstein (1994).

[33] The European Union countries will implement it in 2008; in the United States, as in many other countries, implementation will only occur some time during the next decade.

1.5 THE PLAN OF THE BOOK

After the context and scope of the book have been set out in this introductory chapter, Chapter 2 provides a brief introduction into the peculiarities of the banking sector and the principal tools states have at their disposal for regulating it. It also addresses the challenges states faced in the period after 1973 when liberalization of capital and currency markets, computerization, and a telecommunications revolution fundamentally altered world capital flows, thus creating new banking opportunities and risks.

The four case studies which follow form the empirical core of the book. They follow the same structure for each country by providing a brief historical background for banking system and regulatory system, followed by a description of the specific new challenges, a description of the sectoral policy network, a narrative, and a concluding analysis. Chapter 3 argues that in the United States a political reform of the restrictive 1930s New Deal banking regulation largely failed in the 1980s and 1990s. Deadlock was caused by path-dependent "lock-in" even though there was, by and large, agreement on the necessity of change, as evidenced by the crisis of the Savings & Loans sector in the late 1980s. As Congress with its adversarial political style and many veto-players produced blockade, courts and regulatory agencies provided safety-valve functions in the system through reinterpretation of existing regulations. Chapter 4 argues that in Germany, a consultative, often informal, policy style and a high degree of both self-regulation and institutional continuity have contributed to a successful policy outcome with no major bank failures after the 1974 case of Herstatt Bank. This success, however, had its own costs as the administrative system was not forced to enhance state capacity in this area and thus found it difficult to project its interests onto the European and international level which both grew in importance. Chapter 5 argues that regulatory policy in the United Kingdom was largely characterized by reaction to crises in the banking sector (such as the *Secondary Banking Crisis* in the 1970s, the failure of *JMB* in the 1980s, and *BCCI* and *Barings* in the 1990s). A weak role for Parliament let the *Bank of England* initially dominate a "club-style" sectoral policy network. After repeated piecemeal reforms failed to provide long-term stability, however, the latter was disempowered in favour of a new unified financial regulatory agency, thus providing an example of major institutional change. Lastly, Chapter 6 argues that the consensual style that is generally characteristic for policy-making in Switzerland also applies to banking regulation and has produced a largely positive policy outcome in the face of a high potential risk caused by concentration of the banking system. The highly federal political system does, therefore, not lead to political deadlock, since a strong element of centralized self-regulation manages to balance the fragmentation. Influence of European regulations is considerable, however, despite being concealed in the euphemistic phrase "autonomous adaptation".

The concluding chapters of the book draw together the analyses and comparatively evaluate the findings. Chapter 7 compares the structures and outputs of the four policy networks, arguing that country-specific contingencies lead to different outcomes in the face of similar challenges during the period of investigation. In the United States, a pluralist system of associations in combination with a fragmented regulatory and legislative system leads to policy failure and blockade; in the United Kingdom, market concentration and a concentrated regulatory and legislative system create high state capacity despite a pluralist system of associations. In Germany, a concerted associational system is weakened by market fragmentation, but combined with concentrated regulation creates policy success; in Switzerland, a segmented but concentrated market combines with comprehensive concertation to create flexible adaptation with minimal resource requirements. Compared with these factors, standard political institutions (parliamentarism versus presidentialism; party system; unitary versus federalism) show little influence on their own, but a mediated one depending on context. Different "varieties of capitalism" show an influence through their differences in associational systems, but overall do not have much explanatory value, as the substantial differences between the two "Anglo-Saxon" cases of the United States and United Kingdom demonstrate. Finally, Chapter 8 evaluates the outcome of the study in terms of the competing hypotheses of policy convergence and diversity. It argues that a distinction between the dimensions of policy, politics, and polity helps to gain new insights here: while there is substantial, if far from perfect, convergence in the policy dimension (the content of regulation), no such effects can be found in the other two dimensions (the processes and institutional aspects of banking regulation). The chapter further advances hypotheses to explain the lack of institutional convergence and concludes by arguing that state capacity varies considerably in the field of banking regulation. National institutional situations thus function as filters of globalization, complicating outcomes beyond sweeping assessments of convergence or divergence.

2

The State and the Regulation
of the Banking Sector

This chapter is an introductory overview of state regulation in the banking sector. It describes some of the political and social challenges which have confronted policy-makers in the sector.

2.1 WHY THE BANKING SECTOR IS SPECIAL

Banks have become essential to the economic life of every modern society. A successful banking system has not only become crucial for the functioning of every business, it has also become central to the daily routine of most people. While the possession and use of a bank account still remained limited to the better off four or five decades ago, it has now become impossible to participate in the economic life of most industrialized societies without a bank account. Today, most people have a bank account with which they receive their salary, pay their bills, and invest their savings. This is particularly the case in modern, democratic, and industrialized nations—but not only there. As a result, the security of bank deposits has become a matter of great political and economic importance, with governments doing their best to ensure their security. This process shall be explored in greater detail below.

However, this section will first examine why the banking sector has attracted such a great amount of official attention. This has mainly been the result of factors specific to the banking sector:[1]

- First of all, banks provide all other parts of an economy as well as the consumers on which all businesses ultimately depend with credit. An efficient and well-performing banking sector is therefore fundamental to the health of any economy.
- Secondly, the banking industry is one of the most vulnerable parts of the modern economic system. The collapse of a bank has a very different and

[1] On this, see Baltensperger (1988) as well as the economics literature cited below.

often much deeper impact than the failure of firms belonging to other sectors of the economy. While the bankruptcy of a company normally benefits other companies in the same industry by giving them an opportunity to take over its customer base, the collapse of a bank can seriously damage its competitors. The constant flow of capital from financial institution to financial institution has created a high level of interdependence within the finance and banking sectors. A bank unable to live up to its financial commitments can therefore cause serious difficulties and disruption for the rest of its industry. Moreover, the reaction of a wider public often unable to differentiate between "good" and "bad" banks to a major bank collapse or banking scandal can lead to a so-called "bank run". Such a massive withdrawal of money from accounts by normal consumers is likely to have knock-on effects on "healthy" banks, since the liquidation of an "unhealthy" bank's assets and liabilities (a process which in itself can incur heavy losses) is neither a quick nor an easy process.

All things considered, the collapse of a bank can have catastrophic consequences for an entire banking industry and even a country's economic performance as a whole. Moreover, the credit system could come under threat in such a situation, leading to potentially crippling financial and ultimately social turmoil.

Economic theorists have recognized both the special position of the banking industry and the need to treat the problems banks face differently from those of other parts of the economy.[2] Of particular interest to economists have been those aspects of banking policy involving access to information and institutional change. Banks can only play their crucial role as financial intermediaries if they enjoy the trust of their depositors. However, depositors have normally found it very difficult and often prohibitively expensive to acquire detailed information about the quality, solvency, and reliability of the assets of any bank. This has led to a relationship between banks and depositors shaped by what has become known as "asymmetric information": a situation where the former has considerably more information about the creditworthiness of the latter than the latter has of the former. Such asymmetry is particularly strong when it comes to the position of less well-informed consumers of deposit banking services. Since most depositors are aware of the underlying risks resulting from a business relationship based upon "asymmetric information", the collapse of a single bank can bring about the contagion or domino

---

[2] In the field of economics, the standard reference work on bank regulation is Dewatripont and Tirole (1994). A good overview of the core literature on this topic can be found in Canals (1997: chapter 11) and Goodhart et al. (1998: chapter 1). Studies of bank regulation in Germany can be found in Burghof and Rudolph (1996) and Waschbusch (2000).

effect described above. This process can often lead to deposit and liquidity losses that can do major damage to an economy.

In economic theory, state regulation of the banking sector has been justified by the need to prevent such external events from damaging banks and minimizing the effects a major banking crisis can have on the wider economy (Benston and Kaufman 1996). The need to maintain a competitive and stable economic market has also been used as an argument in support of state regulation of the banking sector (Goodhart et al. 1998: 4–9; OECD 1992: 31ff.). Yet controversy has continued to rage between economists over issues involving bank regulation.[3] One of the main reasons for this recurring debate is the fact that state regulatory agencies supervising the banking sector have failed to prevent banking scandals or bank collapses in several countries. In particular, bank crises in the United States in the 1980s and 1990s[4] as well as the Asian financial crisis of 1997[5] have attracted attention to the costs incurred by state regulation. Critics of current forms of oversight have also pointed to how regulatory structures can distort financial markets, which often try to anticipate state intervention in the banking industry. Sceptical economists have emphasized the fact that the very existence of state regulatory bodies often hampers competition for customers, thus making it more difficult for individual depositors to find more efficient alternatives to their own banks. Some economic theorists have even recommended that national and international bank regulation systems should either undergo a fundamental process of reform or be entirely dismantled.[6] The current system of deposit insurance has come under especially heavy criticism for contributing to "moral hazard" behaviour,[7] as it can lower the incentive of banks to monitor the quality of their assets. Deposit insurance can also discourage depositors from gathering informing about the business conduct of their banks which may lead to failing loans and ultimately put the deposit insurance systems under heavy strain.[8]

---

[3] See, e.g. the debate between Dowd (1996) and Benston and Kaufman (1996).

[4] See Bonn (1998) and Chapter 3 of the present study.   [5] See Terberger-Stoy (2000).

[6] See Dowd (1996) or Knorr (1999). The complete elimination of all state regulation based on a blind trust of the market mechanism has been implemented in New Zealand. See Brash (1995) and McKenzie and Khalidi (1996: 642f.).

[7] The term "moral hazard" denotes the existence of certain behavioural incentives for individuals to achieve their own personal goals by incurring costs which they do not have to take responsibility for. Typical of this kind of dynamic are changes of behaviour conditioned by the possession of insurance. For example, the possession of insurance against theft tends to decrease an individual's willingness to secure his or her own property since any damages can be covered by the insurance policy. This can lead to "adverse selection" which seriously distorts the market mechanism. See Akerlof (1970).

[8] See Knorr (1999) as well as Zimmermann and Barbrock (1993) who focus on deposit insurance issues. A justification for the existence of deposit insurance schemes can be found in Zimmer (1993).

Despite such widespread reservations, the great majority of economists accept the necessity for deposit insurance and some form of state regulation of the banking sector. Many would probably agree with the pragmatic stance of two American experts in the field:

> We would prefer a world in which the government does not provide *de facto* or *de jure* deposit insurance. But, this is not the world in which we live.

(Benston and Kaufman 1996: 696)

Indeed, most states—who do not often pursue their actions in order to maximize economic efficiency—have largely ignored such economic advice and have given preference to political considerations.[9] The nature of such political factors will be briefly examined in the next section.

2.2 STATE REGULATION OF THE BANKING SECTOR

As we have seen, special circumstances have led governments to intervene regularly in the banking sector. In this context, two policy goals have been of particular importance:[10]

1. The instrumentalization of the banking system either to maintain control of monetary policy or to steer structural change through intervention in the credit allocation process
2. The protection of bank deposits in order to maintain the stability of the wider banking system and secure the investments of individual depositors

State institutions have used a wide variety of methods to achieve these goals, which are listed here in diminishing levels of intervention:

- The partial or complete nationalization of the banking system. This is often followed by direct intervention in the credit allocation process and coupled with an implicit state guarantee for all deposits.
- Intervention in the credit allocation process through legislative or administrative mechanisms. Such a policy approach is usually undertaken in

---

[9] As the historical sections of the following four case studies demonstrate, regulatory measures are usually only introduced in response to acute crises, where little time exists for rational debate about the pros and cons since the need for crisis management subsumes all other considerations.

[10] For further information on the following, see Busch (2001).

combination with state-backed redirection of financial resources into politically favoured sections of the economy.

- The introduction of controls on capital movement in order to ensure the success of the measures described above.

- The reduction of competitive risk through the introduction of a legally enforceable separation of commercial banks from their investment banks.

- The reduction of the level of business risk faced by banks through restrictions on the extent to which they can compete with one another. This is achieved by such measures as the establishment of strictly regulated cartels, geographic monopolies or maximum or minimum limits on debit and credit interest rates.

- The introduction of a system of general deposit insurance financed through set contributions made by each bank which can provide compensation to depositors who have suffered serious financial losses because of a bank collapse.

The manner in which governments have applied these different forms of state intervention varies from country to country. The extent to which these measures are implemented as well as the respective "policy mix" reflects the different political preferences of governments as they have developed over time. This process has resulted in a wide variety of nationally specific bank regulation systems. While macroeconomic factors have dominated the thinking of some governments (particularly as part of a wider Keynesian attempt to exert influence over the transmission mechanisms of monetary policy), in most countries the historical legacy of major banking crises as well as social concerns over the deposits of small investors have shaped banking policy.[11]

The reorganization of the international financial order after the Second World War had a major impact on these many different forms of bank regulation. Though this was accompanied by much rhetoric about the need for free trade, in reality, most governments did their best to shield their domestic financial markets from external competition. Controls over the movement of capital were used as a tool with which to steer domestic rates of interest. Such an approach was designed to provide the state with the means to both shape the development of its national economy and protect recently established welfare provisions from the risk of capital flight exacerbated by accompanying increases in rates of taxation (Helleiner 1994: 33ff.). While this "post-war settlement" had remained more or less stable during the 1950s and

---

[11] A detailed description of the different national forms of bank regulation in OECD countries can be found in Pecchioli (1989).

1960s—resulting in little pressure for reform—the economic and political turbulences of the 1970s put the international financial order under massive pressure.

2.3 THE CHALLENGES OF LAST THREE DECADES

The closed national capital markets of the post-war era, which had been an instrumental part of the international financial framework of the "Bretton Woods System", went through a comprehensive process of change in the course of the 1970s:

The internationalization and integration of capital markets has been the most significant change in the political economy of the industrialized countries over the past three decades. [...] No other area of the economy has been so thoroughly internationalized as swiftly as have capital markets since the 1970s.   (Simmons 1999: 36)

This process was initially triggered by the elimination of fixed exchange rates in 1973, fundamentally altering the structure of international financial markets. Simultaneously, the oil crises of 1973–4 and 1978–9 caused major recessions in most countries. The decrease in economic growth combined with a sharp rise in levels of unemployment and inflation, the disappearance of fixed exchange rates, and the sudden rise in oil prices, posed a massive challenge to the further survival of the international financial system. As a result, capital markets were liberalized to remove barriers to international trade, and many states started to dismantle controls over capital movements which had been based on the logic of a system of fixed exchange rates.[12] Though some countries implemented these reforms more quickly than others, almost all countries belonging to the OECD had dismantled any remaining legal or administrative impediments to the free movement of capital by the mid-1990s. Figure 2.1 demonstrates the progress of this liberalization process between 1973 and 1995.[13]

 These developments had a considerable impact upon international capital flows. Where bank loans to foreign clients had played a negligible role in the nationally oriented financial systems of the immediate post-war era, the

---

[12] A detailed analysis of this process, primarily driven as it is by political motives, can be found in Kapstein (1994).

[13] After Freitag (1999: 159). The calculations are based on the number of capital controls: the index reaches from 0 (totally closed economy) to 4 (complete lack of any limitations on capital movement). See also Simmons (1999: 42).

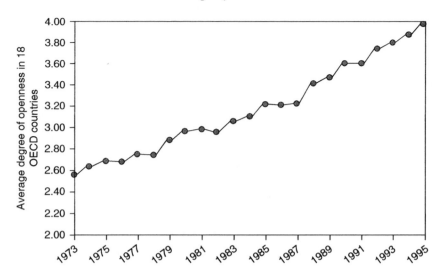

Figure 2.1. The liberalization of capital movements, 1973–95

volume of trading in the international loans market increased twenty-fold in the two decades after 1973 (see Figure 2.2).[14]

In the 1980s and 1990s, the speedy pace of innovation in the computer and telecommunications sectors spurred the development of ever more complex trading tools used by bankers and stock brokers, leading to further changes in the international economic system. Ironically, many of these technologically driven shifts in the operational approach approach of banks and other major financial players had their origin in efforts to decrease levels of risk in an increasingly volatile marketplace.

To sum up, in the last three decades of the twentieth century international financial markets have experienced revolutionary change. New business opportunities as well as new risks have emerged. In parallel, the level of competition in the banking industry has increased considerably while profit margins have shrunk.

Institutions responsible for bank regulation have been forced to deal with the challenge of adapting to new conditions in the marketplace. Since the circle of those who have a bank account has expanded from the upper levels of the social hierarchy in the 1950s to the great majority of the population today, the political importance of safeguards designed to protect depositors from the

---

[14] After Herring and Litan (1995: 26).

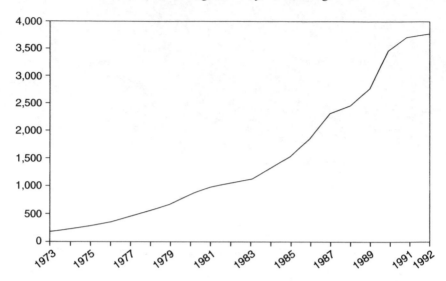

Figure 2.2. Growth of cross-border bank credits and loans, 1972–92 (in bn. US dollars)

consequences of a bank collapse has increased (Gardener 1992: 156).[15] By giving the banks new profit opportunities and simultaneously increasing the risks to which they are exposed, the failure of a bank regulator to exert the necessary level of oversight is much more likely to lead to a bank collapse with all the negative consequences this entails. The liberalization of the financial system and the regulation of the banking industry have thus become intextricably linked.

Not all state banking regulators have been able to cope with these new challenges, a state of affairs which has led to bank collapses and sometimes even the destabilization of entire banking systems. The International Monetary Fund claims that over two thirds of its 181 members have suffered problems with their banking systems (Lindgren, Garcia, and Saal 1996). Though the extent of these crises differs from case to case, at their worst they have inflicted enormous costs upon vulnerable economies.[16] The crisis of the local banking system in the United States has, for example, caused over $160 billion worth of financial damage, of which $130 billion was passed on to the taxpayer (FDIC 1997: 39). In terms of GDP, the impact of these crises on other countries has been even more financially crippling (see Table 2.1).

---

[15] See German case study below: especially Section 4.2.1.

[16] Further information about the wider international context can be found in Caprio and Klingebiel (1996) as well as Dziobek and Pazarbaşioğlu (1998) and in the appendix of Goodhart et al. (1998: chapter 1).

Table 2.1. Costs of banking crises in
per cent of GDP

USA	3.2
Finland	9.9
Spain	15.0
Chile	33.0

Source: Dziobek and Pazarbaşioğlu (1998: 4).

As such figures indicate, the success or failure of state regulators is not merely a technical matter. Rather, a functioning bank regulation system has a distributive element, since the bank collapses which it is designed to avert can cause considerable financial and social costs which the state, taxpayers, and individual depositors ultimately have to cover. The transition from heavily regulated and almost exclusively national markets to the internationally oriented, relatively open financial systems of the last thirty years has therefore posed a significant challenge to the ability of bank regulators' ability to achieve their stated aims.

However, as business uncertainty caused by technological innovation has grown, these shifts have also created considerable incentives for banks to maintain higher standards of probity. How the political systems of the United States, the Federal Republic of Germany, the United Kingdom, and Switzerland have coped with these challenges will be described and analysed in the following four case studies.

3

The United States: Deadlock Through Fragmentation

In the 1980s and 1990s, repeated attempts to modernize the bank regulation system ended in failure despite being declared a key strategic aim by successive American governments. Yet this was not the result of any limitations upon the state's capacity for action. Rather, the fragmented nature of state authority in the United States paralysed the ability of competing regulatory agencies to monitor and control the banking sector. Their failure was the product of domestic political factors instead of any shifts in the market created by greater international integration. Trying to prevent anything that might damage their own economic or political interests in an extremely complex political environment, an assortment of players hindered further progress by focusing on conflict rather than consensus. This, in short, is the main hypothesis of this case study.

Contrary to popular conceptions of economic life in the United States, American banks operate in a highly regulated business environment. The reasons for this are not just to be found in the depression of the 1930s, which had a traumatic effect on other banking systems as well; they stretch back as far as the late eighteenth century. Stretching back to the founding years of the United States, we find debates about the extent of state intervention in financial institutions and markets. This historical legacy has been a major ideological burden on the political process right up until the end of the twentieth century.

Despite the at times impenetrably complex nature of the bank regulation system, which, under the banners of liberalization, deregulation, and globalization, has undergone a massive process of change in the last few decades, several academics have produced extensive studies of its structures and development. With the work of bank regulators being of equal interest to legal experts, economists, and political scientists, the considerable amount of research work dealing with the state regulation of the banking sector is an indicator of the wider significance of the American case.[1] A comparative study

---

[1] Important studies in this field dealing with these issues include Cerny (1994), Reinicke (1995), Coleman (1996), Khademian (1996), Worsham (1997), and Bonn (1998).

can, of course, neither achieve these studies' level of detail nor can it aspire to be a full depiction of the American financial system in all its complexity. This is not the aim of this book in any case. The main focus of this analysis will therefore be upon the regulatory structures monitoring and controlling commercial banks and not upon those regulating depository institutions such as Savings & Loans firms or credit unions.[2] Even with these limitations, it is possible to show support for the hypothesis that in the American case, the ability of the state to intervene in the banking sector was severely limited by the fragmentation and diffusion of power inherent to the American political system.

This chapter will first examine the historical development of state policy towards the banking sector and its implications for the new challenges which have emerged in the last few decades. It will then describe the different private and state actors who have tried to exert influence over the bank regulation system. The final section will analyse the ongoing debate over the implementation of regulatory reforms of the banking system before looking at the defining characteristics of this policy field in the United States.

3.1 HISTORICAL BACKGROUND

This section will first sketch out the historical development of the banking sector together with the political and institutional context that had an impact upon the debates and decisions which shaped banking policy after the 1970s.[3]

3.1.1 The Establishment of the Banking System

Commercial banking only began to play a significant role in the American economy after the end of the War of Independence in 1783. As in the United Kingdom, most of the banks established in the late eighteenth and early nineteenth centuries were relatively small and geographically close to their customer base. The exceptions to this rule were banks and investment houses based in rapidly expanding cities. Yet the emerging American banking system was far less centralized than its British counterpart, in which the Bank of England (founded in 1694) played a central role. This was the consequence of

---

[2] A detailed description of the highly complex American financial system can be found in Baer and Mote (1992), Berger, Kashyap, and Scalise (1995), and Saunders and Walter (1994).

[3] The following section is based on information from Cerny (1994), Spahn (1990), Spong (1994), and Robertson (1995). A general overview can be found in Bonn (1998: 66–87).

the predominantly rural nature of early nineteenth-century American society combined with the weak role of the central government in Washington. The strength of populist movements, which exerted considerable influence over the structure of the banking industry because of their opposition to all forms of centralization, was also of great significance. After the first and second *Bank of the United States* (see below) failed to survive concerted opposition, the federal government abandoned attempts to establish either a central bank or any other form of bank regulation. Instead, the administrations of the 1830s adopted the "free banking" doctrine, which led to the devolution of responsibility for the banking sector to the individual states. In this, the federal government was following the lead of the legislatures of Connecticut, Michigan, and New York which had all passed "free banking" legislation. This allowed any man who fulfilled certain legal conditions and a loosely defined set of minimum business standards to open a bank.[4] In this way, then, the states simply established a legal framework rather than a detailed system of licensing and regular oversight.

Since the states were responsible for bank licensing, they did their best to limit the area in which their banks could operate to inside their own state boundaries. As a corollary of this, state governments introduced other restrictive practices designed to limit growth such as a ban on the establishment of branches. This resulted in a large number of very small banks. Since these banks issued their own legal tender, the value of banknotes fluctuated considerably from region to region, depending on such factors as time of issue, the reputation of the issuing bank, and its distance from the place in which its banknotes were being used. Nevertheless, with the economy being highly localized during the early and mid-nineteenth century, such anomalies did not cause any major problems for either businesses or private citizens.

The sudden upsurge in industrialization and continental trade after the late 1840s increased demand for a uniform national currency. Yet it took the financial pressures created by high levels of military expenditure during the Civil War to bring about the necessary majorities in the House of Representatives and Senate to pass the National Currency Act of 1863 and the National Bank Act of 1864. This legislation enabled the federal government to establish a framework for a national banking system underpinned by a uniform currency and a licensing scheme overseen by the Office of the Comptroller of the Currency (OCC). As the banks licensed by the states still remained in existence, the foundations were laid for the current dual banking system based on the

---

[4] During the "chartered banking" era of the eighteenth century, every new bank concession had to be confirmed by legislation. This meant that each bank had to conform to regulations set up specifically for it alone (Bonn 1998: 66).

coexistence of a financial infrastructure organized by the states with a network of banks under federal oversight.

The economic boom driven by accelerating industrialization in the 1870s did not lead (in great contrast to developments in Europe) to a wave of consolidation or concentration in the banking sector. Moreover, the doctrine of free banking, the dual structure of government, geographic diversity, and the existence of a wide variety of business sectors led to the preservation of a regionally oriented banking system with a surfeit of small banks. As the federally licensed banks were banned from establishing branches (or any other forms of franchising for that matter) until the beginning of the 1920s, the extension of a ban on interstate banking in the late nineteenth century contributed to the fragmented nature of the American banking sector. By 1921, there were over 30,000 commercial banks spread across the country (Spong 1994: 20). Philip Cerny has compared the American financial system with a pyramid where thousands of small banks make up the base and a small number of very powerful institutions are at the apex. While this system can display considerable flexibility, it remains vulnerable to exaggerated expectations and financial panics (Cerny 1994: 182). Even after the financial panic of 1907 led to the establishment of a central bank, this system was still characterized by strong cyclical fluctuations.

The Great Depression which followed the stock market crash of October 1929 was a watershed whose legacy has helped to define banking policy to this day. Repeated waves of bank closures between 1930 and 1933 forced over 8,800 banks to go out of business (Robertson 1995: 125). Many small depositors lost their savings. The resulting atmosphere of fear and insecurity triggered a set of bank runs which led to the collapse of further banks. The Roosevelt administration finally had to enforce a nationwide temporary closure of all banks in 1933 in order to calm the situation before reorganizing the financial infrastructure of the United States.[5]

This comprehensive process of reorganization was coordinated by the government and led to the division of the financial market on a functional basis with strong regulatory barriers keeping its different sections apart (see below). The New Deal in the financial sector remained stable for several decades and managed to end the cyclical crises of boom and bust so prevalent in the late nineteenth and early twentieth centuries. The fact that the stock markets remained relatively weak and the federal government had a highly activist economic policy after the Second World War helped to stabilize the economy and encouraged the investment of private capital. The general framework of the international economic order with its highly protected capital markets also

---

[5] A detailed description of these events can be found in Dale (1992: chapter 2).

helped to stabilize the situation. Only the loosening of the world financial system based on the Bretton Woods accords, which ended with their final termination in 1973 by the Nixon administration, led to new challenges for the American banking system and growing clamour for change.

3.1.2 Development of State Regulation

As has been explained above, in contrast to the general image of the US economy, the American financial system is subject to a high level of regulation whose organizing principles are deeply rooted in the economic history of the United States. Even American commentators have found it remarkable that an economic system, in which the principle of *laissez faire* is enshrined in theory, saw the first attempts at regulating the banking sector only two years after the foundation of the United States. The first "Bank of the United States" operated both as a commercial company and a state-backed central bank which was supposed to increase the influence of the government over credit allocation:

From that day to this, legislators in both federal and state jurisdictions have continued their intervention in the private market place, with the consequence that the American banking system today is surely different from the one that would have emerged in the annealing fires of unregulated competition.   (Robertson 1995: 183)

Alongside this predilection for state intervention in the financial system there has also been a strong strand of opposition fuelled by a fear of any potential of political or financial concentration of power. Established with the support of Alexander Hamilton and other members of the Federalist Party, the "Bank of the United States" encountered fierce resistance from Senators and Congressmen with a strong agrarian background under the leadership of Thomas Jefferson. Those opposed to this first central bank feared that it would be ultimately dominated by urban industrial interests (Ginsberg, Lowi, and Weir 1997: 629). Even though the bank had successfully achieved all its goals, in 1811 the Jackson administration refused to extend its licence. A second "Bank of the United States" was quickly founded a year later because of the financial pressures of the war of 1812. Despite its exclusive focus on its role as a central bank, the same conflicts as those which emerged in response to the first "Bank of the United States" led to its break-up in 1836, ushering in an era of free banking and financial systems run by individual states. Two subsequent attempts by Congress to pass bills for the creation of a third "Bank of the United States" were quashed by presidential vetoes.[6]

---

[6] The conflict over the first and second "Bank of the United States" is described in Robertson (1995: chapter 2).

Hostility towards banks in large parts of the United States because of their perceived embodiment of financial power is perhaps best reflected by the fact that in the 1840s and 1850s, nine states banned *every* form of banking either through laws or amendments of their state constitutions. In some states, banks could not be established legally until after the Civil War (Robertson 1995: 23). The growing pace of economic growth and the emergence of a continental market should have necessitated major changes in the financial system. Yet only the financial pressure on the state caused by military expenditure during the Civil War brought about the decisive step towards a reorganization of the American financial and banking sectors through the National Currency Act of 1863 and the National Bank Act of 1864. Since there was no support for any moves to set up a central bank again, a national banking system was established based upon government bonds and a uniform national currency.[7]

As part of this reform, the Office of the Comptroller of the Currency (OCC) was established as a regulatory body whose responsibilities included monitoring the issue of currency by the banks. Though this federal system was set up in parallel to the pre-existing banking structures overseen by the individual states, it was still based upon the principles of "free banking" doctrine. This meant that it was still remarkably easy to set up both commercial and investment banks (Spong 1994: 16). Because the federal bank regulations were more rigorous compared with those of the states,[8] only a small number of banks chose the federal option. Congress tried to rectifiy this imbalance in 1865, levying a 10 per cent tax on all banknotes issued by a state bank. This measure quickly led to a shift away from state and towards nationally licensed banks. While there were only 467 national banks in 1864 compared to 1,089 banks licensed by the states, by 1866 the ratio had significantly changed with 1,634 national banks to 297 still operating on a state level (Robertson 1995: 53).

Even after these considerable changes, the American financial system remained dogged by cyclical bank crises and financial panics, becoming "one of the worst financial systems in the world" (Broz 1999: 39). These financial crises usually took place in conjunction with major economic recessions.[9] The inelasticity of the gold supply, the main reason behind these recurring economic difficulties, could only be ameliorated through a central bank acting as a lender of last resort. Yet the possible foundation of a central bank remained a matter of considerable controversy (see above). Only after the financial

---

[7] This ensured that American currency remained largely free of risk, which solved the growing problems caused by the fluctuating value of banknotes. These measures also increased demand for state bonds and thus helped to finance the war against the Confederacy.

[8] Details in Robertson (1995: 52).   [9] See table in Broz (1999: 45).

panic of 1907 were there serious moves towards the establishment of a central bank which, despite serious resistance in Congress, was finally founded in 1913. This final settlement contradicted the ideological convictions of all those opposed to any form of central banking. While the radical wing of the Democratic Party had demanded some form of direct political control over financial markets in order to put Wall Street in its place, the majority of small bankers did their best to resist even the lightest political intervention or compulsion to obey instructions from a central bank by threatening to leave the federal licensing system (Robertson 1995: 88f.). Conversely, representatives of the largest banks, mostly based in New York, provided covert support to the political campaign for the establishment of a central bank in the hope that it would enhance the international role of New York as a financial market (Broz 1999).

Out of these conflicting pressures emerged with the *Federal Reserve System* something that might aptly be described as a "decentral bank"—for due to its federal structure it was split into twelve semi-autonomous districts coordinated by a relatively weak board of directors.[10] Since 1917, the Fed and the OCC have shared responsibility for bank regulation. While the former monitors banks licensed by the states, the latter acts as regulator for those banks which were part of the national licensing scheme.[11] Instead of fostering structural change, this arrangement has shored up the pluralistic foundations of the American financial system (Cerny 1994: 180).

As the economy expanded at a rapid pace in the 1920s, commercial banks began to circumvent many of the restrictions that had been placed on their business operations in the previous fifty years. In particular, the National Bank Act of 1864 which prevented banks from becoming involved in the stock market, became increasingly seen as outdated once a trend known as "department store banking" began to take hold of the industry. This reflected widespread attempts by American banks to emulate European universal banks which were active in all aspects of the banking and finance industries. In the American case, the largest banks usually set up subsidiary firms in order to expand into the trade in stocks and securities while observing the letter of the law (Dale 1992: 21ff.). Though the speedy integration of the United States helped to fuel an economic boom after the First World War, it also contributed to the stock market crash of October 1929 which precipitated the Great Depression.

---

[10] The original structure of the Federal Reserve System, which was changed in order to increase central control, is described in Robertson (1995: 93).

[11] However only if they were members of the Federal Reserve System. See Figure 3.3 for details.

The economic depression of the 1930s was a traumatic experience for the United States with GDP falling by a third, industrial production being halved, and consumer prices falling to a quarter of their 1929 levels. Unemployment grew rapidly from 1.5 million to over 13 million. The banking system was hit particularly hard with almost a quarter of all banks becoming insolvent. These were mostly small banks based in rural communities with less than 25,000 inhabitants (Robertson 1995: 117f.; Kareken 1992: 315). Countless small depositors lost over $800 million in total.[12] The widespread nature of these losses led to a resurgence of traditional fear and contempt for banks and bankers who many Americans believed to be responsible for the economic crisis. The idea that the Great Depression had been brought about by risky and irresponsible speculation on the financial markets, spurred on by excessive competition between banks, gained growing support among the electorate as well as in the political establishment.[13] Public hearings in Congress gave credence to this hypothesis, concentrating especially on how commercial banking had become intertwined with securities trading at several major banks.[14]

A potent combination of economic misery and public anger created a political window of opportunity for a fundamental shift in the balance of power in the financial sector. The consequence "was the most comprehensive attempt ever to restructure the American financial system" (Cerny 1994: 181). The consensus that "excessive competition" had caused the crisis provoked lawmakers into imposing a comprehensive regulatory regime upon the financial and banking sector. Banks had to submit to stringent controls on their geographical area of operations, the products they offered, and the prices they charged which locked them into a very well-defined part of the financial market. The ultimate aim of these regulations was to prevent the further spread of universal banking in the United States. After the introduction of the New Deal, four factors characterized the banking industry:[15]

- Commercial banks were not permitted to conduct securities trading. They were also forbidden from buying shares in any other companies and were to provide short-term credit exclusively to small private businesses. In

[12] In 1990 terms, this would be $6 billion (United States Department of the Treasury 1991: 1).

[13] In recent times this interpretation has been questioned since economic historians have come to put more emphasis on the responsibility of the central bank for such major miscalculations because of its unwillingness to fully use its powers as "lender of last resort". See C&N (1990: 119), Dale (1992: 27f.), as well as Baer and Mote (1992: 505).

[14] See the description in C&N (1990: 118f.).

[15] The exact stipulations of the Glass–Steagall Act can be found in Dale (1992: 77–9). See also Spong (1994: 19–22) and Bonn (1998: 82–5).

turn, commercial banks received a monopoly over the market in current accounts.

- Savings accounts provided by banks had to stick to a strict ceiling on rates of interest set by the federal government in order to prevent any form of competition based on price. Interest payments on sight deposits were banned.

- The establishment of branches was only permitted within the home state of a bank. The McFadden Act of 1927 made sure that federally licensed banks were also forced to conform to this stipulation.[16]

- A compulsory examination of local needs and demands before banks were granted a licence ended the era of "free banking".

Another key element of these reforms was the establishment of the Federal Deposit Insurance Corporation (FDIC) which was a state institution to help banks in times of crisis. This was the direct consequence of the high losses experienced by bank customers and was intended to restore public confidence in the banking system. With the creation of a third regulatory body on a federal level, it is not surprising that the first years after the New Deal settlement witnessed considerable conflict over spheres of jurisdiction between the Federal Reserve, the OCC, and the FDIC (Robertson 1995: 134).

Under this new regulatory regime, the American banking system went on to experience an era of stability in the decades after 1932. The number of bank insolvencies sank drastically (see Figure 3.2). The emphasis upon a high level of regulation became the basis of state banking policy.

In the 1950s, legislation dealing with the banking sector focused on issues raised by the growth of "Bank Holding Companies". This form of business organization enabled several corporations to circumvent the strict guidelines concerning interstate banking and the state-enforced separation of banks from all other forms of business enterprise. This form of evasion was banned by the Bank Holding Company Act of 1956, which was strengthened through a second bill in 1970, while existing Bank Holding Companies were put under the oversight of the Fed (Spong 1994: 23f.). Other issues began to play a more central role when it came to regulatory legislation. Concerns over consumer protection and social welfare legislation forced Congress to pass such bills as the Truth in Lending Act, the Equal Credit Opportunity Act, and the Community Reinvestment Act (see ibid., chapter 7).

---

[16] According to the principles of "unit banking", the latter had until then been completely banned from setting up branches.

3.1.3 The Political Context Until 1970

Throughout the history of the United States, banking policy and bank regulation have been characterized by three key factors.

First of all, the issue of bank regulation in the United States has been continuously plagued by a high level of political polarization. As described above, the first political clashes over bank policy took place in the years after the Declaration of Independence and played an important role in several presidential elections. Both the conflict over the extension of the licence of the second Bank of the United States in 1832 and the battle for the introduction of the gold standard in 1896, had a particularly direct impact upon elections which represented watersheds in American history (Robertson 1995: 20; and Cerny 1993: 179).

The first years of the American Republic also saw the emergence of a political fault-line which shaped debate over bank policy for a very long time. This is perhaps best defined as a regionally focused conflict between centre and periphery which first emerged with the debate over the foundation of the Bank of the United States. It saw the commercial interests of the East Coast, with their preference for big business and stable markets, pitted against the agrarian interests of the West which demanded an easy credit policy. Towards the end of the nineteenth century, two coalitions had taken shape, of which the first comprised urban financiers, industrial conglomerates, and trusts together with the federal government, while its opponent consisted of a loose alliance of rural interests including farmers, small banks, and businessmen (Cerny 1994, see also Figure 3.1). Elements of these two coalitions still played a role in the conflicts of the 1980s and 1990s over reform of the banking industry. If one applies Philip Cerny's pyramidal model, this could be described as a conflict between the base and its apex.

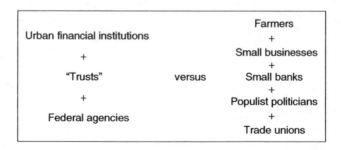

Figure 3.1. Conflict formation in the financial sector by the end of the nineteenth century

The final factor was the manner in which different groups with opposing aims could block each others' interests, thus preventing any reform of such key issues as the creation of a uniform currency, leading to policy deadlock which hampered economic development. Symptomatic of such inertia has been the fact that only acute crises, such as the Civil War, the financial panic of 1907, or the collapse of the banking sector in the 1930s, were able to force otherwise reluctant legislators to initiate reforms. In each case, the threat which these crises posed to the stability of the United States led to the establishment of regulatory agencies. Yet this was largely a process of piecemeal adaptation rather than the result of the continuous evolution of a policy strategy. The consequences were recurring conflict over jurisdiction between competing government agencies and a continuation of political tension in this policy area, though the first decades after the Second World War experienced a period of relative stability. Yet the collapse of the international post-war settlement based on the Bretton Woods system brought this era of tranquility to an end when it came to banking in America.

3.2 THE CHALLENGES

The major changes experienced by the banking and finance sectors since the mid-1970s have been explored above. The American system was confronted by an especially complex set of challenges which shall be examined in the following section.

The American banking system, with its regional rather than national orientation, was particularly vulnerable to the changes wrought by liberalization and internationalization. Both these factors led to a considerable increase in the market share held by foreign banks in the United States, while the (previously substantial) position of American banks in international markets came under pressure from European and Japanese competitors.

Parallel to these shifts, the banking industry in the United States continued to operate under a comparatively heavy regulatory regime. A wide variety of regulations controlling the products, prices, and the geographic extent of American banks created a highly specialized market which was now confronted by a general trend towards international deregulation. Though originally intended as a stabilizing factor, under changed circumstances these regulations proved counter-productive. Since the prevalence of geographic and product-oriented market segmentation led to an insufficient level of portfolio and risk diversification, most small and regional banks found it difficult to cope with recessions and heightened market volatility. In particular, banks

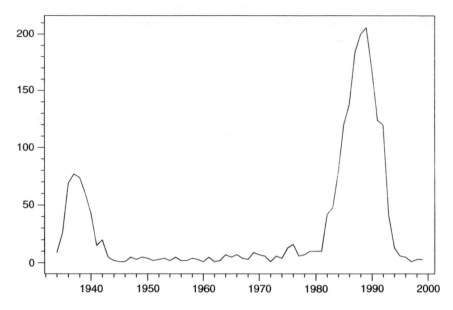

Figure 3.2. Bank insolvencies per year, 1934–99
Source: FDIC

based in Texas and Mid-Western states such as Kansas and Iowa found it very hard to cope with changing market conditions.[17] With a rising rate of inflation, price controls imposed by several regulatory agencies made refinancing an increasingly arduous process for many banks.[18]

In the 1980s and 1990s, these developments resulted in a massive crisis in the American banking system, as the number of business insolvencies rose even higher than during the Great Depression (see Figure 3.2). Between 1980 and 1994, 1,617 banks went bankrupt. This constituted 9.14 per cent of all banks in the United States with combined deposits of over $206 billion, a proportion of 8.98 per cent of the deposits of the entire banking system (FDIC 1997: 14 f.). With financial damage of this magnitude, this was far more than a mere structural adjustment of the market that only affected unviable small banks.

These developments challenged a policy consensus over bank regulation which had its origins in the New Deal in two ways. The drastic process of change which enveloped both domestic and international markets created severe problems for private financial institutions. Conversely, the problems

[17] See the study by Neely and Wheelock (1997) as well as the respective chapters in FDIC (1997).
[18] See the description in C&N (1981: 253f.).

bank regulators had in adapting to new market conditions brought the ability of politicians, civil servants, and state institutions to cope with economic change into question (Reinicke 1995: 2f.).

3.3 THE POLICY NETWORK

The policy network[19] was made up of a combination of private institutions including banks and their representative associations as well as public institutions such as regulatory agencies and legislatures. These will be described and analysed in the following section.

3.3.1 The American Banking Industry

3.3.1.1 *The Structure of American Banking*

If one examines the historical background of the American banking industry's current structures, considerable continuities emerge despite the changes that have taken place in the last two decades. The following section will first illustrate how these structures have evolved as a result of measures taken in response to shifts in the financial market. It will then go on to describe the distinguishing features of the network of interest groups which have shaped banking policy.

One of the main characteristics of the American banking system, focused on by most studies, is its extreme complexity and fragmentation.[20] This is particularly evident in the large number of independent commercial banks, of which there are over 10,000, together with the coexistence of a diverse set of financial institutions. Historical circumstances, the influence of constitutional federalism, and political lobbying have all had an equal share in creating these conditions. Consequently, the United States has developed very distinct financial structures that differ markedly from other countries with a similar level of socio-economic development. The United States Department of the Treasury itself came to this conclusion in a report produced in 1991: "If the United States had the same ratio of banks to population [as Canada], it would have about seventy-five banks of which about fifty-six would operate

---

[19] In this study, the term policy network is used to describe all those players and interest groups involved in a certain policy area without trying to take sides in the theoretical debates surrounding this term (Thatcher 1998).

[20] As one example of many, see Baer and Mote (1992: 470ff.).

Table 3.1. Number of American retail banks, 1934–93

	1935	1960	1980	1985	1993
Number of banks	14,125	13,126	14,435	14,417	10,957
Number of banking organizations	–	12,747	12,368	11,047	8,375

Source: Baer and Mote (1992: 522); Nolle (1995: Table A-1)

nationwide."[21] Conditions in the United States were not just distinct from those in Canada. A systematic comparison with other OECD members demonstrates the extent to which the American banking system has become an exception to the global rule. In 1993, there was one bank for every 23,508 inhabitants of the United States, the lowest ratio of all eighteen OECD member states. Among G8 nations, the average is double that at 53,192 inhabitants for every bank while the ratio in the EU is six times as high with 143,023 inhabitants for every bank.[22] If one takes other industrialized nations as a yardstick, then the wave of consolidation across the international banking system described in the other case studies has not yet taken place in the United States.

As indicated in Table 3.1, from the end of the Great Depression to the mid-1980s the number of commercial banks remained roughly the same. The shift in the proportion of individual commercial banks to organized banking groups[23] of 1.03 in 1960 to 1.30 in 1985 reflected a nominal tendency towards concentration in the form of holding companies in the decade leading up to the mid-1980s.

From this point onwards, both the number of commercial banks per inhabitant as well as the proportion of independent banks to banking groups quickly declined to about a quarter of what they had been in the 1970s. Although one can hardly speak of a real process of consolidation when one looks at events in other industrialized nations, the American banking industry has undergone a traumatic process of structural change. Table 3.2 demonstrates how these changes have largely taken place at the expense of small banks, whose total asset share of the banking industry sank drastically by the end of the 1970s.[24] In the face of such a massive set of changes, one can only describe these two decades as "the most turbulent period in U.S. banking history since the Great Depression" (Berger, Kashyap, and Scalise 1995: 57).

[21] United States Department of the Treasury (1991: XVII–17).

[22] Calculated by the author in accordance with Barth et al. (1997: table 3).

[23] In this context these bank organizations are made up of the sum of independent commercial banks plus the number of bank holding companies (which could own more than one bank).

[24] The figures of $100 million and $100 billion are based on the combined assets of these banks.

Table 3.2. Indicators of American retail banks, 1979–94

	1979	1994
Number of banking organizations	12,463	7,926
– of which: small banks (<$100 m.)	10,014	5,636
Overall assets banking industry	$3.26 trn.	$4.02 trn.
– of which: big banks (>$100 bn.)	9.4%	18.8%
– of which: small banks (<$100 m.)	13.9%	7.0%

Source: Berger, Kashyap, and Scalise (1995: 67, 132ff.)

3.3.1.2 *Interest Groups Involved in Banking Policy*

While economic studies usually limit themselves to an analysis of banking structures, political scientists need to focus more on the structure and organization of the different interest groups involved in this industry. Banks in the United States are entirely owned and run by the private sector. This is in great contrast to many European countries, where the existence of either cooperative or state-owned institutions almost predetermines a disunited interest representation. Despite the advantage of not having to deal with such segmentation, the American banking sector is not characterized by a single organization representing the entire industry. Instead, a highly fragmented system with over 200 associations representing different parts of the banking industry exists.

The reason for this level of fragmentation lies in the sheer number and diversity of American commercial banks. This has made it almost impossible for any single association or federation to represent the entire banking industry. This has not stopped the oldest and largest organization, the American Bankers Association (ABA), which was founded in 1875, from claiming to do so. The ABA employs over sixty lobbyists in Washington alone, giving it considerable influence over the legislative process.[25] Yet with growing divisions in the American banking system in the late nineteenth century, several rival associations with a much narrower focus were established.[26] The association which has become the main rival to the ABA and most strongly opposed to its agenda when it came to the development of bank regulation policy is the Independent Bankers' Association of America (IBAA). Founded in 1930, the IBAA mostly represents smaller "community banks", changing its name in 1998 to the Independent Community Bankers of America (ICBA). It has

[25] Interview ABA, 9 August 1998.
[26] Worsham (1997: 27) claims that the dominant factions within the ABA are New York banks, banks in the Midwest, and rural or small-town banks.

mostly aimed to preserve the licensing systems organized by the states and has consistently opposed any measures which might reduce the level of legal protection which community banks currently enjoy.

Other important associations representing different parts of the banking industry include the Association of Bank Holding Companies (which represents holding companies), the Coalition of Regional Banking and Economic Development (a lobby group for medium-sized banks in regional centres such as Boston, Houston, or Atlanta), the Association of Reserve City Bankers (a representative group for banks in major financial centres), the Bankers Association for Foreign Trade (an organization with banks operating in foreign markets), and the Consumer Bankers' Association (representing banks dependent on individual consumers). Founded in 1927, the National Bankers' Association which was originally intended to defend the interests of Afro-American bankers has also come to represent banks owned by women, Hispanic- or Asian-Americans, and other ethnic minorities. The membership of the Financial Services Roundtable (which was called the Bankers' Roundtable until 1999) is exclusively made up of the hundred largest banks,[27] while an organization called America's Community Bankers (ACB) represents those small banks who do not consider the ICBA to be sufficiently progressive. Recent technical innovations have led to the creation of an Online Banking Association (OBA),[28] while every one of the fifty states has its own set of bank associations.[29]

The main problem arising from the large number of different interest groups in the banking sector is the lack of any clear jurisdictional boundaries between them. For example, the ACB claims to represent the "nation's community banks of all charter types and sizes" yet it does not explicitly define "community bank" as a term.[30] The ICBA also maintains that it defends the interests of these banks while the ABA has set up the Community Bankers Council in order to include the "special needs" of small banks in its own work. Though most studies claim that size is the main dividing line when it comes to the interests of American banks,[31] the constant competition for members between rival associations is another factor making it impossible to sustain united and effective action on behalf of the interests of the banking industry as a whole. This in itself has become a defining characteristic of the

---

[27] Since this change, conglomerates, banks, and companies operating in the insurance and securities sectors are now allowed to join. There are however strict quotas designed to ensure that banks remain the dominant group (see http://www.bankersround.org).

[28] See http://www.obanet.org.

[29] A list of bank associations (though incomplete) can be found in Table A-4 in Coleman (1994).

[30] See http://www.acbankers.org.

[31] See Lehner, Schubert, and Geile (1983: 373); Coleman (1994); Worsham (1997: 21f.).

American case when compared to the international scene (Coleman 1994: 34). At congressional hearings, the ABA and ICBA are the most important players[32] and are regularly invited to testify, though the ABA has at times had to send two separate delegations in order to properly cover the interests of both its smaller and its larger members. The biggest banks often have their own representative offices in Washington to make sure that their concerns are heard during the legislative process (Reinicke 1995: 26). It is therefore not surprising that these associations have never been able to exert the level of influence needed to impose any form of "private interest government" (Coleman 1994: Table A-4).

3.3.2 The Regulatory Agencies

When it comes to the regulatory agencies, the American system of bank regulation is hampered by a similar amount of complexity.[33] In particular, the dual system of regulation with its separate licensing regimes on the federal and the state level has led to the creation of a multitude of regulatory agencies. As is the case with the bank associations, this is a highly fragmented system where different actors oscillate between cooperation and competition.

On the federal level, there are three regulatory agencies responsible for commercial banks. The oldest is the Office of the Comptroller of the Currency (OCC) founded in 1863 which, as the name indicates, was originally responsible for issuing the United States dollar. Since the establishment of a central bank system in 1913, the OCC is the only one of the three federal regulatory agencies whose area of jurisdiction exclusively concerns the supervision and regulation of banks. As part of the Department of the Treasury, the OCC possesses the least amount of formal autonomy of all the federal agencies dealing with the banking sector. The Comptroller is appointed by the President and confirmed by the Senate for a term of five years. This agency is responsible for over 2,800 banks operating under national licence as well as sixty-five US licensed subsidiary branches of foreign banks, overseeing combined assets of over $2.4 billion. The OCC controls the licensing process for new banks as well as applications concerning changes in the business model of established ones. Its area of jurisdiction also gives it the power to issue directives dealing with credit allocation, lending, and investment as well as to enforce adherence to the basic principles of bank management. Another key aspect of the OCC's work is monitoring the compliance of banks to federal laws such as the Equal

---

[32] Lehner, Schubert, and Geile (1983: 373); and Worsham (1997: 21f.).
[33] An overview can be found in Kareken (1992), Reinicke (1995: chapter 3), Khademian (1996), and OCC (n.d.). This section is largely based on information from these sources.

Credit Opportunity Act or the Community Reinvestment Act. Most importantly, the OCC conducts on-the-spot investigations in even the most far-flung locations to gather information about the solvency and credit standing of banks in order to make sure that their deposits remain secure. If inspectors discover serious discrepancies in the course of such an investigation, the OCC has the power to withdraw the licence of an offending bank.[34]

Along with regulatory responsibilities, the OCC represents the United States on a number of international regulatory bodies such as the Basel Committee, the Group of 30, the International Monetary Fund (IMF), and the World Bank. The bulk of the OCC's operations are financed through the inspection fees which it levies on the banks it monitors. Though such methods of raising revenue can endanger the objectivity of a regulator (Khademian 1996: 51), self-financing gives the OCC a semi-autonomous position within the executive. This has made it less dependent on the allocations of tax revenue controlled by the President and Congress. This relative independence is heightened by the fact that a Comptroller cannot be fired by the President without the consent of the Senate.

The Federal Reserve System (FRS or Fed) is the second federal-level institution whose responsibilities include bank regulation. Founded in 1913, the Fed is run by a Board of Governors whose seven members are appointed for a term of fourteen years by the President after consultation with and confirmation by the Senate. The twelve Reserve Banks, each with its own geographic district, which make up the Fed have been deliberately given considerable autonomy in order to minimize the influence of the executive over its decision-making process. Though the Fed is mainly responsible for the formulation of monetary policy, the central bank is also the regulatory agency for those banks that belong to the Federal Reserve System and are licensed by the states as well as bank holding companies (BHCs). The approximately 1,000 banks with a state licence which belong to this system hold about 25 per cent of the total asset value of the commercial banking sector. The 6,010 holding companies under Fed scrutiny control over 7,000 banks, with 94 per cent of all capital assets (FRS 1997: 217). It is therefore its responsibility for BHCs that gives the Fed such a crucial role when it comes to bank regulation. In comparison to its international counterparts which are only responsible for monetary policy, the Fed's role as regulator makes it something of an exception in the world of central banking. However, the Fed has claimed that its regulatory remit is essential to its ability to fulfil its tasks as a central bank.[35]

---

[34] A list of its powers can be found in OCC (n.d.: 3).
[35] See Coleman (1996: 157f.) as well as Peek, Eric, and Tootell (1999).

The third federal agency involved in the supervision of commercial banks is the Federal Deposit Insurance Corporation (FDIC). It is also the newest, having been established in 1933 to administer the recently established deposit insurance fund financed by contributions from the banks participating in this state-backed insurance scheme. The FDIC is also authorized to borrow $30 billion from the Department of the Treasury in order to fulfil its insurance obligations in a financial emergency. While three members of the FDIC board of directors are appointed by the President, the other two are *ex officio* members of which one is the Comptroller of the Currency. Along with the responsibility for stepping in as compulsory administrator of failed banks, the FDIC also oversees the 5,500 banks which are licensed by individual states who are insured by the FDIC but are not members of the Federal Reserve System. It also has the right to inspect the books of all those banks who have signed up to its deposit insurance scheme. These inspections can either be initiated by the FDIC alone or in cooperation with individual state and federal supervisory bodies. As part of this system of inspection, the FDIC has the right to recommend administrative action against transgressing banks to federal government agencies.

Parallel to these three federal agencies, there are also fifty-four supervisory bodies operating in the individual states.[36] These have been represented on the federal level since 1902 by the Conference of State Bank Supervisors (CSBS), whose aim is to ensure the survival of the dual banking system, claiming in the process that this fosters competition and innovation as well as a more consumer-friendly approach. Altogether, these regulatory bodies in the individual states monitor around 6,500 commercial banks and another 400 state-licensed branches of foreign banks, which with a sum of $2.1 billion contain over 40 per cent of the total assets of the commercial banking system.

3.3.2.1 *Interaction Between Regulatory Agencies*

When examining the many agencies involved in the supervision of the banking industry it is important to look at how they have interacted with one another. Since 1979, the Federal Financial Institutions Examination Council (FFIEC) has helped to develop a more uniform approach towards bank regulation on the federal level.

That such an institution is necessary is demonstrated by the fact that though the three federal bank regulatory agencies use the same set of five categories when classifying banks, the same standards of assessment only exist for one

[36] This figure includes agencies in all fifty states of the Union as well as the District of Columbia, the Virgin Islands, Puerto Rico, and Guam (Interview CSBS, 8 July 1998).

of these categories. This means that the regulators are using very different sets of criteria when examining the same banks and financial institutions (Coleman 1996: 169f.; see also Benston 1995: 18). The establishment of shared assessment methods and categories accepted by all federal regulators was only achieved in 1997.[37] A lack of cooperation between agencies is therefore not surprising if one looks at the fact that they are often in a position where they have to compete with one another for the support of the banks they are supposed to regulate. This means that a bank's decision about which system of regulation it joins can have a direct impact upon an agency's budget (see above). In order to improve its image and attract more "clients", each of these agencies does its best to emphasize its own strength and importance in its annual reports while advertising the size of the market share of those banks which it already oversees.

This system gives banks the opportunity to play regulatory agencies off against each other. This kind of manipulation has been fostered by the fact that a distinct bureaucratic culture exists in each regulatory agency which is shaped by its specific role and administrative tradition. Since the FDIC deals with small banks, licensed by individual states, which are particularly vulnerable, this agency tends towards caution and conservatism in order to keep failed banks from putting pressure on the deposit insurance fund administered by it. The FDIC therefore approaches major issues from the perspective of individual banks rather than from that of the banking industry as a whole (Coleman 1996: 159).

In comparison, the OCC is more open to innovation because it is focused on heightening the competitive edge of the federally licensed banks which belong to its area of jurisdiction. The OCC is able to maintain such a stance because of the greater stability of the banks it monitors. Under pressure from Congress, the OCC moved towards a more liberal licensing regime in the early 1980s. This led to considerable conflict with the FDIC, which has always tried to balance the encouragement of greater competition with the preservation of market stability (FDIC 1997: 12, 85). As a consequence of these bureaucratic battles, the OCC's reputation as a particularly progressive agency has made it popular with bankers. The Fed, which is more interested in the banking system as a whole rather than the fate of individual banks, has become increasingly anxious that the ability of banks to move from one regulator to another could lead to the flight of banks to the OCC's more generous regime.[38] With their large share of the total assets of the commercial banking sector, the central

---

[37] See a report in http://www.fdic.gov:80/banknews/fils/1997/fil9717.html.
[38] Interview with Bob Glauber, 5 June 1998.

Table 3.3. US federal banking supervision agencies and their responsibilities

Agency	Type of bank	Role
OCC	Banks with federal licence	Lead supervisor
	Subsidiaries of foreign bank with federal licence	Lead supervisor
FRS	Bank Holding Companies	Sole supervisor
	Banks with state licence	Lead supervisor
	Banks with federal licence	Auxiliary supervisor
	Domestic business of foreign banks	Auxiliary supervisor
FDIC	Banks with state licence (members of FDIC, but not FRS)	Lead supervisor
	Banks with federal licence	Auxiliary supervisor
	Banks with state licence (members of FRS)	Auxiliary supervisor
	Subsidiaries of foreign banks (members of FDIC)	Auxiliary supervisor

bank believes that the retention of holding companies in the Fed system is crucial to its task in monetary policy (Reinicke 1995: 34).

This chapter has examined how regulatory agencies monitoring banks in the United States have become part of a highly complex and fragmented system. Both Table 3.3 and Figure 3.3 try to summarize its conflicting structures.[39] This system is distinguished by overlapping areas of jurisdiction, the necessity for cooperation between agencies, and a competitive framework in which banks can engage in "regulatory shopping" and regulators in a kind of "competition in laxity". Such regulatory disorder is not just problematic on a theoretical level. In practice, dealing with the demands of a wide variety of regulatory agencies can be an expensive process for a bank. For example, a holding company that owns banks with both federal and state licences is not only under the legal obligation to join the Federal Reserve System, it will also find itself within the jurisdiction of the OCC, the FDIC, and the regulatory agencies of the individual states. Seen from the perspective of both the regulatory agencies and the banking associations this is not necessarily a sign of inefficiency. Rather, bureaucratic pluralism is often seen as a positive phenomenon, creating checks and balances which can prevent the dominance of any one government agency. A typical comment reflecting these attitudes in American banking circles is: "The benefits outweigh the costs" or "Bankers

[39] Sources for this data are Spong (1994: 41–50), Bonn (1998: 88), Reinicke (1995: 25–6), OCC (n.d.: 1) as well as FRS (1997: 216). The numbers in Figure 3.3 show the number of banks which fall in this category and their share of the sum total of commercial banks in 1978/9. This information can be found in Bonn (1998: 88). As a result of the bank crises of the 1980s and 1990s, the number of banks has gradually decreased but these percentages have remained relatively stable (see Spong 1994: 43, for data relating to 1993).

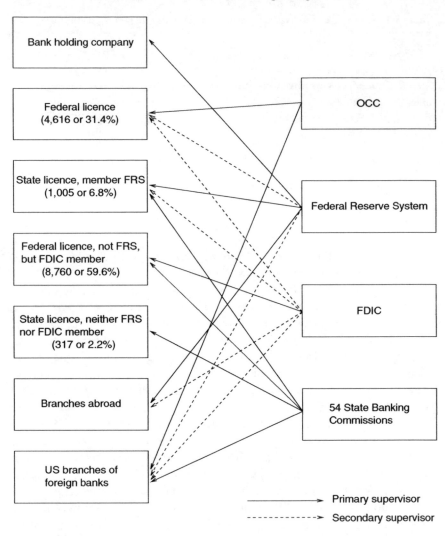

Figure 3.3. Overlapping jurisdiction in the regulation of different types of banks

want regulatory choice. Three heads are better than one, and you get better rules and better policy if the three get together and work it out."[40] This opinion is shared by many politicians, reflecting the deep-rooted fear in the United States of any form of concentration of power, especially when it comes to the world of finance.

[40] Interview CSBS, 8 July 1998; Interview IBAA, 9 July 1998. See also the quotations in Coleman (1996: 160).

3.3.3 The Legal Framework

The responsibility for legislation in the area of bank regulation lies mainly in the hands of Congress, where committees in the Senate and the House of Representatives determine the direction of policy-making. In the Senate, the key committees responsible for this area of policy is the Committee on Banking, Housing and Urban Affairs while the main committee for these issues in the House of Representatives is the Committee on Banking, Finance and Urban Affairs. Since both committees' areas of jurisdiction can be at times quite limited, other committees are also consulted with great frequency when it comes to questions involving bank regulation. This is particularly the case in the House of Representatives, where questions concerning trading in stocks and bonds are dealt with by the Committee on Energy and Commerce while the futures and options markets are covered by the Agriculture Committee (Coleman 1996: 154). When issues concerning monopoly and bankruptcy law arise, then the Judiciary Committees of both the House and the Senate come into play (Reinicke 1995: 24). The lack of any systematic division of responsibility between committees—which is a particularly acute problem when it comes to banking policy since committee jurisdictions have remained ill-defined—exacerbates the inefficiencies of the Congressional legislative process. With so many players involved in, and affected by, the development of bank legislation, the policy network focused on the banking sector has fragmented in a fashion comparable to its counterparts in the banking industry and the regulatory agencies.

3.4 THE BATTLE FOR REFORM

If the American system of bank oversight and regulation seems extremely complicated, then it is because it has come into being through a long process of accretion rather than through systematic planning:

No central architect was assigned to design the overall system or lay out a single set of principles. Instead, many people with many viewpoints, objectives, and experiences have been responsible for the current supervisory framework. As a consequence, bank regulation has evolved to serve numerous goals—goals which have changed over time and on occasion even been in conflict with each other.   (Spong 1994: 5)

Most academic studies of this system are highly critical of its deficiencies, describing it as "an oddly parochial set of laws and regulations that both impair competition and shield inefficiency" (Baer and Mote 1992: 469), "a triple threat to the national interest in being comparatively inefficient, uncompetitive and unsafe all at the same time" (Saunders and Walter 1994: vi) and "the most mis-regulated in the developed world" (Benston 1995: 18). Interviews with experts in regulatory practice as well as with staff at the various agencies often lead to even more drastic descriptions of American bank regulation such as "this crazy mess" or "fucking insane".[41] This kind of hefty criticism is not some recent phenomenon. In the mid-1970s, a senior economist who compiled a report commissioned by the House of Representatives bank committee on "Financial Institutions and the Nations Economy" (FINE) came to the conclusion that the system of regulation was out of date, over-complex, unfocused, and made up of incompetent agencies fighting constant turf battles (Pierce 1977: 605).

The FINE report was not the first study that criticized the entire framework of financial regulation and recommended fundamental reforms of the system. As early as 1949, a task force belonging to the Hoover Commission suggested that the entire system of bank regulation and deposit insurance should be merged with the Federal Reserve. In 1961, the Commission on Money and Credit recommended that the supervisory duties of the OCC and FDIC should be handed over to the Federal Reserve while the Hunt Commission made further proposals for consolidation and reform in 1971. However, the 1975 FINE report made the most far-reaching recommendations, proposing the fusion of all regulatory agencies into a single "Federal Depository Institutions Commission" (Chandler and Jaffee 1977). Further reform initiatives were launched in the 1980s and 1990s. In 1984 the Bush Task Force, headed by Vice-President George H. W. Bush, examined further possibilities for regulatory consolidation.[42] The subsequent first Bush administration made a variety of proposals for the modernization of the regulation system in 1991 designed to improve competitiveness and security in the banking industry (United States Department of the Treasury 1991).

Since the New Deal, there has been no lack of proposals for reform when it came to the serious problems which have continued to afflict the system of bank regulation in the United States. In order to explain why these recommendations for change were not translated into action, the following sections will examine how the debate over the abolition or preservation of a variety of regulatory restraints on the American banking industry in the 1980s and 1990s has been conducted.[43] These regulations constrained banking threefold:

[41] Interview Brookings Institution, 10 July 1998; Interview Federal Reserve Bank, 10 July 1998.

[42] See their report: Task Group on Regulation of Financial Services (1984).

[43] This description is largely based on detailed studies by Reinicke (1995) and FDIC (1997) as well as several volumes of C&N (1981, 1985, 1990, 1993, 1998).

through price regulation (interest rate caps), through geographical regulation (strict limitations on the opening of branches), and through product regulation (bans on stock-brokering and entering the insurance or real estate businesses).

This debate unfolded in three different areas of policy-making. Fierce conflicts over whether the existing legal framework should be reformed took place in the legislative arena of Congress. In the various bureaucratic institutions involved, battles over administrative jurisdiction merged into a wider argument over the necessity for fundamental reform. Finally, the courts were often drawn into this debate through cases submitted by different interest groups, ensuring that each new measure was tested by the judiciary. Linking each of these conflicts were attempts by individual banks and bank associations to exert influence over these various state actors.

The period between 1980 and 1994 saw the largest amount of legislation dealing with bank regulation enacted since the reforms which emerged in the 1930s as part of the New Deal (FDIC 1997: 87). In fact, there was a direct connection between these two eras of reform. Five major banking laws came onto the statute books between 1980 and 1991 while two more were enacted between 1994 and 1999 (see Table 3.4). This does not mean that Congress played a proactive role in shaping this process of consolidation and change. As shall be demonstrated below, its role was that of a reactive institution responding to or confirming changes rather than initiating them. This process can itself be split into four phases: the first was one of deregulation from 1980 to 1982 which was followed by legislative deadlock until the end of the 1980s; this deadlock was overcome in a phase of cautious re-regulation between 1989 and 1992 which was followed by another period of deregulation until the mid-1990s.

3.4.1 The First Phase of Deregulation

Although commercial banks were unable to make any significant progress in the 1970s, they continued to push for the repeal of regulations concerning the financial products they could offer. However, the first wave of deregulation in 1980 took place in another part of the financial sector. This was the "thrift" or Savings & Loans (S&L) industry which had come under considerable pressure because of higher interest rates set by the Federal Reserve and the recession of the early 1980s.[44] In order to ameliorate this situation, Congress passed the

---

[44] These financial institutions began to emerge in the United States after the 1820s and were intended to enable those parts of the population, such as workers and small landholders, who were usually neglected by the commercial banks to set up their own savings accounts. Since

Table 3.4. Selection of important American banking laws

National Bank Act (1864)	Sets up a federally licensed banking system
Federal Reserve Act (1913)	Sets up the Federal Reserve System (FRS) as the United States' central bank
McFadden Act (1927)	Outlaws interstate banking
Banking Act (1933)	Also known as *Glass–Steagall Act*. Sets up the FDIC; enforces the separation of retail and investment banking; strict product regulation in banking
Bank Holding Company Act (1956)	Mandates the FRS to supervise *bank holding companies*; rules out their acquisition of retail banks outside their home state
International Banking Act (1978)	Subsidiaries of foreign banks to be supervised by US agencies and mandated to join the deposit protection fund FDIC
Depository Institutions Deregulation and Monetary Control Act (1980)	Ends price regulation in banking; deregulation gives S&Ls same rights as retail banks in most areas of business
Financial Institutions Reform, Recovery, and Enforcement Act (1989)	Mandates FDIC with deposit protection for S&L; sets up new agencies to clear up the S&L crisis
Federal Deposit Insurance Corporation Improvement Act (1991)	New money and competences for FDIC; re-regulation of business areas of federally licensed banks
Riegle–Neal Interstate Banking and Branching Efficiency Act (1994)	Enables bank holding companies under certain conditions to acquire retail banks in any state; banks can merge across state borders
Financial Services Modernization Act (1999)	Also known as *Gramm–Leach–Bliley Act*. Lifts product regulations of *Glass–Steagall Act* and allows the merger of banks, deposit houses and insurances in one company

Depository Institutions Deregulation and Monetary Control Act (DIDMCA) which allowed S&Ls to expand into new areas of business. Suddenly, they were allowed to offer consumer credit, pay interest on sight deposits (like commercial banks), allow customers to open current accounts and offer them credit cards. The cap on interest for savings deposits of 5.25 per cent for banks and 5.5 per cent for the S&L sector was to be gradually removed over a six-year

they were unable to acquire federal licences until 1982, they operated on a regionally limited basis. After the New Deal they were largely responsible for the mortgage business. The fact that their long-term loans were financed through short-term deposits meant that the S&Ls were particularly vulnerable to sudden rises in interest rates. For more information on the S&Ls sector see Baer and Mote (1992). To prevent any confusion between this American sector and the German *Sparkassen* who share some of its attributes, this study will use the terms *thrift* and S&L when describing it.

period. These new directives were supposed to increase competition in the financial sector by enabling S&Ls to enter more profitable (as well as riskier) areas of business in a bid to improve their position.[45] At the time, the cap on raising the interest of deposits also known as "Regulation Q" was one of the main administrative instruments for regulating prices in the financial sector.[46] The elimination of these measures, which had been under discussion for over ten years, was the centrepiece of the laws enacted as part of the DIDMCA (C&N 1981: 262).

This legislation fitted well with the Reagan administration's belief in the benefits of deregulation. It decided to use any opportunity to remove the restrictions on the banking industry which had existed since the New Deal. Of particular interest to Reagan officials was the dismantling of the controls on the products banks could offer which had been the centrepiece of the Glass–Steagall Act. With the Republicans attaining a majority in the Senate, the appointment of a Republican to chair its Banking Committee seemed to provide an environment conducive to those who wanted to reduce the influence of the state over the banking sector. Yet the Reagan administration was quickly confronted with scepticism from the Federal Reserve[47] and members of Senate committees whose jurisdiction included banking issues (C&N 1990: 89f.). Securities firms, real estate agencies, and insurance companies exerted considerable political pressure to keep unwanted competition from the banks out of their own areas of business while the House of Representatives' own banking committee openly declared its opposition to the Reagan administration's various initiatives. The end product of this debate was the Garn–St. Germain Act, which led to a further wave of deregulation for banks and S&Ls but did not include any changes when it came to product controls.

3.4.2 Legislative Deadlock and Administrative Action

Following this failure in the legislative arena, commercial banks began to focus their attention on the regulatory agencies, where a recent influx of Reagan appointees in leading positions continued to push for further deregulation

---

[45] For a more detailed description of the DIDMCA can be found in C&N (1981: 261f.) as well as FDIC (1997: 91–5).

[46] For an analysis of its history and the reasons for its gradual elimination see Gilbert (1986).

[47] The Fed was concerned that further liberalization might cause problems for its monetary policy, see Reinicke (1995: 64).

from within the system.[48] This was especially the case in the upper levels of the OCC and FDIC though the Fed remained less enthusiastic about this reform agenda (C&N 1985: 84). The FDIC went on to fulfil the hopes of most banks by deciding that the guidelines of the Glass–Steagall Act were not applicable to banks licensed by the states. Commercial banks also enjoyed a string of successes in the courts, where several rulings confirmed reinterpretations of existing regulations by officials who advocated further reform (Reinicke 1995: 66). Both developments led to further tension between federal regulatory agencies as a growing number of banks changed their allegiance to more liberal and pro-reform regulators in a process known as "charter switching". The commercial banks also backed a series of initiatives which encouraged deregulation at the state level. This lobbying effort was crowned with success in 1983, when a bill was passed in South Dakota which allowed state-licensed banks to, among other things, own insurance companies as long as these only operated outside of the borders of this sparsely populated state (ibid.).

Most academic literature on the banking sector has maintained that institutional deadlock was the end result of these different legislative measures.[49] The relevant committees in both the Senate and the House of Representatives were bitterly divided. The Banking Committee in the Senate was dominated by supporters of reform who confronted more sceptical Senators worried about the possible risks of deregulation, the lack of consumer protection, and the need to protect the interests of securities firms. In the meantime, Congressman St Germain, who chaired the Banking Committee in the House, vocally demanded stronger safeguards for the interests of workers, consumers, and small businessmen in any new reform programme. There was also disunity in the ranks of the regulatory agencies, with the OCC and FDIC supporting further reform and the Fed trying to block it. No agreement could even be reached on a suggestion made by the Treasury that further rules and regulations should not be enacted until an agreement on their basic principles could be reached by all government agencies concerned. Though the Fed supported this initiative, the OCC and FDIC opposed it while it caused fierce debate in Congress over whether this moratorium should only involve administrative measures or also encompass a bar on further legislation (Reinicke 1995: 71). The failure to come to any consensus on this Treasury initiative meant that there were no restraints on pro-reform regulators who wanted to achieve further deregulation.

---

[48] See interviews with the chairmen of the OCC and the FDIC, C. T. Conover and William Isaac, in Miller (1982: 35, 42).
[49] See C&N (1985: 83), FDIC (1997: 96), and Reinicke (1995: 58).

In 1982, the FDIC promptly allowed banks licensed by the states to establish subsidiaries that could trade in stocks and bonds. These subsidiaries were subsequently allowed to enter other areas of business in 1983. This was a direct challenge to the Fed as it potentially encouraged a further bout of "charter switching", as well as to Congress, whose position as primary policy-maker was undermined. The Fed had already been warned by Treasury Secretary Regan that the states would take the initiative if there was further Congressional deadlock:

States will shape the financial services industry of the future. And it will be inconsistent, inefficient, costly and less effective in delivering services to the consumer and once again the process will go to those who are swiftest in finding the loopholes.

(Cited after Reinicke 1995: 75)

Banks had in fact shown great ingenuity in finding legal loopholes,[50] which the banking industry went on to manipulate to its own advantage through the establishment of subsidiaries in several business areas. In 1984, there were over 300 applications to the OCC for permission to set up "non-bank banks" after a bill designed to close this loophole was unable to find enough support in the Senate (Reinicke 1995: 78).

The collapse of the Continental Illinois National Bank in Chicago made it impossible for those who had drafted this bill to get it through the House and the Senate. This bank was one of the largest regional banks in the United States, and its bankruptcy meant that the regulators had to pay out over $7.5 billion in order to save it. Even if there was no direct connection between this scandal and the campaign for legislative reform of bank regulation, it did provide its opponents with fresh ammunition for their arguments (FDIC 1997: 97). Always sceptical about the need for reform, the banking committee of the House of Representatives therefore refused to vote on the

---

[50] The three most important loopholes were:

1. The "non-bank bank" loophole was the Bank Holding Company Act of 1956, which defined a bank as a company which provided deposits and business loans. If a company only focused on one of these two areas, it could avoid regulations limiting the scope of regular banks.

2. The "South Dakota" loophole, which allowed a state-licensed subsidiary of a bank belonging to the federal licensing scheme to sell insurance (C&N 1985: 92).

3. The "town of 5000" loophole in the National Bank Act of 1864, which allowed banks with federal licences to sell insurance of towns with less than 5,000 inhabitants (possibly because towns of that size rarely had insurance agents in the nineteenth century). This stipulation was interpreted by the OCC in such a flexible fashion, that many banks were able to sell insurance policies as long as one of their subsidiaries was based in a small town.

"non-bank bank" bill. At the same time, the growing Savings & Loans scandal which enveloped that industry began to dominate proceedings in Congress. The polarized atmosphere caused by the conflict over reform even hindered moves to solve the S&L crisis. As a result, policy-making was largely shaped by decisions made in the regulatory and judicial arenas.

Court rulings, including several by the Supreme Court, confirmed reform-friendly initiatives implemented by the regulatory agencies at the same time that the OCC began to license "non-bank banks" at the federal level. After the elections of 1986 restored the democratic majority in the Senate, the return of the chairmanship of the banking committee to democratic hands ended any further prospect for banking reform legislation being passed in Congress. The new chairman, Senator Proxmire, did not see any need for reform: "We've got to do everything we can to maintain the banking system we have. I think it's worked very well." (Reinicke 1995: 84).

Paradoxically, the preservation of the system which Proxmire professed to admire made a certain level of reform necessary. In the 1970s, foreign banks were the fastest growing segment of the American banking industry, with a market share of 40 per cent in New York alone. Whereas in the 1970s six of the ten biggest banks in the world were American, by 1980 there were only two in the top ten (Reinicke 1995: 91). The growing market share and competitive challenge posed by foreign banks began to force the pace of change. The cathartic effects of the deregulation of financial markets in London (known as the "big bang") began to make themselves felt in the United States. Implied threats made by American banks that they had developed an exit strategy and would move to deregulated markets, especially when their foreign competitors could engage in all forms of financial marketing and speculation in the United States,[51] forced both the Fed and Congress to reconsider their positions. In the wider context of a growing academic and political debate over supposed "American Decline", a new set of priorities and criteria began to dominate the discussion over reform of the banking system.[52]

Rather than protecting "private profit", policy-makers began to speak of preserving the "national interest" while the term "deregulation" began to be used by those who had previously emphasized the need for "reform". This made it much easier for many members of Congress to change their position.

---

[51] This usually took place within the framework of the "grandfathering"-rule for all foreign banks who were licensed to operate in the United States before the International Banking Act was passed in 1978. See statements made by Senator Proxmire in Reinicke (1995: 99).

[52] This debate led to criticism of the American financial system as a whole. The relatively low level of inward investment was seen as the main reason for industrial decline. A study which reflects these concerns was produced by Michael Porter under the aegis of the Washington-based Council on Competitiveness (Porter 1992).

The most important defection from the anti-reform front was that of Senator Proxmire in the summer of 1987, which led to the final elimination of the Glass–Steagall Act's restrictions on the banking industry (C&N 1990: 114). Proxmire argued that in the changed circumstances of the 1980s, the controls imposed by the Glass–Steagall Act, which had originally been designed to stabilize the American banking system, needed to be repealed because they were now having the opposite effect. Although the attitude of the bank committee remained negative when it came to reform, as a concession it held several hearings on the topic for the first time. In the course of these hearings however, representatives from small bank associations as well as their counterparts in securities firms and the insurance industry were given more space to express their opposition to change. By contrast, in Senate hearings on the same issues representatives of the large banks pointed to the decline of the steel, automobile, and textile industries in the United States as examples of what might happen if their own industry was not allowed to adapt to new conditions.

The most significant change in position was that of the Federal Reserve in 1987. Abandoning its sceptical stance, the Fed gave banks permission to set up nationwide subsidiaries that could trade in stocks and bonds as long as their worth did not exceed 5 per cent of a bank's net profit.[53] Suddenly, the Federal Reserve was in the vanguard of the coalition for reform. Although the Fed was accused by many Senators and Congressmen of arrogating powers which actually belonged to the legislative branch, it did not retract this decision. The resignation of the Fed chairman Paul Volcker and his replacement by Alan Greenspan, whose pro-reform views were well-known, represented the final step towards the abandonment of the Glass–Steagall Act by the central bank. Combined with further judicial successes enjoyed by advocates of deregulation, this policy shift in the Fed helped foster a general consensus for reform which was not even dampened by the stock market crash of 19 October 1987.

With the support of his successor as chairman of the Senate banking committee, Senator Garn, another attempt at getting reform legislation through Congress was started by Proxmire in March 1988. This initiative succeeded, as a reform bill passed with a margin of ninety-four votes to two in the Senate (C&N 1990: 116). The political pressure on the House to follow the Senate's lead was so great that committee chairman St. Germain submitted a piece of reform legislation with a strong emphasis on consumer protection backed

---

[53] This reinterpretation was a sophistic definition of section 20 of the Glass–Steagall Act. The relevant sub-clause ("no member shall be affiliated [...] with any corporation [...] engaged principally in the issue, flotation, underwriting [...] of stocks") has always been treated as an absolute ban on such activity.

by a majority of the Banking Committee in 1988. Since this bill contained several directives dealing with trading in stocks and bonds, it also fell under the jurisdiction of the House Energy and Commerce Committee whose chairman John Dingell was deeply opposed to any reform. Though Dingell's motivations were tactical rather than ideological (Reinicke 1995: 109f.), his hostility was enough to delay Proxmire's bill until the end of that Congressional session. A final attempt to pass at least part of this legislation failed to overcome the resistance of New York Senator D'Amato, who did his utmost to protect the interests of the New York stock market (C&N 1990: 120). The end of that session of Congress marked the final failure of this bill, leading Senator Proxmire to explicitly demand that regulatory agencies fill the legislative vacuum that Congress had created: "Congress has failed to do the job. Now it's time for the Fed to step in" (Reinicke 1995: 110).

With changes in the personnel of the Senate and House banking committees making the chances for reform legislation look increasingly remote, in September 1989 the Fed decided to follow Proxmire's advice by raising the limits defined by the section 20 interpretation of the Glass–Steagall Act from 5 per cent to 10 per cent (Reinicke 1995: 114). This resulted in sharp criticism of the Federal Reserve from Congressman Gonzales, the new chairman of the House banking committee.

3.4.3 Legislative Re-Regulation

Despite (or perhaps because) of this legislative deadlock, the competitive position of the American banking industry continued to come under pressure. Japanese banks in particular expanded their market share, controlling 25 per cent of the market in California alone. Those foreign banks not subject to the grandfathering-directive began to lobby American legislators for further liberalization of the US financial market. Pointing to the phenomenal growth of the London market after it was deregulated in 1986 as well as the strength of European forms of universal banking (where banking and securities trading could be undertaken jointly by financial conglomerates), a sub-committee of the House Banking Committee recommended that the interests of small banks, which had been so successful in blocking further reform, should be given less consideration by legislators. This stance hardened as fears grew in Congress that American banks might be locked out of the single European market after 1992 if they could not guarantee reciprocal treatment of their European competitors in the United States. This forced the association representing stockbrokers and securities firms to change sides; a policy shift it confirmed publicly by stating that it would no longer oppose a repeal of the Glass–Steagall Act.

Though two major barriers to reform had therefore fallen away, Congress was still preoccupied with the massive financial losses which had been incurred by the S&L industry. Passed in 1989, the Financial Institutions Reform, Recovery and Enforcement Act (FIRREA) put aside $50 billion to ameliorate these losses and put in motion a fundamental restructuring of the way in which S&Ls were regulated, placing new limitations on the kind of products and services they could offer.[54] Discussions between regulators and Congress over the high costs caused by such major problems as well as the sudden increase in the number of bank insolvencies (see Figure 3.2) led to a reorientation of the wider debate. Instead of "competitiveness", policy-makers were now more focused on the issue of "security".

This shift in the general framework of the debate was a bad omen for the wide-ranging reform initiatives of the first Bush administration which had been unveiled in 1991 as part of the "Brady Plan". These reforms included a cap on levels of deposit insurance, new powers for regulators that would enable them to intervene more quickly in a failing bank, consolidation of the regulatory infrastructure, a removal of barriers to inter-state banking, permission for commercial banks to offer new services, and the repeal of the Glass–Steagall Act (United States Department of the Treasury 1991; see also FDIC 1997: 102). Yet the wide scope of this plan helped mobilize a broad coalition of interest groups opposed to further reform. While the IBAA did everything to prevent the revocation of service and product controls and the removal of geographic regulations, the agriculture lobby expressed concerns that their clientele might face serious difficulties if rural banks were unable to survive the new competitive environment created by these reforms. This led to an intervention against the "Brady Plan" by the House Agriculture Committee which was dominated by opponents of the Bush administrations reform agenda.

The S&L crisis had also mobilized consumer rights groups, who were worried about the possibility that major changes in the banking system might endanger savings and lead to an increase in bank charges (Reinicke 1995: 122). Since another part of this legislative package contained measures to save the FDIC from a financial crisis which was enveloping it, the first Bush administration had to accept a compromise stripping the "Brady Plan" of the most controversial reform measures in order to refinance the deposit insurance system before it ground to a halt. As in previous cases, the failure of

---

[54] See C&N (1993: 117ff.), FDIC (1997: 100ff.). A detailed description of FIRREA directives can be found in Gail and Norton (1990).

this reform initiative was again the result of an unwillingness to compromise among all those involved (ibid.: 124). Thus, a once ambitious plan ended as the rather limited Federal Deposit Insurance Corporation Improvement Act (FDICIA) which passed in 1991.[55]

As with previous reform initiatives, legislative deadlock ultimately led to renewed attempts to change the system by regulatory agencies. This culminated in the Fed allowing the commercial banking arm of J. P. Morgan to offer a whole set of securities and stock trading services. Treasury Undersecretary Robert Glauber, who had been responsible for the "Brady Plan", was remarkably upbeat when he looked back upon the reform agenda of the first Bush administration: "[I]t eventually will get to the situation where Congress will ratify what has already happened" (Reinicke 1995: 126).

3.4.4 Ratified Deregulation

Almost ten years later in 1999, this prediction was fulfilled. Yet in the preceding decade, several of the reform initiatives launched by the Clinton administration would also end in failure. In 1993, its attempt to merge the regulatory arms of the Fed, the FDIC, and OCC as well as that of the Office of Thrift Supervision into one "super-agency" experienced considerable resistance from several sides. While the Fed was deeply opposed to losing its regulatory responsibilities, the banks resisted any initiative to end their right to choose between different regulatory agencies (C&N 1998: 130). After a second attempt to push these measures forward, the Clinton administration abandoned this initiative in 1994 (Vogel 1996: 228). This was accompanied by another stab at repealing the Glass–Steagall Act supported by a broad coalition of Republicans, Democrats, and Fed officials, as well as banks, securities firms, and stockbrokers. The House Banking Committee voted for repeal but added a stipulation that banks should be permanently banned from selling insurance as a sop to the insurance industry. Faced with such limits on their expansion, the banks quickly lost interest in this legislation as the reform effort ground to a halt yet again (Vogel 1996: 228; C&N 1998: 133 ff.). As in the aftermath of previous failed reform initiatives, the Fed raised the cap on the section 20 interpretation of the Glass–Steagall Act; this time it was raised from 10 per cent to 25 per cent (*Neue Zürcher Zeitung*, 2 August 1996: 11).

---

[55] A detailed description of this process can be found in the article "FDICIA: The Wheels Came Off on the Road through Congress" (Glauber 1993). The contents of the FDICIA are explained in FDIC (1997: 102–24), and an evaluation of this legislation can be found in Kaufman and Litan (1993); a more critical view of this law is expounded in Khoury (1997).

The Clinton administration also had its policy success when it came to bank regulation. Legislation such as the Riegle–Neal Interstate Banking and Branching Efficiency Act of 1994 that removed geographic regulation controlling the opening hours of bank branches between states led to a major change in the way bank transactions were conducted in the United States (FDIC 1997: 129ff.; see also *The Economist*, 6 August 1994: 59–60). Yet legislators were only confirming developments which had already taken place on the ground. On the one hand, the number of states permitting intrastate banking had risen massively in the course of the 1980s, while on the other hand, all states with the exception of Hawaii had passed laws allowing banks to be sold to holding companies based outside state borders (FDIC 1997: 130; see also Coleman 1996: 164f.). The Gramm–Leach–Bliley Act passed in 1999 finally managed to abolish the product and service controls of the Glass–Steagall Act. As this chapter has demonstrated, however, this success simply reflected changes, fostered by the actions of regulatory agencies as well as court rulings, which had already taken root in the previous fifteen years.

3.5 CHARACTERISTICS OF THE POLICY FIELD

The policy field of bank regulation in the period we have examined is characterized by four factors: a high degree of politicization, a confrontational political style in the legislative arena, extreme diversity in the number of interest groups and policy-makers involved (many of which were in a position to veto change) along with a willingness to try to impose reform through administrative or judicial means. These factors and the way in which they interacted with one another will be examined in the next section.

3.5.1 High Politicization

What is particularly striking when viewed in international comparison is the high level of political and public attention received by the issue of bank regulation in the United States. This topic has led to a considerable mobilization of resources by interest groups and has sparked fierce political debates in the media and among the public. By contrast, in most European countries bank policy is primarily seen as a technical matter which rarely arouses political passions.[56] As we have seen in the introductory section of this chapter, the

---

[56] See the overview in Busch (2001).

reasons for this unusual level of politicization in the United States have deep historical roots based on a traditional distrust of concentrations of power, be they in politics or finance. The political divisions of the nineteenth century (see Figure 3.1) can still be seen in the battles over reform of the regulation system in the last three decades, especially when it comes to the collision of interests between large and small banks. The long-term historical development towards a low level of consolidation when it came to the banking sector created a set of interest groups which had an incentive to stabilize the system. These tendencies were heightened by the regulatory interventions of the New Deal that had fostered severe market segmentation. The continuing large number of banks means that the topic has remained of interest to the broader population, so that the conflict can still be seen to mirror deeper tensions between the centres of finance and the economic periphery. To sum up, one can say that the situation has remained constant over the past century while these issues have continued to be highly politicized in the last thirty years despite major social change.

3.5.2 Confrontational and Legalistic Policy Approaches

As Section 3.4 has shown, the style of policy-making in the area of bank regulation must be described as confrontational. A tendency towards confrontation is certainly a general characteristic of the American political system. In this case, however, a tendency towards confrontational rhetoric had been strengthened by the high level of politicization when it came to bank regulation. The large number of policy goals which bank regulation is supposed to fulfil in the United States exacerbates this problem. There are effectively five separate policy goals which have been focused on by all those involved in this process:[57]

1. Protecting the integrity of individual deposits and the banking system as a whole
2. Consumer protection
3. Fostering competition within the banking system
4. Prevention of concentrations of power
5. A fair process of credit allocation

Consumer protection (a policy goal resulting from high levels of politicization) was supposed to be secured by forcing banks to act in a transparent manner, giving their customers access to as much information as possible. At a regional level, the fairness of credit allocation was to be ensured

---

[57] Spong (1994: chapters 5–7); interview at the Brookings Institution, 10 July 1998. See also the "core beliefs" in Worsham (1997: 32, 42, 91, 108).

through a ban on discrimination at an individual level which was maintained by a ratings scheme enshrined in the Community Reinvestment Act. These goals are, in one sense, compatible (a competitive banking system should ideally be consumer-friendly by keeping prices low), and yet, in another, incompatible (competition can lead to heavy concentrations of power; state intervention in credit allocation can reduce competitiveness and distort the marketplace).

Moreover, the sheer number of different policy goals necessitates a great many laws if they are to be achieved. The large number of laws resulting from these pressures, the most important of which are set out in Table 3.4, have created an almost impenetrable legal framework. This has led to a situation where significant legal factors are not clearly defined or are defined in a contradictory fashion, where loopholes are frequent and where interactions between different legislative initiatives have not been thought through. For example, deregulation which took place under the auspices of the DIDMCA in 1980, was brought about without any measures taken to reduce the resulting level of risk (FDIC 1997: 10). This resulted in the raising of the deposit guarantee from $40,000 to $100,000, a decision which has subsequently been made responsible for some of the moral hazard problems which helped to cause the S&L crisis (Scott and Weingast 1992).

The plethora of banking laws has also helped to shape the political style of the debate on banking regulation since these laws have precisely defined the responsibilities of the state and can be scrutinized by the courts. This has fostered an extremely formalistic administrative approach where legal challenges from interest groups have become frequent. This political style has been termed "legalistic" and is considered by many to be an impediment to major change because it makes the political process dependent upon openness, lack of trust, and a willingness to fight over issues. This means that it has become very difficult for the different players involved to come to a consensus on a common strategy for action (Coleman 1996: 156).

3.5.3 Variety of Players

Openness is in itself central to the pluralistic nature of the American political system (Peters 1999: 50) and is of great significance to the policy field of banking regulation. Conversely, it also works against cooperation between interest groups since individual associations or banks find it easier to be heard when working alone than in a coalition with other institutions. As we have seen above, the sheer variety of different players, who are in constant competition with one another, is a problem for both banking associations and regulatory agencies. While it is difficult for the state to coordinate such a large number of different interest groups, it is in theory directly responsible for the number of regulatory agencies involved. Most attempts to reduce their number have failed. On the contrary, lower down the hierarchy new committees and agencies are constantly being formed to deal with new problems on an ad hoc basis.

Examples of further fragmentation of state authority are the Depository Institutions Deregulation Committee created by the DIDMCA to implement its directives (FDIC 1997: 92), the Federal Financial Institutions Examination Council (FFIEC) or the Resolution Trust Corporation (RTC) responsible for dealing with the S&L crisis. One could surmise that this approach is taken because it is easier to set up new committees or agencies to deal with new crises rather than handing over such responsibilities to established regulators who are already in fierce competition with one another. However, this has only worsened the conflicts over jurisdiction that have helped make the system of regulation evermore chaotic. The observation made by one expert sums up the end result of this tendency: "They never close an agency down."[58]

Congress has not covered itself with glory either. The sheer number of Congressional committees involved in banking policy mirrored the multitude of regulatory agencies competing for turf and attention. The conflicts between different committees are given an added edge by the fact that their chairmen are very powerful, effectively able to veto legislation of which they disapprove (Shell 1990: 304–8). While these positions were filled on a strict seniority basis until the mid-1970s, in the last three decades they have been determined through majority voting on the House and Senate floors. However, the chairmanship is usually still held by the most senior members of the majority party although there are some exceptions to this rule (Ginsberg, Lowi, and Weir 1997: 411). Since it has given committee chairmen greater power and access to a larger number of staffers, this democraticization has led to a greater fragmentation of power, making it even more difficult to reach agreement over policy.

Chairmen have almost absolute control over the agenda of their committees, and can even block policy initiatives supported by a majority of other committee members. Acting as "gatekeepers", their powerful position gives them an informal veto over any kind of policy initiative. Other committee members also have the means to block legislation through their power to add amendments and organize filibusters. It is therefore not surprising that over

[58] Interview OCC, 10 July 1998.

95 per cent of all proposed bills fail to survive the committee stage (Ginsberg, Lowi, and Weir 1997: 417). Since committee members are usually chosen through a process of self-selection where Congressmen or Senators who have expertise or are close to interest groups dominate committee proceedings, little consideration is taken of the consequences their policy initiatives have for the wider national interest (Worsham 1997: 64).

The legislative process in Congress is therefore highly dynamic and subject to a range of influences including presidential action, judicial rulings, international developments, or media coverage. Its imperatives make it necessary to find a new majority at every legislative step in an environment where such majorities can fall apart at any time (Oleszek 1989: 283). Under these conditions, the whole process has come to resemble some kind of highly complex game, whose attributes are described by the chairman of the Energy and Commerce Committee, John Dingell:

Legislation is like a chess game more than anything else. It is a seemingly endless series of moves, until ultimately somebody prevails through exhaustion, or brilliance, or because of overwhelming public sentiment for their side.

(cited after Oleszek 1989: 283)

The short duration of Congressional sessions exacerbates this situation, since any legislation which has not passed at the end of a session has to be resubmitted at the beginning of the next one. The resulting tactical means to block bills have already been illustrated in Section 3.4.2 through the example of John Dingell's attempts to kill off legislation, demonstrating that he knows how to play the rules of the game he describes.

The short Congressional sessions also ensure that Congressmen (who have two-year terms while Senators serve for six years) are constantly reminded of the concerns of their own constituents. Electorally vulnerable, most Congressmen are usually more interested in defending the interests of their electorate than in objective facts and necessities (Scott and Weingast 1992: 12). It is, therefore, no coincidence that since the nineteenth century, the House of Representatives has traditionally been more hostile to bank reform than the Senate (Worsham 1997: 29). This is largely because Congressmen usually represent a specific territorial district, containing its own small banks whose local influence cannot be ignored during primaries and elections. The principle that "all politics is local" is therefore as relevant to bank regulation as it is to other aspects of American public life.[59]

---

[59] Interview with Ray Vernon, 13 May 1998.

3.5.4 Circumventing Deadlock at the Administrative
and Judicial Level

The actions of regulatory agencies and the courts in response to Congressional deadlock is the final characteristic of the American case to be explored in this case study. New definitions and reinterpretations of existing law created considerable movement in bank policy despite the legislative inertia displayed by the House and Senate. The ability to use these means was largely the result of the legalistic policy style described above. Yet these efforts to circumvent the legislature were of an ambiguous nature. On the one hand, it was a form of safety valve, which enabled the system to adapt to international pressures despite the inability of politicians to implement meaningful reform over decades. On the other hand, reform initiatives driven forward by the work of unelected bureaucrats and judges had little democratic legitimacy. Yet these caveats are balanced by the many investigative committees set up by Congress, whose work on problems in the banking system has often provided the information upon which administrative or judicial decisions for change have been based.

3.6 SUMMARY: THE AMERICAN CASE

The American policy network dealing with banking issues reacted with deadlock to the many challenges of the 1980s and 1990s. This fostered attempts to circumvent a legislative blockade on the administrative and judicial levels through the reinterpretation of existing regulations. This deadlock is largely the result of the existence of a "path-dependent lock-in", that is a policy framework which has developed over a long period of time and thus possesses a high degree of stability. Each initiative to deal with these challenges posed a threat to the agenda of different interest groups, who thus did their best to thwart any further progress towards a solution.

Nevertheless, there was considerable movement under the surface. The pro- and anti-reform coalitions were in a constant state of flux, as different interest groups moved from one coalition to the other whenever regulatory reinterpretations changed their position within the banking system. While in the 1980s, insurance companies and stockbrokers fearful of competition from commercial banks were opposed to any reform which might abolish controls on bank products and services, in the 1990s, they came to support a repeal of product and service controls as long as it created greater regulatory clarity through the closure of remaining legal loopholes. By contrast, banks that had initially supported change began to resist further reforms which were not compatible with their plans for the future.[60]

Movement was also created by changes in the "framing" of the political discourse (Rein and Schön 1993). The widespread discussions over American decline in the late 1980s led to a general change in the national mood, a development that had a considerable impact on attitudes in Congress:

Congress remains the "people's branch", and when it hears the citizens "loud and clear", it will heed their voices.   (Rieselbach 1986: 270)

Yet in order to make further changes possible certain conditions must be fulfilled such as, according to Rieselbach, a consensus about the way forward between different interest groups and Congress committees involved (ibid.). As we have seen, such a consensus has rarely been achieved.

Although there has been no concerted reform of the chaotic consequences of competing state agencies and overlapping jurisdictions—a shift that has been demanded by several Congressional commissions over the past decades—piecemeal measures such as the abolition of product and service controls, the repeal of price regulations and the removal of geographic limits on bank operations have changed the nature of the financial marketplace. Despite these limited successes, in the 1990s the banking system of the United States was, when viewed in international comparison, still one of the most heavily regulated in an industrialized country, superseded only by the Japanese financial sector (Barth, Nolle, and Rice 1997: table 5). Moreover, many academic experts and regulators have expressed serious doubts over the current system's ability to cope with (and survive) the challenges posed by a serious recession.

For the state's capacity for action, when it comes to the policy field of banking regulation, has remained limited in the United States (Coleman 1996: 77). This should not lead to any generalizations about the regulatory power of the American state as a whole. When it comes to regulation of the stock markets, US regulators are willing and able to intervene decisively in a crucial part of the American economic system.[61] In the area of bank regulation itself, one should differentiate between domestic and international developments. The same banking lobby which proved so obstructive when it came to domestic reforms played an instrumental role in the creation of international standards

[60] Interview with Bob Glauber, 5 June 1998.
[61] Coleman (1996: 161) believes that the main reasons for this is the fact that there is less pressure on all the main players to conform, a much stronger central regulatory agency, and a far less complex policy network.

for bank capital enshrined in the Basle Accords.[62] The behaviour demonstrated by iron triangles of interest groups, members of the executive, and legislators depended on the situation at hand. The ability to act internationally does not necessarily mean that a state or government could impose its will domestically.

This case study has, therefore, demonstrated that in the United States, a set of domestic factors ensured that there was no long-term strategy guiding reforms of the regulatory system. Major changes took place, but attempts to steer policy towards a well-defined aim were few and far between.

---

[62] Reinicke (1995: chapters 7 and 8); see also Vernon, Spar, and Tobin (1991: chapter 6) as well as Genschel and Plümper (1999).

4

The Federal Republic of Germany: Keeping the State at Arm's Length

Despite preconceptions in the English-speaking world that Germany is a country in which the state intervenes in all aspects of economic life, the German banking system has traditionally been characterized by a relatively low level of state regulation. In fact, state regulations covering debit and credit interest rates as well as controls on capital movement were lifted at a comparatively early point in time.

Consequently, the transformation of international financial markets in the last few decades has not led to any great pressure upon banks and state regulators in the Federal Republic to adapt to new circumstances. Germany is—in marked contrast to the United States—a case in which one single law, the *Kreditwesengesetz*, has codified state regulation in the banking sector. In the 1960s, this law already contained those stipulations which were fostering the international harmonization of regulatory structures in the banking sector: equity quotas and controls on the maximum amount of major loans. Moreover, the universal bank system which has increasingly predominated in most European states, has historically been the largest element of the banking sector in Germany.

Most academic studies have therefore come to the conclusion that in comparison with other countries, German banking policy has not had to confront any major problems (Vogel 1996: 250; Coleman 1996: 128). As the following case study will show, however, the German finance and banking sectors have experienced moments of crisis which threatened existing patterns of regulation. In the following section, the historical background of banking regulation as a policy field will be examined first, the specific challenges which policymakers in the Federal Republic have had to face in recent decades will then be described in the second section. Next, this case study will move on to take a look at the relevant actors involved in the banking policy network before examining a key political moment, the *Herstatt Bank* crisis. The final part of this case study will offer some conclusions about the defining characteristics of this policy field in the Federal Republic.

4.1 THE HISTORICAL BACKGROUND

This case study will begin with a short examination of the historical background of both the banking industry and bank regulation in Germany which provided the foundations for the new developments that have taken place in this policy field in the last twenty-five years.

4.1.1 The Establishment of the Banking System

The modern German banking system first emerged in the nineteenth century.[1] The development of increasingly complex banking structures was both the result as well as the cause of the economic integration of Germany in that period (Tilly 1994: 299). In the process, the banking sector itself experienced fundamental changes. At the beginning of the nineteenth century, the banking sector was still dominated by individual private bankers who largely traded in government bonds. Though this group played a significant role until the 1870s, by the mid-point of the century a new set of incorporated banks were established which managed to attain a dominant position in the sector after German unification in 1870. At the same time, the close relationship between many banks and major industrial companies led to the creation of a specifically German form of universal banking.

Initially, however, banks had not done much to help finance the first steps of the industrialization process in Germany. Typical of the difficult conditions in which the first German industrialists had to finance their projects was the fact that in 1811 Friedrich Krupp had to borrow the start-up capital for his first major factory, a steelworks in Essen, from his mother and his siblings. His company only received its first bank loan in 1835, a comparatively small sum of 8,000 Thalers (Gall 1995: 26).[2] Yet by the 1840s, banks began to take an increasing interest in expanding industrial companies. The rapid growth of the railway network and the heavy industry needed to supply it led to the emergence of what has become known as the "leading sector complex", a part of the economy in which the banks became heavily involved (Tilly 1990: 50). Leading bankers played a key role in the foundation of the *Rheinische Eisenbahngesellschaft* (REG) in the 1830s, which, with a net worth of 3 million Thalers, was the largest private business in Prussia (ibid. 61f.). This level of

---

[1] This part of the chapter is partly based on information from Gall (1995), Pohl (1993), and Tilly (1990, 1994). A comprehensive examination of the banking and financial system in the nineteenth and twentieth centuries can be found in Born (1977), while its role in the historical development of Germany is analysed in Wehler (1995: 85–91, 622–37, 662–80).

[2] This loan came from a bank based in Cologne called the *Herstatt-Bank*, which will be examined further below.

involvement was matched by the banking community in a whole set of similar companies. As a consequence of this massive financial commitment, which was often financed from their personal fortunes, bankers usually received seats on the board of directors in order to help them oversee and secure the assets into which they had invested such massive sums.

Yet the demand for capital generated by the railway industry was so high that private bankers were unable to provide sufficient funds to finance it alone. This necessitated a number of comprehensive mergers which consolidated the industry by turning a large number of smaller private banks into several large corporate banks. Though the first such corporate bank, the *A. Schaafhausen-scher Bankverein*, was only established in order to save a private bank threatened with insolvency (Tilly 1990: 64), in 1853 the *Bank für Handel und Industrie* based in Darmstadt was specifically set up to help finance industrial projects. This initiative emulated the highly successful French *Crédit Mobilier*, whose primary focus on financing major manufacturers had helped kick-start the industrialization process in France.[3] With their greater financial and administrative resources, corporate banks could act as capital accumulators in order to help provide much larger long-term loans than had previously been possible. Since most German banks after 1870 provided venture capital and issued stock while still conducting regular deposit transactions, they developed the kind of universal banking model which has shaped the German banking system to this day.

While in countries such as the United States (see Section 3.1.1) commercial banks had the right to issue banknotes, in Prussia the state kept total control of the currency, issuing banknotes and coins produced in government-owned mints (Tilly 1990: 66). Implemented in 1875, the first banking law enacted after the foundation of a German nation state led to the establishment of a single central bank (based on the Prussian central bank) which had branches in every major urban centre of the German *Reich* (Born 1977: 35). This resulted in a systematic division of labour between the commercial banks and the state-run central bank.[4] While the latter controlled the great bulk of paper currency payments and cashless transactions as well as the growing number of

---

[3] Its founders, the Péreire brothers, were heavily influenced by the ideas of the early socialist Saint-Simon, who believed that banks could become the ideal instrument for the non-revolutionary transformation of society. This was to be brought about through the creation of cartels, which were to minimize competition and enable governments to control the economy through the banking system.

[4] The singular is used here for the purpose of simplification. In 1850, there were in fact over thirty banks issuing currency in Germany. However, the number of banknotes issued by these institutions was negligible when compared with the sheer volume put into circulation by the Prussian bank. Of 179 million Thaler banknotes in circulation in 1866, 125 million came from the Prussian bank (Born 1977: 32).

short-term business loans through its extensive network of branch offices, the former mostly concentrated their resources on venture capital projects, loans, and the issue of stock for the industrial sector. The initially cash-strapped universal banks were therefore able to use the state-run payment system for their own financial transactions.

Concentration upon certain business partners, particularly first-rate banking houses, industrialists of significance, and wealthy private citizens, was a defining characteristic of German commercial banks in the second half of the nineteenth century.[5] It was only through close relationships with these different elements of the German business elite of that period that commercial banks were able to play such an important role in the industrialization process.[6] However, this meant that market segments such as the rural population, the credit needs of the real estate sector, or the savings of the working class were not catered for by the commercial banks. This created a vacuum which was filled by two forms of banking that had also emerged in the course of the nineteenth century, credit unions and the municipal savings and deposit banks known as *Sparkassen*.

The first *Sparkassen* were established by municipal and local district governments after 1820. By 1850, almost 1,200 existed in every German-speaking state. They were supposed to enable the middle classes as well as the poorer elements of the population to open small, interest-bearing savings accounts which could help provide them with financial security in case of illness or after retirement. They were often founded for both charitable and pragmatic reasons, since increasing the savings rate of the great bulk of the urban population could ultimately help reduce the amount of money city governments had to spend for social welfare purposes (Born 1977: 199f., 207). Moreover, it quickly became apparent that *Sparkassen* could prove instrumental in helping

---

[5] See citations from business memoranda of the *Bank für Handel und Industrie* in Tilly (1990: 65).

[6] In Germany, the financing of industrial development took place in a very different fashion to the methods used for this purpose in England, where economic expansion was driven by direct investment from private capital. As a result, the bank system there became split between deposit banks on the one hand and finance, issue, and investment banks on the other.

In his ground-breaking analysis, Alexander Gerschenkron has pointed out that these divergent economic paths were largely the result of a considerable difference in levels of demand for capital. While it was low in an early industrial England dominated by the textile industry, the late industrialization of Germany, based as it was on heavy industry, could only be achieved through high levels of capital expenditure. Major projects also needed capital over very long periods of time, turning banks into permanent partners of the companies they were helping to finance: "A German bank, as the saying went, accompanied an industrial company from the cradle to the grave, from establishment to liquidation throughout all the vicissitudes of its existence" (Gerschenkron 1966: 14).

municipalities satisfy their demand for credit and meet their financial obligations (Tilly 1994: 305). Though initially only intended to provide savings accounts, by the end of the nineteenth century the introduction of health and disability insurance along with a national pension scheme enabled *Sparkassen* to move more and more into commercial banking focused on the middle classes.

Credit Unions were founded in the 1840s and 1850s for very different reasons. Their aim was to provide small traders, craftsmen, and farmers with loans and other financial services. Based on the principles of self-help and shared liability, several credit unions were founded by Hermann Schulze-Delitzsch in 1850. Run under the aegis of registered societies, these credit unions were usually called *Volksbanken* or *Vorschußvereine*. In the countryside, the decisive step towards this new banking model came from Friedrich Wilhelm Raiffeisen. After a failed harvest in 1846, Raiffeisen founded charitable associations to help farmers buy seed and fertilizers which were swiftly converted into credit unions once it became apparent that rural communities needed long-term financial help. By 1883, over 500 such rural credit unions were operating in the countryside (Pohl 1993: 188).

Cyclically recurring economic crises had a considerable impact on the German banking industry in general and commercial banks in particular. Though the boom of the early 1870s led to the establishment of over 183 corporate banks (Pohl 1993: 189),[7] the subsequent recession (known as the *Gründerkrise*) triggered a wave of consolidation. Unable to cope with changing business conditions, most private banks either slid into insolvency or were taken over by the corporate banks that had survived, and in some cases even thrived in the nationally integrated market of the Wilhelmine period. A second wave of consolidation took place between 1895 and 1913, as provincial banks first combined forces with, and were then taken over by, larger national banks.

At the end of this process, a small number of banks and banking groups dominated the landscape to a much greater extent than in any other comparable country. In 1913, the three largest German companies were banks while seventeen of the twenty-five largest companies were all involved in banking (Tilly 1994: 304). Beyond their sheer size, the introduction of measures shoring up accountability and control such as supervisory boards of non-executive directors for incorporated companies and the introduction of proxy voting rights further strengthened the position of banks within the wider

---

[7] This wave of bank foundations was influenced by the removal in 1870 of the need for joint-stock companies in Prussia to get a state licence.

economy. As a result, the first calls for action to curb the "power of the banks" were made at the beginning of the twentieth century, which became increasingly widespread after Rudolf Hilderding's attack on financial circles (*Das Finanzkapital*) was published in 1910. Whether this specifically German intertwining of corporate banks with industrial corporations really meant that corporate banks controlled the private sector has been a matter of controversy to this day. Most historians have, however, maintained that rather than one-sided control, the relationship between banks and industry was characterized by a form of mutual dependence (Wehler 1995: 630; see also Gall 1995: 51).

The system of universal banking which dominates the German banking sector today, with its three pillars consisting of the commercial banks, *Sparkassen* and cooperative banks, came into existence between 1895 and 1926.[8] The major banks expanded their network of branches by taking direct control of their regional affiliates, a move which shored up their already strong presence in every part of the country.[9] The *Sparkassen*, of which there were over 3,300 by 1913, had become able to conduct most forms of banking by 1921 by integrating their financial transactions and working together in current account associations. This ensured that they were able to operate in as modern a fashion as their corporate competitors. The founding of the *Deutsche Girozentrale* in 1918, as a central coordinating institution for the *Sparkassen*, was the final step in this process. The *Volksbanken*, of which there were 1,500 by 1913 with 815,000 members in total, and the *Raiffeisen* credit unions, of which there were 9,800 in 1900, also moved towards a higher degree of centralization and coordination. All three constituent parts of the German banking industry founded associations to represent their interests. While the commercial banks were represented through the *Centralverband des Deutschen Banken- und Bankiergewerbes* which was founded in 1901, the *Volksbank* sector had the *Hauptverband deutscher gewerblicher Genossenschaften*, which was founded in 1924, the same year in which the *Sparkassen* established the *Deutscher Sparkassen- und Giroverband*.

The hyperinflation crisis of the early 1920s, which weakened the capital base of the banking industry, initiated another wave of consolidation that culminated in several major mergers. Growing competitive pressure and sinking profit margins forced banks to engage in increasingly risky business ventures and financial transactions. With the onset of the Great Depression, this higher level of risk increased the vulnerability of many banks and led to a deep crisis

---

[8] Detailed information about the balance sheets of these banking groups between 1884 and 1913 can be found in Wehler (1995: 631).

[9] For example, the number of *Deutsche Bank* branches rose from 15 in 1913 to 173 in 1926 (Pohl 1993: 190, which also provided the other statistical data in this paragraph).

in the banking sector.[10] After the *Darmstädter und Nationalbank* declared bankruptcy in 1931, the central government in Berlin hastily decided to act as guarantor of this bank's liabilities and installed an official receiver to try to restore its finances. Despite this intervention, in the following days thousands of depositors stormed banks and *Sparkassen* in order to empty their accounts and withdraw their savings. This bank run threatened the stability of the entire banking system, forcing the central government to make further financial guarantees and impose a forced closure of every bank in Germany for several days. One result of this intervention was a quasi-nationalization of the major banks by the state, at the end of which the Reich and the *Reichsbank* held a 91 per cent stake in the *Dresdner Bank*, 70 per cent of the *Commerzbank* and 35 per cent of the shares of Deutsche Bank. Simultaneously, a comprehensive system of bank regulation was established for the first time, initially through emergency directives which were finally codified in 1934 in the *Reichsgesetz über das Kreditwesen*. This did not, however, lead to further structural changes in the banking sector. By 1936, most bank shares in state hands had been sold back to private investors, ending this temporary nationalization.

The end of the Second World War was a watershed of far greater significance. The Allies dismantled the three largest corporate banks because they believed that a concentration of power in the banking sector had helped create the conditions for the National Socialist takeover of power. The largest banks were decentralized and split up into ten banks that could only operate within the borders of their respective states (Pohl 1983: 231–41), though these measures did not affect the rest of the banking system. Yet this policy of decentralization was short-lived since it simply did not command the support of the West German political establishment. In 1952, a legal directive from the new West German government (called the *Großbankengesetz*) decreased the number of successor banks to three per pre-war corporate bank. These subsequently drew closer together in order to combine their profits in a so-called *Gewinnpool* (Pohl 1993: 191). The limits on the opening of bank branches were repealed in 1956 through a legal initiative on the federal level, paving the way for the reestablishment of the *Deutsche Bank*, *Commerzbank* and *Dresdner Bank* in 1957. This did not mean that the corporate banks would be able to reattain their pre-war dominance. In 1957, the major corporate banks only controlled a seventh of the national credit market. As we shall see below (Section 4.3.1, especially Table 4.1), the three main sectors of the German banking industry, the private commercial banks, the state chartered institutions such as the *Sparkassen*, as well as the cooperative and credit union sector have maintained the same level of strength in the last few decades.

---

[10] A detailed description of this crisis can be found in Born (1977: 482–502).

4.1.2 The Emergence of State Regulation

In Germany, as in many other countries, state regulation of the banking system was a twentieth-century phenomenon.[11] The nineteenth century saw, by contrast, no moves towards specific government oversight of the banks, a fact that has surprised many current experts in the field.[12] However, this period witnessed considerable debate over the necessity of regulatory measures. This began to have an impact on policy-making during the policy discussions which led to the enactment of the bank law of 1875 (Fischer 1997a: 3721).[13] But the proposal to place all banks under state supervision ultimately failed to gain any headway, since its opponents argued that economic freedoms codified in the trading guidelines of 1869 made such a form of regulation a legal impossibility. Most lawmakers believed that the protective stipulations of the civil code would be enough to keep the banks in check (Niethammer 1990: 41).

After the collapse of several private banking houses in the 1890s, the protection of deposits once again became a serious issue for those determining economic policy. A proposed bill for the introduction of state banking regulation failed to pass in 1896. At the same time, another planned law for the regulation of deposit banks, which demanded that banks publish their balance sheet on a quarterly basis as part of the legal framework for the stock and bond markets, was also shelved (Mayer 1981: 9f.). After a wave of bank consolidation led to further bankruptcies, the prominent economist Adolph Wagner circulated a detailed proposal for the establishment of a regulatory agency he called the *Reichs-Bankkontrollamt*. Yet opposition to Wagner's plan quickly emerged in the banks, *Sparkassen*, and credit unions as well as among senior academics. Together with growing worries over the level of concentration in the banking sector, this controversy led to a commission of inquiry which undertook a survey of the banking industry in 1908–9 and submitted reform proposals to the government. Its final report advocated the creation of an insurance scheme for deposits run by a *Reichsdepositenversicherungsanstalt*, which was to be financed through contributions from banks and *Sparkassen*, together with a call for banks to release regular balance sheet reports. However, this did not lead to any legislation making such action mandatory since most banks voluntarily followed the survey's recommendations (Niethammer 1990: 42).[14]

---

[11] This part of the chapter is largely based on the corresponding sections in Mayer (1981) and Niethammer (1990).

[12] See Schwintowski and Schäfer (1997: 132).

[13] Despite its name, this bank law did not focus on commercial banks. It largely dealt with the establishment of the *Reichsbank*, the central bank of the new German Empire.

[14] Another plausible reason is the fact that the deposit business was still quite limited.

During the First World War there was further state intervention undercutting the principle of economic freedom which the banks had used to shore up their position. These interventions were not undertaken for regulatory reasons. Rather they were intended to shore up the currency and Germany's external balance of trade. In this fraught environment, a compulsory registration scheme was introduced for all deposit banks. Any bank going through this process needed to prove that it had a minimum amount of funds and that its non-executive directors were competent and reliable before it could register successfully. Several of these regulations remained in force until 1929 (Mayer 1981: 11f.).

At the same time, special regulatory agencies were set up for specific parts of the credit market. The *Sparkassen* were supervised by state regulators which had their origins in regulatory agencies set up when the Prussian legal code had been enacted in 1839. Control over this aspect of banking regulation gradually shifted from municipal institutions into a special national agency, which included an auditing office set up in cooperation with the *Sparkassen* associations. The mortgage banks were placed under a separate national legislative framework in 1899, which put limitations on the extent of long-term loans, established firm directives on the kind of lending and borrowing services banks could offer, and led to supervision on the state level (Mayer 1981: 13).

Despite these directives, the regulatory system has to be classified as liberal until the first decades of the twentieth century. Fundamental change only took place after the bank crisis of 1931.[15] Once a succession of bank collapses had forced the state to undertake immense financial exertions to secure the solvency of the surviving banks, the Brüning government decided to impose a strict regulatory regime on the banking sector in order to prevent a repetition of the events which led to this crisis. At the time, most economists identified the tardy intervention of state authorities and ignorance among policy-makers of conditions within the major banks as the central reasons behind the escalation of this crisis. As a consequence, most experts in the field believed that a licensing system and a strong regulatory regime could prevent a recurrence of such a system failure (Born 1977: 501). Yet the way in which these recommendations were implemented was very different from the regulatory structures that emerged at the same time in the United States, which experienced its own banking crisis in the 1930s. While the solution put forward in Washington consisted, on the one hand, of a state-run deposit insurance system, which was based on a compulsory membership scheme designed to protect the depositor

---

[15] The following sections are based on Alsheimer (1997), Fischer (1997a: 3721), Mayer (1981: 13–15), Niethammer (1990: 45f.), Ronge (1979: 69–81), and Wagner (1976: 34–46).

from losses incurred by a bank, and on the other hand, a legally imposed segmentation of the market (cf. Section 3.1.2), the German model focused on the limitation of competition in the credit system and the stabilization of bank profits.

Several emergency decrees issued by President Hindenburg in 1931 and 1932 led to the creation of a new agency called the *Amt des Reichskommissars für das Bankgewerbe*. The *Reichskommissar* was also responsible for the *Kuratorium für das Bankgewerbe*, in which the central bank or *Reichsbank* and the Ministry for the Economy coordinated their banking policy with each other. Since the *Reichskommissar*'s responsibilities also included "influencing bank policy in the interests of the general German economy",[16] at the beginning of 1932 his office initiated a comprehensive cartel through a written agreement between associations representing different parts of the financial industry. It contained detailed directives determining the level of fixed interest rates for deposits and loans. In 1933, a commission of inquiry called the *Untersuchungsausschuß für das Bankenwesen* was set up. Submitted in the following year, the recommendations of its report formed the core of a law enacted in September 1934 called the *Reichsgesetz über das Kreditwesen* (KWG). This piece of legislation created a uniform legal framework for banking and finance and codified a set of regulations and emergency decrees. It also included caps on the maximum level of interest for loans and directives concerning the liquidity and capital requirements of banks. In order to conduct business, a bank now needed a state concession, which gave regulators considerable room for manoeuvre when it came to determining who could operate a bank. For example, both national and local regulators could now block the opening of local branches if they believed that a local or regional community did not need them.

In the following years these regulatory structures underwent further centralization twice (1939 and 1944) while the major banks were re-privatized in 1933 and 1936. After the end of the Second World War, the KWG was kept in place because the Allied occupation authorities did not believe that it constituted a genuinely National Socialist piece of legislation. Yet the lack of any central state in the immediate post-war era meant that responsibility for bank regulation had to be taken over by the *Länder*. Although the *Länder* agencies quickly started coordinating their activity, this form of decentralization suited the wider plans of Allied officials who wanted to split up the larger German corporate banks. Yet as we have seen in Section 4.1.1, this policy ended when the three main banks of the pre-war era were reconstituted in 1957. This was followed by the re-centralization of the regulatory system

---

[16] Cited from Mayer (1981: 14).

which was sealed by a law enacted on 10 July 1961 called the *Gesetz über das Kreditwesen*. This restored the structures within the banking industry that had existed before 1939 and provided the state with the means to control rates of interest as well as business terms and conditions, to be overseen by the newly founded *Bundesaufsichtsamt für das Kreditwesen*. The power to coordinate interest rates could be found in the regulatory frameworks of many other developed countries, too.[17] They were based on the assumption which had predominated in the 1930s that "competition between banks and between other financial institutions ultimately imperilled their existence, threatening the security of most creditors" (Boos, Fischer, and Schulte-Matler 2000: 95). However, in the course of the 1960s major changes were made to this system. In 1967, the last decree determining rates of interest issued in February 1965 was repealed as the Federal Republic became one of the first states to liberalize the setting of interest rates.

4.1.3 Key Aspects of the Policy Field Until 1970

What is particularly interesting when looking at these issues is the tension that existed between the emphasis upon state action and the desire to limit state power. This stress on limiting state power in the nineteenth century was the result of the hold economic liberal doctrine had upon governments during that period. Even though the banking system was developing at a breakneck pace and was coming to play a central role in the economic life of the country, initiatives that encouraged the establishment of different models of state control ended in failure. Only the massive bank crisis of 1931 created the political atmosphere in which moves towards the creation of regulatory measures could come to fruition. Nevertheless, this remained limited to a broad legislative framework which neither included any detailed legal directives nor fostered intervention into market structures. While such crises led to major structural change in the banking sectors of other European countries as well as the United States, the situation in Germany remained comparatively stable (Tilly 1994: 307)—even though the preconditions for sweeping change were particularly favourable: after all, the big banks had been socialized to cope with the crisis. Yet that was quickly repealed and the major banks were restored to private ownership. After the Second World War, West German policy-makers continued to conform to this liberal tradition.

On the other hand, a considerable segment of the German banking sector (including the *Sparkassen* and the *Landesbanken*) has remained close to the

---

[17] See "regulation Q" in the United States (see p. 59 above) or the regulations and guidelines in the United Kingdom before 1971 (p. 141 below).

state, in so far as they are chartered companies operating under a public-law framework for which the city and provincial governments who own them are liable. As has been explained above, this form of state-backed banking has a long history in Germany. These banks have often been used as instruments of local and regional economic policy. Nonetheless, in contrast to France and other centralized states, federal governments have been unable to use such state influence in their attempts to achieve a coherent economic strategy because of the decentralized nature of the German state and the many different players involved in policy-making (Coleman 1996: 44). State influence can therefore largely be described as diffuse rather than concentrated.

The fact that so many different political actors have profited from the diffuse nature of this state influence limits the extent to which this policy field has managed to provoke controversy. When compared to developments in the United States in particular, the relatively low level of political conflict surrounding banking policy in the nineteenth (as well as by and large in the twentieth) century becomes noticeable. If one takes the influence banks had on industrial expansion as well as wider economic development into consideration, this quiescence is remarkable. Although there have been periodic disputes over the "power of the banks" since the beginning of the twentieth century they have had little impact on state policy, diminishing pressure for such measures as nationalization.

A third aspect is the banking sector's positive contribution to German economic development. Research by economic historians has indicated that by the late nineteenth century, the creation of cartels in heavy industry helped spur economic growth, enabling a belatedly industrializing Germany to "catch up" with established industrial nations like the United Kingdom (Tilly 1994: 310).[18] The traditional long-term relationships between banks and industrial corporations continued after the Second World War. According to empirical studies, this has been a trend that has had a positive effect upon economic development:

West German banks provide industry with substantial long-term finance, have extensive control over shareholders voting rights and are widely represented on company boards. Empirical estimates show that, despite the banks' denial of exercising control over industry, there is a significant positive relationship between the degree of bank involvement in leading industrial companies and their financial performance.

(Cable 1985: 129)

As well as acting as a stimulus for further investment and greater profitability, the stability of the financial sector has also contributed to economic

---

[18] A detailed description of this "cartel movement" can be found in Wehler (1995: 632–7).

development by minimizing the negative effects of such major problems as banking crises or bank collapses.

Banks which were strong, successful, and well-represented by their associations, cooperated with a liberally oriented state, producing a preference for self-regulation and little legal regulation. From voluntarily acquiescing to the publication of quarterly results suggested by the bank commission of 1908–9 to the positive reaction of banks to the formation of a state-coordinated cartel organized by the main banking associations, a tradition was formed. As will be seen below, the reactions to the challenges posed by globalization from the 1970s onwards were very much a continuation of this pattern.

4.2 NEW CHALLENGES FACING BANK REGULATORS

The West German system of bank regulation did not need to adapt in any great way to the new systemic and socio-economic challenges which emerged after the 1970s. As we have seen, the German banking system had already undergone a process of liberalization and codification before these trends began to have an impact on the international scene. This does not mean that this policy field did not generate any controversy. At several key moments, serious debates took place over the measures state institutions or banks should take to cope with different challenges. Nevertheless, these debates were sparked by issues which had caused controversy over a long period of time in a national context rather than new problems caused by globalization. Public discussion in the Federal Republic of Germany was dominated by two issues in particular: the first was the extent to which depositors should be protected from the consequences of increasing deregulation of the banking sector, while the second concerned the long-running controversy over the power of the banks and the established system of universal banking.

4.2.1 Liberalization and Depositor Protection

The issue which linked the liberalization of the banking market with the administrative responsibilities of bank regulators was depositor protection. The liberalization process created new business opportunities for many banks while simultaneously increasing the level of risk to which they are exposed. A system of bank regulation unable to exert its influence over the industry in these new market conditions could bring about a bank collapse and cause serious financial losses for depositors. As a result, increasing liberalization has paradoxically forced bank regulators to take on new responsibilities.

In the Federal Republic, this causal relationship has been the subject of political debate since long before the 1970s.[19] Enacted in 1961, the KWG had originally contained directives regulating the levels of interest of debit and credit rates. As was the case in many other countries, these measures were seen as essential to the protection of banks from excessive competition and were intended to ensure that the cost of credit did not become too high for consumers. However, banks which broke the rules set by the KWG were rarely punished by West German regulators, eventually leading to much higher levels of interest paid on deposits than anticipated by this legal framework (Franke 1998: 296f.). As a result, senior officials in the *Bundeswirtschaftsministerium* decided to repeal the cap on rates of credit interest in January 1967, taking a considerable step towards the liberalization of the West German financial markets in the process.[20] Yet at the time the KWG was first being drafted in March 1961, debates in the *Bundestag* had shown that considerable concerns existed within the West German political elite over the possibilty that greater competition might have adverse effects upon depositors. Consequently, the federal government came under pressure to explore whether improvements to the deposit insurance scheme were necessary (Ronge 1979: 98).

Partly to assuage such concerns, one of the most important associations representing the interests of the private banking sector, the *Bundesverband deutscher Banken* (BdB), established a nationwide special fund known as the *Feuerwehrfond* to help insolvent banks which was made up of voluntary contributions from commercial banks. The BdB described this step as

a trust-building exercise [...] which would work in conjunction with the comprehensive forms of liability used by public-law credit institutions and cooperative banks.

(Landesbank Rheinland-Pfalz 1983: 195)

The latter had already established deposit insurance funds in the 1930s (Coleman 1996: 125).

A government report reviewing these various developments was made public in November 1968.[21] It accepted that a growing need existed for measures to increase the security of deposits, since the intensity of competition in the banking industry had increased for a variety of reasons: the disappearance

---

[19] As Section 4.1.2 has shown, the policy debates over the establishment of a state-backed deposit insurance system had been taking place since the nineteenth century.

[20] The banking industry's representative associations had great reservations about this step and continued to oppose any further moves towards liberalization (Landesbank Rheinland-Pfalz 1983: 195).

[21] *Deutscher Bundestag*, Drs. V/3500, 18.11.1968.

of the traditional division of labour between locally oriented *Sparkassen* or the cooperative banks and the commercial banks, with the former suddenly offering the full spectrum of banking services; the rise in the number of local branches after state powers to block the opening of bank branches had been abolished; growing variability in business conditions and interest rates after the repeal of interest regulation; and the removal of strict rules on advertising which led to greater efforts on the part of banks to attract new customers.[22] In its conclusion, this report stated that the introduction of a new deposit insurance scheme would protect the banking system from bank collapses that might lead to demands for restraints on competition. Such a scheme would therefore be able to serve two distinct purposes. On the one hand, it would help to preserve a market regime based upon competition, while on the other, it could neutralize the competitive advantage public-law banks had as a result of their more secure position. The report went on to state that, if necessary, legislative intervention might be needed, since a voluntary approach was not sufficient to deal with the changing nature of the banking industry. This effectively meant that if banks did not improve their own safeguards, a state-run deposit insurance scheme would need to be established.

The banking industry reacted to these stinging criticisms in the following years. The banks increased their contributions to the *Feuerwehrfonds* in order to ensure that the fund could guarantee individual savings deposits of up to DM 10,000 in each bank that contributed to them.[23] While the BdB admitted that it was following recommendations made by a government body, it emphasized that it was taking these actions on a private and voluntary basis (Bundesverband Deutscher Banken 1975: 17).

4.2.2 Left- and Right-Wing Critiques of the "Power of the Banks"

Along with the continuing controversy over the need for a system of deposit insurance, in the first half of the 1970s there emerged a much more fundamental debate in this policy field as criticism grew of the extent of the "power of the banks". Intriguingly, these underlying worries existed in two very different parts of the political spectrum, with fierce criticism of the major banks expressed by both prominent economic liberals and left-wing thinkers. In both cases, important aspects of the banking system such as the influence which banks could exert over companies in which they owned shares, voting by proxy, and the many seats held by bankers on the boards of major corporations came under attack. Although the criticisms made by all sides were

---

[22] See pp. x and 138ff. of the report as well as Ronge (1979: 98f.).
[23] All other forms of deposit banking were not protected.

remarkably similar, there were substantial differences between the various proposals for reform.

Economic liberals emphasized the detrimental effects of the influence which the three largest corporate banks could exert on companies. In particular, they believed that the close relationship between the three largest banks and big companies could give these bankers access to inside information which would put them at an advantage over their smaller competitors. Moreover, the influence an individual bank could exert over several companies which were in competition with one another could lead to serious conflicts of interest.[24] According to liberal economic theorists, such a concentration of power had potentially negative consequences for consumers, who might have to pay higher prices for banking services than in a system which was prepared to accept a greater level of competition. Airing these kinds of concerns, many economic liberals came to the conclusion that banks should only be permitted to offer banking services and ought to leave parts of the financial sector to other forms of business organization. Liberal critics also demanded that legislation should be enacted in order to ensure that banks could only hold minority shares in firms outside of the financial sector. These proposals were put forward by the monopolies commission (*Monopolkommission*) which was founded through an amendment of the federal competition law in April 1974 (§24b GWB). Its first report contained detailed information about the extent of banking interests in other business sectors and demanded a cap of 5 per cent on the amount of shares which banks could hold in other companies (Monopolkommission 1976: 296f.; see also Eckstein 1980).

By contrast, though left-wing criticism also focused on this concentration of power, it usually led to policy proposals designed to give the state a much more active role in relation to the major banks. This policy stance was directly expressed in a medium-term policy programme presented by the SPD in 1975 which was called "*Orientierungsrahmen '85*".[25] This paper demanded a restructuring of the banking sector, the abolition of the universal banking system and strict separation between credit transactions and the broader investment business. It went on to suggest that the state use its infrastructural resources and investment guidance powers to create much tougher bank

---

[24] The former chairman of *Deutsche Bank*, Abs, became famous for sitting on the boards of more than twenty different companies. When an amendment to the relevant law was enacted in 1965, which limited the number of directorships that any one individual could hold to ten, it quickly became known as the "*lex Abs*".

[25] The discussions surrounding this programme as well as its text are documented in Oertzen, Ehmke, and Ehrenberg (1976). The quotations from *Orientierungsrahmen '85* used here can be found in Sections 2.6.3–2.6.7.

regulation agencies than existed at the time. In particular, the Social Democratic politicians who supported this proposal believed that it was necessary to create a registration scheme and issue permits which could be withdrawn in order to prevent banks from gaining control over other companies. They also recommended the establishment of incentives which would encourage banks to invest in some areas and discourage them from investing in others. Repeated allusions were made in this document to one of the key passages of the Godesberg programme of 1959 (which had confirmed the SPD's acceptance of a moderated form of market capitalism) which stated that the existence of public enterprises was right and necessary, "when a healthy [social] order based on an economic balance of power cannot be achieved by other means". This constituted a barely hidden threat to the commercial banks who might oppose these plans.

The private banking sector participated in these political debates in order to confront both their critics in economic liberal circles and those on the left. Representatives of the major banks argued in favour of the status quo while emphasizing that banks would use their power responsibly, which would in any case be limited by the competitive pressures of a relatively deregulated market (Gall et al. 1995: 645–62). Nevertheless, it had become clear that the groundswell of criticism from economic liberals and left-wing thinkers had to be taken seriously. This was especially the case after the FDP, in which economic liberalism had strong advocates, and the SPD, where left-wing suspicion of the private banks was still strong, formed a coalition after winning the federal election of 1969.

4.3 THE POLICY NETWORK

The political challenges described above confronted a policy network which was typified by a high level of continuity. In this respect, little has changed throughout the period examined by this study. The following section will therefore examine the elements of the banking industry, regulatory agencies, and legislators who were involved in this policy network.

4.3.1 The German Banking Industry

The banking industry in the Federal Republic of Germany is the most well-established example of the universal banking model (Kloten and Stein 1993;

Table 4.1. Banking industry sectoral market share, 1957–97 (%)

	1957	1967	1977	1987	1997
Commercial sector	27.7	22.1	23.0	21.6	29.0
—of which big banks	13.8	9.6	10.4	8.7	13.8
Public law sector	36.1	38.1	38.5	37.4	36.6
—of which *Sparkassen*	21.5	23.2	22.0	21.7	—
Cooperative sector	8.5	10.6	14.0	17.1	13.1
—of which credit cooperatives	5.6	6.9	9.8	12.5	—

Source: Deutsche Bundesbank (1988: 181, 1999: 104).

Canals 1997). As a result, German banks offer a wide range of financial services including every form of deposit or portfolio banking, loans, investment opportunities, and share trading.[26]

These banks can be split into three dominant groups: the *Sparkassen* administered under public-law, privately run commercial banks, and the cooperative banking sector.[27] As indicated in Table 4.1, the relative proportion of market share held by these three sectors has largely remained unchanged in the last forty years.[28] The over 600 *Sparkassen* and 12 *Landesbanken/Girozentralen* that make up the public-law sector cover over a third of the market, while 320 commercial banks have a market share of approximately one quarter. However, over 50 per cent of the commercial banking sector is dominated by the largest three corporate banks (*Deutsche Bank*, *Dresdner Bank* and *Commerzbank*),[29] a proportion of market share which equals that of the over 2,400 credit unions (1997). Containing the largest number of individual financial institutions, the

[26] A certain set of special banks exist as well (such as banks entirely devoted to mortgages or partial payment banks, see Scheidl (1993)). These will largely be ignored below, since they were not affected by the change in the regulatory framework described in this chapter.

[27] A good overview of the structures of the German banking sector can be found in Deeg (1999: chapter 2).

[28] Unfortunately, in several of its publications the *Bundesbank* only provides aggregate information about the public-law and cooperative sectors. Yet the reports produced by these sectors' representative associations indicate that the relative proportion of *Sparkassen* to credit unions in comparison to previous years has remained relatively stable. The main source for the statistical data in this section is Deutsche Bundesbank (1988, 1999) along with the author's calculations.

[29] The 1999 merger of the *Bayerische Hypotheken- und Wechselbank* with the *Bayerische Vereinsbank* to the *Bayerische Hypo- und Vereinsbank* meant that the number of banks classified by the *Bundesbank* as "major banks" has risen to four with a combined share of the market of 20 per cent.

credit unions have proven particularly adept at expanding their share of the market in the last few decades.

Despite this relative market stability, the banking industry has experienced major changes since the establishment of the Federal Republic in 1949. Two central factors stand out in this context, namely a movement towards greater concentration of resources and an expanding number of branches. While there were 13,359 independent banks in 1957, by 1997 there were only 3,577 left. This was mostly the result of a decline in the number of credit unions from 11,570 to over 2,400. At the same time, the number of bank branches has risen from 25,000 to approximately 50,000.

The process of concentration experienced by the German banking sector may seem dramatic, but these figures are quickly put into perspective if one compares them with developments in other countries. In this context, the German banking sector must be considered to have a remarkably low level of concentration. In comparison with other countries of the European Union:

The Germans and their banking sector are a truly exotic phenomenon...we [the Germans] are quasi unique.[30]

Yet when it comes to the associations representing the banks, the German banking system exhibits a high level of concentration. Each of the three dominant sectors has its own representative association. While the commercial banks belong to the *Bundesverband deutscher Banken* (BdB), the *Sparkassen* are represented by the *Deutscher Sparkassen- und Giroverband* (DSGV), and the cooperative banks cooperate under the aegis of the *Bundesverband der Deutschen Volksbanken und Raiffeisenbanken* (BVR). Together with the *Bundesverband Öffentlicher Banken Deutschlands* (VÖB) and the *Verband Deutscher Hypothekenbanken* (VDH), these three associations coordinate their work on behalf of the industry as a whole in the *Zentraler Kreditausschuß* (ZKA).[31] This body deals with a variety of important issues (including tax, trade law, regulatory legislation, and securities trading), and develops a coordinated response across the industry to the actions of the *Bundestag, Bundesrat*

---

[30] Interview VÖB, 3 February 2000. If one takes the share of customer deposits held by the five largest banks as a measure, then in 1989 it only came to 18.4 per cent of the West German market, while in the United Kingdom it was almost double at 38.4 per cent and four times as high in France with 69.6 per cent and Belgium at 71.2 per cent. In the Netherlands it even comes to 74.4 per cent (Valdez 1993: 50).

[31] The last two associations are only of minor importance. This can be seen in the fact that the control of the ZKA only lies in the hands of the first three associations (Interview VÖB, 3 February 2000). The VDH is quite small, representing twenty-four private mortgage banks as a member of the BdB.

(the second chamber of the federal parliament), federal government, regulatory agencies, and the *Bundesbank*.[32]

Members of the ZKA are always invited to *Bundestag* committee hearings and other major parliamentary set-pieces. Such extensive cooperation between the different associations is not just the result of historical tradition. Rather, it is strengthened by the fact that there is little or no competition between them when it comes either to their ideological agendas or the recruitment of new members.[33] The only potential exception is the anomalous position of the *Landesbanken*, who oscillate between the DSGV and VÖB. Yet even here the relationship is as complementary as it is competitive, since all *Landesbanken* are members of both associations. Both associations go to great lengths to coordinate their work with one another, with the president of the DSGV receiving a seat on the board of the VÖB and vice versa (Coleman 1996: 52).

The association with the greatest internal tensions is the BdB, since the interests of the major corporate banks are not always compatible with those of their smaller commercial counterparts. As a result, the leadership of the BdB is often preoccupied with trying to reconcile different elements of their constituency with their broader agenda since the relationships between different member banks has continued to be difficult.[34] A certain level of dominance within this organization is reflected by the fact that the four largest corporate banks automatically hold seats in the board of the BdB. The internal framework of the other sectors is rather different. Based on a three-tiered system, there is considerable structural uniformity within the public-law and cooperative sectors, especially since there is so little competition between them.

The well-equipped headquarters of each of these associations gives them the ability to lobby legislators and regulatory agencies in a highly effective manner.[35] There is intensive cooperation on this level, with the banking associations taking an active part in the work of governments and regulators. For example, directives and information issued by the BAKred (*Bundesaufsichtsamt für das Kreditwesen*) are passed on to banks via these associations. Cementing their position, the legislatory framework set out in the *Kreditwesengesetz* makes it mandatory for governments to consult the banking associations in advance of major regulatory shifts such as changes to basic guidelines dealing with equity and liquidity (Mayer 1981: 34f.).

---

[32] The ZKA was founded as a result of a decree of the *Reichspräsident* during the banking crisis in 1931 as a cartel of banking conditions (Born 1983: 134).

[33] That this is not necessarily typical is demonstrated in Section 3.3.1.2 of the American case study.

[34] Interview BdB, 3 February 2000; interview DSGV, 4 February 2000.

[35] For example, the BdB currently employs seventy staffers at its headquarters (interview BdB, 3 February 2000).

4.3.2 The Regulatory Agencies

Mirroring the clearly delineated structure of interest representation embodied by the German banking associations, there is a similarly defined division of responsibility between the different regulatory agencies. The three main institutions responsible for regulation, the *Bundesaufsichtsamt für das Kreditwesen*, the *Bundesbank*, and the *Bundesministerium der Finanzen* each have their separate areas of jurisdiction with little overlap between them. Moreover, on the policy level these institutions share a liberal outlook which discourages direct intervention into the affairs of individual banks (Vogel 1996: 251; Becker 1998: 57).

The only institution which is exclusively focused on bank regulation is the *Bundesaufsichtsamt für das Kreditwesen* (BAKred).[36] Established as a result of the banking and finance law (*Kreditwesengesetz* or KWG) of 1961, it was initially supposed to be housed in the *Bundesbank* building but was finally moved to West Berlin for political reasons (Mayer 1981: 17).[37] According to §6 (2) of the KWG, the responsibilities of the BAKred include "to counteract irregularities in the areas of banking and financial services, which threaten the security of the assets of those institutions in its area of responsibility, hamper the orderly conduct of banking transactions and create difficulties for the wider economy". Its president made the same point more succinctly in 1962: the BAKred should "ensure that the banking sector continues to function and protect individual bank creditors" (Kalkstein 1962: 125).

The BAKred discharges the sovereign responsibilities of the German regulatory system which includes the granting and withdrawing of permits and licences. Throughout recent decades the BAKred has remained a relatively small agency. Although its level of staff has doubled in the twenty years after 1980 from 240 to 530 officials, this still seems minuscule when one takes the 3,400 different banks it oversees into account.[38] Yet the German system of banking regulation has always remained focused on registration and notification rather than on-the-spot investigation and intervention (Mayer 1981: 42f., General Accounting Office 1994*b*: 25f.). Although the KWG law permitted on-the-spot investigations in 1961, these were only to be initiated after a problem had arisen, giving such inspections the character of measures that were only to be taken in extraordinary circumstances. Instead, this regulatory agency

[36] General descriptions of the BAKred and its work can be found in Schneider (1978) and Mayer (1981). Unfortunately, both studies are nearly thirty years old and only reflect the situation at the time of this study in limited ways. A more up-to-date overview can be found in General Accounting Office (1994*b*).

[37] As a result of the Berlin–Bonn law, the BAKred moved from Berlin to Bonn in 2000.

[38] The figures can be found in Mayer (1981: 29), Gläser (1999: 41), as well as Bundesaufsichtsamt für das Kreditwesen (1999: 104).

has preferred to analyse annual reports submitted by the banks which are legally obliged to fully disclose all essential information and have it certified by independent auditors. Able to rely on this groundwork, the BAKred usually restricts itself to examining whether these reports conform to legal guidelines and stipulations. Despite the fact that the BAKred's area of responsibility is in the economic sphere, it has therefore been largely dominated by legal experts rather than economists.[39] Along with the help it receives from private auditors for its oversight of private commercial banks, in its dealings with the *Sparkassen* and credit unions the BAKred also relies on support from the auditors of the representative associations who do much of the essential preliminary work (Schneider 1978: 42ff.; see also Kalkstein 1962: 125).

The BAKred is financed through contributions (set by §51 of the KWG law) from the banks it oversees, usually proportional to their size, while 10 per cent of its funding is covered by the federal budget. It is entirely devoted to the public weal and has no obligations towards individual investors.[40] It is an independent federal level agency (*selbständige Bundesoberbehörde*) and consequently does not have a nationwide infrastructure. When it comes to collecting economic data and information from the banks, the BAKred is dependent upon its legally delineated relationship with the *Bundesbank*.

Despite the *Bundesbank*'s decentralized structure in which the *Landes-zentralbanken* (the central banks of the Länder) play a key role, it also has offices in almost every part of the Federal Republic. In §7 the KWG law makes it obligatory for the *Bundesbank* to cooperate with the BAKred, though it usually operates only in a supportive capacity rather than becoming actively engaged in investigations which could distract from its focus on monetary policy.[41] Nevertheless, if the *Bundesbank* wants to be able to successfully implement its monetary policy, it depends on a functioning banking system. What increases the attractiveness of cooperation with the *Bundesbank* for regulatory agencies is its ability to acquire information about specific banks and the sector as a whole through its role as "bank of banks". This dependence means that the BAKred needs regular infusions of information from the *Bundesbank* if it wants to know about the internal affairs of banks before it receives their annual reports.[42] Both institutions share information and cooperate more widely with one another. The *Bundesbank* president still possesses

[39] Interview BAKred, 3 February 2000.
[40] This was questioned in several judicial rulings made by the BGH in the 1970s, however the legal basis was clarified through the inclusion of §6 section 3 in the third amendment of the KWG (Mayer 1981: 40; Gläser 1999: 40).
[41] This came to an end with the third stage of European Monetary Union, when responsibility for monetary policy shifted to the European Central Bank. The structures described here are relevant to the period examined by this study.
[42] Interview, BAKred, 3 February 2000.

considerable influence over the selection process for each new president of the BAKred, who has the right to take part (though not vote) in meetings of the central bank council in which issues within his area of jurisdiction are under discussion.[43] Major decisions in a variety of policy areas can only be made jointly through a process of negotiation between both institutions.[44]

The responsibilities of the federal finance ministry (BMF) have included bank regulation since 1972.[45] Its area of jurisdiction mostly involves the development and amendment of laws regulating the sector such as the KWG, though the ministry is not directly involved with the administrative details of banking regulation. Though in principle entitled to issue decrees when faced with a banking crisis, and to issue directives towards the BAKred, it makes no practical use of these powers (Fischer 1997b: 132). The ministry believes that it ought to be responsible for those aspects of banking connected to general economic policy and can thus leave the details of direct oversight to the BAKred (Coleman 1996: 132).

In summary, the structure of the bank regulation system in Germany is based on a division of labour between agencies such as the BAKred and the *Bundesbank*, which act as unpolitical technocratic experts overseeing the banking sector, and a BMF which sees itself as responsible for the political aspects of this policy field. Each institution's area of jurisdiction has been set out in such a fashion that these different actors do not end up in conflict with one another over bureaucratic turf. These factors have created relatively good conditions for a smooth coordination of policy which one would associate more with the political structures of a centralized state. By contrast, the American case demonstrates that regulatory stability, which has become a hallmark of the German system, cannot be taken for granted in a federal state.

4.3.3 The Legal Framework

As stated above, the federal government has exclusive responsibility for legislation dealing with the financial sector and banking regulation. This state of affairs has been challenged several times. After the implementation of the KWG in 1961 centralized a bank regulation system which had been run by the *Länder* since the Second World War, the *Land* governments took a legal challenge to the federal constitutional court (*Bundesverfassungsgericht*), claiming that these measures were unconstitutional. This legal challenge ultimately

---

[43] §7 (3) KWG.
[44] An exact description of the powers of the *Bundesbank* can be found in Deutsche Bundesbank (2000: 38), Mayer (1981: 33), and Becker (1998: 59).
[45] Responsibility previously lay with the Bundesministerium für Wirtschaft (Mayer 1981: 28).

failed, ensuring that the federal government became exclusively responsible for the regulation of this sector.[46] This meant that banking policy is one part of German public life which has not become drawn into the complexities of policy-making in a federal political environment. Yet despite these initial disagreements, there has been a high level of consensus between the parliamentary parties and the different levels of government in Bonn and the *Länder*. Because of this low level of politicization, a study of the legislative process in the Federal Republic came to the conclusion that the KWG and related banking laws cannot be considered as key decisions shaping the political development of the Federal Republic (Beyme 1998).

The key body on banking matters in the *Bundestag* is the finance committee (*Finanzausschuß*) but other committees (particularly the ones dealing with economic and home affairs) also take part in an advisory capacity. Committees have the power to make recommendations for change to pieces of legislation, though this rarely leads to surprises since such consultations are usually predetermined by decisions endorsed by the parliamentary parties (Beyme 1998: 21, 42f.). There are therefore few stages at which any one side can block proceedings, tactics which are unlikely in any case in such a depoliticized policy field. According to the rules and procedures of the *Bundestag*, committees are obliged to discharge their responsibilities as quickly as possible (§62 (1)). Delaying tactics are therefore rarely crowned with success, even though the smaller parties usually have enough members of the *Bundestag* to demand that a report be submitted to the plenum. Moreover, decisions made in this policy field have never been particularly controversial since banking legislation has usually been limited to technical adaptation of regulatory structures to new developments such as the consequences of European integration. In the context of bank regulation, the role of parliament is primarily that of a ratifying body rather than a space in which detailed discussion over policy alternatives takes place.[47]

Once the relevant committees decide to hold hearings on a specific issue, the associations belonging to the ZKA are automatically invited to take part in order to ensure a balanced representation of interests. There are no firm alliances or specific tensions between political parties and the three different banking sectors. There is a broad political consensus in support of the three-tiered banking system, though there are some nuanced differences when it comes to the attitudes of political milieux. Though the FDP demonstrates some scepticism towards the lobbying efforts of public-law banks, the other

---

[46]   An exact analysis of these developments can be found in Büschgen (1983: 372f.). The legal ruling is described in BVerfGE 14: 197–221 (July 1962).

[47]   See interview BVR, 24 March 2000.

parties tend to be rather supportive of this sector: the CDU has always believed that the *Sparkassen* embody the principle of subsidiarity, while the SPD has tended to emphasize their role as public-law bodies upholding social solidarity in local communities and the Green Party considers their decentralized structure to be an excellent antidote to the concentrations of power which can be found in other parts of the banking industry.[48] What the governing parties of the *Länder* all have in common is an awareness that locally rooted *Sparkassen* and credit unions (in contrast to commercial banks operating on an international basis) are not in the position to develop tax avoidance strategies. Of equal importance to regional politicians is the large number of well-paid jobs which the existence of *Sparkassen* provide in every part of a *Land* because of their legal inability to withdraw from less profitable regional markets in times of crisis.

Just as in the case of interest groups within the banking industry and the regulatory agencies, the legislative arena is exemplified by clearly defined areas of jurisdiction and the lack of any kind of institutional competition. Furthermore, the regulatory framework has been codified by laws that have become a central point of orientation creating an environment which is conducive to the effective implementation of further regulatory initiatives. The positive assessment arrived at in the previous sections, namely that the German policy network displays a high level of efficiency, has been confirmed here.

4.4 THE CALM AFTER THE STORM: CONTINUITY RATHER THAN FUNDAMENTAL CHANGE

As we have seen above, the bank regulation system in the Federal Republic did not need to go to any great lengths in order to adapt to the new economic challenges which emerged after 1973. However, this did not mean that this policy field was quiescent during this period. In 1974, a very early point in the post-Bretton Woods period, the *Herstatt Bank* scandal erupted, creating a fluid situation which had the potential to trigger major changes. A regulatory regime based on sectoral self-regulation could have undergone a major transformation if it had succumbed to shifts in the balance of power between the market and the state which had been made possible through this political episode. The next section will therefore examine in detail a banking scandal which has no equivalent in the other three case studies.

***

[48] Interview VÖB, 3 February 2000.

4.4.1   The Herstatt Crisis and its Consequences

In June 1974, Germany experienced its worst bank collapse since the crisis of 1931. It was caused by drastically changed circumstances in international markets. The resulting increase in exchange rate volatility created profitable new business opportunities in a very short period of time. Conversely, this new development made massive losses equally possible. Together with the bankruptcy of the Franklin National Bank in New York, the collapse of the Cologne-based *Herstatt Bank* was one of the great bank collapses of the 1970s to result from forward trading on the currency market (Kapstein 1994: 31, 39f.).

This resulted in financial losses of over DM 1.2 billion. After attempts by the *Bundesbank* to coordinate a rescue plan involving the entire banking sector ended in failure, the BAKred ordered the closure of the *Herstatt Bank* on 26 June 1974. Even though it was only eightieth out of the hundred largest banks in Germany,[49] this collapse had dramatic consequences. In the first five years of its existence, the deposit insurance fund administered by the BdB had only had to pay out DM 7 million in seven incidents in which a small number of depositors had experienced losses or a minor bank became insolvent. Suddenly, DM 100 million were needed to keep the collapse of the *Herstatt Bank* from causing a major crisis (Bundesverband Deutscher Banken 1974: 14ff.). Although the funds to compensate 30,000 depositors were collected within a few days in a remarkable show of solidarity by the banks, the resulting crisis rocked the entire banking system. In a short period of time, commercial banks experienced withdrawals of deposits, particularly by insurance companies and public institutions, on a massive scale. This crisis of confidence hit the entire banking system and created the potential for a major crisis of liquidity which was only prevented after the *Bundesbank* agreed to extend its rediscount and lombard facilities. These events demonstrated that even well-run banks with a good credit rating could experience serious difficulties as a result of the indirect consequences of the collapse of a single bank, forcing the *Bundesbank* to act in its capacity as lender of last resort.[50] Moreover, this crisis showed that the existing deposit insurance scheme[51] was not capable of coping with a bank run (Franke 1998: 297f.).

---

[49]   According to Bundesverband Deutscher Banken (1974). Other statistical evidence (Wagner 1976: 98) has ranked the bank as thirty-fifth. This does not necessarily matter, since even according to these figures, the bank was not one of the largest in the country.

[50]   Though the *Bundesbank* has always emphasized that it will provide healthy banks with liquidity in principle, it has remained wary of using the term "lender of last resort" (Coleman 1996: 74). Yet the *Herstatt* crisis has shown that it is prepared to act in such a capacity.

[51]   As of January 1974, it guaranteed deposits up to DM 20,000 per person and also included term deposits and sight deposits at non-banks (Wagner 1976: 98). The BdB, in consultation with

The *Herstatt Bank* case turned the issue of deposit insurance into a major political issue. In the same year, debate over deposit insurance subsequently intensified after major losses came to light which had been incurred in the currency markets by two public-law banks. In the case of the *Hessische Landesbank* (HeLaBa), almost DM 2 billion was needed to save it from collapse. Half of this sum was paid by the Hessian *Land* government, which had to pass a special budget in its parliament in order to raise the necessary funds, while the other half was covered by Hessian *Sparkassen* (Ronge 1979: 86f.).

The political debate over the consequences of this crisis was characterized by expressions of solidarity, procedural delays, and tactical manoeuvring. This process can be split into three phases:

- The initial reaction in the first six months after the scandal up to the end of 1974, during which emergency measures were taken and the ultimate direction of the following phases began to take shape.

- The main phase, in which state institutions and private actors came to an agreement over new regulations for the sectoral regime. This process ended with the passing of an amendment to the KWG in March 1976 known as the *Sofortnovelle.*

- The final phase lasted until the third amendment to the KWG was passed in 1984. During this period, several regulations were modified, although there were no basic changes to this new framework for a variety of reasons.

Although this episode took ten years to work itself out, the central decisions in reaction to it had actually been taken relatively quickly. The contours of future regulation designed to prevent a repeat of such a scandal already became evident within a year after the collapse of the *Herstatt Bank*.

In the initial stages however, crisis management was the main priority. Immediately after the collapse of the *Herstatt Bank*, the BdB created a liquidity consortium, in order to help coordinate the provision of guarantees for *Herstatt* deposits. It was made up of fifteen corporate banks, regional banks, and private banking houses which declared their willingness to provide short-term loans to banks suffering from a liquidity shortage (Wagner 1976: 99).[52]

This consortium was expanded and formalized in September 1974. In conjunction with the *Bundesbank* (which played an important role in planning these new measures, cf. Franke 1998: 298) and other parts of the banking industry, this consortium was transformed into the *Liquiditäts-Konsortialbank*

---

the BMF and BAKred, had doubled the sum covered in the guidelines (Bundesverband Deutscher Banken 1974: 14).

[52] The "liquidity-consortium" proved to be the right invention at the right time, since it was able to compensate depositors when three small banks collapsed in August 1974.

GmbH (LiKo-Bank). It provided a broader basis for the safety mechanisms protecting domestic and international financial networks by providing financial to banks experiencing liquidity problems. This new bank (which was not permitted to undertake any form of business) had capital reserves of over DM 250 million, with access to over DM 750 million if necessary. While the *Bundesbank* and the BdB each controlled over 30 per cent of the LiKo's shares, the DSGV held 26.5 per cent and the BVR had a smaller stake with 11 per cent. The *Verband der Gemeinwirtschaftlichen Geschäftsbanken* and the *Treuhandfonds der Teilzahlungsbanken* also had a stake in the LiKo, with the former holding 1.5 per cent of its shares and the latter holding 1 per cent (Wagner 1976: 99f.). The costs of this means of intervention were therefore not carried by the three big corporate banks alone, since the arrangement also involved regional and local banks in its maintenance. The other sectors of the banking industry, the *Sparkassen* and the credit unions were also included in this scheme. That inclusion became characteristic for the further development of this policy episode—both for the commercial banks and the banking industry as a whole.

4.4.1.1 *Political Initiatives: Threats to the Status Quo*

Faced with public controversy and declining confidence in the German banking system, the government did its utmost to calm down the situation.[53] By the end of August 1974, it issued a set of proposals to amend the KWG as well as other regulations. In a press conference on 3 September the Finance Minister Hans Apel (SPD) explained these plans:

1. Amendments to the KWG should be implemented as quickly as possible. The powers of the BAKred should be strengthened while directives, including a cap on credit levels, for reducing risk in the deposit and loan business in the banks were issued.

2. For the first time, a legal framework was to be created for a comprehensive deposit insurance scheme covering all sectors of the banking industry and providing total protection for all depositors in order to prevent bank runs from recurring in the future. This would have the advantage of creating equal competitive conditions for commercial and public-law banks.

3. A commission of experts should be established to examine "fundamental issues involving the banking system" and make recommendations for further reform.

---

[53] For below see Knapp (1976); Wagner (1976: 100f.).

These proposals entailed a complete transformation of the system of bank regulation. Their implementation would have turned the existing liberal regime into a regulatory system with much stronger state influence. Though banks and their representative associations acknowledged the need to strengthen the regulatory powers of the BAKred, the introduction of a state-administered deposit insurance system with mandatory membership for every bank would have signalled the failure of a fifteen-year lobbying effort in favour of a privately organized scheme based on voluntary participation. With political criticism of the influence the banks had on the economy as a whole becoming increasingly strident, the commission of experts had the potential to become a means with which to change the structure of universal banks and limit their deep involvement in the affairs of industrial corporations. If such a commission were to come under the control of left-wing thinkers, it could even become the first step towards a nationalization of, at the very least, parts of the banking industry, emulating the kind of measures taken by the French and Austrian governments in response to the crisis of 1931.

4.4.1.2 *Damage Limitation: The Reaction of the Banking Industry*

Following the collapse of *Herstatt Bank*, deposit insurance became a central issue confronting the private banking sector as a whole. It was no longer just about deposit security. Rather, in the BdB's assessment, the issue was remaining competitive in the face of that issue having gained a hitherto unknown importance for consumers (Bundesverband Deutscher Banken 1975: 17f.). For the BdB, the fact that the *Sparkassen* and credit union sectors both had functioning schemes of their own meant that it was imperative for commercial bank systems to set up efficient safety mechanisms as well.

Once the establishment of the LiKo bank had reduced problems surrounding the availability of liquid capital in times of crisis, the issue of deposit insurance therefore rose to the top of the industry's policy agenda. Finding a solution was not an easy process since technical problems exacerbated the difficulties involved in coordinating collective action. With the deposits of each bank effectively covered by its competitors, there was also some incentive for the major players to engage in moral hazard behaviour. This could tempt a bank into offering depositors higher credit interest rates in order to increase its market share. Since this practice necessitates a much higher level of income from interest, it can often force banks into providing much riskier loans in order to maintain stable revenue levels. Deposit insurance schemes therefore have the potential to change the behaviour of individuals or institutions in the market place, increasing the general level of risk. These kinds of market distortions caused by deposit insurance schemes are often mentioned in academic literature dealing with such issues.[54]

The West German government's proposal tried to solve this problem by only providing complete protection to the deposits of non-banks. This was intended to provide banks (whose deposits were only partially covered by other banks) with an incentive to monitor the actions of their competitors. Yet these measures created a further set of technical questions: How high should protective quotas be for deposits that are not fully covered? How should one examine and ensure a bank's adherence to proper banking practice? How should the costs of an inspection regime and the regulatory framework for a deposit insurance scheme be covered?

Of even greater importance was the central problem of coordinating collective action within the banking industry. There were hefty protests from the *Sparkassen* and credit union sectors against compulsory membership in a general deposit insurance system. Afraid of having to cover massive losses incurred by their competitors in the private banks, the representative associations of these two sectors pointed to their own well-functioning safeguards (Deutsche Bundesbank 1976: 22; Ronge 1979: 124). The BdB which, by contrast, was likely to profit most from an industry-wide arrangement, reacted positively to this government initiative and expressed its willingness to help in its implementation (Wagner 1976: 101).

However, if the efforts of the banking industry to prevent these extensive government initiatives were to have a chance, it would have to act in a united fashion. This led to negotiations between the constituent parts of the banking industry over the next months. Considerable barriers to a consensus position emerged, since any model based on voluntary participation would force banks to give their competitors access to internal financial information. Other problems included the need to find a mechanism which could stop banks from defying this framework (a form of "moral hazard" behaviour) and the need to ensure that all banks contributed to the deposit insurance scheme in order to prevent a bank from attaining a competitive advantage by opting out.

Faced with the threat of state intervention, the BdB managed to unite its members behind a set of policy proposals. This plan consisted of a voluntary system created by the private banking sector and run by the BdB. It was designed to improve the position of individual depositors since coverage was extended to all forms of deposits and each depositor would be covered up to 30 per cent of the own capital of the affected bank. Moreover, in a move away from existing practice, even deposits which exceeded this limit would still be protected up to that level. In practice, this meant that all deposits benefited

---

[54] See the references in Section 2.1.

from a level of protection which, even for smaller banks, went far beyond what had existed in the past or in other countries.[55]

This proposal made it possible to overcome many of the collective action problems involved in uniting the private banking sector. Those working in the private banking industry accepted that certain limits to their autonomy had become inevitable. Yet they preferred limitations imposed through their own representative associations over any form of state action. Furthermore, this proposal was also considered acceptable by all other sectors of the banking industry, paving the way for a united front against the government initiatives.

4.4.1.3 *The Final Compromise: Voluntary and Group-Specific Safeguards, Not State Control*

In the political sphere, similar proposals had been made by the parliamentary opposition. Instead of the comprehensive system of deposit insurance suggested by the government, the CDU/CSU presented a plan in November 1974 which was based on a fund administered by specific banking groups. A further debate over these issues in December 1974 demonstrated that the FDP, which was part of the governing coalition, also preferred a voluntary scheme run by the banking associations (Ronge 1979: 124ff.). The *Bundesbank*, however, called for a comprehensive deposit insurance system based on a legislative framework since it would provide a good level of protection for the entire banking system (Deutsche Bundesbank 1976: 22). Simultaneously, the government was conducting secret negotiations with the BdB. As a consequence, the government-backed amendments made to the KWG in December 1974 did not include proposals for a deposit insurance scheme.

In April 1975, the BdB presented its final plan for a voluntary, group-based deposit insurance system based on many of the ideas that had been developed in the previous six months. It was enhanced by several measures agreed with the government which were intended to make it more practical. These included:

- The stipulation that all banking and credit institutions (notwithstanding their size and the legal framework under which they operated) had to publish their annual results and business reports which disclosed the size of their capital stock.

- Giving representative associations the right to be heard by officials whenever a new bank applied to the BAKred for a licence.

---

[55] Information about the different levels of protection in OECD countries can be found in Deutsche Bundesbank (1992: 36).

- Finally and most importantly, several significant changes were made to company law. The BAKred was given the power to impose a respite of payment on banks that are experiencing serious trouble. Furthermore, only the BAKred was to have the right to start bankruptcy procedures against a bank. Both directives were supposed to give failing banks the necessary time to take the restructuring and refinancing measures needed to ensure their survival (Deutsche Bundesbank 1976: 22f.).

When the *Bundesrat* criticized the absence of a comprehensive deposit insurance scheme in this amendment, the government declared its preference for the compromise it had struck with the BdB. It even went on to state that it did not believe that a comprehensive scheme was necessary.[56] Government ministers pointed to several factors in their attempts to justify this policy shift. The representative associations of the *Sparkassen* and credit union sectors had increased the size of their safety funds to DM 500 million for the former and DM 350 million for the latter. Moreover, in neither sector had any deposits ever been lost through a member institution's insolvency.[57] The BdB proposals promised a much better level of coverage for individual depositors than what could have been achieved through a state-administered scheme that had no state subsidy.

In the first reading of this piece of legislation, Finance Minister Apel reassured the *Bundestag*:

When these regulations take effect, ladies and gentlemen, there will be coverage for savers in the Federal Republic whose extent will be unmatched in the rest of the world.[58]

He went on to explain that the achievement of a compromise with the banking industry was largely due to the threat of a "very comprehensive legal settlement for a deposit insurance scheme" if they were unable to come to an agreement. However, Apel went on to emphasize once more that he preferred the compromise that had been achieved with the BdB (ibid.). The impression that the original government proposal had largely been of a tactical nature was strengthened during the second reading when a spokesman for the SPD parliamentary party stated that: "the Federal government had wanted to throw a fat stone in the waters in order to make certain that something more

---

[56]   See *Deutscher Bundestag, Drucksache 7/3657, Anlage 3*, p. 23.

[57]   Both *Sparkassen* and credit unions have set up mechanisms whereby their guarantee funds provide the financial means to prevent their member institutions from going insolvent. This also protects creditors from suffering major losses (Deutsche Bundesbank 1976: 22).

[58]   See *Deutscher Bundestag, Stenographische Berichte, 7/176, Sitzung*, 5 June 1975, p. 12357f..

happened than a few small ripples on the surface."[59] The achievement of this compromise appeared to be the result of an exemplary process of cooperation between government, parliament, and the banks (ibid.).

Indeed, several factors indicate that the original wide-ranging government proposals had primarily been introduced for tactical purposes. In particular, the fact that they had been announced at a press conference and the subsequent immediate launch of negotiations with the bank associations showed that there was a tactical element to this initiative. If this was the case, then this approach was rewarded with success since even experienced observers admitted that from the perspective of 1976, the extent to which the *Bundesverband Deutscher Banken* was prepared to compromise was far greater than it had been two years previously (Knapp 1976: 876). The other advantages of this settlement included the speed with which it could be put into practice,[60] the avoidance of state subsidies and its compatibility with the principle of subsidiarity which was so vital to the existing economic system.[61] The opposition, which had insisted upon a state-run system in the first reading,[62] dropped this demand. This paved the way for a unanimous vote in favour of the legislative proposal. Along with some of the directives mentioned above, the most important changes set in train were new guidelines for major loans[63] and the introduction of the *Vier-Augen-Prinzip*, that is, the stipulation that every bank now needed two full-time chief executives (Deutsche Bundesbank 1976; Knapp 1976).

The high level of deposit protection—up to 30 per cent of the capital stock of any bank for *every depositor*—led some to openly doubt the ability of this system to cope with the collapse of a major bank. Yet these critics were silenced when the first test case in 1976 (the closure of the *Pfalz-Kredit-Bank*) demonstrated the positive aspects of these new regulations. There was no run on this bank nor did the rest of the banking industry experience serious trouble. The attempts at restoring trust in the banking system had clearly succeeded. At the same time, the banking industry demonstrated that it would

[59] Statement by Member of the *Bundestag* Heinz Rapp (SPD), *Deutscher Bundestag, Stenographische Berichte*, 7/219, *Sitzung*, 30 January 1976, p. 15248.

[60] The legal problems involved in the establishment of a deposit insurance system were considerable and such a project would have been delayed by any eventual challenge in the courts. The Justice Ministry had even suggested that the original plan might contravene the constitution (Deutsche Bundesbank 1992: 31f.), while the BAKred had also expressed its displeasure with this initiative (Franke 1998: 298). It would therefore have probably been very difficult to implement this plan.

[61] See the debate at the second reading of this law (*Deutscher Bundestag, Stenographische Berichte*, 7/219, *Sitzung*, 30 January 1976, pp. 15245–55).

[62] See *Deutscher Bundestag, Stenographische Berichte*, 7/176, *Sitzung*, 5 June 1975, p. 12360.

[63] After these changes, major loans *had* to be limited to 75 per cent of own capital, while the previous guidelines had stipulated that they *should* be limited to 100 per cent.

stick to its commitments. Although the changes made to the KWG and the deposit insurance funds were not yet in force, the banks made certain that the depositors were given compensation in accordance with the basic principles of the agreement between the government and the BdB (Knapp 1976: 874).

4.4.1.4 *All's Well that Ends Well: The Commission on "Basic Principles of the Banking Industry"*

The third element of the initial reaction of the Finance Minister to the collapse of the *Herstatt Bank* was the establishment of a commission to investigate the basic principles of the banking industry and make recommendations for reform. This commission was called the *Studienkommission Grundsatzfragen der Kreditwirtschaft* and began work in November 1974, the first phase of reaction to the crisis.

As has been described above, this commission had been a potential threat to the existing banking system, and there were some indications that the banking industry perceived it as such. In its 1974 annual report the BdB hoped "that in the face of a discussion which has continued for some time [...] over the supposed 'power of the banks' [...] this commission will be made up of real experts', and it offered to answer all questions and provide all necessary documentation" (Bundesverband Deutscher Banken 1974: 16). The BdB also pointed out that the universal banking system had demonstrated its high level of efficiency and its ability to provide a wide range of financial services at comparatively low cost. It ended this report by expressing doubt over whether the kind of strict system of separation which existed in Britain and the United States was any better (ibid.).

At the very same time that the members of this commission were announced in November 1974, the government was already negotiating with the banking industry. Real experts were therefore appointed in order not to endanger these negotiations. Of the eleven members of this commission, none had their professional competence questioned when their participation was announced. It included[64]

- Four government representatives who came from the Justice Ministry, Finance Ministry, BAKred and *Bundesbank*, respectively.
- Two academics specialized in credit and banking issues.
- Five representatives from the banking sector. This included two from the private commercial banks (one representing a major and one representing

---

[64] Studienkommission Grundsatzfragen der Kreditwirtschaft (1979: 2f.).

a small bank), one from the public-law *Sparkassen* and *Landesbanken*, and two from the credit union sector.[65]

The remit of the commission encompassed three main issues:[66]

1. The controversy over whether the banking system should be restructured. This was to include an exploration of potential alternatives such as a regime based on strict separation in which banks would either focus exclusively on loans and deposits or on stock-and-bond trading.

2. An investigation of the complex debate over the power of the banks. This was to be done with specific reference to proposals for a ban or the imposition of limits on the ability of banks to purchase a stake in industrial and retail corporations. It also examined the issue of proxy voting, the large number of directorships held by senior bankers and the issue of domination of the securities and bond markets.

3. Amendments to the legal framework enshrined in the KWG when it came to the own capital and liquidity requirements of banks and other financial institutions.

The commission had originally been supposed to submit its report at some point in the spring of 1977 after a two-year deliberation period. The results were to be discussed in detail and recommended changes to be implemented before the federal elections of 1980 in order to keep its findings from becoming a topic of contention during the election campaign.[67]

But the commission handed the report in two years late—in May 1979. Over 600 pages long, it contained a detailed account of different critiques of the banking system as well as various reform proposals. Yet the recommendations made by the commission itself were remarkably modest. While the BdB expressed relief at their unspectacular nature, the response of the trade press was laced with sarcasm.[68] Even though this report did not deny that

---

[65] Coleman (1996: 135f.) overestimates the extent to which members of the banking industry in general, and representatives of the private banks in particular were able to "capture" the commission. Some of the most controversial decisions made by the commission—such as the recommendations dealing with the curbs on bank investment in companies outside the financial sector (see Studienkommission Grundsatzfragen der Kreditwirtschaft (1979: 282f.))—were only passed by the slimmest of majorities (six votes for to five votes against). Therefore it is important to point out that representatives of the banking industry did *not* have an own majority within the commission.

[66] See Studienkommission Grundsatzfragen der Kreditwirtschaft (1979: 3).

[67] As announced by Finance Minister Apel. See *Deutscher Bundestag, Stenographische Berichte*, 7/219, *Sitzung*, 30 January 1976, p. 15255.

[68] One comment made in the *Zeitschrift für das Kreditwesen* (volume 13/1979) began under the title "The Mountains Laboured..." with a short commentary dealing with the commission report that stated: "One could describe it with this picture: a team of architects and structural

there were some structural problems with universal banking, it claimed that a system change was not indicated and might be risky:

> The universal banking system has proved its worth. Both putative and actual defi-ciencies of the current banking system are not sufficient to necessitate a change of system [...] A transition to a system based on separation might be able to eliminate the kinds of conflict of interest which exist within the universal banking system. However, major structural change of this nature would have such detrimental effects that it can ultimately not be justified.
>
> (Studienkommission Grundsatzfragen der Kreditwirtschaft 1979: 26)[69]

It also came to the conclusion that nationalization or the imposition of public ownership upon the financial infrastructure of the Federal Republic would not be a suitable means for the achievement of the government's agenda (Studienkommission Grundsatzfragen der Kreditwirtschaft 1979: 249). The commission made few concrete proposals. Among its few recommendations were suggestions that a limit of 25 per cent plus one share should be set on the stake a bank could acquire in a company outside of the financial sector, and a reform of proxy voting.

Both initiatives did not require quick action. In addition, there was a personnel change at the Finance Ministry, with the new Finance Minister Matthöfer (SPD) announcing that any amendments to the KWG based on the recommendations of the commission would only take place after the election of 1980. The change of government in 1982, when the SPD was replaced by a coalition between the Christian Democrats and the FDP, meant that further delays prevented the enactment of these amendments to the KWG until 1984. At this point, ten years after the commission had been set up and five years after it had submitted its report, none of its recommendations were included in the amending legislation (Deutsche Bundesbank 1985: 38).

Considering this meagre result, there is room to speculate whether the entire commission was also essentially a tactical instrument that had already served its purpose long before the report had been submitted. Since continu-ing stability meant that fears of further bank crises had not been confirmed, none of the relevant actors in this policy field had any interest in questioning the compromise that had been achieved. It had also become clear that, as the commission report had suggested, a change of system would have created even greater political, legal, and economic difficulties than the introduction of a

---

engineers is called in to investigate the reasons why two buildings have collapsed. They find nothing, yet decided that a third building next door needed a new doorbell" (p. 617). The BdB's reaction to the report can be found in the same journal (volume 11, p. 516).

[69] A more comprehensive description of these arguments can be found on pp. 222–45.

state-run deposit insurance scheme—even though already that option had been treated with some scepticism by the Justice Ministry.

4.4.2 Gradual Europeanization: Further Amendments to the KWG

After the political episode described in Section 4.4.1, which covered the decade between 1974 and 1984, the policy field of bank regulation remained quiet for a long period of time. Though there were a further three amendments to the KWG before the end of our period of investigation, there were considerable differences between these and the legislation surrounding the *Sofort-Novelle* of 1976, which enshrined the changes in regulatory guidelines that had resulted from the *Herstatt* crisis. For after the middle of the 1980s, the legislative actions of the Federal Republic were largely limited to the implementation of European Commission directives as well as other aspects of European integration.

As Figure 4.1 shows, state action (under the timeline) reacted to external influences (above the timeline) which were emerging at the European level. In the last decade, the influence of the European Commission upon policy-making has been intensifying, resulting in a growing number of regulations and directives. German legislators have reacted to this European pressure with further amendments to the KWG every two to four years.[70] The third amendment of the KWG, which came into force in January 1985, led to a consolidation of regulatory indicators and made the inclusion of assessment of equity demands in balance sheets obligatory for every bank. It also revoked decree powers to regulate interest levels that had not been used since 1967. By contrast, the recommendations made in the report of the *Studienkommission Grundsatzfragen der Kreditwirtschaft* (the commission which had brought about the amendments in the first place) were not implemented. The fourth amendment package, enacted in January 1993, converted the Second Consolidated Supervision Directive produced by the European Commission into German law.

This was a fundamental reconfiguration of KWG guidelines dealing with equity ratios. This reform introduced the idea of a "European passport" which enabled German banks to offer financial services and open branches across the European Union without having to apply for special permission in every individual country. After this law was passed it became clear that a further set of amendments would have to follow, since the Second Consolidation Directive had already been put in place by the European Commission while

---

[70] More information about changes to the KWG can be found in Fischer (1997*b*, 1999), Gläser (1999: 38–41), as well as Deutsche Bundesbank (1985, 1993, 1994, 1998).

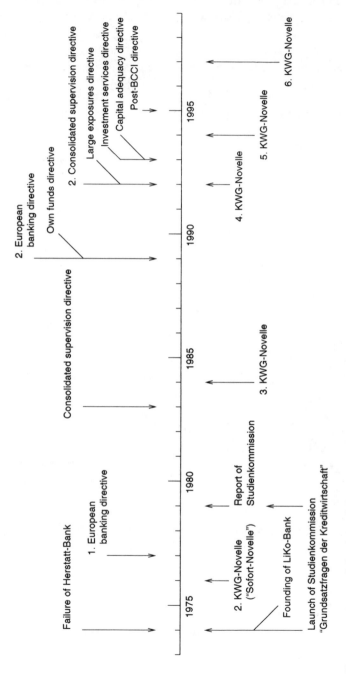

Figure 4.1. External shocks and domestic reactions in banking regulation policy, 1973–99

further directives dealing with major loans, investment services, and capital adequacy were already on the cards. The first two measures were converted into German law through a fifth amendment of the KWG which effectively led to a redrafting of its legal framework. Together with the so-called Post-BCCI Directive, the directives concerning investment services and capital adequacy were turned into German law through a sixth amendment, which had already been in the pipeline when its predecessor was still being examined in the *Bundestag*. The removal of such regulatory barriers at a European level was extended to stock-broking firms, which also received a "European passport".

What has become increasingly evident in the course of this case study is that control of important aspects of the bank regulation system has shifted from the national to the supranational level. This sea change has been recognized by members of the German policy network:

The music is not being made by the legislative bodies of the Federal Republic in Berlin any longer. Rather the most important initiatives are coming from Brussels and even Basel.[71]

This process of step-by-step Europeanization in the decade after the creation of the European common market has heavily influenced the legal basis of the German system of bank regulation. The KWG in its current form is "largely the product of European guidelines" (Boos, Fischer, and Schulte-Matler 2000: v). At the moment, there is no end in sight for this Europeanization process.

4.5 CHARACTERISTICS OF THE POLICY FIELD

In the last twenty-five years, the policy field of bank regulation in the Federal Republic has been characterized by a high level of integration and consultation, success with regard to its output, recurring debates about the power of the banks and a considerable amount of institutional continuity despite changing circumstances. The following section will examine these defining characteristics in more detail.

4.5.1 Integration and Consultation

As we have seen in the description of the relevant actors and their behaviour in the crises of the 1970s, the German policy network focused on banking

[71] Interview BVR, 24 March 2000. Similar statements can be found in other interviews with bank executives.

regulation issues is characterized by clear divisions of responsibility and broad consultation of all participants. Although the latter was legally required, it is not the only reason why the system seems to function reasonably well. Historical tradition and good experience are of equal importance, since there are few "turf battles" either in terms of interest groups competing for members or regulatory agencies trying to protect their areas of jurisdiction in the course of the legislative process. In fact, the American case study demonstrates that this is not a state of affairs generally to be expected.

Both formally and informally, there is constant contact between the different constituent parts of the policy network.[72] Senior representatives of the ZKA membership and the chief executives of the largest banks meet annually with the Finance Minister in the course of the so-called Bristol Discussions,[73] while on the working level the banking associations are in constant contact with the government. Consequently, the associations are able to obtain detailed knowledge about new regulations when they are still being drafted, giving them significant time to prepare their response to them despite the relatively short amount of time provided in the legislative process for interest groups to react to new initiatives. With the Finance Ministry and BAKred relatively remote from day-to-day developments in the banking system, such input from the associations has become particularly important for regulators. This gives banks the ability to exert influence over the legislative process, though only if the banking associations can maintain a united front: "Whenever we cannot come to a consensus on regulatory questions, we find ourselves in a bad position."[74] Yet the associations themselves maintain that they have remained united. The relationship between the DSGV and VÖB has remained particularly strong, since the *Landesbanken*, which belong to both groups, have bound them closely together. A similar level of close coordination exists between the DSGV and BVR because of the decentralized structures which both have in common. All in all, one can describe the three sectors of the German banking sector as a "cohesive power triangle".[75] The German policy network is characterized by associations that are both horizontally and vertically integrated and have been regularly included in the formulation and implementation of government policy. The classification of this network as a system characterized by corporatism—used by many experts in this field (Ronge 1979; Lehner, Schubert, and Geile 1983; Coleman 1996: 82)—has been confirmed by the findings of this case study.

---

[72] The following statements are based on different interviews with the BdB, VÖB, DSGV, and BVR.

[73] Though these continuing consultations were named after a Bonn hotel, they kept this name after the federal government moved to Berlin.

[74] Interview BdB, 3 February 2000.   [75] Interview BVR, 24 March 2000.

While banks in the *Sparkassen* and the cooperative sector are very similar to one another, the commercial banks vary enormously in size and interests. In this context, the ability of the BdB to integrate the diverse set of banks involved in this policy field is remarkable. In the crisis after the collapse of the *Herstatt Bank*, the BdB made one of its main goals the preservation of a diverse private banking landscape which included both small- and medium-sized institutions working parallel to the major banks (Bundesverband Deutscher Banken 1975: 18), even though a competitive environment in which the smaller banks could be put under pressure would have been more profitable for the major players.[76]

The state does not play a very prominent role in this sector, opting for self-restraint (in comparison with other states) when it comes to bank regulation. It often limits itself to a moderating role when dealing with the associations: "The BAKred is trying to maintain a consensus."[77] Significant aspects of the bank regulation system are controlled by the representative associations. For example, the inspection reports of the different oversight bodies belonging to the representative associations have to be handed over to state regulators (Mayer 1981: 34f.), and the relevant association must be heard in the licensing process for any new bank.[78] The *Herstatt* episode demonstrated that the state has not used moments of crisis as a means with which to acquire new powers and areas of jurisdiction and has worked to preserve the existing system which has functioned for decades. This form of voluntary self-restraint is intriguing, since most observers have pointed out that the German state's capacity for action in this sector is considerable (Coleman 1996: 75). Instead of using its influence, the state has allowed the associations to expand their own area of jurisdiction. This process led Volker Ronge to comment already nearly thirty years ago that—in contrast to claims of theories of late capitalism that state regulation is constantly expanding—developments rather indicated a growing importance of associations, "political self-administration of capital" and "self-organising capitalism" (Ronge 1979: 46).

4.5.2 Successful Policy-Outcomes

A further characteristic of the German case is the extent of its success in terms of policy outcome. If one takes the number of bank collapses as an indicator,

---

[76] It is possible, that this policy position may have been influenced by the fact that the head of the BdB in 1974 was Alwin Münchmeyer from the banking house of *Münchmeyer & Co.*, Hamburg, one of the smaller commercial banks. In 1975, he was replaced in this function by a senior executive from the *Deutsche Bank*, one of the three major banks (Wagner 1976: 81, 104).
[77] Interview DSGV, 4 February 2000.   [78] See §32 (3) KWG, which was added in 1976.

then one sees a situation where there were no collapses in the *Sparkassen* and cooperative sectors[79] and thirty-seven such collapses in the private banking sector between 1973 and 1997, of which only twenty-five took place after 1976.[80] Of these instances, the *Herstatt Bank*, which was in size only eightieth out of the hundred major banks, was by far the largest institution to be hit. If one examines the assets of these failed banks, during the most acute period in 1974 they consisted of over DM 2,885 million, less than 1 per cent of the total assets of the banking system as a whole, which were worth over DM 291,678 million. In 1995, the deposits of failed banks were worth over DM 2,619 million, the second highest amount in the period examined during this study. Yet this was less than 0.1 per cent of the total deposits of a banking industry which had undergone a massive process of expansion. If one adds all deposits of failed banks since 1977 and compares them with the value of the total deposits in 1987 (the mid-point of the period examined in this section), then they only make up 0.7 per cent of the total deposits of that one year.[81]

After the *Herstatt Bank* crisis, the German system has, therefore, been spared major or even medium-sized problems during the period examined by this study. In international comparison, this represents a unique level of success (Busch 2001). Most scholarly analyses have been correspondingly positive:

The German banking system is one of the most stable in the world; it is internationally competitive and records high levels of earnings. To date there have been no instances in Germany of crisis-like developments, as have occurred in some other countries because of speculative bubbles in the real estate or share markets, with serious repercussions for the entire economy.   (Becker 1998: 65f.).

The assessment of the new president of the *Bundesaufsichtsamt für das Kreditwesen*, Jochen Sanio, at the start of his term was similarly positive:

[79] As has been explained above, the safeguards within these sectors are designed to maintain the solvency of each bank, providing indirect protection for depositors. If serious problems arise in a bank belonging to these groups, then a merger between such a bank and another institution in the group is arranged. One prominent case in recent times were the problems experienced by the *Mannheimer Sparkasse*, which had to write down its value by DM 830 million because of a series of bad loans (Rhein-Neckar-Zeitung, 25 January 2000, p. 8). It was quickly forced to merge with the *Bezirkssparkasse Weinheim*, becoming the *Sparkasse Rhein-Neckar-Nord* with considerable help from the *Badische Sparkassen- und Giroverband* (the association representing the interest of *Sparkassen* in the Southwest of Germany) and the DSGV (vwd, 26 July 2000).

[80] Information passed on from the *Deutsche Bundesbank* to the author, 22 February 1999.

[81] Author's calculation based on information from the *Deutsche Bundesbank* (see above) as well as Deutsche Bundesbank (1988: 180) and Deutsche Bundesbank (1999: 107).

The record of German regulatory bodies as guardians of the banking industry can be considered faultless. At no point since the founding of the *Bundesaufsichtsamt* [...] has the German banking trade experienced the symptoms of crisis despite intensive competitive pressures and the resulting higher levels of risk.[82]

This success has also been positive for the banks involved and even brought them competitive advantages in the international market. While contributions to the deposit insurance scheme in the Federal Republic only make up 0.3 per thousand of bank assets, in the United States the level of contributions is seven times as high at 2.3 per thousand of all bank assets (Deutsche Bundesbank 1992: 35).

The compromise agreement of the mid-1970s has demonstrated itself to be stable and successful. The deposits of every insolvent bank were restored to customers at their full value, so that since 1975 no depositor in any German financial institution had to experience any losses whatsoever. Bank runs have not taken place since the collapse of the *Herstatt Bank*. As a consequence, the issue of deposit insurance, which was still a matter of controversy in the 1960s, arouses little interest among policy-makers today.

4.5.3 Ongoing Debate about the "Power of the Banks"

Despite these positive policy outcomes, the other issue which shaped debate at the beginning of the period examined here has continued to be a matter of public controversy. The questions surrounding the so-called "power of the banks" have regularly returned to become a topic of public discussion.[83]

With a highly competitive banking market and low level of concentration, wider banking issues have not played a central role in this debate. Rather, it has largely focused on controversial aspects of the universal banking system such as proxy voting, the presence of bank representatives in company boardrooms and the possession by banks of major stakes in corporations outside of the financial sector.[84] While in the 1970s the question of nationalization provoked considerable discussion, since the 1980s, the emphasis has shifted to the establishment of legal limits on banking power through alterations to existing guidelines of commercial law (particularly the stock corporation act,

---

[82] See: http://www.bakred.de/texte/praes/r_280600_2_htm (25 August 2000).

[83] Similar conditions existed in the early twentieth century. See Section 4.1.1.

[84] See Büschgen (1983: 360–7) as well as the journal *Der Bürger im Staat* 1/1997 (which focuses on the "power of the banks"). A detailed description of this debate can be found in Engenhardt (1995), which includes excerpts from party programmes and position papers published by interest groups.

the commercial code and antitrust law). In 1997, for example, the SPD/FDP coalition governing the *Land* of *Rheinland-Pfalz* introduced a draft bill in the *Bundesrat* for a law designed "to heighten the efficiency of company directors and limit the concentrations of power in the hands of banking institutions through the purchase of shares in other companies".[85] This legislative initiative was largely intended to impose an upper limit of 10 per cent on the amount of shares a bank could purchase in a non-banking company. The SPD parliamentary party in the *Bundestag* introduced a similar proposal in the twelfth and thirteenth legislative sessions of the federal parliament.[86] Both proposals were unsuccessful, while the law for greater transparency of companies ("*Gesetz zur Kontrolle und Transparenz im Unternehmensbereich*" or KonTraG) enacted in April 1998 did include some recommendations for the control of company directors but did not contain any stipulations putting limits on the extent to which banks could invest in other companies.[87]

The fate of both these initiatives is symptomatic of the debate as a whole, with a great amount of legislative effort and discussion having little or no impact on the legal framework of banking regulation or the universal banking system. Twenty years after the commission on the "fundamental issues of the banking industry" had first recommended limits on bank investment in other companies this proposal has still not been put into place. The potential for fundamental reform which the recurring debates over the power of the banks represent have, however, repeatedly reminded banks of how a sudden shift of popular opinion could threaten their interests.

4.5.4 Institutional Continuity

Continuity is a characteristic of German policy in this area not only because of the developments in the banking system described above. It is also characteristic of state institutions involved in banking regulation and the wider sectoral policy network.

Very little has changed after the initial shock of the crisis at the beginning of the period analysed by this case study. The collapse of the *Herstatt Bank* had greater consequences at the international level by encouraging senior bankers to establish the Basel Committee than it had had on the German system. Once the critical phase had been overcome and sectoral reform had been implemented, the state continued to play a small role as it had done before these crises. The established structures remained in place throughout

---

[85] BR Drs. 561/97.   [86] See BT Drs. 12/7350 and 13/367.
[87] See *Bundesgesetzblatt Teil I* 1998, Nr. 24, 30 April 1998, p. 786.

the remaining twenty years of our investigation when it came to cooperation between representative associations and other institutions as well.

This high level of continuity was made possible through the stability of the banking sector and the successful policy outcomes mentioned above. Further crises would probably have forced the pace of change in a manner similar to events in Britain (see Chapter 5). While this kind of long-term stability certainly has its positive aspects (Coleman 1996: 123, 144f.), one also needs to examine the possibility that it may have had negative effects. For stability and success can paradoxically hinder necessary adaptation to changing circumstances.

The position of the BAKred is particularly significant in this context. Although its personnel numbers have been progressively increased (see above), it has largely remained an administrative body whose workforce has little practical experience of modern banking. This state of affairs is seen as a problem even within the BAKred itself.[88] Even after its powers for on-the-spot inspections were expanded in the amending bill to the KWG of 1976, it did not lead to the establishment of its own independent team of investigators as this organization remained dependent on external auditors (Mayer 1981: 42f.). When the BAKred wanted to be able to cope with the accelerated pace of change at the end of the 1990s by creating a department exclusively responsible for monitoring big corporate banks (Bundesaufsichtsamt für das Kreditwesen 1999: 103), it experienced serious difficulties in recruiting suitable personnel. It had already found it difficult to find staff after its expansion in the course of the sixth amendment of the KWG: of the applicants who had been accepted, over seventy (!) preferred to accept other jobs (Bundesaufsichtsamt für das Kreditwesen 1999: 104). For well-qualified specialists in the field, mid- to upper-level positions in the German bureaucracy were simply not as attractive as equivalent positions in the private sector. Compounding these kinds of problems (and legal limitations on the size of civil servant salaries), the federal government's move from Bonn to Berlin led to a further haemorrhaging of qualified staff (ibid.).

The banking associations have expressed concern about the difficulties the BAKred has had in acquiring the necessary level of resources, largely because of anxieties that less qualified personnel would be more likely to make decisions that damage banking interests.[89] This has also led to problems on the international level. Since negotiations on the international level have become of great importance to national legislation, the fact that such a key institution is under-resourced puts German representatives involved in such discussions in a disadvantageous position. While the relevant department in

---

[88] Interview BAKred, 3 February 2000.   [89] Interview BdB, 3 February 2000.

the BAKred only has a staff of twenty-eight responsible for covering over forty international organizations and committees, the Federal Reserve Bank in New York has an international research department with over 280 employees.[90] Since only 10 per cent of the BAKred's budget is covered by federal funds, it is even more surprising that there has been no expansion of its resources. That members of a representative association like the ZKA had to send a joint letter to the budget committee of the *Bundestag* begging it to prevent further cuts in the BAKred's funding, the agency responsible for monitoring them, must be a unique event in the annals of banking history.[91]

4.6 SUMMARY: THE GERMAN CASE

The German policy network in the area of banking regulation managed to develop an effective strategy in reaction to an early shock.[92] It had been remarkably fortunate in so far as the early liberalization and codification of the banking system as well as the lack of legally enforced market segmentation meant that there was little pressure for different German banking sectors to adapt to new circumstances.

The "iron triangle" made up of state administrators, interest groups, and legislators[93] is typified by a focus on consensus, a perception which is shared by many of those involved in bank regulation.[94] In this triangle the emphasis has remained upon self-regulation and keeping the state at a distance, reflecting the tradition which spanned over a century described in the opening section of this chapter.[95] This is beneficial to the interests of both sides: while it puts less pressure on state resources, it gives the interest groups involved a great deal of freedom of action. As a consequence, they also have to share a part of the costs, as the *SMH-Bank* crisis demonstrated in 1983. Under the pressure

---

[90]   Interview BAKred, 3 February 2000.   [91]   Interview BAKred, 3 February 2000.

[92]   This is also the conclusion arrived at in Coleman (1996: 123).

[93]   Klaus von Beyme (1997: 12) has argued that in Germany we should use the term *ungemütliche Fünfecke* ("uncomfortable pentangles", which include the *Länder* and political parties) when describing conditions in the Federal Republic rather than "cosy iron triangles", a term coined by American specialists in this field. However, in this policy field American terminology does match German conditions, since the *Länder* do not play a role and the political parties adhere to a general consensus on these issues.

[94]   Interview BVR, 24 March 2000.

[95]   There are extraordinary parallels between reactions to the crises of 1908–9 and 1974. In both cases, a commission of inquiry was put into place, whose report did not lead to any new legal regulations, since voluntary safeguards put into place by the banking sector pre-empted state action.

of the BAKred, the banking community paid out large sums to help deal with
the final liquidation of this bank (General Accounting Office 1994*b*: 30). This
delegation has prevented the kind of politicization and the use of delaying
tactics which exacerbated the S&L crisis in the United States.[96] Nevertheless,
the German banking industry has consistently expressed a preference for associational authority over state authority. The political debates over the "power
of the banks", which from the banks' perspective often seemed irrational, may
have contributed to that position.

While this case study has shown how the German policy network attained a
high level of efficiency, it remains unclear whether its policy style can be classified as "active" or "reactive" (Richardson 1982: 13). While the comparatively
early introduction (in Europe at least) of a deposit insurance scheme points to
the former, the fact that it was only established after the *Herstatt* crisis can be
taken as evidence of the latter.[97]

The literature dealing with the state's sectoral capacity for action has
demonstrated a similar level of ambivalence. While Coleman classifies it
as high because of institutional conditions (Coleman 1996: 75), Vogel has
emphasized its limitations by pointing to the fragmented nature of the German state and its dependence on the cooperation of the private sector (Vogel
1996: 254f.). If one looks at the scepticism with which various policy-makers
treated their ability to achieve a state-backed deposit insurance scheme (see
Section 4.4.1.3), then one is tempted to accept the latter argument. Yet when it
comes to this factor, it is difficult to reach a final conclusion, since the German
state has never tried to impose its will against the massive resistance of the
private banking sector.

As this case study has demonstrated, in the last fifteen years the state
system of banking regulation has been shaped by a gradual process of Europeanization. If the German state's capacity for independent action has become
increasingly limited in this policy area, one could argue that it is because
of this process. However, this issue has not been raised in the course of
the many parliamentary debates surrounding successive amendments of the
KWG. Rather, the desire for a strengthening of Germany as a financial centre
has been expressed in parliament across party lines, with new legislative initiatives portrayed as a further step towards the integration of European markets.
Yet this process, too, is not without its problems. The growing frequency of
amending legislation puts all participants under pressure, since they are forced
to develop a response and adapt to new circumstances in ever shorter intervals.

---

[96] See the American case study as well as Scott and Weingast (1992).
[97] See relevant data in Barth, Nolle, and Rice (1997: Table 10).

These changes go much further than the term amendment indicates, often becoming complete reconfigurations of a major law.[98]

The end of the 1990s has also witnessed wider cracks in the stability of the sectoral regime. The sixth set of amendments to the KWG led to a diminishing of the informal relationship between regulators and the banking industry by increasing the BAKred's scope for intervention in the affairs of individual banks (Fischer 1999: 8). The creation of a specific regulatory agency for the stock market[99] in a universal banking system was considered to be illogical and has been heavily criticized by the banks[100] while the *Bundesbank* has begun to compete with the BAKred by increasing the number of its staff working on banking issues.[101] Yet, few further concrete steps have been taken before the end of the period of investigation (1999).

In conclusion, a state which was being kept at a distance from the banks profited from the continuing stability and security provided by the banking industry and the reduced financial costs governments had to face when dealing with banking issues. The success of this model manifested itself also in the fact that, unlike the banking systems of other countries, there was no forced adaptation to new challenges. This was almost the opposite of developments in the United Kingdom, where a forced transfer of regulatory power to an integrated body responsible for all sectors of the financial market took place (which will be examined in Chapter 5). However, the successful and stable development of the banking industry and its low level of politicization in the twenty-five years examined here have taken a less obvious toll. Both trends have diminished the ability and willingness of state institutions to acquire vital information about events in the financial markets and the internal life of banks (Coleman 1996: 135; Lütz 1999). How the impact of these factors can be measured remains a difficult question. Only when these developments have played themselves out over the next years will it be possible to come to some firmer conclusions over whether this strategy has proved acceptable and affordable, or whether in hindsight it will be seen as a missed opportunity.

---

[98] According to the representative of the ZKA, Lehnhoff, at a public hearing of the *Bundestag's* finance committee on 19 March 1997, the first draft of the sixth amendment to the KWG was over 600 pages long (see *Gesetzesdokumentation* BD XIII/285).

[99] The agency responsible for the stock market, the *Bundesaufsichtsamt für Wertpapierhandel* (BAW) was founded in accordance with the legal stipulations of the *Wertpapierhandelsgesetz*, a key part of the second *Finanzmarktförderungsgesetz* of 26 July 1994. Since January 1995, the BAW has 140 staff working in Frankfurt am Main (see http://www.bawe.de/bas_neu.htm).

[100] Interview BAKred, 3 February 2000; interview BVR, 24 March 2000.

[101] Interview *Bundesbank*, 24 March 2000. See Deutsche Bundesbank (2000).

5

The United Kingdom: Late Codification, Early Reform

The British banking system and its regulatory regime have been traditionally characterized by a high degree of continuity. Over the past centuries, both have evolved in a manner unique to the United Kingdom. Moreover, the British tendency to treat what has become known as "the City" as a kind of quasi-metaphysical entity reflects besides continuity also the geographical concentration of financial power in the square mile of the City of London. In none of the other cases examined in the course of this study, not in Frankfurt, Zurich, or even New York's *Wall Street*, is there such a high concentration. While Germany, Switzerland, and the United States each have several important financial centres, in the United Kingdom only "the City" counts. Many in Britain consider it to be a national treasure, a view which is justified by its contribution to British GNP and the national balance of payments.[1]

In recent decades, the tradition-bound British financial community milieu has been exposed to the shock of financial globalization. This is not to be understood in the passive sense, for the internationalization of the financial marketplace has been actively shaped by London bankers through the establishment of the so-called Euro-markets at the beginning of the 1960s along with a whole range of other financial innovations. Throughout this process, the international contacts enjoyed by the London financial sector—a product not least of the former British Empire—enhanced the City's global position.

But the transformation of the market has also had a direct impact upon the financial community in London. The internationalization of money markets in the 1960s and 1970s undermined the City's informal coordination and regulation mechanisms. The world of the City had originally been based on unwritten rules, which were rooted in modes of socialization and upbringing shared by those who belonged to it. As ever more financial players who were

---

[1] On the other hand, this focus on the City has also at times had negative economic effects partly as a result of a tendency to foster an excessively high exchange rate, which has had an adverse impact upon the international competitiveness of British industry (Hall 1986: chapters 3 and 9).

ignorant of, or uninterested in, these rules arrived in the City, the importance of this unwritten compact as a steering device began to decline. In particular, the old order was no longer able to meet heightened demands for transparency and clarity in an internationalized market structure. These pressures led to a growing emphasis upon formalization and codification, described in more detail below, which was effectively a consequence of the internationalization process.[2] The mixture of a social milieu which was interwoven with local financial structures turned into an unfettered marketplace.

In the course of this chapter, a description of the historical development of the banking system and its regulatory structure will be followed by an examination of the relevant protagonists involved in this policy field. This case study will then consider the interplay between crises and reforms which have influenced bank regulation during this period. Although the policy outcome of this process was ultimately positive, it has has been characterized by "some high profile accidents".[3]

5.1 HISTORICAL BACKGROUND

5.1.1 Creation of the Banking System

The British banking system and its central institutions look back upon a long history. Founded in 1694, The Bank of England is the second oldest note-issuing bank after the Swedish *Riksbank* (founded in 1668) and the oldest organized in the form of a joint-stock company (Born 1977: 17f.). It was established through a vote of parliament in order to help finance the war against the France of Louis XIV. That the sum of £1.2 million needed to finance this project was collected in only eleven days and in amounts between £25 and £10,000 was an early sign of the power of London's financial market (Pohl 1994: 1190). In 1707, the Bank of England provided the government with a further loan to pay for the War of Spanish Succession and was rewarded for this with a special privilege when their royal charter was renewed: apart from this institution, no bank with more than six shareholders was to be allowed to issue banknotes in England and Wales (Born 1977: 18). As a consequence, the other banks which were created in the course of the eighteenth century either remained small or accepted that they could not issue banknotes. The special role of the Bank of England as a private bank with a public-law charter, which

---

[2] Interview with Lord Burns, 14 October 1999.
[3] Ibid.

from the middle of the eighteenth century onwards became the bank of the government, will be considered in more detail below.

In the final third of the eighteenth century the number of banks in England and Wales rose sharply.[4] In 1800 there were around 70 banks in London and around 280 in the rest of England and Wales (Cottrell 1994: 1139). The main difference between the city banks and the rural banks was that the latter issued banknotes (because the Bank of England could not guarantee the circulation of its banknotes outside the south-east metropolitan area), whereas the banks located in London had given up the right to issue their own banknotes. The banks (which rarely possessed branches) were mostly private bankers, that is, they utilized only their own capital and retained exclusive control over the decision-making process. These men often came from businesses with the kind of high profit margins which facilitated significant capital accumulation. This is clear from the names which came to be used for these groups of bankers: thus merchant bankers were involved in the wholesale trade and goldsmith bankers came from the goldsmith industry.

With the founding of the *Commercial Bank of Scotland* in Edinburgh in 1810, the first joint-stock bank in Scotland was created and others were soon to follow. The motivation for this move was the desire to involve a wider section of the population in a banking system which had previously been dominated by the rich (Cottrell 1994: 1139). After the Napoleonic wars and the economic crisis of 1825–6, when many private note-issuing banks in England and Wales discontinued their payments and were no longer able to convert the banknotes they had issued into gold, the foundation of capital rich note-issuing banks, that is, joint-stock banks, was also proposed.[5]

It first became possible to found joint-stock banks in England after a change in the law in 1826. At first this did not apply to London or an area within a radius of 65 miles from the city. This restriction was lifted in 1833, leading to the establishment of the *London & Westminster Bank*. This innovation met with strong resistance from the established private banks and the Bank of England because the new joint-stock banks offered interest on deposits for the first time.[6] This resistance was so persistent that the *London & Westminster Bank* only gained access to the London Bankers Clearing House in 1854. Yet such obstruction was unable to check the increasing success of banks with a

---

[4] Banking in Scotland and Ireland developed independently from the policy direction in England and Wales. This will only be examined here in so far as is relevant to our topic of study.

[5] In the two years before the commercial crisis, the private note-issuing banks had more than doubled the circulation of their banknotes. The Bank of England solved the crisis with a considerable investment of their own gold reserves and granted all loan requests (Born 1977: 19).

[6] Hitherto, protection from theft was considered an adequate return for depositing money.

larger capital base. In particular, after the reform of corporation law in 1862, which limited the liability of each shareholder to his deposit,[7] the joint-stock bank became the dominant type of bank. Other types of credit institution had also been introduced by this time, but did not, in contrast with other European countries, manage to survive in the long term. At the beginning of the nineteenth century, savings banks were created in England for similar reasons as in Germany, namely to create investment opportunities for small savers. However, in contrast to developments in Germany, private individuals (often with a religious background) rather than municipal savings banks took the initiative in England. By 1816, seventy-eight savings banks had been created (Born 1977: 211). The savings bank law of 1817 obliged these private institutions to invest their funds in national debt bonds. There was, however, no governmental supervision to ensure the fulfilment of these stipulations. After the economic crisis of 1847, it became clear that many of the 600 savings banks operating in Britain had not conformed to government guidelines. In addition, some national debt bonds had suffered a loss in value. This ongoing systemic crisis was finally resolved through the creation of the Post Office Savings Bank in 1861, which led to the centralization and nationalization of a significant aspect of the banking system.[8] Credit Unions were not created in the United Kingdom because of the large number of rural country banks.

From the 1840s onwards, there was a growing division of labour between the rapidly developing deposit banks, concentrating on domestic business, and merchant banks which had continued to expand since the end of the eighteenth century and focused on financing international trade (Cottrell 1994: 1143). The latter also specialized in financial services and the provision of state loans. In 1803, for example, London's *Barings Bank* arranged a loan of $1 million to the United States for the purchase of Louisiana from France. The specialized nature of these different types of bank fulfilled the requirements of the highly complex financial and industrial networks which provided the economic base for Britain's colonial and trading empire. This was facilitated by the fact that in Britain, unlike continental Europe or the United States, the process of industrialization and the construction of the railways were financed without the aid of banks. Unlike the new financial systems on the continent, the growth in middle-class savings in Britain was characterized by the direct investment of small amounts of capital in the stock market without

---

[7] Previously, each shareholder had been liable with his entire estate (Born 1977: 19).

[8] There is a clear contrast with the German case in which public-law was anchored in municipal government. Due to centralization, there was no development of a local credit cycle through credit lending to local small businesses which provided the basis for German savings banks since the second half of the nineteenth century. On the other hand, the local demand for credit in England and Wales was met through the high number of country banks.

the involvement of banks as accumulators of capital (Born 1977: 86f.). The rest of the industry was also either self-funded or raised investment capital through long-term loans from non-banks (ibid. 96). Therefore, banks did not play an important role in the financing (or control) of the savings industry as they did in Germany for example. As a result, Britain did not experience the introduction of the universal banking model.[9]

The number of joint-stock banks in Britain was at its highest in 1880.[10] Only shortly afterwards, a massive process of concentration led to a major drop in their number. Because most banks had no branches ("unit banks"), they only began to become an important factor in British banking after a wave of mergers between various banks created several sizeable financial networks. In 1900, twelve major banks had come into existence in this fashion which each possessed over 100 branches across the country. After 1910, the concentration process reached a new level with the merger of two of these major banks. This trend came to a climax with a wave of mergers between 1917 and 1918 which led to the creation of five major banks (the Big Five): Barclays Bank, Midland Bank, Westminster Bank, Lloyds Bank, and the National Provincial Bank (Born 1977: 133f.).

In view of this concentration, political fears about a monopolization of the market arose. The government set up a investigatory commission (the Colwyn Committee) and began preparations for the drafting of a law prohibiting further mergers between big banks (Cottrell 1994: 1147). However, assurances from these banks that they would undertake no further mergers between themselves prevented a legal ruling. Until 1923, however, mergers with smaller banks continued to take place with the result that by the end of the 1920s around 80 per cent of the English banking business was concentrated in the hands of the five big banks. On the eve of the Second World War, apart from the "Big Five", only eight banks in the whole of the United Kingdom remained completely independent (Born 1977: 135, 445). Moreover, the major banks extended their operations into Scotland and Ireland while Lloyds and Barclays even attempted tried to set up a global financial network (Cottrell 1994: 1150f.).

After 1939, banks were increasingly subjected to state control. Controls on the movement of capital and the provision of credit after the Second World War led to a cartelization of the banking system. In 1968, the number of major banks was reduced to four through a merger between the *Westminster Bank* and *National Provincial Bank* which created the *National Westminster Bank*.

---

[9] See on this in more detail Section 4.1.1, and in particular p. 78 of this study.

[10] Statistical information varies substantially in the secondary literature. However, it is of little consequence in this context (Born 1977: 131; Cottrell 1994: 1144).

These banks were not just big by British standards. When it came to net assets, Barclays Bank was the world's fourth largest bank in 1970, and National Westminster Bank the sixth (Cottrell 1994: 1155). However, the English banking world in general, and London in particular, was beginning to change. With the influx of more and more foreign banks from the middle of the 1960s onwards,[11] the internationalization of the London financial market began the process which would lead to fundamental changes in the following decades. The major English banks responded to these challenges with, among other things, a diversification strategy as a part of which a growing involvement in industrial investment and finance precipitated a wider shift towards the adoption of the universal banking model.

5.1.2 The Development of State Regulation

It is difficult to determine the exact point at which a system of banking regulation worthy of the name took shape in the United Kingdom. Though it has only existed in law since 1979 (see below), the Bank of England (BoE) has acquired responsibilities involving banking issues over a long period of time. Because it is an institution that has been in existence for such an extraordinarily long time (the Bank was founded over 300 years ago), it is not easy to determine the exact manner in which certain practices and traditions came into being. The following section will therefore mainly focus on certain key incidents as well as the official approach towards banking regulation in the United Kingdom until the beginning of the 1970s.[12]

As has been mentioned above, the Bank of England was founded as a private bank in the form of a limited company under Royal charter. By the mid-eighteenth century, it had become the main provider of financial services to most ministries and administered the state debt (Pohl 1994: 1190). In the nineteenth century the bank gradually acquired the functions of a central bank: in 1833 its bank notes were declared legal tender; in 1844 the Peel government's Banking Act ended the practice of handing concessions for the production of banknotes to private banks and decreed that as these banks ceased to issue notes or merged, their contingent for the issuing of notes fell to the Bank of England (Born 1977: 19ff.). By 1900, this had led to a de facto BoE monopoly when it came to these issues, cementing its position as central note-issuing bank.

---

[11] In 1960 there were 77 foreign banks resident in London. By 1970 the total had risen to 159, by 1974 to 256, and by 1979 to 330 (Cottrell 1994: 1156, 1159).

[12] A comprehensive overview can be found in Gardener (1986*b*: chapter 4) and Reid (1988: chapter 10).

The same law also imposed a fixed ratio between the level of gold reserves and the circulation levels of the Bank of England's banknotes. In the crisis years of 1847, 1857, and 1866, the gold reserves of the Bank of England shrank so quickly that strict adherence to these coverage guidelines for the English economy would have led to a credit squeeze in a recession where easy credit was needed, a course of action which would have worsened the economic crisis. Yet the combined intervention of the government and bank managed to solve this problem by temporarily suspending the relevant guidelines when these crises reached their peaks (Born 1977: 24). Thus even shortly after the first legal guidelines for monetary policy had been put into place, the political decision-makers dealt with them in a highly pragmatic fashion, an approach which can be seen as early evidence of a key characteristic of the entire British system of banking regulation.

Faced with a succession of further problems in the British financial system throughout the nineteenth century, the Bank of England effectively grew into the role of crisis manager without actually having received an explicit mandate from parliament. When Barings Bank tumbled into a liquidity crisis after overinvestment in Argentine government bonds began to cause it problems, the Bank of England came to the conclusion that this event put the British banking system as a whole at risk and promptly organized a financial aid package. Within twenty-four hours it was able to collect a combined amount of £10 million pounds from all major London banks for a guarantee fund which prevented the spread of panic across the financial markets and saved Barings from bankruptcy (Born 1977: 238f.).

When major political change after the First World War began to threaten the privileged position of the City, the Bank of England served as a buffer between City interests and the government:

The Bank served as spokesman both for the City within the government and for the government within the City. (Vogel 1996: 98)

Throughout, it claimed that flexibility and informality were the only proper basis for dealing with the highly complex world of finance and banking and did everything to oppose the introduction of regulatory legislation (Moran 1991: 61ff.). After the Second World War, the central bank was nationalized by the newly elected Labour government through the Bank of England Act 1946. Although several official inquiries openly questioned whether this would influence the workings of the bank and its relationship with the Treasury under whose aegis it now operated,[13] it was promptly integrated into the mechanisms of government in a much more comprehensive fashion. This

---

[13] See statements in the Radcliffe-Report of 1959, cited in Reid (1988: 207f.).

development was strengthened by a whole set of laws and regulations, such as the limitations on capital movements as a result of the Exchange Control Act 1947, which directly intervened in the economic cycle and therefore impinged on the work of the central bank.

Yet the Bank of England Act 1946 did not contain any stipulations dealing with bank regulation. Though it gave the central bank the power to demand information from the banks and give them "recommendations" and (with the assent of the Treasury) "directions", a bank that decided to ignore these kinds of interventions could not be threatened with sanctions. These instruments were never used by the Treasury anyway (Reid 1988: 207; General Accounting Office 1994a: 12f.; Kloten and Stein 1993: 301). Rather, the system continued to be based upon informal relationships, in which the "raised eyebrows" of the Governor of the Bank of England was a powerful form of sanction that could compel obedience. The "long-standing tradition of allowing the banking industry a high degree of self-regulation", which alone could provide both cheap and competent oversight, was usually used to justify the continued existence of this traditional order (Hall 1999: 3).

While a variety of different laws defined the rights and responsibilities of banks, a generally accepted definition of what constituted a bank did not exist. Instead, several ministries created a set of lists which contained the names of firms that had to conform to the directives of the Exchange Control Act 1947, the Companies Acts 1948 and 1967, as well as the Depositors Act 1963 (Gardener 1986a: 71f.; Coleman 1996: 176f.; Hall 1999: 3ff.). There were several levels of "recognition" within these laws, which decreed that the Bank of England must be consulted before a ministry put a bank on any one of the three lists. These procedures secured the informal power of the Bank of England, since the privileges accruing from "recognition" could not be received in any other way. The monitoring of companies which had been recognized as banks by the BoE only took place, at the very most, through informal meetings with senior managemers from these firms (see below).

5.1.3 The Policy Field Until 1970

Until 1970, four factors in the policy field of British banking regulation stood out in particular. First of all, there was the development of a segmented system of banking which evolved historically and was not (as in the United States and Japan) imposed through legislative means (Klein 1991: 70). These developments were largely shaped by the fact that the industrialization process had taken place without universal banks acting as places in which capital could be accumulated for major projects. Of equal significance were the highly specialized demands of a world power's international trading network. This resulted in a strict division of responsibility between deposit banks and merchant banks.

Second, there is the extraordinary stability (particularly in comparison to the other cases studied) of British banking structures over the decades. In 1970, the system was dominated by a handful of banks with a first-class reputation that had operated in a practically unchanged fashion for over half a century. Even during the global depression of the 1930s, which had caused turmoil in all the other countries examined in this study, there had been almost no problems in Britain.

In the light of this stability it seems understandable that the practice of self-regulation in the finance and banking markets, which had developed over such a long period of time, continued to be maintained, since the flexibility and informality of this system seemed to have proven its worth. This policy approach was centrally executed by the Bank of England, an amorphous institution caught between the market and the state which had to constantly work to prevent the imposition of the limits on its room for manoeuvre which would have resulted from any form of codification.

Finally, this stability was heavily influenced by the economic and monetary policy of whichever government was in power at any one time. Direct intervention in the allocation of credit through the imposition of borrowing limits lowered levels of competition within the British banking system. Yet such measures also lowered levels of risk, since within this controlled framework loans were only given to the most financially secure borrowers.[14] After 1971, an interest rate cartel coordinated by the banks ensured good profit margins for the industry and decreased the danger of an individual bank collapse; a mechanism which was used in a similar manner (if in a more formalized way) by many other countries.[15] In the context of these different forms of influence, the success of the British system of banking regulation until 1970 is not only the result of the informality and flexibility mentioned above, it has also been made possible by limits upon competition which were imposed by the state.

5.2 NEW CHALLENGES FOR BANK REGULATORS

At the beginning of the 1970s, major shifts took place in the global financial system as a result of increasing internationalization and decentralization. Yet

[14] Interview with Brian Quinn, 8 October 1999. See also Hall (1999: 5).
[15] See the other case studies in this book.

along with these general challenges, many countries had to deal with problems that had more to do with their own specific development. There were four major issues which caused serious difficulties for regulators in the British case: changes in the banking landscape as a result of the sudden influx of foreign capital into the City; a fundamental restructuring of British state institutions leading to substantial changes in monetary policy; a trend towards the codification of banking regulation; and finally, the increasing prevalence of the universal banking model.

The most recognizable changes resulted from the growing number of foreign banks which were setting up branches and subsidiaries in London. As we have seen, the number of foreign banks in London quadrupled in the twenty years after 1960. The reason for the speed with which this trend took hold was the creation of so-called Euro- or offshore markets in which assets denominated in foreign currencies were traded.[16] These markets came into existence in the City of the late 1950s with the active support of the Bank of England.[17] This has been described as one of the most important developments in the evolution of the London financial market since the Second World War (Reid 1988: 8). As we shall see below, however, it also led to a complete transformation of the City's underlying structures.

In the course of the 1970s, another fundamental shift took place in the formulation of monetary policy. The introduction of the Competition and Credit Control (CCC) system by the Conservative government in 1971 led to the abolition of limits on loan levels and the interest rate cartels set by the clearing banks in order to heighten levels of competition and efficiency in the financial system. Rather than the availability of credit, now the governance of the money markets via the setting of interest rates was to be the main task of monetary policy.[18] Restrictions on competition, which bank regulators had hoped would act as safeguards, were abruptly dismantled. This led to a sudden change in levels of risk which had the potential to destabilize the entire banking industry.

---

[16] The Eurodollar market is a term which describes the trade in dollar assets outside of either the United States or the currency zone of the United States dollar. The term "Euromarket" therefore has nothing to do with the common European currency of the same name.

[17] Several theories have tried to explain the origin and growth of these markets. While several focus on the growing extent of international trade and investment transactions, others have emphasized the expanding gap between transactions on the financial markets and conditions in the economy as a whole. Other studies have portrayed their establishment as the result of widespread avoidance of attempts to regulate financial markets (such as interest rate caps) in other countries such as the United States (Kapstein 1994: chapter 2). An example of such interest rate caps is the "Regulation Q" in the Unites States (see above, p. 59).

[18] A detailed examination of this episode and its consequences can be found in Hall (1983: chapters 1 and 2).

Further challenges to a British system based on informal relationships emerged as a result of the harmonization of international guidelines that made codification inevitable. Of equal importance in this respect was the pressure to adopt the universal banking model in order to stay competitive with other members of the European Community (Cottrell 1994: 1156).

5.3 THE POLICY NETWORK

These challenges were faced by a policy network which tended to operate with a high degree of informality, flexibility, and centralization (at least when it came to the regulators). The following sections will describe the underlying structures of both the private (bank associations) and public (regulatory bodies and the legislative framework) elements of this network.

5.3.1 The British Banking Industry

As we have seen, the British banking sector has developed in a relatively steady way and has managed to avoid major disruptions.[19] It has traditionally been seen as the classic example of a system with a strong history of clear divisions of responsibility which (unlike the United States, France, and Japan) are not legally imposed.

Such a strict segmentation of the banking market emerged as a result of the existence of sharp differences between commercial banks and investment banks as well as the lack of interest commercial banks have displayed in the housing and mortgage markets (Coleman 1996: 177f.). This created space for the establishment of so-called building societies which managed to gain control of over 90 per cent of this market by 1970. These building societies are structured in a very different fashion from the commercial banks. While the latter were characterized by a high amount of concentration resulting in the dominance of the market by a handful of banks, the building society sector was characterized by considerable diversity, with national groups coexisting alongside medium-sized or even smaller, locally based competitors. As non-profit organizations, they benefited from tax breaks and managed to acquire a significant share of the savings and deposit market.

The British market has also been characterized by the absence of a significant state banking sector that can be found in many European countries,

[19] Overviews can be found in Campbell (1974) and Llewellyn (1992).

where state-backed major banks or public-law savings banks often have a significant share of the market. The only exception to this rule is a current account bank owned by the Post Office. This bank was established because of government concerns over the possibility that the dominance of the banking market by a small number of institutions was diminishing competitiveness. Yet in the context of the different forms of interest representation which are the main focus of this study the Post Office bank does not play an important role since it did not, for example, form its own representative association.

Even though the British financial sector as a whole has been characterized as comparatively fragmented when it comes to the nature of its different representative associations (Coleman 1996: 50ff., 248f.), this is not the case with the commercial banks. Only a small number of associations represent the interests of this sector, with little competition between them for members. The most important association is the British Bankers Association (BBA), which was founded in 1919 and only allowed foreign banks to join in 1972 (and then only as associate members). In 1991, the BBA also took over the Committee of London Clearing Bankers, which had existed since the nineteenth century. In the same year, the Committee of London and Scottish Bankers (CLSB, the association representing the six largest clearing banks) was also integrated into the BBA, which began to allow foreign banks to become full members of all of its organizations. In 1972, the BBA already opened itself up to investment banks, which meant that its membership came to encompass all main sectors of the banking industry. With a large number of foreign members, it ceased to be an exclusively national organization. In the period under examination, the BBA has therefore taken part in the wider internationalization of banking in the City of London. By 2001, 178 of the 295 banks represented by the BBA were foreign banks, which meant that the majority of its membership was now based outside the United Kingdom.[20] Further evidence of the BBA's ability to help integrate different parts of the banking sector is the fact that it treats the association representing investment and merchant banks (the British Merchant Banking and Securities Houses Association or BMBA) as a part of its own organization, giving it seats in the BBA executive board.

The only competition the BBA has to face is the activity of the Building Societies Association (BSA), whose members have come into increasing competition with the major banks after the late 1970s by offering customers such bank services as cheque books, credit cards, and automatic telling machines. Of equal significance was the Council of Mortgage Lenders when it came to mortgages, though this organization was created as a result of a BSA initiative.

---

[20] Information provided by the BBA to the author in June 2001.

Nevertheless, conditions in Britain do not have much in common with those in the United States, where a large number of different bank associations compete for access to the legislative process. In this respect, the British banking industry has much more in common with its European counterparts, where a relatively small number of strongly differentiated associations try to avoid unnecessary competition.[21]

Even if the size of a bank was no longer of much institutional importance after the merger of the CLSB with the BBA, this factor clearly plays an important role in the wider market. In the highly concentrated sphere of banking, the autonomous influence of the BBA is limited: "Associations are not as important as the big players in the United Kingdom."[22]

Moreover, only the relationship between the commercial and investment banking sectors has been given an institutional foundation; cooperation with other sectors (such as building societies and finance houses) over issues that are of mutual interest is usually conducted on an ad hoc basis.

Though this does not bring the advantages of the kind of long-term cooperation developed by the German *Zentraler Kreditausschuss*,[23] it does give the relevant actors a considerable amount of flexibility. This reflects the interests of the large commercial banks to a greater extent than any form of cooperation with their closest competitors would. In the British regulatory environment, which has been shaped by informal contact and consultation, senior bankers have access to information concerning plans for regulatory changes anyway, at the latest during meetings between the board of the BBA and the leadership of the main regulatory agency that take place every three months.[24] In general, the industry is largely satisfied with its level of influence, which it considers to be an integral part of the underlying rules and customs of British democracy: "Our philosophy is that it is the role of the government to decide how it wants to regulate, and then the role of the industry is to respond to that."[25]

5.3.2 The Regulatory Agencies

Another defining characteristic of the British system of bank regulation is the high level of centralization when it comes to the role of the state, with the

---

[21] See the case studies examining developments in the Federal Republic of Germany and Switzerland.

[22] Interview Bank of England, 13 October 1999.

[23] For information about the ZKA, see above, p. 93.

[24] Previously the Bank of England and currently the Financial Services Authority.

[25] Interview BBA, 6 October 1999.

Bank of England the only state institution responsible for state oversight and control.[26]

Originally a commercial bank in possession of a Royal charter, then a bank controlled by the state and government, the BoE draws much of its self-confidence from 300 years of experience with London's financial market. In 1844, the Banking Act passed by the Peel government was the first attempt to separate its commercial banking arm (banking department) from the section responsible for currency matters (issue department) (Pohl 1994: 1190). The bank runs the former on an independent basis, paying out a dividend to the Treasury, which directly supervises and pays for the latter.

The BoE claims that its activity as a commercial bank, of which it is extremely proud (Vogel 1996: 96), gives it a better understanding of the market and bolsters its role as the natural supervisor of the banking industry. When the merchant bank Lazard's asked for help in 1931, the BoE acceded to this request in order to prevent panic in the City. But in turn, it committed Lazard's and several other banks to providing the BoE's discount office with vital information about their capital commitments. Failure to do so would result in unfavourable terms in any refinancing agreement (Coleman 1996: 176). As a result, the discount office effectively became the main regulatory body of the BoE.

The Bank is run by a Court of Directors, which consists of a governor, his deputy and sixteen further members. Four of the directors (the so-called executive directors) are directly employed by the bank and are responsible for banking regulation, monetary policy (for which two of these directors have primary responsibility), and the wider infrastructure of the financial system. The twelve non-executive directors come from companies involved in the financial and banking industries. All members of the Court of Directors are appointed by the Crown (which follows the recommendations of the Prime Minister), giving Downing Street a high level of influence over the internal workings of the central bank.[27] Though it is theoretically possible for the

---

[26] Since the Bank of England has been responsible for regulation for the great bulk of the period described in this case study, this section will largely focus on its development. The Financial Services Authority, which has taken over these responsibilities in the 1990s, will be described in the section examining the reform of bank regulation (see Section 5.4.3, especially p. 154).

An overview of the regulatory regime can be found in Pecchioli (1989: 256f.) and General Accounting Office (1994a); a description of the role of the Bank of England can be found in Quinn (1993); a comprehensive analysis of the evolution of bank regulation in the United Kingdom can be found in Hadjiemmanuil (1996).

[27] Before the nationalization of the bank, its twenty-four directors were appointed by its shareholders (Born 1977: 23). Both the Governor and the Deputy Governors serve five-year terms while the directors served for four. It is possible for a director or Governor to be renominated to the same post.

Crown to fire these directors, in reality such a contingency has never taken place (General Accounting Office 1994*a*: 17). The decision over who should be offered the governorship is determined by unwritten rules as well. Since the Governor must not be perceived to have a bias when dealing with conflict and crisis situations, no chairman of a major bank had ever occupied the post until the appointment of Robin Leigh-Pemberton in 1983.[28]

When the Bank of England was nationalized by a Labour government in 1946, the law on which this measure was based did not explicitly define its role, a turn of events which led Eddy George, the Governor in the late 1990s, to comment: "It seems to have been taken for granted that everyone knew what our role was." (George 2000) However, this law did give the bank the power to give "directions" (i.e. order a certain course of action) to commercial banks, though this power has never been formally used.[29] Instead, the bank chose to make its "preferences" known through friendly letters or "nods and winks and eyebrows"[30] in the cosy and closed world of the City's club culture. Indeed this has fostered doubts over the extent to which nationalization led to any change in the behaviour of the central bank (Reid 1988: 207f.). It continued to put a much greater emphasis on cooperating with, rather than controlling, the banks and tried to keep its preferred role, which it had developed in the 1920s, of mediator between government and the City without entirely belonging to either: "The bank has been transferred to public ownership in 1946, but this had produced little alteration in either its relationship with Government or in its regulatory style." (Moran 1991: 66) The former remained informal, non-legalistic, and was maintained through networks based upon a socially homogeneous and distinctive oligarchy. The amorphous position of the Bank spurred one observer in the late 1980s to speak of an "ill-defined constitutional position", which gave its governing body considerable room for manoeuvre (Reid 1988: 220).

This informality was also reflected in the approach taken towards banking regulation. Since practical experience was considered to count more than theoretical training in this environment, a greater emphasis was put upon "informed judgement" rather than "analysis of figures".[31] From the 1960s onwards, pressure grew (largely in reaction to the findings of investigative commissions such as the Radcliffe Committee) for the bank to behave more as a state institution and abandon the mentality of a private enterprise. This led to increased concentration upon economic analysis and formal organization,

---

[28] See Born (1977: 23), Reid (1988: 222). Leigh-Pemberton had previously been chairman of the National Westminster Bank.

[29] See Reid (1988: 207), Coleman (1996: 176), Hall (1999: 3), as well as Dow (1970: 236). Such directives could only be issued with the permission of the Treasury.

[30] Interview Bank of England, 13 October 1999. See Vogel (1996: 96).

[31] Interview Bank of England, 13 October 1999.

with the Bank issuing its own academic journal, the *Bank of England Quarterly Bulletin*, from 1960 onwards. Its personnel base became more professional as well, increasing the influence of its executive directors at the expense of their non-executive counterparts. Yet even after the codification of regulatory practice in the 1970s (see below), the Bank continued to stress the need for flexibility, an attitude reflected by a statement made by a deputy governor who was in office in the 1980s:

> To specify in legislation the way in which capital and risk should be measured; how financial instruments should be treated; the control system banks should use; the amount of capital they should have; and so on: all that detail would be both clumsy and inflexible. In some minds, of course, flexibility is only one step away from weakness and inconsistency. We remain convinced, however, that flexibility is essential to effective and fair supervision.   (Blunden 1987: 382)

As has been mentioned above, rather than being clearly defined in law, the BoE's responsibilities have evolved over a long period of time. What is extraordinary in international comparison is the manner in which it has acquired responsibility for both monetary policy and bank regulation.[32] The possibility that this double role can lead to a conflict of interest[33] has never been seen as particularly problematic by the Bank of England.[34] Though its leadership was aware that this gave the BoE an unusual role internationally, it believed that this strengthened its wider position (Blunden 1987: 385).

The BoE has also considered the promotion and support of London as a financial marketplace to be one of its primary responsibilities (Bank of England 1997: 12; George 2000). These exertions on behalf of the City paid off when the Euromarkets began to establish themselves there (Moran 1991: 55; Vogel 1995: 95). Nevertheless, this role created another potential conflict of interest as well, since the Bank was simultaneously both promoter and regulator of the financial industry. Although the Bank has denied that it was susceptible to such problems, this lack of institutional clarity has become the subject of major political debates.

---

[32] Among the countries examined in this study, the United Kingdom is the only one in which the central bank is the sole body responsible for bank regulation. Though the Fed's area of jurisdiction includes banking issues along with monetary policy, other agencies are responsible for bank regulation as well. The central bank is involved in bank regulation in the Federal Republic and Switzerland, however, in both countries the great bulk of work involving bank oversight is undertaken by separate agencies.

[33] This can be the case, for example, when a tightening of monetary policy is abandoned in order to spare weaker banks or when an interest rate decision is swayed by concerns over the profitability of the banking sector. Mistakes made in the course of bank oversight can also damage the reputation of a central bank, which can be crucial to the perceived legitimacy of decisions concerning monetary policy.

[34] Interview with George Blunden, 7 October 1999.

5.3.2.1 *The Relationship Between the Bank of England and the Treasury*

Along with the Bank of England, the Treasury is another key state actor when it comes to banking policy.[35] While the Treasury plays a dominant role within the British ministerial hierarchy, it does—like its German counterpart—keep its distance from the day-to-day workings of the regulatory system. It only intervenes when it believes that legislative change has become necessary, leaving the formulation of banking policy to the central bank and, when necessary, using the BoE's expertise and experience to its own advantage. New initiatives are often proposed by the Bank and then taken on and implemented by the Treasury.[36] Communication has always been regular and intensive between both institutions, giving the ministry a clear picture of new developments in the field of banking.[37]

The Treasury is formally integrated into the regulatory process in so far as the BoE's directives to the banks need to gain the legal assent of the ministry before being made public. Yet, as we have seen above, the relationship between the central bank and the banks it oversees is shaped by a reliance on informal cooperation, which has made the use of this power to issue directives unnecessary. The influence of the ministry is more of a theoretical nature, creating an asymmetrical relationship between the two regulatory bodies (Coleman 1996: 76). The industry sees the Bank as the more important actor as well, since it is responsible for the implementation of rules and directives, acting as patron of the City and buffer against overregulation.[38] Since the Treasury has a wider perspective than the BoE because of its responsibility for economic policy as a whole, crises involving the regulatory system come to be seen as chances to correct the balance between these two institutions, mostly to the detriment of the central bank (see below).

5.3.3 The Legislative Process

British parliamentary life has always been dominated by its plenum. Though the Houses of Parliament also contain several different kinds of committees, the main focus of parliamentary activity is on the fierce partisan debate in the

---

[35] The relationship between both institutions is described comprehensively in Committee to Review the Functioning of Financial Institutions (Chairman: Sir Harold Wilson) (1980: chapter 25).

[36] Interview with Brian Quinn, 8 October 1999. See Coleman (1996: 76).

[37] Ibid., as well as interview with Lord Burns, 14 October 1999.

[38] Interview BBA, 6 October 1999.

plenum which has become so characteristic of Westminster-style democracy (Norton 1998: 143). Since it is very difficult to conduct informed debate on the details of a bill in the debating chamber of the House of Commons, after their first reading bills are passed on to a stage where they are examined in so-called Standing Committees. Despite their name, the makeup of these committees is constantly changing as new members leave and join with every new piece of legislation.[39] As a consequence, few Members of Parliament with specialist knowledge can be found on the committee level, a situation which undermines any kind of continuity in policy-making: "There are no specialised committees in the British system. Rather there are specialists in ad hoc committees." (Jann 1989: 180) The main beneficiary of this arrangement is the government: "The ad hoc nature of standing committees serves the purposes of the government—wary of informed scrutiny by specialist committees—and successive governments have blocked moves to provide for a greater degree of institutionalisation" (Norton 1998: 144).

The Standing Committees work in public and do not have the right to initiate legislation. Compared with the power of committees in other West European parliaments, their position is decidedly weak (Strøm 1998: table 4). Furthermore, the kind of confrontational politics typical of the House of Commons and party discipline imposed by party "whips" predominate on the committee level as well. As a result, the majority party in parliament is usually able to impose its will (Jann 1989: 181). The kind of specialization that exists in many other parliaments (at its strongest in the American Congress) is not necessarily of any great advantage to the career of individual MPs. Rather, British politics has traditionally been dominated by generalists rather than specialists.[40] The fact that successive studies have demonstrated that changes to legislation are very rarely made in the committee stage is therefore not surprising (Peele 1995: 164, 166).

Party political confrontation is less evident in the Select Committees (Norton 1998: 150). These act purely as collectors of information for Parliament as a whole. Their activity usually culminates in reports on different issues which, as we shall see below, were often used to help formulate banking policy in the course of the 1990s. While Select Committee members do acquire

---

[39] Though MPs can express their preference for membership of a certain committee, there is no guarantee that attention will be paid to such a request (Jann 1989: 180).

[40] On the one hand, this is exacerbated by the British electoral system as British voters demand that their constituency representatives have a strong grasp of all important political issues. On the other hand, generalists are far more likely to be promoted to the party leadership on the front bench of the House of Commons rather than specialists in a specific policy area (Peele 1995: 177f.).

a considerable amount of specialist knowledge in the course of their work and can have some indirect influence on policy-making through their reports, they cannot intervene directly in the legislative process.

Legislation usually emerges as a result of the manifesto commitments of a governing party or initiatives backed by individual ministers. Because of the institutional weakness of Parliament, few amendments are introduced to parliamentary bills, since governments have a high level of control over the legislative process (Jann 1989: 193; Peele 1995: 162; Helms 2001). As we shall see below, parliament can hardly be considered as an independent actor in this policy network.

5.4 THE INTERACTION BETWEEN CRISIS AND REFORM

In the British case, the period between 1974 and 1999 can be split into three phases, which roughly match the respective decades. The 1970s was a phase in which the establishment and consolidation of the bank regulation system took place; in the 1980s, major legislative amendments altered the system; finally, in the 1990s fundamental reforms were undertaken as a result of two major bank collapses that had attracted public attention. This can also be seen as an attempt to solve problems that had become evident from the crises of the previous two phases. Whether these efforts will be crowned with success remains to be seen.

5.4.1 The Secondary Banking Crisis and Codification

The first phase of crisis and reform in the British bank regulation system took place in the 1970s. To a certain extent, the events of those years marked some of the most fundamental shifts in the entire period, leading to the emergence of structures that had not existed previously: "Up to the 1970s, there was effectively no system of bank supervision as we know it today" (Gardener 1986a: 70).

Until then, the United Kingdom had belonged to a group of countries, in which bank regulators operated without any fixed legal rules.[41] The other countries in this group (Canada, Australia, New Zealand) also belonged to the

---

[41] For information on developments described in the following section, see Pecchioli (1989: 45ff.).

family of English-speaking nations,[42] which share British-style legal structures and whose close relationship with one another was strengthened through their membership of the Commonwealth. Yet international trends pointed in the direction of further formalization and codification of bank regulation, forcing the United Kingdom to adapt to new circumstances. As we shall see, the impulse for this change in course did not come from the international sphere; instead it was domestic turmoil in the banking industry known as the "Secondary Banking Crisis" which heightened pressure for reform.[43]

The British banking system, as we saw above, has over a long period of time been characterized by a high amount of stability and the absence of crisis. Even in the 1930s, when most other countries in the Western world were experiencing major banking crises, the British did not have any serious structural difficulties. Though several banks had their problems, this did not lead to a wider systemic crisis. Only three banks failed between the Second World War and the 1970s. Every one of these cases was "escorted" into relatively painless bankruptcy with the help of financial aid packages from the Bank of England, whereby the BoE quickly got its money back after the matter had been brought to a close.[44] This was all taken as proof that the informal approach is an effective one. The crisis, which hit parts of the banking system between 1973 and 1975, was therefore a traumatic experience for many in the industry and has been rated as the crisis which was "the most serious to hit the industry this century" (Metcalfe 1986: 126).

One of the main reasons for this crisis was the introduction of Competition and Credit Control (CCC), a major change in the direction of monetary and banking strategy carried out by the Heath government.[45] Until this point, the monitoring of banks was closely linked to monetary policy. Through the setting of lending limits, the government could intervene directly to determine what the level and growth of total lending should be and those economic sectors which should have first priority when it came to lending (Campbell 1974: 98f.). As a result of these guidelines, banks gave loans to what they specified to be the best targets, creating a low level of risk that made risk evaluation virtually unnecessary.[46] The implementation of these measures

---

[42] On the "families of nations" approach see Castles (1993). For a recent reassessment, see Castles and Obinger (2008).

[43] This interpretation of events is shared by Sir George Blunden, one of the key figures responsible for the creation of a formalized system of bank regulation at the Bank of England (interview with Sir George Blunden, 7 October 1999). See also the assessment of Vogel (1996: 98f.): "The banking reforms [...] responded primarily to domestic and economic pressures."

[44] Interview Sir George Blunden, 7 October 1999.

[45] For information about the system of Competition and Credit Control see Hall (1983: chapters 1–4).

[46] Interview with Brian Quinn, 8 October 1999.

created a cartel made up of the largest clearing banks that became a de facto arm of the government.

The wave of liberalization caused by the CCC was intended to introduce a market system in which a price mechanism could have an allocative effect that would enable banks to freely compete with one another. Deregulation of interest rates for loans and deposits (which had been linked by an oligopolistic consensus to the central bank rate since the 1950s) was the consequence.[47] Furthermore, the big banks were freed from the administrative burdens which had been imposed on them as favourite members of the "banking family" (and which had caused them losses in market share to building societies—see Vogel 1996: 99).

Increasing competition led to a sudden expansion in the amount of available credit which gave a further group of institutions, the so-called fringe or secondary banks, a more significant role in the banking system.[48] They had been established in the 1960s as an indirect result of the informality which had shaped the British regulatory regime. The lack of any clear legal rules meant that there was no strict definition of what constituted a bank. In practice there existed lists of companies compiled by state bodies, which defined the nature of a bank according to a loose set of guidelines in business law and consumer protection guidelines.[49] For example, recognition as a bank according to the terms of section 123 of the Companies Act of 1967 was determined by the Department of Trade and Industry in conjunction with the Bank of England. Yet this did not mean that either the BoE or the DTI believed that they were under any regulatory obligation when it came to banking. The central bank remained true to its philosophy of self-regulation (though it did not maintain the kind of close contacts to fringe banks that it had with established banks), and the DTI did not see itself as either properly equipped or responsible for the formulation and execution of banking policy (Metcalfe 1986: 129). However, these new banks were exactly the kind of financial organizations that needed close oversight, since they often provided mortgage loans which were then refinanced in the money markets, a financial technique which included risky term transformations (Reid 1982).

When the Heath government tried to bring an increasingly chaotic credit market under control through a tightening of monetary policy in the second

---

[47] For information concerning the problem of credit control see Dow (1970: 235–42). A short description of the main problems confronting British economic policy in the post-war era and the political strategies used to overcome them can be found in Busch (1989: chapter 2).

[48] A comprehensive examination of this crisis can be found in Schultze-Kimmele (1978) as well as Reid (1982).

[49] For further information concerning the composition of these lists see Gardener (1986a: 71ff.).

half of 1973, many of these secondary banks were suddenly thrust into a dangerous situation. With rising interest rates and a crash in housing prices, the result was liquidity and even solvency problems for several secondary banks. This led to an intervention by the Bank of England in order to prevent this crisis from spreading to the established "primary banks" which might cause a loss of trust among bank customers that could lead to a bank run. In conjunction with the major banks, the BoE arranged a "life boat" by offering large loans to the twenty-six secondary banks that had come under pressure. Though the bulk of these standby credits were paid back, the costs of this operation still came to several hundred million pounds (equivalent to over £1 billion in current spending terms).[50] Many of these secondary banks were—with help from the BoE—taken over by or merged with larger banks. Those which could not be rescued had to close.

What made this rescue operation extraordinary was its informality along with the ability of the Bank of England to get the major banks to make a massive contribution. While the losses incurred by the central bank came to £50 million, the amount the four clearing banks had to write off topped £200 million (Metcalfe 1986: 127). Their willingness to contribute without any legal obligation shows how well an informal system could function based on a strong sense of solidarity and common interest between members of key "clubs" who were prepared to follow "suggestions" made by the BoE.

Although the informality and club atmosphere of the regulatory system had helped to bring the crisis under control, considerable criticism was voiced over lack of transparency when it came to issues of jurisdiction and institutional responsibility. Further avoidance of change would have probably had a counter-productive effect, politicizing the issue to the extent that root-and-branch change in the sectoral regime might have become inevitable.[51] In order to anticipate such a turn of events, the Governor of the Bank of England decided to put a formal system of bank regulation into place.[52]

---

[50] See Metcalfe (1986: 127), Reid (1986: 100f.), and Reid (1988: 218).

[51] This was considered threatening because of the nature of the debate over the reform of the banking system in the governing Labour party. While one party faction wanted to strengthen the regulatory regime and improve levels of competitiveness, another wanted to nationalize the clearing banks and establish a National Investment Bank in order to systematically channel capital investment into manufacturing industry. A demand for the nationalization of the "big four" was included in Labour's electoral manifesto of 1974 (Schultze-Kimmele 1978: 31). For the justification of these different positions in debates at the Trades Union Congress see Committee to Review the Functioning of Financial Institutions (Chairman: Sir Harold Wilson) (1980). There are interesting parallels to debates in Germany at the same time (see Section 4.2.2 on page 89).

[52] Information on the following was gleaned from an interview with Sir George Blunden, 7 October 1999 as well as Reid (1986: 103f.).

This new system was fully operational within three months. It included quarterly reports and formal interviews of senior bank executives by the Bank of England in which, for example, the structure of their assets and liabilities would be analysed and questioned. This was supposed to enable regulators to anticipate and prevent future problems. Around a hundred banks and sixty finance houses took part in this new system (even though it was not legally binding) as they feared that non-cooperation might lead to unfavourable treatment from the central bank. Moreover, membership in this BoE scheme was quickly used as a further means with which to attract customers in a highly competitive environment. The Bank of England separated the department responsible for regulation from the Discount Office and increased its staffing numbers from fifteen to over seventy employees. The declared aim of these new measures was to monitor all institutions which accepted deposits and improve the quality of oversight mechanisms.

In order to achieve better control over the use of the term "bank", the government also announced new legislation as part of a new "Banking Act". This was partly motivated by the impact of the secondary bank crisis as well as the growing number of foreign banks operating in the London markets.[53] In 1976, the Treasury presented the main goals of legislation affecting this policy field in a White Paper (H.M. Treasury ⟨*United Kingdom*⟩ 1976). It particularly emphasized that in future, the existing form of informal bank oversight should be preserved and that self-regulation (the banks' preferred option) should continue to play an important role.[54]

The Banking Act 1979 came into force on 1 October 1979. It created a legal basis for the regulatory powers of the Bank of England and introduced a licensing scheme as well as new guidelines for the administration of deposit accounts. The traditional BoE approach to bank regulation still survived within this framework. The set of criteria anchored in this law remain relatively general while their interpretation and implementation was left to the central bank (Pecchioli 1989: 46). Precise measures dealing with such issues as owners' equity were not put into place (Reid 1986: 105). The Treasury had originally wanted to create a department of its own responsible for the implementation of bank regulation in order to keep the Bank of England from getting caught up in any possible conflicts of interest. The difficulties involved in simultaneously trying to be the regulator and friend of the banking industry were also recognized within the BoE. Yet Governor Gordon Richardson succeeded in imposing his view that it would not be sensible to transplant the established system from the BoE to another institution.[55]

---

[53] See Schneider, Böttger, and Uebe (1980: 15). See also above, p. 128. The government's plans were made more concrete in a White Paper a year later.

[54] See Schneider et al. (1980: 15 ff.).   [55] Interview Sir George Blunden, 7 October 1999.

The law differentiated between two categories of bank: "recognized banks" and "licensed institutions". This effectively reproduced the old distinction between primary and secondary banks. However, the turmoil caused by the secondary bank crisis led to the imposition of much stricter regulations for new forms of banking than for "recognized" banks. For example, the latter were not required to submit information over their business dealings since the law simply assumed that they would provide such information voluntarily (Schneider, Böttger, and Uebe 1980: 24ff.). Despite formalization and codification, significant elements of the old informal "club" system had therefore survived.

5.4.2 Johnson Matthey Bankers and Reform of the Regulation System

At the beginning of the 1980s deposit protection, a further element of the banking regulation system, was formalized through a set of guidelines in the Banking Act which came into force in 1982. Under the administrative control of the Bank of England, a "Deposit Protection Fund", which guaranteed 75 per cent of deposits up to £10,000, was established by the banks (Reid 1986: 106). In stark contrast to the informality which usually dominated proceedings, the membership of this scheme, its claims mechanism, as well as its modalities of payment were all subject to highly detailed regulations.[56] This reflected the controversy which surrounded this deposit protection scheme and concerns that its impact might lead to such negative consequences as "moral hazard" behaviour. In the wake of this debate, only a moderate level of protection (particularly in comparison to regulations in the Federal Republic: see Section 4.4.1.3 on page 105) was agreed upon.

This newly formalized system of banking regulation had to cope with its first crisis in October 1984, when Johnson Matthey Bankers (JMB), a bank classified as a recognized bank, began to experience serious financial difficulties.[57] By itself not a particularly large or important bank, it was heavily involved in the London gold market through its parent company, Johnson Matthey plc. This increased the Bank of England's fears that a collapse could have wide-ranging negative effects. Yet the attempt to force other banks to take over JMB in order to solve the problem ended in failure. The central bank had no other option than to purchase JMB itself for the symbolic price of one

---

[56] With thirteen paragraphs, the regulatory framework for the deposit protection fund is only slightly shorter than the guidelines for the oversight of the entire deposit business (Schneider, Böttger, and Uebe 1980).

[57] On the following see Reid (1988: 224–33) and Hall (1999: chapter 5).

pound along with a cash infusion of £50 million from its parent company. Though the clearing banks had committed themselves to sharing the costs in principle, they had not specified the amount of money they would commit to such a rescue operation. Since the estimated losses of JMB amounted to £250 million (much larger than the net equity of the bank), a guarantee of £150 million was needed to stabilize the situation.

The difficulties encountered by the Bank of England in its efforts to distribute the costs of a potential rescue operation were an indication of a change of atmosphere in the City. The central bank's original proposal, which would have essentially been a repeat of the strategy developed ten years previously, when the BoE covered 10 per cent of the costs and the major banks dealt with the rest, was rejected by the banking community. The commercial banks put the blame for the collapse squarely on the shoulders of the regulators and therefore on the central bank (Reid 1988: 227). After some negotiation, an agreement was finally reached whereby the latter contributed £75 million, the clearing banks provided £35 million, the gold banks £30 million, and the investment banks £10 million.[58]

Yet the row over the collapse of JMB did not remain limited to the financial community. It also caused a serious rift between the Bank of England and the Treasury because of disagreements over regulatory quality. For JMB had blundered into near bankruptcy through the incompetence of its management rather than as a result of unforeseen circumstances (Hall 1999: 31). Political factors also came to play a role, since the strict market-based approach of the Thatcher government was threatened by the fact that a bank that had encountered difficulties had to be nationalized and saved with public funds. Particularly dangerous to the position of Chancellor Lawson was a false statement he made at the House of Commons, since the central bank only informed him about an additional deposit of £100 million pounds made by the Bank of England in order to provide JMB with operating capital after the fact (Lawson 1992: 405ff.). The resulting criticism in parliament of the Chancellor's handling of the crisis laid bare the tensions that existed between the two institutions.

After this crisis, it became clear that the existing system of regulation had to be overhauled and that such a task could not be solely left to the Bank of England. Lawson not only set up a commission of inquiry under the stewardship of Governor Leigh-Pemberton, he deliberately placed senior officials from the Treasury on its main committee (ibid.). This commission began its work in December 1984 and handed in a report six months later which recommended

---

[58] Because of further arrears, the total sum needed sank to about £60 million, reducing the total payments made by all participants by about a half (ibid. 228).

a series of reforms (Committee Set up to Consider the System of Banking Supervision (Chairman: Robin Leigh-Pemberton) 1985: 22ff.):

- The dual system of regulation was dismantled so that all banks could be treated equally.

- Auditors were to be integrated into the regulatory system and able to report in future directly to regulators when dealing with criminal behaviour or management failures.[59]

- Making a false declaration to the Bank of England was to become an offence under the criminal code.

- The department responsible for regulation should get an increase in staff and be made more familiar with the practices of commercial banks.

In December 1985, the Treasury signalled its acceptance of these proposals in a White Paper. Furthermore, major institutional changes to the regulatory process were put into place despite the resistance of the Bank of England. Within the central bank, a Board of Banking Supervision was established (BoBS) that could advise the Governor and implement the Banking Act (after it had been amended). Along with three members of the BoE (the Governor, his deputy, and the head of the regulatory section), this board also had six independent members who, as specialists in banking issues, were supposed to bring external expertise to the regulatory process.[60] Though the Governor does not have to follow the recommendations of the Board, when he decides to take an alternative course of action, he has to explain his reasons for ignoring the Board's advice in a report to the Chancellor. The Board also produces a report of its own as part of the wider BoE annual report. Both administrative mechanisms strengthened the position of the Treasury (which now indirectly received access to the regulatory process) and weakened the bank, though not to the extent that had been originally intended.[61] In any case, these changes

---

[59] Until this point, it was only possible to do this with the assent of the relevant bank for confidentiality reasons.

[60] The external members of the board were jointly appointed by the Governer and the Chancellor of the Exchequer for a term of five years (General Accounting Office 1994a: 18). The original White Paper had proposed that the Board should only consist of five members (H.M. Treasury (*United Kingdom*) 1985: 11).

[61] In the run-up to this amendment package, Chancellor Lawson tried to transfer responsibility for bank oversight to an agency outside the Bank of England. According to the deputy governor (who shared Lawson's views), this initiative failed because of the resistance of the Governor and Prime Minister (interview with Sir George Blunden, 7 October 1999). However, Lawson presents a different version of events in his memoirs. According to Lawson, the Prime Minister wanted to strip the bank of its regulatory powers after it had failed to prevent several bank crises, a course of action prevented by Lawson himself. He claims that, although he shared the Prime Minister's interpretation of events, he had not wanted the bank to suffer a loss of prestige which might damage British national interests (Lawson 1992: 408f.). Nevertheless,

created an incentive for the BoE to coordinate any future policy with major players in the government and the industry in order to gain the approval of the Board of Banking Supervision (Coleman 1996: 85).

The amended Banking Act of 1987 adopted the positions of the White Paper and came into force at the end of the same year.[62] The introduction of a new obligation for every bank to send an annual report to auditors at the Bank of England as well as the creation of the Board of Banking Supervision led to a further reduction in the scope for informal decision-making within the regulatory system.

5.4.3 BCCI and Barings Bank: Impulses for Fundamental Reform

Yet the reforms described above did not manage to calm the world of British banking regulation. Two bank collapses, which took place in the first half of the 1990s, led to a further examination of regulatory practices that resulted in fundamental reforms and wide-ranging institutional changes.

The first case was the scandal surrounding the Bank of Credit and Commerce International (BCCI).[63] Founded in 1972, this bank was an international conglomerate based on a holding company in Luxembourg which consisted of two financial entities, of which one was incorporated in Luxembourg and the other in the Cayman Islands. Though the bank had branches in the Unites States, France, and Hong Kong its main place of business was London while its majority shareholders lived in Abu Dhabi. Such a structure was ideal for avoiding the attention of bank regulators and, as it turned out, was used for exactly this purpose. After the collapse of BCCI, investigators discovered that the bank had been used to make fictitious loans, set up hidden deposits, launder profits from the drugs trade, and provide financial support to terrorist groups.

Although rumours about these nefarious dealings had started to circulate in 1988 and shareholders had had to make a supplementary payment from their own capital in order to cover bad loans, the bank was only closed on 5 July 1991 after a report (demanded by the Bank of England) by the BCCI's auditor, Price Waterhouse, uncovered "massive and widespread fraud" in the bank. Yet even in April of the same year, the BoE had assured the Chancellor that

since Lawson was unable to grant the Bank of England greater independence when it came to monetary policy because of a veto by the Prime Minister, there is some doubt over whether he had the power to set policy in the fashion described in his memoirs.

[62] It also included an increase in the deposit guarantee from £10,000 to £20,000 (Hall 1999: 39).

[63] A more comprehensive analysis of this case can be found in Dale (1992: 196–204), Bingham (1992), Herring (1993), and Hall (1999: 121–35).

BCCI's British branches were in solid financial condition (Hall 1999: 121ff.). The closure of the bank when it was on the brink of insolvency meant that many of its British customers lost their deposits,[64] forced major changes in international regulatory structures,[65] and led to widespread criticism of the regulatory practices of the Bank of England.

An independent investigation headed by Lord Justice Bingham and a report by the Treasury and Civil Service Select Committee of the House of Commons both found serious deficiencies in the methods used by bank regulators and criticized the manner in which the central bank handled the entire BCCI case. The recommendations included such improvements as:[66]

- A substantial increase in the number of on-site bank inspections.
- The development of personnel skills and technological tools essential for the early recognition of fraudulent and criminal business practices.
- An improvement of internal communication and cooperation with the Treasury.
- An enhanced role and better working conditions for the Board of Banking Supervision.

Though it had been considered, the transfer of regulatory powers to an independent body was not included in these proposals.[67]

While the BoE claimed that it had acted properly within the framework of existing law, it did accept the reforms recommended by the Bingham Report. It announced the creation of a Special Investigations Unit under the leadership of a former executive of KPMG (a major auditing firm) along with the establishment of a specialized Legal Unit run by a specialist recruited from outside the bank (Hall 1999: 133f.). This led to a more differentiated and formalized regulatory structure.

The lengthy legal battles between the different actors involved in the BCCI affair had not yet died down[68] and the scandal was still fresh in the memory of the public, when the next major collapse hit the headlines and led to further

---

[64] Most heavily hit were import–export traders from the Pakistani community, who had entrusted their deposits with BCCI because of its Muslim ownership (interview Maximilian Hall, 12 October 1999). If these deposits were over £20,000 or were held in other currencies such as US dollars, they did not enjoy the protection of the deposit insurance scheme.

[65] As a direct result, new "minimum standards" were put in the Basel Accords in July 1992; this led to a "BCCI directive" on the European Union level, which enshrined these changes in European law in 1995 (Herring 1993: 84ff.).

[66] See Bingham (1992: chapter 3) and Hall (1999: 130f.)   [67] See Bingham (1992: 181).

[68] Trials took place both in the United States and the United Kingdom. Along with the criminal cases, the receivers, shareholders, and former BCCI customers decided to sue the Bank of England (because of alleged negligence).

questions over the competence of British regulators. This was the collapse of Barings Bank.[69]

While BCCI had always had a shady reputation, Barings Bank (also known as Baring Brothers & Co.) had been one of the City's most venerable institutions. Founded in 1763, it was among the oldest banks operating in the United Kingdom; even the Queen had an account there. Barings was also famous among insiders for being the cause of the first major financial rescue operation in the City coordinated by the BoE, after Barings executives had caused a major liquidity crisis through a disastrous transaction involving Argentine state bonds in 1890. It is not without irony that the failed attempt of a similar rescue operation a century later ended the era of clubby solidarity which had been started with a crisis at the very same bank a century earlier.

Ostensibly known for its conservative approach, the bank had set up a subsidiary registered in the Cayman Islands which owned a company in Singapore called Baring Futures Singapore. This subsidiary was specialized in the highly complex area of derivatives trading, with particular focus on options warrants in the Japanese Nikkei index. This business was initially very successful, making up over a quarter of the earnings of the Barings group (Tickell 2001: 425). However, when a heavy earthquake destroyed the Japanese industrial town of Kobe, the value of stocks on the Nikkei index began to tumble causing massive losses for Baring Futures Singapore. In order to conceal them, Nick Leeson, the head of the Singapore office, made a succession of trades on the stock and derivatives markets with ever-greater sums of money in the hope that the prevailing trend in the Japanese financial markets might change again. When this failed to take place and Leeson's miscalculations were discovered, the positions he had taken were so high that Barings had to be declared insolvent on 26 February 1995, forcing the Bank of England to send receivers in to save as much of the bank as they could.

Before having to take these measures, the central bank had tried to organize a financial "lifeboat" in the traditional manner. In a late night session, the Governor begged the financial community to come to the aid of a bank which had until then been a pillar of the British establishment. Though senior bankers who took part in this meeting declared themselves prepared to commit contributions of up to £600 million to any rescue attempt, this was not nearly enough to cover the unlimited and potentially many billions of pounds covered by Leeson's derivative contracts (Tickell 2001: 427).[70] Since there was

---

[69] Case studies on the Barings affair can be found in Hall (1999: chapter 12), Tickell (1996), and Tickell (2001).

[70] The technical details of the Barings affair as well as an exact explanation of how derivatives contracts are structured can be found in a case study by Chew (n.d.) for the International Financial Risk Institute accessible at http://riskinstitute.ch/137550.htm [8 Dec 2007]. This study

no way to predict how these contracts might develop until their due date, any guarantee would have had to have been of an unlimited nature, a commitment that neither the BoE nor the major private banks were prepared to make. Unlike the Johnson Matthey Bankers affair, this collapse ended in insolvency rather than a takeover by the BoE. Any use of public funds in this affair would not have received the support of the Chancellor of the Exchequer, a stance which was made clear in a statement he made to the House of Commons on 27 February.[71] Instead, he commissioned a detailed report on the Barings case from the Board of Banking Supervision.

While this collapse was caused by the unauthorized actions of a single rogue trader, the conclusions of the official investigation, which were made public in July 1995, indicated that (along with serious mismanagement in Barings itself) regulators at the Bank of England had been negligent in their dealings with Barings Bank. BoE officials believed the verbal assurances of senior executives at Barings and gave informal assent to the circumvention of the rule stating that financial commitments exceeding 25 per cent of a bank's net assets needed to be registered with British authorities (Board of Banking Supervision 1996: 197, 244f.). The 300-page report contained a detailed list with seventeen recommended improvements to the system and demanded that a further report on their execution should be submitted by the end of the year.[72] By January 1996, the BoE announced the complete implementation of these proposals (Hall 1996*a*). The independent investigation of the regulatory process was conducted by Arthur Andersen, a major management consultancy. The approach of this management consultancy brought, as one responsible department head in the BoE admitted, "fresh wind" into the discussion (Foot 1996: 359).[73] The results of this investigation together with a general assessment were presented in July 1996 (Arthur Andersen & Co. 1996). Once again, detailed suggestions for further improvements of the system were included.

puts the net worth of the contracts when Barings was declared bankrupt at $27 billion at a point when the bank's assets only came to $615 million.

[71] See the transcript of the relevant debate in Hansard, House of Commons Debates, Volume 255, 27 February 1995, col. 693ff.. It can be found online (including the Chancellor's statement on the insolvency of Barings) at http://www.publications.parliament.uk/pa/cm199495/cmhansrd/1995-02-27/Debate-1.html [8 Dec 2007].

[72] Among them were a strengthening of the powers to monitor conglomerates; an examination of balance information demanded from banks; the establishment of internal guidelines for certain regulatory procedures; an increase in the numbers and powers of on-the-spot inspections of banks; and finally independent oversight of the regulatory process itself.

[73] If the different factors named by Foot (discussions with banks over their perceptions of the regulatory process; discussions with regulators monitoring other sectors of the economy or other countries; and generally a "comprehensive and open debate") already merited such characterization, then this throws a rather unfavourable light on the reforms so far.

Much that was in this list of improvements sounded familiar. It included the formalization and making public of goals and standards for bank regulators, an increase in the number of on-the-spot inspections and an increase in the number of staff, which should contain better trained and more experienced experts in the field (Arthur Andersen & Co. 1996: Attachment).[74] Such recommendations had already been made in previous reports. The most constructive innovation was a proposal to introduce a so-called RATE system (*Risk Assessment, Tools of supervision, and Evaluation*), a model based on nine factors which could help restructure and streamline the regulatory process.[75] Such impulses for the formalization of the regulatory regime received support from both experts and the government.[76] As a consequence, the Bank of England announced a fundamental restructuring of the department responsible for regulation and committed itself to the implementation of the recommendations made by the management consultants (Bank of England 1996).

After the crises of the 1990s and an avalanche of reports and investigations, a strong foundation for the future work of bank regulators in the United Kingdom seemed to have been established. While Arthur Andersen had provided the basis for a systematization and streamlining of the bank regulation system, it had not recommended that any relevant tasks should be transferred to other institutions. Yet such drastic proposals were not to be expected, since the central bank had itself commissioned the review produced by the management consultancy. By contrast, after the Barings case the Treasury and Civil Service Select Committee took a significantly more critical position towards the regulatory structures of the BoE than they had done in the wake of the BCCI affair. It expressed serious concerns over the possibility that the Bank of England had become susceptible to "regulatory capture", and demanded more distance between regulatory agencies and the banks, which, according to the committee's report, did not necessarily deserve the level of understanding they had received from the regulators. Finally, the report threatened that "it may be

---

[74] The report demonstrated that the regulatory department had considerable staffing problems. Most of its employees did not consider it a place where they could enjoy a promising career because of its low promotion opportunities and low prestige. This led to rates of staff turnover which were double that of regulatory agencies in other countries, while the average age of a regulator was under thirty. According to Arthur Andersen, another cause for low morale was the fact that the BoE kept transferring personnel into other departments. Though this was supposed to increase their horizons, it meant that they could rarely get in-depth experience of any specific department (Arthur Andersen & Co. 1996: 29).

[75] It is telling that an institution which was supposed to ensure that banks maintained certain control mechanisms as part of their management structure, did not have any comparable system itself!

[76] "This was their bright idea." (Interview FSA, 15 October 1999); (Hall 1996*b*: 529). Cf. also the CAMEL approach (*Capital adequacy, Asset quality, Management competency, Earnings, and Liquidity*) used in the United States, which follows a similar structure (Khademian 1996: 25ff.).

necessary that in order to bring about the necessary cultural change banking supervision will have to be taken away from the Bank of England" (Treasury Select Committee 1996: xxxvi).

The committee report was produced by a group which was mostly made up of Members of Parliament from the governing Conservative Party, a sign that patience with the existing system of banking regulation and the crisis that surrounded it was beginning to dry up in the political sphere. This also reflected a raging debate among academics and journalists over whether the Bank of England, with its many duties,[77] was overextended and should only focus on its responsibilities in the area of monetary policy (*The Economist* 1993). The BoE leadership had already rejected such ideas and emphasized the advantages of having responsibility for monetary policy and bank regulation in the hands of one authority. They even went on to announce their belief that "the British system of bank regulation [...] in its present form is the best in the world" (*Neue Zürcher Zeitung*, 20 Nov. 1996: 10).

Nevertheless, and to the surprise of many involved in banking, a fundamental institutional reform was implemented in 1997.[78] When in opposition, Labour Party politicians had already declared their doubts over the ability of the Bank of England to oversee ever more complex financial transactions competently in parliamentary debates dealing with the Barings case, going on to declare that a "culture of complacency" was endemic in this institution.[79] Labour's massive victory in the national election of May 1997 created the conditions for its leadership to make what it considered to be essential reforms. On 20 May 1997, the new Chancellor of the Exchequer, Gordon Brown, announced a complete reorganization of the oversight mechanisms for all companies involved in financial services.[80] The regulation of banks, stock

---

[77] Next to monetary policy (for which at that time the Chancellor of the Exchequer bore ultimate responsibility and not the central bank) and bank regulation, the BoE was also responsible for administering the deposit insurance system, the printing of banknotes, the management of government finances, strengthing London's position as an international financial centre, and arbitrating disputes between companies and creditors. This is far more than is usual for central banks in comparable countries (*The Economist* 1993: 67).

[78] Even the head of the bank regulation department was surprised by this initiative (interview FSA, 15 October 1999). Similar sentiments were voiced in interviews with experts (Professor Goodhart, 30 September 1999) and representatives from the industry (BBA, 6 October 1999).

[79] See Hansard, House of Commons Debates, Volume 255, 27 February 1995, col. 695f. as well as Volume 263, 18 July 1995, col. 1458.

[80] This took place two weeks after the Chancellor of the Exchequer had given the Bank of England the power to set interest rates and monetary policy independently. After increasing its prestige enormously, he promptly transferred many of its responsibilities into the hands of other or new bodies. Many senior members of the BoE would have preferred it if these measures had been announced at the same time as part of a more balanced package (interview Bank of England, 13 October 1999). Instead, the removal of regulatory powers was seen as an affront, leading the Governor to even consider resignation (*Financial Times*, 22 May 1997).

exchanges, and insurance companies was to be in the hands of a single agency. This reflected the fact that the distinction between these different sectors of a modern economy was becoming less and less relevant:

[I]t is clear that the distinctions between different types of financial institution— banks, securities firms and insurance companies—are becoming increasingly blurred. Many of today's financial institutions are regulated by a plethora of different supervisors. This increases the cost and reduces the effectiveness of the supervision.

There is therefore a strong case in principle for bringing the regulation of banking, securities and insurance together under one roof. Firms now organise and manage their businesses on a group-wide basis. Regulators need to look at them in a consistent way. That would bring the regulatory structure closer into line with today's increasingly integrated financial markets. It would deliver more effective and efficient supervision, giving both firms and customers better value for money, and would improve the competitiveness of the sector and create a regulatory regime to genuinely meet the challenges of the 21st century.[81]

Banking regulation and the system of self-regulation for stock and bond markets overseen by the Financial Services Act of 1986,[82] were accordingly to be merged together into a newly formed Financial Services Authority (FSA).[83] While the legal framework of bank regulation was not changed, these measures led to major institutional reforms. This ended a century of informal oversight and a quarter of a century of BoE regulation of the banking industry.

The implementation of these reforms were not yet finished by the time the period of investigation of this study ends. The relevant Financial Services and Markets Act 2000 was only a passed a year later.[84] A comprehensive process of consultation with consumer representatives, industry and professional associations, as well as specific companies and individuals took a considerable amount of time. After it came to a close, however, the reform package was implemented with great speed and in a pragmatic fashion described by one expert[85] as "the traditional British way of doing these things". Passed in 1997, the Bank of England Act[86] transferred control over banking regulation to the Securities and Investment Board (SIB) and changed its name to the Financial Services Authority (FSA). At the same time, the different self-regulating bodies

---

[81] Hansard, House of Commons Debates, Volume 294, 20 May 1997, col. 510. See also the Treasury press release at http://www.hm-treasury.gov.uk/newsroom_and_speeches/press/1997/press_49_97.cfm [8 December 2007].

[82] For further information on the Financial Services Act 1986 see Vogel (1996: 108–14).

[83] First under the aegis of the Department of Trade and Industry and then the Treasury.

[84] Detailed information about this law and its guidelines, its legal text and the negotiations in the Houses of Parliament as well as the reports from the different committees can be found in http://www.fsa.gov.uk/development/legal/fsma/.

[85] Interview Lord Burns, 14 October 1999.

[86] This Act gave independence in monetary policy to the BoE.

under the oversight of the SIB,[87] which were about to lose many of their responsibilities anyway, decided to subcontract their work to the FSA. With 500 officials from the bank regulation department of the BoE transferred to the FSA, a highly effective new agency was quickly established which began work even before its legal basis had been confirmed by parliament. The fact that its head office was located in the London Docklands rather than the City also marked a geographic break with long-standing traditions.

5.5 CHARACTERISTICS OF THE POLICY FIELD

During the period of 1974–99 and when compared to the other cases covered in this study, it was probably the United Kingdom in which banking regulation as a policy field experienced the greatest upheavals. An extremely informal and, in the strictest sense, almost non-existent system of banking regulation went through a series of transformations that led to the establishment of new regulatory bodies, further codification as well as several reform initiatives launched in reaction to different crises which finally led to fundamental institutional change. This policy field seems to have been generally characterized through shifts in regulatory style, a reactive approach to policy-making, and the capacity for the implementation of fundamental change when the political will for reform existed.

5.5.1 Changes in the Style of Regulation

In the years after 1974, the British system of bank regulation has experienced major changes. This process could, with some qualifications, be described as "the end of informality". For a long period of time, this system had been focused on cooperation,[88] close relations with the industry, and permanent, though informal, dialogue enhanced by the geographical concentration of the financial world in London. Many of these characteristics have had positive effects, leading the newly reconstituted FSA to announce that it wishes to preserve many elements of the traditional approach to regulation. Yet the transformation of a close, 300-year-old relationship between banks and the Bank of England, where the proverbial "raising of the governor's eyebrows" was perhaps one of the most effective instruments of control and shared bonds

---

[87] Securities and Futures Authority (SFA); Investment Management Regulatory Organisation (IMRO); Personal Investment Authority (PIA).

[88] In the academic literature this has been described as "meso-corporatism" (Moran 1991).

were shaped by a club-like social environment, into a purely working relationship between banks and a new and geographically distant agency represents a substantial cultural shift.

Nevertheless, these institutional changes have largely constituted a reaction to fundamental changes that have taken place in the London financial markets in the last quarter of the twentieth century. They are a good example of how the regulatory response to banking crises changed over time. Where the Bank of England had been able to organize a concerted rescue operation with the help of the financial community in which the costs were shared during the secondary banking crisis in the 1970s, it came to experience resistance to such measures in the course of the 1980s. This ultimately led to a situation where the BoE had to take over Johnson Matthey Bankers, and to cover the great bulk of the costs needed to restore JMB's financial health. When it came to the Barings Bank crisis in the 1990s, the Bank of England was no longer even capable of conducting a unilateral rescue, since an increase in potential costs was accompanied by a commensurate decline in the level of solidarity. After all avenues explored by the BoE had failed, Barings was finally taken over by ING, a Dutch banking consortium, for the symbolic price of £1 and cover of all its liabilities.

The Barings crisis symbolized the final demise of the informal club system. The key players in the City no longer felt themselves bound to customs and traditions which had existed for generations; their actions were now purely determined by the interest of their own specific banks and corporations, making it impossible for them to cover losses incurred by a competitor. The sudden dominance of the market principle had therefore altered the mechanisms of governance. The process of codification that took place at the end of the 1970s (along with the BoE's dual role of regulator and main source of refinancing) had already resulted in an increasingly distant relationship between the senior executives of major banks and the Governor of the Bank of England.[89] As a result, his power—based as it was on soft power factors such as trust and prestige—over the financial community began to decline. This became evident in a series of crisis situations. For example, when in 1981 the foreign bank HSBC wanted to take over one of the largest British banks[90] despite the fact that there was already a domestic bidder, the HSBC board contacted the Governor. Yet despite the Governor's negative response to its takeover plans, HSBC still put in a bid. Such open defiance of unwritten rules undermined the authority of the BoE even further (Reid 1988: 216, 218).

[89] Interview Sir George Blunden, 7 October 1999.
[90] It was the Royal Bank of Scotland.

While the regulatory efforts of the Bank of England had initially remained limited to discussions with senior bank executives, it gradually expanded the spectrum of its contacts lower down the management hierarchy, giving it access to a much wider store of information. This naturally made it necessary to expand staffing levels in the central bank's regulatory department. While there had only been twenty regulators in the 1970s, the codification process led to considerable growth in their numbers. In the early 1980s personnel numbers had expanded to 60 and increased again to over 300 in the 1990s. By 1997, over 450 regulators were transferred to the FSA.[91]

Yet the end of a regulatory regime based on informality, which resulted in the growth of the formal power and decline of the informal influence of regulators, had its costs as well. Many experts believe that the BoE could have discovered the management failures that beset BCCI and Barings Bank much earlier within the context of the old system, giving it the necessary time to take rescue measures before the point of no return had been crossed by both banks.[92]

Conversely, the extent and impact of these changes should not be exaggerated. The British regulatory style is still characterized by a stronger emphasis on management interviews than the American system, where regulators rely almost exclusively on statistical data (Hall 1999: 143f.). The combination of "objective" figures with "subjective" judgement in the formulation of analyses of current trends is one of the great strengths of London as a financial marketplace; a fact that was highlighted by the Arthur Andersen report. The FSA has therefore declared that one of its main priorities is to continue working in this manner.[93]

5.5.2 Reactive Policy-making

A further distinguishing feature of this policy field is that bank regulators only acquired new powers and developed new techniques in reaction to major crises. They therefore acted in a *reactive* rather than an *anticipatory* fashion. The means to undertake on-the-spot inspections were only put in place after the Johnson Matthey Bankers affair, a fraud unit was only established in the wake of the BCCI scandal, while a group specialized in complex financial transactions was only set up after the collapse of Barings Bank.

The fact that policy-making was reactive should not be surprising, since the first steps towards the establishment of a formal system of banking regulation

---

[91] Figures stem from an interview with Brian Quinn, 8 October 1999, as well as an interview with the FSA, 15 October 1999.

[92] Interview Brian Quinn, 8 October 1999.   [93] Interview FSA, 15 October 1999.

took place in reaction to the secondary banking crisis, the first bank crisis to hit the United Kingdom after a long period of stability. Although these banking crises in the final quarter of the twentieth century were not nearly as damaging as the banking crises experienced by other industrialized nations in the 1930s, as we have seen above, the sudden emergence of instability within the banking sector was a major shock for the British financial establishment. On the other hand, the differing level of intensity of such crises may explain why there were such divergent reactions to them. While in the 1930s the United States, Switzerland, and Germany established separate institutions with an elaborate legal framework dealing with regulatory questions, in the United Kingdom regulatory powers were conferred upon the established and inherently conservative Bank of England, with accompanying legislation merely a codification of pre-existing regulatory practices. This resulted in a kind of "muddling through", in so far as political action was defined by reactive adaptations to new problems, an approach which has often been seen as typical of the British style of policy-making (Richardson 1982; Coleman 1996: 176).

5.5.3 The Weak Role of Parliament

Another characteristic of the British case is the fact that parliament has only played a minor role in various attempts to adapt this system to new challenges. The contrast becomes quite pronounced when one compares it with conditions in the United States. Advice for the executive often comes from outside through recommendations from ad hoc external committees or independent investigative commissions. The Radcliffe Report in the late 1950s, the Wilson Committee in the late 1970s or the Leigh-Pemberton Committee in the 1980s are examples of influential proposals for reform in this policy field. Yet parliament hardly played a role in them.

This is less the result of the fact that this is a highly technical policy field—though this certainly explains its relatively low politicization in an era of overwhelming change (Busch 2001). The crises of the 1990s did however lead to a certain level of politicization reflected in the investigations and reports of the Treasury and Civil Service Committee. The losses incurred by individual depositors in the BCCI affair and public attention attracted by the role of Nick Leeson in the Barings scandal certainly played a significant role in this respect. Yet the two reports which emerged from these scandals gained much less attention in public and institutional debate that the inquiries conducted by Lord Bingham and Arthur Andersen, even though the recommendations made by all of these different committees and reports were remarkably similar. The role of Arthur Andersen particularly reflected the weakness of the British parliament, since a massive reorientation of the state's regulatory approach was initiated by a management consultancy rather than the legislature.[94]

5.5.4 The Easy Implementation of Fundamental Reform

A final characteristic typical of the British case is the comparative ease with which fundamental reforms were implemented. This becomes particularly evident when contrasted with the United States, the other "Anglo-Saxon" case examined in this study. While changes in American banking policy got ground down to such an extent during the course of the legislative process that they usually ended in failure, in the United Kingdom even the most fundamental reforms have been implemented without any great difficulty. A government with a strong parliamentary majority can act swiftly and decisively without having to take the views of other relevant actors into account. This has always been considered as one of the key elements of the Westminster system, and has been confirmed in the course of this case study.

Most intriguing is the existence of a kind of "pre-emptive" obedience. Once a political decision is made in principle, its precepts are followed even before legislation has been passed in parliament. One example of this kind of behaviour is the establishment of banking oversight structures by the Bank of England after 1974, the creation of the Board of Banking Supervision in 1986 (even before the Banking Act 1987), and the establishment of the Financial Services Authority in 1997. In all these cases, everyone behaved "as if" (at times for years) the legal framework was already in force, even when this was not the case.

As has already been pointed out, the contrast to the American case (in which all veto points were used extensively) could not be stronger. In the United Kingdom, however, this form of institutional behaviour is usually commented on with the statement that "it is the traditional British way of doing these things",[95] although it is usually admitted that this would "probably not be possible in many other countries".[96]

5.6 SUMMARY: THE BRITISH CASE

Since the reforms of the Thatcher era, the British economic system has been regarded as one strongly shaped by economic liberalism. This has led many to

---

[94] Jann (1989: 354–7) speaks in the British case (already for the 1980s) of an "exclusion of parliament" or an "outsourcing of formulation of law" when it came to the legal framework.
[95] Interview Lord Burns, 14 October 1999.   [96] Interview FSA, 15 October 1999.

falsely conclude that Britain had always been characterized in this way. In fact, state intervention and a considerable emphasis on economic planning played a central role in policy-making from the end of the Second World War to the mid-1960s at the very least (Shonfield 1965: chapter VI; Dow 1970; Hall 1986: chapters 3 and 4).

As described above, at the beginning of the 1970s credit steering in the domestic financial sphere was abandoned in favour of greater liberalization.[97] The result was a crisis of adaptation exacerbated by a shift in the strategies of market participants and state responses to their actions. Those in charge of monetary policy tried to prevent a credit explosion by raising interest rates, triggering the secondary banking crisis. Since this crisis took place in the phase of early liberalization of the 1970s, it had far less drastic consequences than similar events experienced by other European countries in later decades such as Spain in the 1980s and Sweden in the 1990s.[98]

Matching developments in the German case, this British crisis took place shortly after conditions on international markets were transformed by the end of the system of fixed exchange rates. Yet in contrast to the collapse of *Herstatt-Bank*, these events were not causally linked to turmoil on the international markets; rather, they were caused by domestic reforms. This is probably the reason why the reforms initiated as a consquence did not include any attempt to grapple with the potential problems emerging from changes on the international level.[99]

Another reason was the strong position of the Bank of England, which had traditionally dealt with issues involving banking regulation and had responded so quickly to the crisis of 1973–4. The existence of an established institution in this policy field made the creation of new bureaucratic competitors unlikely. Yet in the face of desegmenting markets and growing competition, the problems inherent in this decision became increasingly obvious in the dynamic environment of the City. The BoE relied upon its long-standing experience and intimate knowledge of the London markets, an approach which quickly proved to be "too close to the industry, too trusting".[100] The piecemeal introduction of changes in reaction to a succession of crises did not help: "New statutory powers were grafted on to the Bank's older habits of informality, and with equal regularity proved inadequate to the task" (Story and Walter 1997: 235). When it came to essential reform of the system of banking regulation,

---

[97] The liberalization of rules dealing with international markets took place with the removal controls on capital movement in 1979.

[98] For further information on these cases see Busch (2001), Tranøy (2001), and Pérez (2001).

[99] In contrast to the German reaction, which led to the development of strict guidelines for major loans and the imposition of the equal treatment of speculation in shares with credit risks.

[100] Interview Maximilian Hall, 12 October 1999.

London proved far less innovative than it was when it came to the introduction of new forms of financial trading and services.

Whether the reform that led to the creation of the FSA will lead to the transformation of the "culture" of regulation which has been demanded so often is not yet clear. The first studies conducted on this new system indicate that this might be the case.[101] What has probably changed is the state's approach towards this policy field, from an emphasis on adaptation and reaction towards an attempt to plan for and pre-empt future problems. Whether this new system will work better than the old order has not been proven yet. Nevertheless, though the United Kingdom was once a latecomer to the codification and formalization of the regulatory regime, when it comes to the concentration of unitary financial oversight into the hands of a single agency that has become increasingly popular in other countries, the British have proven to be early starters.

[101] Interview Maximilian Hall, 12 October 1999.

6

Switzerland: High Risks, Joint Responsibilities

In the popular imagination, the banking industry has become synonymous with Switzerland. Seen as a haven of stability and security, the Swiss confederation offers the qualities that banks most highly prize. Equally important is a reputation for centuries-long experience in domestic and international banking. Aside from its important place in Switzerland's national image, the banking sector also contributes significantly to the country's net domestic product and comprises an unusually large proportion of its work force.[1] With an annual growth rate of 5.5 per cent between 1960 and 1992, double that of the entire Swiss net domestic product (2.0 per cent), there was a fivefold increase in the net value of the banking sector product. In parallel, the number of bank workers increased annually by 3.8 per cent, tripling the number of those employed in the banking industry during this period. The banking sector's share of Swiss GDP amounted to 11 per cent in 1998, thereby enjoying a larger share than almost every other industry with the exception of the retail and wholesale trades. In the banking sector, worker productivity is double that of manufacturing and three times that of the service sector. As Table 6.1 indicates, in international comparison the level of employment in the Swiss banking sector is very high: approximately 50 per cent more than in the Federal Republic of Germany and double that in the United Kingdom or the United States.

Yet, given the massive changes in the world of international finance over the last thirty-five years, economic dependence upon an internationally first-class banking sector represents a considerable risk. The resulting exposure to foreign capital flows coupled with the banking industry's sizeable share of the net domestic product and general workforce could have a negative impact upon the Swiss economy in the event of a crisis. Moreover, there exists a strong tension between the heavy involvement of a traditionally export-oriented Swiss economy in an ever more integrated global economic system and the refusal by

---

[1] The following figures stem from Hirszowicz (1996: 32) and Schweizerische Bankiervereinigung (2000*b*).

Table 6.1. Banking employment as share
of total workforce (in per cent, 1994)

Switzerland	3.14
Federal Republic of Germany	2.07
France	1.86
United Kingdom	1.53
United States	1.21
Japan	0.64

Source: Schweizerische Bankiervereinigung (2000*b*)

the Swiss state to take part in the process of international political integration. The manner in which Switzerland deals with such apparent contradictions and how the Swiss define and achieve their goals is, in the context of the globalization debate, a particularly interesting conundrum. The following section will first explore the historical development of the Swiss banking system and those state institutions charged with overseeing and regulating it before moving on to an examination of the relevant actors in the political sphere. A closer analysis of the decision-making process in the area of bank policy will bring to light a combination of liberal consensus and partial politicization. While the latter may at times cause considerable public controversy, it has not yet led to any lasting consequences. Despite the high risks mentioned above, the policy outcomes of the Swiss state have largely been crowned with success.

6.1 THE HISTORICAL BACKGROUND

6.1.1 Formation of the Banking System

The origins of the Swiss banking system can be traced as far back as the fourteenth century.[2] In the late Middle Ages, bankers and moneylenders were already practising their trade in the area around Geneva. By the second half of the eighteenth century, a similarly early point when compared to the financial development of other European states, Switzerland had already acquired a good reputation in international financial circles. This was largely due to the export by private bankers of vast amounts of surplus capital belonging to the Swiss urban patriciate (made up largely of the vast sums paid for Swiss mercenaries by major European powers). Underpinning this growing involvement

---

[2] The information on the establishment and structure of the Swiss banking system stems from Bänziger (1985), Bänziger (1986), Birchler and Rich (1992), Born (1977), Cassis (1994), as well as the ground-breaking study by Ritzmann (1973).

in foreign financial markets was the low domestic demand for capital in a country whose avoidance of major military conflict had prevented the accumulation of significant state debt. By contrast, massive demand for capital generated by a spendthrift French court and government channelled the great majority of Swiss capital investment into France via Geneva (Ritzmann 1973: 31). In German-speaking Switzerland there followed a conscious attempt to emulate this profitable Genevan example. As a result, banking houses were also established in Zurich, Basel, and Bern towards the end of the eighteenth century.

The structure of the major finance and credit institutions at the beginning of the nineteenth century had therefore been shaped by a combination of low domestic demand for capital, a lack of state demand for credit, and a surplus of capital accumulated in the hands of a small, socially homogeneous ruling class. The need of this small oligarchy for international financial services was satisfied by highly specialized private bankers who themselves showed no interest in the domestic market.

In the first decades of the nineteenth century, *Sparkassen* (as in Germany these are public-law banks administered by local government) were founded across Switzerland as well as several other European countries. They were supposed to give the less wealthy sections of the population (domestic servants, small tradesmen, traders, and peasants) the opportunity to save and invest in order to secure their financial future. Often founded through the philanthropic work of members of the liberal middle class, these institutions satisfied domestic demand for financial services on a regional basis.[3] Between 1815 and 1830 alone, a hundred *Sparkassen* were established throughout the Swiss confederation (Cassis 1994: 1015). In most cases these local financial institutions proved highly successful, not least because the willingness to save proved very high among the general population. According to the statistics of the *Sparkassen* themselves, in comparison with other European states not only did Switzerland have the highest number of savers per capita, it also enjoyed the highest average amount of accumulated capital per savings account (Bänziger 1986: 6; Ritzmann 1973: 36). By 1840, *Sparkassen* were the dominant form

---

[3] Partly through the so-called *Gemeinnützige Gesellschaften* which were founded at the beginning of the nineteenth century and still exist today. These philanthropic institutions were influenced by social thinkers and provided many services that are now the responsibility of the state social welfare system. In the nineteenth century, their work was focused on such very different areas as the establishment of free public schools, spreading information about healthy eating, material security in old age, the amelioration of poverty in mountain communities, and maintaining the distinct identity of the Swiss Confederation. For example, in 1859 the *Schweizerische Gemeinnützige Gesellschaft* bought the meadow where the Swiss Confederation was founded (known as the *Rütliwiese*) in order to protect it from construction and donated it to the national government.

of banking in Switzerland. Yet, the combination of private banks operating internationally and regionally oriented *Sparkassen* proved insufficient to cover increasingly imminent financial demands generated by the industrialization process. In order to finance major investment projects such as the construction of railway networks, financial institutions with a stronger capital base (such as joint-stock banks) were needed. Furthermore, cantonal governments began to establish their own banks in order to help develop their regional economies. Thus, two types of bank came into existence which have played a dominant role in the Swiss banking system to this day.

The first of these are the major corporate banks. Following the example of the French *Crédit Mobilier*,[4] they were established in the years after 1850. The first joint-stock corporate banks were founded for political reasons. As with the Parisian banks on which they modelled themselves which were founded in order to break the dominance of the Rothschilds, the radical democratic Genevan politician James Fazy hoped that Swiss joint-stock banks could weaken the position of those Genevan bankers who belonged to his political opponents. Through the foundation of the *Banque Générale Suisse* in 1853, Fazy aimed to put these private banking circles in their place. Though the *Banque Générale Suisse* collapsed in 1869 after some initial successes, other corporate joint-stock banks founded during this period proved highly successful. Most of these were established in the German-speaking cantons. In 1856 the *Schweizerische Kreditanstalt* was founded in Zurich; in 1862 the *Bank in Winterthur* (which in 1912 merged with the *Toggenburger Bank* to become the *Schweizerische Bankgesellschaft*); 1872 saw the foundation of the *Baseler Bankverein* out of the merger of five former private banks. After 1897 this bank became the *Schweizerischer Bankverein* through a merger with the *Zürcher Bankverein* and several smaller banks. The *Bank Leu*, which had been founded in 1755 as a state bank only to be privatized in 1798, together with the *Schweizerische Volksbank* founded in 1869 (the only cooperative modelled on the German credit cooperative banks) rounded out the field. These were the five major national banks which survived into the late twentieth century.

The second type of bank, which came into existence in the mid-nineteenth century, was the publicly owned cantonal bank. The earliest to be established was the *Kantonalbank Bern*, founded in 1834, followed by the *Banque Cantonale Vaudoise* in 1846. The aim of cantonal governments was to foster economic development. Their business activity remained limited to their home cantons, and their deposits were protected by cantonal governments which proved an advantage when competing with other banks and *Sparkassen* in

---

[4] For information on the *Crédit Mobilier*, see Section 4.1.1.

Table 6.2. Market share of Swiss bank groups, 1880 (%)

Bank type	Market share
Cantonal banks (14)	28.1
Bodenkreditbanken (64)	21.9
Local banks (148)	24.4
Sparkassen (217)	13.9
Big banks (5)	11.7

Source: Bänziger (1986: 4)

times of crisis. After 1860, a second wave of cantonal banks were formed largely for political reasons. Fears that the growing domination of corporate equity banks was leading to a worsening of the financial plight of indebted farmers, small traders, and tradesmen, led to growing resistance against this part of the banking sector. Under the slogan "The Peoples' Banks Against Masters' Banks", the *Demokratische Bewegung* campaigned against the close relationship between railway companies, banks, and the central government in order to liberate the capital markets from the control of a small circle of major industrialists. The most important result of this campaign was the establishment of the *Zürcher Kantonalbank* in 1870, which quickly became the biggest cantonal bank as well as one of the largest banks in Switzerland (Cassis 1994: 1016).

The basic structure of the Swiss banking system had therefore taken shape by 1880.[5] The economic significance of the *Sparkassen*, which had been so dominant in the first half of the nineteenth century, began to diminish over time since the cantonal banks were able to attract a large number of their savers (Born 1977: 339). In great contrast to the German banking system, credit cooperative banks were only marginal players. The market share of different types of banks (according to balance of payment totals with the respective number of bank institutes in brackets) during this period is shown in Table 6.2.

No one type of bank had attained a position of dominance by the end of the nineteenth century. The high degree of concentration, characteristic of the Swiss banking system a hundred years later (in terms of market share rather than number of institutions), had not yet taken place. This process of consolidation was the result of several major crises, which shall be examined below.[6] What all these different types of bank in Switzerland had in common,

---

[5] With the exception of the foreign banks, which only began to enter the Swiss market in the second half of the twentieth century.

[6] In fact the cantonal banks dominated approximately half of the market at the turn of the century and on the eve of the First World War a third, a market share that was larger than the

however, was a lack of any division of labour between them along the lines of the British financial structures that had developed during this period. By contrast, the "universal bank" model predominated in Switzerland; in other words, all banks offered the full spectrum of financial services, from savings accounts and the administering of financial transactions right up to trading on the stock market. Yet one significant difference did exist between these competing forms of banking. While the major corporate banks and private bankers were not constrained by any geographical limitations (even working on an international basis), the cantonal banks were legally obliged to exclusively focus on their respective cantons. Moreover, the operational scope of local banks and *Sparkassen* did not go much beyond the borders of their respective towns and cities (Born 1977: 336f.).[7]

The 1890s witnessed another expansion of the banking system as a hundred new banks were founded in a ten-year period. This large increase was stimulated by the rapid growth of the electrical power and tourist industries. In proportion to population, there is little doubt that the Swiss banking sector was becoming an overcrowded market. The first phase of what was an inevitable process of consolidation took place in the run-up to the First World War. Between 1910 and 1913, a succession of bank collapses led to the striking of over eighty-five institutions from the commercial register. In addition to bankruptcies, a set of mergers between large cantonal banks also took place. After the First World War and the subsequent economic convulsions of the 1920s major corporate banks expanded quickly because of their heavy involvement in the international financial system. However, with the worldwide economic crisis following the stock market crash of 1929 and the collapse of many German banks in the early 1930s, this international commitment almost crippled the Swiss banking system. The introduction of exchange controls in a desperate attempt by the German state to stabilize its economy froze the great bulk of foreign assets held by Swiss financial institutions. The resulting threat of mass insolvency ultimately forced the Swiss government to follow the German example and issue a state guarantee for the banks in crisis.

This crisis hit the major corporate banks hardest of all, with net profits falling by more than 50 per cent in the following years. Five of the eight biggest

---

quarter held by the major banks. The Swiss major private banks were therefore in a much weaker position than their British, French, or German counterparts. Only in 1962 did their combined balance exceed that of the cantonal banks (Born 1977: 337; see also Albisetti et al. 1977: 84).

[7] This differentiation still exists today (Birchler and Rich 1992). It was moreover the strong domestic competition of the cantonal banks which forced the corporate banks to extend their operations onto the international market and issue securities in other countries at a relatively early point in time.

banks had to be rescued with state funds. The economic crash which followed also hit many smaller banks, sixty of which were either put into liquidation or taken over—more than 10 per cent of the banks operating in Switzerland at the time.[8] The crisis of the 1930s led (as it did in the United States and Germany) to a much higher level of government intervention through the establishment of a banking regulation system, which shall be discussed in more detail later. After the end of the Second World War, the Swiss banking industry attained a central role in the domestic economy, especially in terms of employment figures and contribution to GDP, which it has kept to this day. The international orientation of the Swiss financial sector intensified by the early 1960s and 1970s not only as a result of the growing activity of Swiss corporate banks in international financial markets, but also through an unprecedented increase in the number of foreign banks operating in Switzerland itself (Hirszowicz 1996: 478).

6.1.2 The Development of State Regulation

In the first half of the nineteenth century, Swiss authorities had not believed that it was necessary to set up a state regulatory authority to monitor the newly established *Sparkassen* sector. In tune with the dominant "liberal" approach which dominated policy-making during this period, the general consensus between the governing parties was that such a method of control was not needed, an attitude which seemed to have been validated by the experience of the previous few decades. A statement made by the *Gemeinnützige Gesellschaft* in 1853 claimed that "state protection and state control are not necessary for *Sparkassen* which had been freely founded for the common good, since their fruitful development free of such forms of limitation best proves their vitality".[9] However, even during this period exceptions existed in the cantons of Bern and Freiburg. In both cases, a state licence was mandatory if "over a longer period of time [...] the assets of others were being managed". Yet experiences with these localized regulatory regimes had hardly been promising and they were particularly unsuited for the pre-emption of problems since, as a contemporary observer noted, "the state authorities only discovered that losses had been incurred when it was too late".[10]

The general position of the banking sector changed fundamentally in the mid-nineteenth century; not only because the philanthropic motives of the *Sparkassen* had become increasingly secondary as a more commercial

---

[8] See Bänziger (1986: 88), Birchler and Rich (1992: 412), and Born (1977: 523).
[9] Cited from Bänziger (1985: 7).   [10] Cited from Bänziger (1986: 6f.).

approach began to dominate their operations which led to a commensurate rise in the size of deposits and level of risk. In particular, technological innovations in industry and transport triggered major structural changes in the agricultural sectors. The expansion of Atlantic shipping and the railways made it easier to import agricultural produce from distant producers, leading to a halving of cereal prices over a short period of time. As a result, many farmers started to concentrate more on dairy production, a shift which necessitated high levels of capital investment.

Demands for the cheap credit which a strong dairy industry needed have become a recurring political issue since this period. In 1860, the first political controversy resulting from such agricultural developments led to a politicization of banking policy, which became increasingly directed against the major corporate banks and their growing dominance of the capital market (Cassis 1994: 1016). Under the slogan "The Peoples' Banks not Masters' Banks", which has already been described above, the *Demokratische Bewegung* established several new cantonal banks in order to create a strong alternative (Bänziger 1986: 3).

The issue of deposit protection was, with the exception of moments of crisis, less significant in political terms in the second half of the nineteenth century than conflicts over how the financial and banking sectors were organized in Switzerland. This debate principally took place between centrally oriented and federally oriented groups as different solutions to this conflict evolved over several decades into the early twentieth century. As in other federal states such as Germany, the standardization of currency in Switzerland took place at a very late point in time. The federal constitution of 1848 did not contain any clauses regulating such matters although currency issues had been discussed at the time. In the revised constitution of 1874, the federal government gained powers to regulate the issuing of banknotes, though it was explicitly refused a monopoly over issuing currency (His 1938: 706f.). Until this moment, control over the issuing of banknotes had lain in the hands of the Cantons (Born 1977: 36ff.). The *Berner Kantonalbank*, a public-law institution, was the first bank to issue currency in 1834, quickly followed by a private bank called the *Bank in Zürich*. Until the mid-1860s, the number of banks issuing banknotes (so-called *Zeddelbanken*) had risen to twenty and by 1880 they numbered over thirty-six. Yet even an agreement between these banks in 1876, whereby each bank would accept the others' banknotes, could not provide a solution to this unsatisfactory situation since only half of the competing banks issuing currency were party to it.

The introduction of the silver Franc as legal tender through the Swiss coinage law of 1850 ensured that Switzerland became a de facto monetary province of France. When the *Banque de France* terminated the discounting privileges enjoyed by Swiss banks in the Paris money markets the Swiss financial sector experienced a major liquidity crisis. Since the Swiss Confederation did not possess a central bank with the power to control the currency, the federal government was unable to print paper money which could have replaced the French Francs that had been taken out of circulation. This forced the Swiss government of that time to pass a law in August 1870 which made the American dollar and British sovereign legal tender in Switzerland (Ritzmann 1973: 93).

This crisis reignited the debate over plans to introduce a central bank that could deal with currency issues. Yet the banknote law (*Banknotengesetz*) of 1875, which implemented the relevant articles of the federal constitution covering the standardization of Swiss currency, was opposed by the issuing banks and was ultimately repealed after its federally minded opponents succeeded in winning a referendum on this issue (His 1938: 707). Thus further standardization of currency in Switzerland did not get off the ground. Only in 1882 was a law enacted which put the issuing banks under the obligation to apply for state licences and present annual business reports. This led to the creation of the first federal regulatory regime for at least a part of the banking sector (Bänziger 1985: 15).

Because of the rapid economic development which transformed Switzerland, a unified currency and monetary policy as well as the establishment of a central bank became a matter of necessity. In 1891, an amendment to the federal constitution that provided the federal government with a monopoly of the issuing of banknotes was finally passed that also granted the establishment of a central bank. Yet this only opened the next round of political debate, which centred this time on whether the central bank should be a public "state bank" or a private "joint-stock bank" under state oversight. While conservatives and federally minded political forces resisted the introduction of a "state bank", the Liberals as well as the political Left supported this model, which was enshrined in the national bank law (*Nationalbankgesetz*) of 1897. Yet that law was overturned by a referendum. Only in 1905 was the privately organized *Schweizerische Nationalbank* (SNB) established as a central bank of which both banks and cantons held a substantial share and whose charter tried to reconcile private and state interests.[11]

The takeover of the issuing of currency by a new central bank forced the thirty-six banks which had issued banknotes in the nineteenth century to find new areas of business. Although the development of a unified monetary policy

---

[11] A detailed description of this conflict, which provides interesting insights into the development of the Swiss association and party systems as well as examples of the pre-parliamentary decision-making process in operation can be found in Zimmermann (1987).

stabilized interest rates and had other "rapidly emerging positive economic effects" (His 1938: 713), it also had a major impact on the commercial banking sector. Tougher discounting conditions and greater competitive pressure led to difficulties in the banking sector which culminated after 1910 with the collapse of over sixty local banks by the First World War (Born 1977: 335f.). This "overcrowded" banking system experienced a period of consolidation which fostered a resurgence of public support for some form of state regulation of the banking system (Bänziger 1985: 28ff.). A moment of crisis in the early 1890s (caused by overspeculation in railway bonds which had crashed the stock market) had already spurred different initiatives for the improvement of deposit protection. These had, however, foundered on the complexities of a cantonal legislative process which could not take such issues further because of the limitations on cantonal power enshrined in federal law (Bänziger 1986: 9–11).

The next initiatives for the creation of a stronger regulatory regime were started on the federal level. With greater public pressure caused by the banking crisis and declining confidence in the industry, a first blueprint for a new banking law was put together between 1914 and 1916. It contained four main points of emphasis:[12]

1. The introduction of bank licences
2. Standardized guidelines for billing and disclosure
3. The introduction of audits
4. The establishment of an agency responsible for all state regulation of the banking sector called the *Bundesamt für das Bankwesen*, which would be overseen by a commission made up of banking experts

However, even this piece of legislation failed before it had reached the parliamentary stage because of the fierce opposition of the central bank and the banking association. Both feared that such forms of control would have undermined the tradition of banking confidentiality to such an extent that it could trigger the mass withdrawal of foreign deposits.[13] This was considered to be such a delicate matter that these legislative proposals were kept secret in order to prevent them from having any negative effects on international confidence in Swiss banks (see ibid. p. 48).

---

[12] See Bänziger (1986: 40–6).

[13] In the face of growing demand for capital after several years of war, both Germany and France had moved towards high levels of taxation. Foreign depositors were therefore particularly interested in ensuring that their domestic tax agencies remained unable to access the money they had deposited in Switzerland.

The pressure for further banking legislation began to subside after the end of the First World War, partly because the banking system had managed to stabilize itself which increased confidence in financial institutions as a whole. Yet this was also accompanied by major political shifts which led to pressure on banks from an entirely new ideological direction. After the replacement of an electoral system based on the first-past-the-post principle with proportional representation, the decades-old dominant position of the Liberal (or *Freisinn*) movement was broken by a resurgent Social Democratic Party. Moreover, many farmers had left the Liberals and joined a new Agrarian party. This resulted in widespread demands for lower rates of interest and stronger state control of the banks. The heavy involvement of major corporate banks in the international bond market led to strong criticism of the resulting export of Swiss capital, which ultimately heightened interest and mortgage costs. Threats by the powerful farmers' association and its political allies to call a referendum on banking issues forced the SNB and the bankers association to make an informal deal to provide consumers with better conditions in the first of several so-called Gentlemen's Agreements.[14] This form of policy-making was considered to be more effective than any piece of legislation, even when further proposed laws were put on the table at the federal level. The major corporate banks declared their readiness to consult the *Nationalbank* in future before providing major loans to foreign clients. Attempts by the SNB to turn this informal deal into a written agreement however failed to overcome the resistance of the bankers association (Bänziger 1986: 76f.).

In the early 1930s, a succession of bank collapses in Germany triggered a massive banking crisis in Switzerland which resulted in the codification of a previously informal regulatory regime. Since the growth of the Swiss banking sector was largely caused by the growing international commitments of the banks, it is not surprising that these banks were most heavily affected by this international financial crisis, effectively "importing" their problems from Germany.

As in the crisis of 1913, there were widespread calls for more state control of the banking sector. The Social Democratic Party made such demands during the elections of 1931, although it avoided making any proposals for nationalization. In reaction, both the *Nationalbank* and the bankers' association did their utmost to prevent any of these proposals from being turned into law and focused instead on putting similar reforms into place in another voluntary "Gentlemen's Agreement". Despite these efforts, proposals for the extension of

---

[14] This term was not chosen coincidentally—in fact the SNB modelled these arrangements on the traditionally informal agreements between the Bank of England and the banks in the City of London.

disclosure requirements to include the cantonal banks as well as 100 further banks (which would therefore cover over 90 per cent of the balance sheet total of the banking system) ended in failure in the autumn of 1931. After several fierce debates and after further state subsidies had failed to prevent the re-emergence of financial instability in large parts of the banking sector in the autumn of 1933, a legal framework for banking regulation in the form of a Banking Act (*Bankgengesetz*) was finally passed in 1934.

This law, which has remained the basis of state banking regulation in Switzerland to this day, did not take shape as quickly as it may superficially seem to an observer.[15] In fact, it was only possible to develop an effective law so quickly because policy-makers could draw on the great amount of research and redrafting which had gone into previous initiatives. To a considerable extent, it simply codified voluntary (by the major corporate banks at least) practices such as the auditing of annual statements, the balancing of financial commitments with liquid assets, and the maintenance of transparent internal management structures. Moreover, the legislative initiatives of the 1930s drew on proposals made in reaction to the crises of the First World War period which included external auditing and the establishment of an advisory commission made up of experts.

This commission, known as the *Eidgenössische Bankenkommission* (EBK), had only five members, with a president and vice-president who were appointed by parliament and had to present regular reports (see below). In conjunction with external auditing, the oversight of banks was thus organized at arm's length from the state, reflecting the wishes of the financial department and the *Nationalbank* (Bänziger 1986: 104, 106). The latter had recommended that an independent commission be created with responsibility for the implementation of the *Bankgengesetz* (Banking Act) as well as oversight of the banking sector. The proposal to develop a deposit protection scheme effectively run by a (yet to be founded) national banking association ended in failure. It encountered resistance from both the Liberals as well as Social Democrats for a variety of different motives: while the former opposed any of these kinds of structures as a dangerous infringement of economic freedoms,

---

[15] Member of the Federal Council (*Bundesrat*) Otto Stich—obviously frustrated by the slow speed of the Swiss legislative process—wrote in an introduction for a book produced for the fiftieth anniversary of the establishment of the *Eidgenössische Bankenkommission*: "An observer today could only boggle at the pace of the legislative process in those days: three weeks after the *Bundesrat* had made its decision to create a specific banking law, the first proposal had been drafted which a year later was submitted to the confederate councils despite a delay in the work of the *Bundesrat*, coming into force (accompanied by an administrative by-law) only a year later on 1 March 1935" (*Eidgenössische Bankenkommission* 1985: v). For a more detailed and realistic description of the process see Bänziger (1986: 102–22).

the latter saw these initiatives as the first step towards the kind of corporatism which in Italy and Austria had ended in the rise of fascist regimes.

The institutional environment in which regulators had to work remained relatively stable in the years after the enactment of the Banking Act. The establishment of a comprehensive system of deposit protection only took place several decades later, and then only on a voluntary basis.

6.1.3 The Policy Field Until 1970

When reviewing the historical development of the Swiss banking system and the state regulatory regime until the beginning of the 1970s, several important factors begin to emerge.

In general, banking policy in Switzerland has often been the subject of substantial political controversy, a fact that is not surprising if one looks at the important economic role this sector plays in terms of employment and GDP. Nevertheless, the level of politicization has remained moderate when compared to the extensive politicization of banking issues in the United States during the nineteenth century. Although there are similarities when one looks at the underlying conflicts in both countries (particularly an agrarian lobby's demands for cheap credit), in Switzerland compromises were usually reached after long periods of negotiation as the debate surrounding the establishment of the *Schweizerische Nationalbank* demonstrates. Characteristic of these debates were efforts by all sides to ensure discussions were conducted in a calm and informed fashion in order to achieve a general consensus that could protect laws from any referendum initiatives. Only rarely do policy-makers display intransigence, even when there might be a tactical advantage in such a stance, since the desire to achieve some kind of agreement usually trumps the particular concerns of an interest group. For example, though Social Democrats regularly demanded stronger state control, they never proposed nationalization of the banking industry (Bänziger 1986: 92). With this moderate stance, they accepted key elements of a political consensus over the principal parameters in the area of state banking policy.

One of these key elements is a traditionally liberal approach to state regulation of the banking sector. The Swiss state never tried to acquire the means to impose government control. As described above, neither the finance department nor the central bank wanted to take responsibility for banking regulation, opting instead for private auditing under the oversight of a small, parastate commission. The lack of any state influence over the development of the commercial banks was in harmony with this tradition, encouraging the major corporate banks as well as smaller and regional banks to adopt the universal banking model.

A third characteristic element is the negative effect the strength of the Swiss banking sector had on the wider economy. Problems resulting from capital export recurred so often during the nineteenth century that informal guidelines had to be introduced. In the second half of the twentieth century the influx of foreign gold created similarly daunting problems which led to repeated upward revaluations of the Franc, threatening Swiss businesses that depended on exports. Since this problem could not be solved by any kind of voluntary domestic guidelines, both the government and the *Nationalbank* had to use administrative measures such as deliberately worsening investment conditions for foreigners (including negative interest rates or even interest bans) in a bid to improve the situation (Kloten and Stein 1993: 312).

6.2 NEW CHALLENGES FOR BANK REGULATORS

As in the German case, there was relatively little pressure to adapt the Swiss system of banking regulation to new conditions. Because of traditionally liberal attitudes and the codification that had already taken place in the 1930s, Switzerland was already on course to match established international trends. Nonetheless, there were several, in some cases quite nationally specific, challenges which this system had to face. In particular, there was the question over the potential effects on Switzerland of growing and widening European integration. From their nucleus in the original six founding nations and throughout their subsequent expansion, the new institutions of the European Community underwent a process of expansion which had a considerable impact on the banking sectors as well as systems of banking regulation of those countries which refused to take part.[16]

The steady influx of foreign money caused considerable economic problems by contributing to a considerable rise in the value of the Swiss Franc. In order to slow this trend down and blunt its negative effects for Swiss exporters, measures such as negative interest rates and even a ban on interest were introduced for foreign investors. Despite these deterrents, in the mid-1970s many foreigners tried to exchange their liquid assets (often held in currencies suffering from heavy inflation) for the comparatively stable Swiss Franc. In the process, many tried to circumvent the restrictions on the export of capital which existed in their homelands.

[16] See Regul and Wolf (1974).

As a result, Switzerland often had to deal with heavy recriminations that the Swiss tradition of banking confidentiality was an incitement to break the law from other countries trying to cope with economic problems. This often led to demands that relevant guidelines should be made to conform to the standards of most other states. Yet the retention of banking confidentiality was considered by the Swiss to be the key to the success of their own banking system, an attitude which increased the potential for conflict with the rest of the international community.[17]

6.3 THE POLICY NETWORK

6.3.1 The Swiss Banking Industry

6.3.1.1 *The Structure of the Banking Sector*

Similarities with the German case and differences with developments in the United States and the United Kingdom emerge from the segmented nature of the banking industry in Switzerland. It was effectively split between privately run commercial banks, a strong cooperative sector, and state-backed banks. In official Swiss bank statistics, these different groups are denoted as the major banks (classified as major corporate banks in the above parts of this case study), cantonal banks and the so-called *Raiffeisenkassen*. There is also a fourth group made up of different forms of mixed bank administration (such as the regional banks and *Sparkassen*) as well as a variety of foreign banks operating in Switzerland.

As Table 6.3 demonstrates, the relative share of the Swiss market held by these different groups has diverged considerably since the 1930s.[18] After losing considerable market share in the crisis of the 1930s, the major banks were able to reconquer lost terrain after the end of the Second World War, becoming the dominant banking group in the course of the 1970s. These gains have been achieved at the expense of two other groups, namely, the cantonal banks on the one hand and the regional banks or *Sparkassen* on the other. While

---

[17] See the article titled "*Bankgeheimnis*" in Albisetti et al. (1977: 98–103). The special nature of Swiss banking confidentiality is (beyond the fact that it enjoys the protection of the civil code when it comes to the secrecy of customer bank accounts) that it is also protected by clauses in the criminal code which in the eyes of the Swiss banks increases customer confidence in the banking system. Breaking banking confidentiality is a crime which automatically leads to official investigation and prosecution by the state. It can result in a six-month jail term and a fine of over sFr 50,000. See Mast (1974: 487ff.) as well as Schweizerische Bankiervereinigung (2000b: 36).

[18] Cf. also Table 6.2.

Table 6.3. Market share of Swiss banking sectors (by balance sheet), 1930–98 (in per cent)

	1930	1945	1960	1973	1990	1998
Big banks	39.8	26.5	31.3	46.6	48.4	66.7
Cantonal banks	35.1	42.4	35.5	23.7	19.8	13.3
Regional banks / *Sparkassen*	23.9	26.4	23.9	12.5	8.7	3.5
Raiffeisen banks	1.2	3.5	3.6	2.7	3.1	3.0
Foreign banks	—	—	—	—	*12.4	8.0

*1989
Source: 1930–73: Albisetti et al. (1977: 84); 1990: Kloten and Stein (1993: 314);
1998: Schweizerische Bankiervereinigung (2000b: 6)

these two groups (in relation to the balance sheet of the Swiss banking system) controlled over two thirds of the Swiss market in 1945, over fifty years later they only had a share of one-sixth of this market. By contrast, the market share of the cooperative *Raiffeisenkassen* has remained remarkably stable while the share of the market held by a heterogeneous group of foreign banks operating in Switzerland stayed at approximately 10 per cent.

Along with the shifting strength of these different groups, the Swiss banking market has also undergone a process of consolidation during this period. As Table 6.4 indicates, this trend has had a particularly significant impact on the major banks in the 1990s. The five major banks operating in the early 1990s[19] were whittled down to three through mergers and takeovers by 1998. In 1990 *CS Holding*, the umbrella company of the SKA, took over the venerable *Bank Leu* (which had been founded in 1755 as a state bank and privatized in 1798) and then went on to buy out the *Schweizerische Volksbank* in 1993.[20]

In order to forestall *CS Holding* dominance, in December 1997 the SBG and the SBV merged to form the *United Banks of Switzerland* (UBS), a deal which cut the number of major corporate banks in Switzerland down to two.[21] Next to the consolidation of the major banks, a less drastic process of consolidation and concentration was taking place among the regional banks and *Sparkassen* in the 1970s and 1980s which led to a massive decline in the number of institutions belonging to this banking group in the 1990s.

The Swiss banking industry is therefore characterized by a high level of concentration accompanied by considerable differences in the size and nature

---

[19] These were the *Schweizerische Kreditanstalt* (SKA), the *Schweizerische Bankgesellschaft* (SBG), the *Schweizerischer Bankverein* (SBV), the *Schweizerische Volksbank* (SVB), and *Bank Leu*.

[20] See Hirszowicz (1996: 76ff.) as well as APS (1993: 110).

[21] These figures overdramatize developments somewhat, since the *Bank Leu* and the SVB were by far the smallest of the major banks and are only included in that category for historical reasons (Swary and Topf 1992: 12; Kloten and Stein 1993: 313).

Table 6.4. Number of institutions in each banking sector, 1973–98

	1973	1989	1998
Big banks	5	5	3
Cantonal banks	28	29	24
Regional banks/*Sparkassen*	237	210	108
Raiffeisen banks*	2	2	1
Foreign banks	101	135	149

*Peak associations
Source: 1973: Albisetti et al. (1977: 92); 1989–98; Schweizerische Bankiervereinigung (2000*b*: 4)

of the different banks operating in the same marketplace. Two dominant major banks had to compete with a great number of small- or medium-sized banks which were not only administered under a distinct legal framework but also had a very different business emphasis and regional focus. If, when, and how far the dominant position of the major banks was translated into control over those interest groups representing the banking industry will be examined in the next section.

6.3.1.2 *The Banking Associations*

In view of the crucial role played by interest groups in Swiss policy-making through the consultation or "*Vernehmlassung*" process,[22] one could expect that such an economically vital sector as the banking industry would have its political position protected by strong representative associations. Yet the considerable segmentation of the Swiss banking industry is mirrored in the structure of its interest groups, leading to the creation of organizations each representing a different part of the banking sector. Commercial banks there-fore all belong to the *Schweizerische Bankiervereinigung* (SBVg), next to which there is also an association representing the cantonal banks, an association for regional banks, and *Sparkassen*, as well as one for the cooperative *Raiffeisenkassen*. Bearing great similarities to the German experience and in great contrast to the banking pluralism which dominated the American scene, in Switzerland there is no institutional competition for members between these organizations even when there are (despite a background of general consensus over banking policy) occasional differences of interest between particular groups (Lehner, Schubert, and Geile 1983: 373).

---

[22] For further information on the consultation process, see Höpflinger (1984: 171ff.) or Linder (1999: 299f.).

Another peculiarity of the Swiss banking system is the fact that the *Schweizerische Bankiervereinigung* acts as an umbrella organization for the representative associations as a whole. The SBVg is therefore by far the most important of all the banking organizations in Switzerland.[23] The following will therefore examine the individual banking associations before taking a detailed look at the *Bankiervereinigung*.

The *Verband Schweizerischer Kantonalbanken*, the association to which the cantonal banks belong, represents the strong public-law element of the system. In contrast to many other West European state banks, which emerged through the nationalization of pre-existing commercial banks, in Switzerland the cantons (as well as several city governments, see below) started their own banks from scratch.[24] As has already been described above, the cantonal banks were established in the second half of the nineteenth century in order to meet public demand—especially among farmers and small businessmen—for financial services. With the commercial banks preoccupied with the financing of massive industrial projects, many Swiss citizens felt that they did not have access to affordable loans and mortgages. The cantonal banks[25] were therefore established to fulfil a social agenda. They were supposed to increase the willingness to save among the population, enable the financing of cheaper housing and reflect the needs of workers, small traders, farmers, as well as other public charter institutions. The main focus of the cantonal banks has remained upon these areas of business to this day (Hirszowicz 1996: 60f.). In return, they benefit from state guarantees covering their assets and liabilities along with special treatment from bank regulators.[26]

The aggregate market share of the cantonal banks declined over time. While they made up the largest banking group towards the end of the nineteenth century (see Table 6.2), the major corporate banks had an equal share of the Swiss market by the 1930s. After the crisis at the beginning of the 1930s, the cantonal banks were able to briefly benefit from their deposit guarantees, leading to a short period of growth in their market share before it began to decline again at the end of that decade. Moreover, there is great diversity among cantonal banks both in size and financial capacity, which can vary to a factor of fifty depending on the magnitude and economic strength of their

---

[23] Interview with Professor Hirszowicz, 29 June 2000.

[24] This points to the existence of strong parallels to the German system of public-law *Sparkassen* and *Landesbanken*.

[25] The first cantonal banks were founded in Geneva in 1816 and Berne in 1832. The final ones were established in Wallis in 1916 and Jura in 1978.

[26] See the Swiss Federal Constitution (*Schweizerische Bundesverfassung* or BV) article 31quater. (A new Swiss Federal Constitution came into force on 1 January 2000. The findings of this case study relate to the Swiss Constitution of 1874, valid throughout our period of investigation.)

home cantons, outside of which none of these respective banks can operate.[27] The long-term consequences of this kind of structural development will be examined later in this chapter.

The *Verband Schweizerischer Kantonalbanken* was established in 1907 as the result of a general compact between the former issuing banks after their operations had been terminated with the transfer of control over the national currency to the *Schweizerische Nationalbank*. Today, this association acts on behalf of the cantonal banks when dealing with Swiss state authorities and has become an integral part of the consultation process ("*Vernehmlassungsverfahren*") whereby different private and public institutions take a direct role in the formation of legislative proposals involving the banking sector (Hirszowicz 1996: 462ff.). The association is also responsible for several cooperative projects involving cantonal banks designed to increase the competitiveness of this entire banking group.[28] Since the cantonal banks are also all members of the SBVg, the *Verband Schweizerischer Kantonalbanken* cooperates very closely with this organization as well.

As a group, the regional banks and *Sparkassen* are quite heterogeneous. It is made up of institutions operating under very different legal conditions from one another; along with joint-stock companies, it contains cooperatives, municipal corporations, and registered clubs (Hirszowicz 1996: 88ff.). Although they are not unique to this group, some of its typical characteristics are the relatively small size of the member banks, their geographically restricted area of operations, and the limited number of services they offer their customers (Mast 1974: 496). The *Sparkassen* were established as self-help organizations for philanthropic reasons in the mid-nineteenth century. Just like the cantonal banks, they were largely designed to fulfil a social agenda rather than the pursuit of profit. From its initial dominance of the Swiss banking market, the market share of this group as well as the number of its member banks has sunk continuously to this day (see Tables 6.2–6.4).

The first association representing the interests of Swiss local banks, savings institutions and *Sparkassen* was created in 1920. The growing convergence in the interests of regional banks and *Sparkassen* led to the merger of their representative associations in 1971 into what since 1981 has been called the *Verband Schweizer Regionalbanken* (Hirszowicz 1996: 464). Since the smaller banks belonging to this group found it especially difficult to cope with the more competitive marketplace of the 1990s, their pressure for

[27] The calculations of the author are based on the balance sheets of cantonal banks in Zürich and Appenzell-Ausserrhoden, measured according to their balance figures in 1994. Data from Hirszowicz (1996: 61).
[28] This includes the mortgage loan centre, the jointly run *Swiss Holding* for asset management as well as cooperation in the areas of training and information technology.

greater cooperation led to the establishment of the *RBA-Holding* by ninety-eight regional banks and *Sparkassen*. As in the case of similar projects in the cantonal bank sector, this subsidiary was designed to increase the ability of regional banks and *Sparkassen* to compete with their private counterparts by coordinating a set of centrally administered nationwide services (ibid.). The *RBA-Holding* acts as a group representative and cooperates closely with the SBVg.

The *Schweizer Verband der Raiffeisenkassen* represents the many very small and rural *Raiffeisen* banks. These are mostly cooperatives and were largely founded in order to provide a further means for "self help" by ameliorating the traditional lack of available capital in rural areas.[29] Up to this day, these banks have remained focused on their traditional areas of business, the provision of cheap mortgages and savings accounts. They fulfil a "niche and developmental function in the Swiss banking landscape" and are often the only banks to be found in small towns and villages in the Swiss countryside (Hirszowicz 1996: 94f.) Their representative association, which was founded in St Gallen in 1902, is responsible for ensuring that the several hundred *Raiffeisen* banks maintain a unity of purpose and remain recognizable through unified methods of presentation (signs, advertising, and so on) and operation. Over 537 small banks currently belonged to this group in the early 2000s,[30] only half of the over 1,000 *Raiffeisen* banks that were still active a decade earlier (Hirszowicz 1996: 94).

Other—smaller and more specialist—bank associations exist parallel to these main organizations. Founded in 1981, the V*ereinigung schweizerischer Handels- und Verwaltungsbanken* has thirty members,[31] while the *Verband der Auslandsbanken in der Schweiz*[32] represents the interests of foreign banks in Switzerland. The *Vereinigung Schweizerischer Privatbankiers*, established in Zürich in 1934, is made up of three sub-organizations,[33] while the *Verband Schweizerischer Kreditbanken und Finanzierungsinstitute*, which is based in Zurich, is a federation of thirty institutions which are specialized in small-business loans and consumer credit.

The Swiss banking industry can therefore be seen as consisting of a heavily differentiated set of interest groups. When it comes to representing banks

[29] The *Raiffeisenbank* concept has its origins in nineteenth-century Germany. See Section 4.1.1 of this study.

[30] See http://www.raiffeisenbank.ch, 15 August 2001.

[31] Membership of the SBVg is a pre-condition for membership of this organization.

[32] This association was founded in reaction to the tightening of *Bankgesetz* guidelines concerning the operations of foreign banks. It tries to act as an arbitrator in conflicts with Swiss banks and takes part in the consultation process.

[33] These are regional associations in Geneva, German-speaking Switzerland, and for private banks in Zürich.

in the political process, however, the only association of relevance is the *Schweizerische Bankiervereinigung* (SBVg) which has been playing a central role in policy-making since 1912.[34] Two attributes of the SBVg are of particular importance in this respect. On the one hand, although it is itself an association, it also acts as the umbrella organization for all other representative associations in the banking industry; on the other hand, since it represents bank directors and other senior personnel in the banking industry, it does not ostensibly represent the interests of banks as institutions.[35]

This association was founded in 1912 through the initiative of a banker from Basel in reaction to the serious difficulties Switzerland as an export-oriented nation had experienced after the American stock market crash of 1907. As the banking industry was going through a phase of consolidation during the same period (see above), several initiatives were launched for a new banking law which did not, however, lead to any lasting legislation. However, the SBVg entered into several "Gentlemen's Agreements" with the *National-bank* in the 1920s and 1930s which were largely integrated in the Banking Act of 1934. And it also cooperated closely with the central bank during the currency problems of the 1930s (Hirszowicz 1996: 450). Long before its role became enshrined in the economic statutes of the Swiss constitution in 1947, this association had therefore been heavily involved in policy formulation and implementation.

According to its own statutes, the SBVg has four main areas of responsibility:[36]

1. The recognition and representation of the interests of the different banking groups when dealing with state agencies and administrators
2. The protection of Swiss savings (even after insolvencies)
3. Ensuring fair competition and a functioning financial market
4. The standardization of business practices through the publication of technical guidelines, etc.

Within the framework of its "code of professional conduct" (*Standesregeln*), the SBVg has always interpreted the last point in as broad a sense as possible

---

[34] "Cooperation on an industry-wide level takes place primarily under the aegis of the SBVg" (Hirszowicz 1996: 443). Similar opinions were voiced in an interview at the think tank *Forschungsstelle Schweizerische Politik*, 15 June 2000.

[35] In the first year of the SBVg's existence, 316 members from 159 banks joined this association. Since 1947, institutional membership is also possible though this did not change the character of this association from a "collection of individuals who each possess great responsibility" (Hirszowicz 1996: 450). Its founding document included as one of its main goals "the fostering of good personal relations between its members" (cited from Hirszowicz 1996: 448).

[36] SBVg statutes §§2 and 3, see Füglister (1993: 232), Hirszowicz (1996: 451), and Schweizerische Bankiervereinigung (2000a: 4).

and has thus taken on a crucial self-regulatory role in the financial sector. This "code of conduct" covers areas such as a bank's duty of care, advertising and limits on advertising in the field of consumer credit, managerial practice in certain forms of business, and even includes "best practice" recommendations on the structures of internal management.[37]

There also existed a set of "conventions" under the umbrella of the SBVg with the aim to "channel competition between banks towards orderly lines and avoid destructive rivalries" (Hirszowicz 1996: 458)—which effectively fosters cartels regulating price levels. This was a vital instrument of sectoral policy until its abolition in the early 1990s (see below). Two important conventions dealing with short-term redeemable bonds and deposit protection continue to exist merely as agreements within the *Bankiervereinigung* (Schweizerische Bankiervereinigung 1993).

In 1999, the association had 5,858 individual members and 509 member banks and institutions (Schweizerische Bankiervereinigung 1999: 104). This indicates that it really can live up to its claim to represent the banking industry as a whole. The intensive activity of this institution can be seen in its many commissions working on such matters as tax questions, the economic aspects of foreign policy, performance comparisons, banking structures, and banking examinations. In total, there are sixteen such commissions and several of them have their own offices and staff (ibid. 12–22). The SBVg also administers a number of joint ventures involving business information and monetary transactions. The SBVg is therefore a very powerful association, whose own resources (as well as the resources of its members) enable it to represent the sector's interests very effectively.[38]

The presidium of the SBVg meets two to three times a year with a delegation from the *Eidgenössische Bankenkommission* (EBK, see below) to discuss a previously agreed agenda. Cooperation with regulators is generally quite intensive since there are close contacts on all levels between the two sides.[39] Because of the heterogeneity of the Swiss banking industry described above, the SBVg has to expend a considerable amount of effort on internal integration as considerable differences exist between the interests of internationally oriented major banks and local or regional banks who only operate domestically or

---

[37] See a more detailed description and analysis in Füglister (1993). Compliance to an association's rules can of course only be imposed through a set of internal sanctions which ultimately culminate in the offending institution being expelled from the SBVg (ibid. 247). The current version is the "*Vereinbarung über die Standesregeln zur Sorgfaltspflicht der Banken* (VSB 98)" which includes a system of fines of up to sFr. 10 million (Schweizerische Bankiervereinigung 1998: article 11, p. 22).

[38] As an example, see the 150-page-long position paper on the consultation process for the amendment of the Banking Act in 1983 Schweizerische Bankiervereinigung (1983).

[39] Interview SBVg, 14 June 2000.

regionally. This is particularly the case when it comes to the implementation of international regulatory requirements. Big banks are often the only institutions involved in these commissions and working groups of the SBVg as they are the only banks who possess the necessary expertise in key areas and can afford to second specialists to the SBVg if necessary.[40] However, the major banks cannot impose their views in the SBVg's board and would not try to do so. In the decision-making bodies of this association there exists a "culture of compromise" and respect for other banking group's interests. This is a legacy of the decades-old tradition of operating banking cartels and reflects the consensus-based approach of Swiss politics as a whole. It is therefore symbolic that the president of a major bank has never been chairman of the SBVg, since this position above all requires an ability to arbitrate disputes rather than allow the pursuit of own interests.[41]

6.3.2 The Regulatory Agencies

Despite a strong federal tradition, in Switzerland the state element of the policy network dealing with banking issues is exemplified by a high level of uniformity. It therefore bears greater structural similarities to the German system rather than the highly decentralized form of banking regulation prevalent in the (otherwise equally federalized) United States (Lehner, Schubert, and Geile 1983: 370f.). This is reflected in the close relationship between the EBK and SNB which is based on strong cooperation—a further parallel to the German and contrast to the American case.[42]

The central state agency responsible for banking regulation in Switzerland is the aforementioned *Eidgenössische Bankenkommission* (EBK). The legal basis for the system of banking regulation as a whole was put into place by the *Bundesgesetz über die Banken und Sparkassen* (Banking Act or *Bankengesetz*) of 1934 and the *Verordnung über die Banken und Sparkassen* (Banking Bylaw or *Bankenverordnung*) of 1972. Both have been altered several times since being originally enacted, though not in any fundamental fashion. Bank regulation in Switzerland has been generally dominated by an indirect approach (see below) shaped by a highly liberal economic environment—there are no fundamental restrictions imposed by the state on the banking sector (as is the case in the United States). The Banking Act, above all, imposes certain minimum

---

[40] The commissions are not made up of full-time staff. Rather, they are staffed according to the "militia principle" which predominates in many Swiss institutions.
[41] Interview SBVg, 14 June 2000.
[42] Interview with Professor Baltensperger, 15 June 2000.

requirements for bank capital and liquidity as well as a mandatory oversight of financial risk held by the major clients of any bank.[43]

Article 23 of the *Bankgengesetz* covers the operations of the EBK. The EBK is responsible "for the independent oversight of the banking sector, investment funds, the stock exchange and financial products offered to the public" (ibid.). The cantonal banks represent the main exception, as the *Bankgesetz* (based on Article 31quater of the Federal Constitution) stipulates that the EBK is not responsible for this banking group. The EBK is financed through fees it charges on those banks it monitors.[44] The commission itself consists of seven to eleven members, which are each appointed for four years by the government. The government also appoints the president as well as the vice-president of the EBK. While the president is the only member who works exclusively for the commission, the other members work there on a part-time basis and are only compensated for the amount of time they have spent working on regulatory matters.[45] Though the EBK is subordinated to the state finance department, it operates independently to the extent that it is banned from following directives from government or parliament (Birchler and Rich 1992: 413; Bodmer, Kleiner, and Lutz 2000: article 23, N4). Although the EBK is a relatively uncontroversial and depoliticized institution, its makeup is designed to roughly represent the different political parties: While the president is usually a figure associated with the centre-right parties, the vice-president is chosen to be close to the Socialists.[46]

According to the commission's annual reports, it meets ten to twelve times a year for one- to two-day sessions.[47] Even if the "militia principle" was taken to extremes, the large amount of work which bank regulation involves could not be processed by the commission members alone during that time and is therefore mostly dealt with by the secretariat of the EBK. In international terms, this is a remarkably small apparatus which at the beginning of the 1990s had only thirty-five employees and by the end of that decade had a staff of ninety full-time specialists.[48]

Such a small regulatory unit cannot undertake regular oversight of every specific bank. The direct inspection and monitoring of banks and bank branches is based on the reports of auditors (see below) and is therefore largely

---

[43] See Birchler and Rich (1992: 414f.). These guidelines are relatively similar to the German KWG.

[44] *Bankgengesetz* article 23. See Bodmer et al. (2000: article 23 N21).

[45] See Birchler and Rich (1992: 413) as well as article 50 of the *Bankverordnung*. These guidelines stipulate that the members of the commission have to be experts in the field and must have worked in a leading position in a bank, an investment fund, a stockbroking firm, or as an auditor (article 23).

[46] Interview SBVg, 14 June 2000.   [47] See EBK Jb (1987) and EBK Jb (1999).

[48] Figures from EBK Jb (1990) as well as interview EBK, 15 June 2000.

of an indirect nature. The main task of the EBK secretariat is to ensure the correct interpretation of the banking regulatory framework by the auditors.[49] This takes place through the circulation of memoranda to all the key actors in the banking industry and the state, which is preceded by the usual process of consultation with all of those involved in banking policy (*Vernehmlassungsverfahren*).

The direct monitoring of the banks is therefore undertaken by auditors known as "*Revisionsstellen*", who produce annual reports of their own. These are almost exclusively large international auditing firms.[50] They effectively act as the extended arm of the EBK, a position encapsulated in the observation of one British expert: "The auditors could be said to act as the eyes of the Commission, or at least to provide extra eyes and ears" (Cooke 1985: 144). Yet they do not have any well-defined legal powers even though they are grouped as a regulatory agency in this section. These auditors have to be independent of their clients both in business and personnel terms and possess specialists with in-depth experience of the banking industry. Throughout they are under the control and licence of the EBK (Schweizerische Bankiervereinigung 2000*b*: 32). Moreover, the auditors can be prosecuted under the criminal code if they file incorrect or fraudulent reports (Birchler and Rich 1992: 413).

Another form of regulation which is equally important and conducted in a fashion that is not heavily formalized is the SBVg's "code of conduct". It can be considered as another form of oversight since its importance in shaping the behaviour of banks augments the banking laws. This "code of conduct" has become a particularly flexible means with which to put new rules and guidelines into place quickly and efficiently (Füglister 1993: 250). These rules play a particularly important role in those areas which have not been covered by legislation or where lawmakers have put an emphasis on voluntary action (Schweizerische Bankiervereinigung 2000*b*: 33). In the face of an often very long and complicated legislative process which has to be passed before new formal regulations can be put into place in Switzerland, such residual steering mechanisms have proven their particular worth.

Finally, there is the *Schweizerische Nationalbank* (SNB). As a central bank, this institution has a natural interest in the security and the functioning of the banking system because of its central role in the transmission mechanisms of monetary policy. The SNB is also focused on the banks because of its function as "lender of last resort", though more on the level of the banking industry as a

---

[49] A further area of responsibility is the licensing and monitoring of the auditing firms, yet this is made easier by their relatively small numbers (see below).

[50] See the list in EBK Jb (1990: 147). Among the fourteen licensed auditing firms are such major companies as Arthur Andersen, Ernst & Young, Coopers & Lybrand, Deloitte & Touche, KPMG, and PriceWaterhouse.

whole rather than individual banks.[51] Despite the fact that the central bank is not involved in bank supervision, it does produce official statements on banking matters and can provide help to any bank or financial company. There is also regular contact between the EBK and the SNB. Meetings between the two institutions take place in which all issues of mutual interest are discussed twice a year.[52] The SNB sees itself as acting more in "the capacity of an observer rather than as a direct participant in the area of banking regulation" and believes that the separation of monetary policy from bank oversight has a positive effect in ensuring that there are no conflicts of interest which could result from interdependent decision-making processes.[53]

Low deployment of state resources, independence from direct political intervention, and a cooperative relationship between state institutions are key characteristics of the approach taken by the Swiss state when it comes to its role in banking regulation. As mentioned above, lack of rivalry between agencies as well as a unitary approach to banking issues on all state levels is not necessarily to be expected in a federal system.

6.3.3 The Legislative Framework

In the area of legislation, the federal system is of much greater significance. The Swiss political system is characterized by a significant separation of powers. The most important elements of this system will be examined here. While members of the government cannot belong to the national parliament or "*Bundesversammlung*", the parliament does not have the power to vote a cabinet out of office during a legislative term.[54] Moreover, the Swiss parliament is marked by total symmetry between both chambers which possess identical legislative powers and areas of responsibility. This is a further strong parallel to the American system[55] and a distinct divergence from both the German and

---

[51] Interview SNB, 29 June 2000.

[52] See descriptions in EBK Jb (1999, 127f.) and Schweizerische Nationalbank (1999: 59).

[53] Interview SNB, 29 June 2000. Interview with Professor Hirszowicz, 29 June 2000.

[54] This stands in contradiction to most classic parliamentary democracies and is normally a characteristic of presidential systems of government, fostering a tendency in political studies to classify the Swiss system as the latter rather than the former (Steffani 1983, 1992). Conversely, the *Bundesrat* is elected by the parliament rather than the people, a tradition that is not a characteristic of presidential systems. The Swiss system is therefore often described as a hybrid between presidential and parliamentary forms of government (Lijphart 1999: 120) or as a directorial and collegiate system that has a dualistic division of power in common with presidential states (Beyme 1999: 29, 53).

[55] In the United States' symmetrically bicameral system the Senate has certain foreign policy powers. However this is not relevant to the policy field considered here.

British models of government, where one chamber has far greater power than the other.

When examining the influence of legislators on policy-making, the implementation of new laws in practice is as important as the theoretical powers of the chambers of parliament. While the Swiss parliament is considered to be more a working parliament rather than simply a place in which debates are conducted without consequences (Lüthi 1999: 136), its lack of resources and other structural limitations have tended to weaken its position (Kriesi 2001: 60).

This has been exacerbated by the "militia parliament" concept, with its emphasis on a part-time legislature consisting of politicians who retain a normal working life. Although this concept has "become a fiction long ago" (Linder 1999: 198) through the legislature's evolution into a "semi-professional parliament" (Riklin and Möckli 1991), this "militia ideal" still exerts a powerful hold over both the public and policy-makers. A reform package designed to improve the pay and working conditions of members of parliament by providing them with part-time staff failed at the hands of a referendum initiated by more conservative elements of the legislature (Kriesi 2001: 62f.). This is evidence of another restriction on policy-makers, the strong plebiscitary component of the Swiss system of government which puts further limits on the power of parliament as final legislative arbiter.

The way parliamentary work was organized in the past did not make it easier for members of parliament to influence the legislative proposals formulated by the cabinet or other state institutions. The four-yearly parliamentary sessions are very short, with each only consisting of three weeks while, influenced by the "militia" concept, there are no established parliamentary committees responsible for specific issues. Every new piece of legislation is examined by an ad hoc committee which prepares the plenary agenda and is wound up after the relevant law has been enacted.[56] This only changed in 1992, when a reform of the commission system led to the establishment of several permanent committees ("*Legislativkommissionen*").[57] These have encouraged legislators to develop greater in-depth knowledge of certain policy areas, enabling the Swiss parliament to increase its influence on the legislative process (Lüthi 1997: 201).

Several studies have shown that as a result, parliament has become much more ready to intervene in the course of the 1990s and has exerted more influence over policy than in the 1970s (Jegher 1999: 206). This is especially the case

[56] In the legislative period 1971–5 there were no less than 225 of such committees in the *Nationalrat* and 239 in the *Ständerat* (Kriesi 2001: 203).

[57] The work of these commissions and the behaviour of parliament has been analysed in detail in a study by Lüthi (1997).

when there is a conflict between a parliamentary majority and the *Bundesrat* (the federal government) or when the *Bundesrat* makes a proposal that fails to unite the affected groups behind it and is thus particularly "endangered by referendum" (Lüthi 1997: 201). Yet such interventions do not lead to gridlock between government and parliament—as is the case in the US Congress— since most legislators are interested in consensual solutions and try to ensure the success of any proposal.[58] The fact that both chambers of parliament share the same committee structures also tends to smooth the path of compromise.[59] This is based on a tradition of consensus in which 90 per cent of all issues are dealt with in only two parliamentary debates (Kriesi 2001: 63).

In summary, one can say that the structural reasons described above and the comprehensive pre-parliamentary consultations and agreements (described in the section on bank associations) weaken the ability of parliament to influence or block legislation in the area of banking policy.

6.4 LIBERAL CONSENSUS AND PARTIAL POLITICIZATION

As in the German case, one specific incident in the period between 1974 and 1999 is of central importance to the development of Swiss banking policy. Yet this is not a bank collapse but rather a scandal which caused one major bank difficulties for a considerable period of time after it incurred some of the largest financial losses in Swiss history. The "Chiasso Scandal" and the resulting politicization of banking issues is the main focus of the following section which will also examine how the banking crisis of the 1990s was overcome. Since a summary of these events in the academic literature does not yet exist, this case study will depend to a much greater extent than preceding sections on primary sources and descriptions in order to illustrate the underlying dynamic behind these political developments.[60]

6.4.1 The "Chiasso Scandal" and the Politicization of Banking Issues

The most notorious scandal to hit the Swiss banking system in the period under examination is unquestionably the "Chiasso Scandal", named after a

[58] According to Lüthi (1997: 203).

[59] The opposite effect created by committees based on thematic structures can clearly be seen in the American case. See Sections 3.3.3 and 3.5.3.

[60] The primary sources used here stem mostly from the 1974 to 1999 issues of *Année politique suisse* (cited as APS), the annual reports of the *Eidgenössische Bankenkommission* (cited as EBK Jb) as well as the *Amtliches Bulletin der Schweizerischen Bundesversammlung* (cited here as AB). The exact references can be found in the bibliography.

branch of the *Schweizerische Kreditanstalt* (SKA) in which questionable and at times criminal financial dealings took place. This incident politicized banking issues in Switzerland for years and has served as a point of reference ever since. The following section will examine this scandal before looking at its political and regulatory impact.

The "Chiasso Scandal" burst onto the scene in the second half of the 1970s in a time when the contrast between the general economic crisis and the simultaneous stormy growth of the banking sector was beginning to gain wider attention. In particular, the role of the banks in the export of capital and its impact on the value of the Swiss Franc on the international currency markets became a matter of discussion once again.[61] In the midst of this growing uncertainty, in April 1977 it emerged that the manager of the Ticino branch of the SKA in Chiasso had over several years accumulated hot money from tax evaders and criminal sources in Italy and invested it in questionable financial dealings in Liechtenstein instead of, as he had agreed with his Italian clientele, in legitimate Euro-markets.[62]

Once massive liquidity problems at one Liechtenstein company brought these illegal transactions—and the losses of over sFr 2 billion that had been incurred in the process—to the attention of the police, public and corporate confidence in the SKA diminished overnight. The bank itself had to cope with the large-scale closing down of customer accounts in its Chiasso branch as consumers in the Ticino region tried to shift their funds to other banks as quickly as possible. This drove the value of SKA shares downwards to the extent that it affected the market value of other Swiss bank stocks as well. A proposal made by the president of the SNB to increase confidence in the solvency of the SKA through a standby loan from the central bank and the other major banks of over sFr 3 billion had the opposite effect and led to serious doubts over the ability of this bank to survive (Jung 2000: 260f.). The arrest of three top managers of the Chiasso branch generated further publicity. The scandal finally reached the Zurich headquarters of the SKA with the resignation of Chief Operating Officer Wuffli in May 1977.[63]

The regulatory reaction of the EBK consisted of an immediate exceptional audit of the SKA's accounts to get a clearer picture of the wider impact of the goings-on in Chiasso. The *Nationalbank* was more concerned about the

[61] See APS (1975, 76f.); APS (1976, 68f.).

[62] A detailed description of this case including its wider consequences can be found in Jung (2000: 245–87). Moreover, further information can be found in APS (1977: 68–70) and an analysis of the consequences in Winter (1977). This section also draws on these sources.

[63] The scandal had consequences for personnel and organizational structures as attempts were made to encourage transparent and responsible decision-making. This led to strengthening of internal auditing and the formalization of the way general management was organized, including the establishment of weekly sessions where detailed minutes were taken in a way that had not been done before (Jung 2000: 280).

damage this scandal had done to the image of the Swiss financial markets. As a consequence, it made an agreement with the *Bankiervereinigung* confirming an extensive code of conduct to which each bank had to conform. Although the SBVg had originally resisted such measures, this agreement was finalized in June 1977 through an accord known as the *Vereinbarung über die Standesregeln zur Sorgfaltspflicht der Banken* (VSB) between the *Bankiervereinigung* and the SNB (Jung 2000: 290). The different parties to this agreement, which was initially only intended to last for five years, committed themselves to certain guiding managerial principles:

1. The principle to know and identify their contractual partners and clients
2. To not actively encourage capital flight and other questionable forms of capital export
3. To not actively encourage tax evasion[64]

The financial community responded to the challenges caused by this crisis with a speedy act of self-regulation which was almost certainly a successful case of pre-emptive action designed to prevent state intervention:

The VSB dealt with certain aspects of banking law in an autonomous fashion and made analogous or similar state norms unnecessary. This action in itself has normative character. Its emphasis is pronouncedly ethical in an immediate way which could not have been achieved by a piece of legislation.   (Jung 2000: 293)

The extent of this scandal nevertheless led to a deeper politicization of banking policy. This was already becoming evident a few weeks after the discovery of the scandal at the June session of the Swiss parliamentary chambers. A plethora of parliamentary proposals to prevent a repetition of this scandal were promptly tabled in the *Nationalrat* (the lower chamber), signalling a general desire among legislators to play an active role in regulatory reform.[65] While the Liberal and centre-right parties expressed concern over the international reputation of the Swiss financial markets and demanded that the government take action in this regard, the parliamentary left took the scandal as an example of deeper flaws in the banking system. The parliamentary spokesman of the Social Democratic SPS spoke of "excess maximisation of profit" and "profit-seeking at any price". His speech ended with the statement:

[64] See the partial reproduction of the original text in Jung (2000: 292). The preamble of 1977, which defines the aims of the document, has not been changed and has been integrated into the last VSB (Schweizerische Bankiervereinigung 1998: 3). The main part of the VSB consists of detailed definitions and practical instructions, making the text a useful handbook for bankers as well. A major sanction for those who ignore these instructions is a fine of up to sFr. 10 million (VSB article 11).

[65] Jung (2000: 291) lists 17 such parliamentary initiatives in the session in which these negotiations had taken place.

"What has come to public knowledge through the Chiasso case is not the exception, it is the rule."[66]

The centre-right and left political camps therefore developed divergent interpretations of these events which resulted in very different demands when it came to possible legislative intervention. While the former focused on the managerial failures of individual bank employees and were confident that the resulting improvements in oversight and control mechanisms would prevent a repetition of this affair, the latter believed that the "Chiasso Scandal" represented a systemic failure in a steadily expanding banking sector belonging to a profit-oriented economic system that could only be overcome through a complete transformation of the entire industry. This led to demands that state representatives should receive a seat on the board of every important bank (Winter 1977: 13).

After these SPS demands for a tightening of legal stipulations concerning internal and external controls as well as an expansion of the powers and personnel of the EBK failed to find a majority in the *Nationalrat*, the Social Democrats announced that they would try to turn these proposals into law through a referendum which came to be known as the "*Bankeninitiative*". The "Chiasso Scandal" therefore triggered an extensive debate over the fundamental nature of the financial marketplace in Switzerland that continued over many years. The referendum was called the "*Volksinitiative gegen den Mißbrauch des Bankgeheimnisses und der Bankenmacht*" (People's initiative against the abuse of banking confidentiality and bank power)[67] and consisted of a demand for the loosening of banking confidentiality in all those areas where it might foster tax evasion or might hinder legal enquiries concerning hot money from abroad. It also tried to impose disclosure requirements on all banks as well as introduce a compulsory deposit protection scheme. Moreover, banks would have to make public all their business commitments and investments in other companies while the state would be empowered to put caps on these investments and restructure a bank if they were surpassed. These proposals were clearly designed to limit the power of the banks.[68]

---

[66] Cited from Jung (2000: 293). See also APS (1977: 68ff.), which contains further information on the following.

[67] The initiative was introduced by the SPS at its party congress on 20 May 1978 in Basel and was handed in on 8 October 1979 with 124,291 signatures (Jung 2000: 294).

[68] See APS (1978: 64, 1982: 61) as well as Jung (2000: 294). The parallels to the demands made in debates in Germany in the 1970s for the dismantling of many of these structures (see Section 4.2.2) are noticeable. This is largely because of the form of universal banking with strong involvement in industry which existed in both countries.

Although certain aspects of these referendum proposals were integrated into banking legislation in the following period,[69] the Swiss government rejected the bulk of its recommendations in a debate in 1982. The only exception was the deposit protection scheme. While centre-right parties and the *Bankiervereinigung* reacted positively to the government's position, the SPS expressed deep disappointment and decided to follow through with the referendum initiative (APS 1982: 61). Though the government did not formulate an explicit counter-proposal, a proposal made by experts advising the parliament for a complete overhaul of banking law was widely taken as a direct response to the referendum proposals. It contained modified accounting rules which were intended to improve transparency along with the creation of a system for savings deposits (APS 1982: 61). Yet the political struggle prior to the referendum on the Social Democratic banking proposals had an impact on the "consultation" process for the *Bundesrat*'s banking law. Social Democrats, trade unions, and development aid non-governmental organizations rejected this legislation, claiming that it had not taken enough of the referendum initiative's ideas into account. By contrast, the employers' federation, the centre-right parties and the banking associations voiced their support for these amendments while opposing any form of obligatory deposit protection system or making duty of care (a measure the SPS supported) a legal obligation (APS 1983: 78).

As with the *Bundesrat* in the previous year, parliament rejected the referendum initiative without making any counter-proposals. The opponents of this initiative pointed to the importance of the banking sector for the Swiss economy and vehemently opposed the imposition of legal restrictions on banks, emphasizing the importance of self-regulation mechanisms. On the other side of the political divide, the supporters of regulatory reform claimed that the Social Democratic banking initiative was not an attack on the banks, while emphasizing that the state had to do something to ensure that their operations were conducted in a moral and ethical fashion since the influx of foreign "hot money" was damaging the reputation of Switzerland as a whole (APS 1983: 77).

In the final stages of the referendum campaign, its opponents went on to claim that this initiative marked a full-scale attack upon the liberal economic system and the freedoms it was believed to entail, while the only groups

---

[69] The *Nationalrat* then decided that when dealing with cases of tax fraud (though not tax evasion) Switzerland should now provide help for its international partners. The desire to develop stronger protection for savers reflected a legislative motion proposed in the *Nationalrat* by the *Freisinn* party for the introduction of compulsory insurance for savings accounts and other deposits which was unanimously adopted in both chambers of parliament (APS 1979: 74f.).

supporting the initiative were the Social Democrats, the extreme left, and the trade union federation. In the referendum of 20 May 1984, over 73 per cent of votes cast and every canton rejected the banking initiative, marking its final failure (APS 1984: 74).

This ended a political process which had begun with the "Chiasso Scandal", but which after seven years had largely faded into the background anyway. The political debate over banking policy had effectively split into two separate spheres of discussion. The first was largely a depoliticized discussion over the reform, integration, and adaptation of the Swiss financial marketplace and its regulatory framework which was largely conducted among academic experts and in parliament. The second was the public debate, in which fierce controversy raged over the issue of bank policy and (from the early 1980s onwards) "hot money" from abroad which helped to politicize banking issues. Though these debates have continued since, the failure of the referendum of 1983 has ensured that this political weapon has so far not been used again when it came to banking policy.

6.4.1.1 *The Reform Debate*

The apparent public support for the arguments of the banks and their supporters, which seemed to have been confirmed by the referendum result of 1983, strengthened the resistance of the banking associations against planned amendments of banking law. In the face of the controversial findings of the "consultation" process, the *Bundesrat* decided to only introduce partial amendments which could be enacted more easily (APS 1984: 75). This new approach gained the support of the banking commission, too, which believed that the existing law was sufficient to ensure "an effective and up-to-date regulatory system" (EBK Jb 1984: 14).

Yet even this reduction of legislative ambitions did not result in the support of banking representatives who continued to support the tightening of existing guidelines (including the integration of the VSB code of conduct into banking law or the codification of improved controls of financial corporations) and, instead, demanded improvements of political and tax conditions in Swiss financial markets. These demands were triggered by growing worries within the Swiss financial community that the competitive position of Swiss financial markets was worsening in comparison to countries like the United Kingdom, where the liberalization of the City through the "Big Bang" gave the markets in London a considerable advantage.[70] At the centre of this debate lay the demand for a reduction of taxes and charges for a whole variety of financial

---

[70] See APS (1984: 75, 1985: 70f.).

services (particularly stamp duty), which the banks believed were putting the financial marketplace in Switzerland at a disadvantage.

As a result, the whole emphasis of this debate slowly shifted from the original proposals for the strengthening of regulatory guidelines towards the reduction of the tax burden. The consequences of this trend became apparent when in December 1986 the *Bundesrat* announced a postponement of the planned partial amendments of the banking law in order to be able to take changing conditions in financial markets into account (APS 1986: 77).[71] One consequence was the announcement by the *Nationalbank* that it would withdraw its involvement in the planned revamp of the SBVg's code of conduct known as the "*Vereinbarung über die Standesregeln zur Sorgfaltspflicht der Banken* (VSB)". Instead of including this code in the banking law, the VSB now became part of a private agreement between the SBVg and the participating banks, leading to greater self-regulation rather than its restriction.

The *Bundesrat* announced that it would now try to achieve its initial intentions through a stricter interpretation of existing laws (APS 1986: 77). Once again, the EBK voiced its support for the government's intitiative, since the banking law "does indeed permit a more up-to-date interpretation" (EBK Jb 1986: 14). In order to be able to put this initiative into practice, the commission began the necessary redrafting for any alteration in the banking by-law. After the obligatory consultation process, the new banking by-law came into force in 1989. It stipulated that securities firms and other financial intermediaries should receive the same treatment as banks under the law (taking changes in the financial markets into account) and adapted guidelines on equity ratios to conform to the rules of the Basel Committee.[72] When compared with the wide-ranging amendments of banking law which had originally been planned, the changes that were ultimately achieved in 1989 can only be described as minor tinkering around the edges.

While the Social Democrats were deeply dissatisfied with this result and tried to achieve further changes in the *Bankgengesetz* (which proved just as unachievable as previous left-wing initiatives), the centre-right parties threw their support behind the banks which wanted further deregulation of the Swiss market.[73] Sweeping demands for a reduction of tax levels for the financial sector and measures to improve the international competitiveness of Swiss markets met opposition in the *Bundesrat*, which believed that such measures would increase the state deficit and hinder plans to reduce the tax burden

---

[71] This initiative was eventually completely put on ice when the *Bundesrat* introduced its legislative plans for the period between 1987 and 1991 and confirmed that it was not going to amend banking law in the near future (see APS 1988: 101).

[72] EBK Jb (1989: 12). On the amendments discussed here see also Schuster (1988).

[73] See APS (1985: 70f., 1986: 76, 1987: 105, 1989: 102f., 1990: 110, 1991: 126, 1992: 119).

for families, making it impossible to decrease stamp duty without finding equivalent sources of tax revenue elsewhere. This led to a compromise in 1989 ending the stamp duty, a move which was now partially to be compensated through the creation of a set of alternative taxes on financial services.

This amendment was passed against heavy resistance from the Social Democrats, but did not come into force immediately because of further consultation in the *Nationalrat*. In the process, the amendment became entangled in the whole discussion over a restructuring of the federal budget. The termination of stamp duty became integrated into the legislative package reforming state finances and thus became caught up in the failure of this reform to win a referendum on 2 June 1991. Although this was quickly followed up by a parliamentary initiative running along established lines, the circumvention of Social Democratic opposition in both chambers of parliament led the SPS and SGB to call another referendum. But they failed, and the new regulations succeeded at the ballot box, receiving 61.5 per cent of the vote.

A further aspect of the reform debate related to the impact of European integration and the plans of the Swiss government to join the European Economic Area (EEA).[74] Already in 1990, the banking commission had compiled a comparative study which indicated that when it came to banking regulation, the Swiss system was largely compatible with those of its European neighbours (EBK Jb 1990: 12). The few adjustments that were necessary, particularly those concerning exchange of information between Swiss and other European state agencies (ibid. 46), were enacted in parliament as part of the wider legislative package on prospective membership of the EEA (*"Eurolex"*).[75] After accession to the EEA was rejected in a referendum in December 1992, these harmonization measures essential to the preservation of Swiss competitiveness in financial services were passed in parliament as part of a bill known as *"Swisslex"*.[76] The only exception was the planned inclusion of cantonal banks into the EBK's regulatory scheme, which ultimately failed to achieve enough support in parliament because of concerns in the centre-right parties that such a measure might undermine federalism (APS 1993: 10). In the face of the financial difficulties which many cantonal banks began to experience in the

---

[74] For the relationship between Switzerland and the European integration process and specifically on the debate over membership of the EEA see Christen (1999: 212–18).

[75] The main changes related to foreign banks operating in Switzerland, which were to be commissioned and licensed by their home countries rather than by the EBK from that point onwards. It also led to the abolition of the privileged position of internal auditing of cantonal banks (see APS 1992: 119). Further details on this material can be found in the plenary debate at the *Nationalrat* on 27 August 1992 (see AB 1992: N 1402–14).

[76] See the debate at the *Nationalrat* on 17 December 1993, in which these proposals were described as having been "warmed up" (AB 1993: N 2492). See also Lutz (1995: 477ff.).

following years (see below), resistance to a firmer regulatory framework for this part of the banking sector was not to be maintained for much longer.

6.4.1.2 *The Controversy surrounding Banking Confidentiality, Money Laundering, and "Hot Money"*

While the reform debate described above largely took place in expert circles and failed to arouse much public interest, the controversy surrounding banking confidentiality and the issue of money laundering and "hot money" was another matter. These issues drew a considerable amount of public attention in the debates over the Social Democratic banking initiative. In the mid-1970s, there had already been considerable public concern over the possibility that banking confidentiality (which had existed since 1934) had brought about an influx of capital which—while profitable for the financial community— contributed to a hefty increase in the value of the Swiss Franc that was doing considerable damage to other economic sectors. This effectively became a debate of "assembly-line Switzerland" (*Werkplatz Schweiz*) versus "financial market Switzerland" (*Finanzplatz Schweiz*).[77]

In the 1980s, this controversy was fuelled by a variety of court cases related to a crackdown in the United States against illegal activity on the stock markets such as insider trading. Although state agencies initially refused to remove banking confidentiality clauses because these activities were not illegal under the Swiss criminal code, they were finally forced to alter this stance when the United States began to exert pressure on the Swiss government.[78] In 1985, insider trading became a criminal offence (APS 1985: 71).

More public attention was attracted to this issue when it emerged in the mid-1980s that several dictators who had been toppled from power had secret bank accounts in Switzerland.[79] In 1986, the banking commission helped to block the accounts of Philippine President Marcos and Haitian President Duvalier who had both been forced to flee their countries. Having in the wake of the banking referendums become more sensitive to the connection between poverty in the Third World and the influx of "hot money" from these kinds of regimes, the commission behaved in a very different manner in these two cases than it had done in the case of the exiled Shah of Iran in 1979. The *Bundesrat* even decided to intervene, using its constitutional powers to take

---

[77] See APS (1975: 76f., 1976: 68f.). For an analysis of the history and the conditions in which legal regulation of the Swiss tradition of banking confidentiality—which was a codification in the 1930s of customs which were deeply anchored in the liberal ideology of the late nineteenth century—see the study by Vogler (2000).

[78] See APS (1981: 66f., 1982: 61).   [79] On the following see APS (1986: 78).

foreign policy initiatives by ordering a freeze of such accounts in order to protect the international reputation of the Swiss banking system.[80]

When the discovery of the "Lebanon Connection" brought the connection between money laundering and the trade in illegal narcotics to light,[81] the legislative efforts in this area were speeded up. The banking commission set up, "without delay", an investigation and eventually decided to only allow professional wholesale trading in foreign banknotes if the bank involved had received a special permit from the commission (EBK Jb 1988: 12, 1989: 12). Although the extent to which the banks were actually responsible for money laundering remained unclear, their role elicited considerable public disquiet. One major bank, the *Schweizerische Kreditanstalt*, even saw itself forced to take out full-page adverts in order to clarify its position. The *Bundesrat* went on to put before parliament a legislative proposal, formulated by its experts in 1986, which made money laundering a criminal offence (Jung 2000: 297ff.). This law was passed in the following year and came into force on 1 August 1990. It effectively integrated the essence of the banking association's VSB code of conduct into the criminal code.[82]

In the mid-1990s, Swiss banks once again became the centre of public (and international) attention because of the continued existence of financial assets deposited in Switzerland by victims of the Nazi regime.[83] These "newless assets" were estimated by Jewish organizations to be worth several billion Swiss Francs. When in 1996 the chairman of the US Senate banking committee, Alfonse D'Amato, joined in demanding that Swiss banks pay compensation to the families of these holocaust victims, and requested them to testify at a Senate committee hearing in the process, the Swiss parliament and *Bundesrat* were forced into action. An international commission of historians was established to investigate these claims. Yet when in October 1996 American lawyers initiated a class action lawsuit with compensation demands that amounted to over $20 billion, a political inconvenience turned into a massive threat to the business interests of the largest Swiss banks. Calls for boycotts against Swiss banks were voiced in the United States, and in the course of heated debates the issues of "newless assets" and the SNB's purchase of gold from the Third Reich were conflated in such a way that the Swiss state also became a

---

[80] The funds still in the Marcos accounts were handed to the Phillipine government only eleven years later (APS 1997: 128). A similar official freeze of accounts was imposed on the assets of the Zairean President Mobutu after his flight from Kinshasa in 1997 and former Palistan Prime Minister Benazir Bhutto after she fell from power in the mid-1990s.

[81] In this context, three major banks were accused of accepting banknotes worth around sFr. 1.5 billion—mostly stemming from the drug-dealing—making these institutions complicit in money laundering through their negligence. See Jung (2000: 297f.) as well as APS (1988, 101).

[82] See APS (1989: 101, 1990: 109) as well as Schweizerische Bankiervereinigung (2000*b*: 36f.).

[83] On the following see APS (1995: 119, 1996: 119–24, 1997: 123–8, 1998: 123–6).

target of international criticism because of its behaviour during the Second World War. A complete public relations disaster ensued when an attentive employee at a security firm working for the *Schweizerische Bankgesellschaft* brought to public attention the fact that documents at this bank dealing with the Second World War period had been shredded—inadvertently, as the bank claimed. The fate of this employee, who was fired by the security firm and had to move to the United States after receiving anonymous threats, further damaged Switzerland's international reputation.

Although the big banks did put a compensation fund in place in which each institution paid over sFr 100 million,[84] attempts to bring about a state boycott of Swiss banks continued in the United States. In 1998, Senator D'Amato even tried to pressure the Federal Reserve into blocking the merger of the *Schweizerischer Bankverein* with the *Schweizerischer Bankgesellschaft* in the United States.[85] By August 1998, however, a compromise was reached between the major banks on one side and the plaintiffs as well as the Jewish organizations on the other. As part of this agreement, the big banks declared themselves ready to pay out over $1.32 billion in four instalments spread over three years. This compromise ended a decade which, even without the controversy surrounding victims of the Nazi regime, had been among the most turbulent for the Swiss banking industry in the twentieth century.

6.4.2 Banking Problems in the 1990s

It was in the first half of the 1990s that Switzerland experienced an economic crisis which also had a major impact on the banking industry. At the same time, significant structural change manifested itself in the removal of the cartel rules which had played an important role in the banking system until this point. The effects of these two factors—the economic crisis and the increase in competitive pressure—intensified each other.

6.4.2.1 *The Abolition of Bank Cartels*

As has been described above, "conventions" about the managing of certain areas of business created under the aegis of the *Schweizerische Bankiervereinigung* had existed for a considerable period of time. Many aspects of these conventions had effectively created cartels about conditions between different

---

[84] This came to sFr 272 million in total, see APS (1997: 125).
[85] See the letter from D'Amato to the Fed Chairman Alan Greenspan of 5 February 1998 (http://www.senate.gov/ banking/corresp/0205fed.htm) and a press statement made by the Senator on the same day (http://www.senate.gov/ banking/pressrel/0205sws.htm).

member banks with the aim of controlling and reducing levels of competition.[86]

In the face of the increasing liberalization of the banking sector in member states of the European Community and the negotiations surrounding accession to the EEA, such practices no longer seemed appropriate.[87] The cartel commission therefore produced a report on the nature and extent of competition in the Swiss financial markets in 1989, in which it recommended that most aspects of the Swiss conventions should be brought to an end since the uniform prices and charges they fostered were hindering competition. The report also claimed that the structural arguments used by the banks to defend the conventions were not convincing, since it had served less to protect the smaller banks than to increase the profits of the larger and more efficient banks.[88] The SBVg tried to react flexibly towards these recommendations and accepted a large part of the cartel commission's suggestions while rejecting others. The commission however stuck to its guns and asked the responsible ministries to turn all of its recommendations into legal directives. With the support of the SNB, the ministry and the commission managed to implement their agenda to create a more competitive environment by removing the cartel regulations in 1990.

This increased the level of competition between the banks. Another effect was the recession that followed the overheating of the European economies in the 1980s. The resulting rise in unemployment forced the banks to reduce the number and extent of the loans they were willing to offer on the market. This was also a reaction to the massive amounts that the banks had been forced to write-off on loans they had provided in the previous decade.[89] Although the

---

[86] Similar measures to control levels of competition were adopted in many other countries at certain points including Germany in the 1930s or the United Kingdom after the Second World War. Certain legal restrictions in the United States had the same aim. This was therefore not a specifically Swiss measure. More typical of Swiss conditions, however, was the development of these measures as a convention within the frame of a top-level association. Moreover, in most other countries these restrictions had been removed by the end of the 1970s.

[87] On the broader trend towards further liberalization in Switzerland in the 1990s see the paper by Mach, Häusermann, and Papadopoulos (2001).

[88] See Hirszowicz (1996: 442, 458) as well as APS (1989: 101).

[89] A survey in 1997 by the EBK came to the conclusion that between 1991 and 1996, write-downs, written-off loans, and losses in the domestic credit market added up to over sFr 42 billion. The big banks incurred three quarters of these losses and the cantonal banks roughly one quarter, while the regional banks incurred only 3 per cent and the *Raiffeisen* banks only 0.6 per cent. As a percentage the losses in the domestic market varied considerably from banking group to banking group with the big banks incurring 12.5 per cent and the *Raiffeisen* banks incurring the much lower figure of 0.7 per cent. The regional and cantonal banks only suffered reductions of 4–5 per cent. The banking commission considered these losses to be the "result of management policy which in many cases was incautious during the speculation boom in the Swiss real estate market in the second half of the 1980s and the ensuing collapse of property prices which helped foster six years of macroeconomic stagnation after the boom years" (EBK Jb 1997: 11f.).

big banks incurred the greatest losses, the smaller and medium-sized banks suffered the most from the contraction of the market, since they were unable to profit from the economies-of-scale diversified sources of revenue that could have protected them from the housing crash (APS 1991: 123). A succession of mergers and takeovers was the result, creating a wider consolidation of the market which was seen in positive terms by the EBK at least: "After the end of this wave of consolidation, the Swiss banking market will find itself in a much stronger position" (EBK Jb 1990: 13).

6.4.2.2 *The* Spar- und Leihkasse Thun

The most prominent victim of this turbulence was the *Spar- und Leihkasse Thun*, which was forced to close (at first on a temporary basis and then permanently) by the commission in 1991.[90] A report by external auditors, which had discovered that the requirement of write-downs on bad real estate loans made by the bank in the most favourable case equalled its whole own capital, set the ball rolling for its eventual closure.[91] Furthermore, the bank's loan records had turned out to be completely inadequate and management at the bank had even failed to fulfil the legal duty to report aggregate risks which exceed 30 per cent of their bank's balance sheet or 400 per cent of its own capital (EBK Jb 1991: 26).

Since these failings entailed high and incalculable levels of risk, no other bank was prepared to take over this 125-year-old institution, whose final closure was accompanied by great expressions of regret from the commission (ibid. 28). This closure was a shock to the system, not only because the *Spar- und Leihkasse Thun* was a medium-sized regional bank whose customer base was spread across the country or the fact that this was the first bank failure for many years, but also because this event for the first time caused financial losses among depositors, in general, and private customers and small businessmen, in particular.[92]

The problems caused by these losses and the convoluted manner in which compensation payments were made triggered a series of political initiatives.

---

[90] Detailed descriptions of this case can be found in the annual reports of the EBK (EBK Jb 1991: 26–9; EBK Jb 1992: 44–6).

[91] A more detailed examination in June 1992 demonstrated that a write-down of assets of around sFr 255 million had become necessary with a bank that had net assets of only sFr 85 million. The *Spar- and Leihkasse Thun* was therefore saddled with debts of over sFr 170 million (EBK Jb 1992: 44f.).

[92] Interview at the *Forschungsstelle Schweizerische Politik*, 15 June 2000. The SBVg's convention on deposit protection only guaranteed up to sFr 30,000 per creditor.

The introduction of an extended compulsory deposit protection scheme as suggested by the president of the EBK was however rejected by the government. It argued that this negative stance was justified by what had happened during the crisis in the American banking system which had "demonstrated the counter-productive nature of such forms of reinsurance, since they would tempt bankers and depositors into overly risky behaviour" (APS 1991: 124). Another proposal to replace the EBK by a stronger regulatory agency to be known as the *Bundesamt für Banken und Finanzen* was also unsuccessful (ibid.).

Nevertheless, the *Spar- und Leihkasse Thun* affair had had a "catalytic effect" on the banks.[93] They came to realize that the EBK was indeed prepared to revoke bank licences. Apart from this instrument, the EBK's powers to intervene were relatively weak, since it was unable to impose its will on recalcitrant managers before an auditor's report had been completed. The Thun case can therefore be seen as a pivotal moment, which heightened the tempo of consolidation in the Swiss banking system—the number of regional banks sank from 204 to 134 between 1990 and 1995 (Hirszowicz 1996: 91). This weeding out process partly took place through mergers and partly through direct takeovers. The establishment of the *RBA-Holding* described above was a further step towards the consolidation of this sector.

6.4.2.3 *Problems Experienced by the Cantonal Banks*

The cantonal banking groups were not spared from the consequences of this economic crisis either, of which the downward adjustment of the value of their asset portfolios was particularly painful. For this reason, the EBK had to make a temporary exception for the *Berner Kantonalbank* when it came to the legal guidelines concerning the level of own capital by allowing the bank to operate with asset levels below the official quota (EBK Jb 1992: 34f.).[94] One reason for its problems was a combination of risky management decisions made by senior executives at this bank and a lack of any effective regulatory agency in the canton in which it was based. As a result, the canton of Berne had to step in and pay out the costly financial guarantees it had made to the bank.[95] At

---

[93] Interview EBK, 15 June 2000.

[94] Cantonal banks were not regulated by the EBK, but the own capital guidelines of the *Bankengesetz* also covered their operations. For information on the special treatment of cantonal banks in the *Bankengesetz* see Hirszowicz (1996: 71).

[95] The compensation payments came to about sFr 5,000 per tax payer (interview with Professor Hirszowicz, 29 June 2000).

the same time, similar problems confronted cantonal banks in the cantons of Solothurn[96] and Appenzell-Ausserrhoden.[97]

These events led to a further set of political debates, both on the federal and the cantonal level. Central to these political discussions was the question of whether, in a changing world, the special position of the cantonal banks was still justified since the original reasons for their establishment had disappeared.[98] Moreover, further questions were raised over the possibility that the cantons' guarantees for the cantonal banks could have adverse effects (especially among the smaller ones) by fostering "moral hazard" behaviour among senior managers. The latter point was particularly emphasized by private commercial banks which considered such state guarantees to be a form of unfair subsidy. The *Bundesrat* and the banking commission particularly emphasized the need to impose external audits also on cantonal banks.[99] While the Social Democratic Party wished to uphold the special status of the cantonal banks,[100] the cartel commission continued to push for the removal of state guarantees and tax privileges.

Rather than waiting for these wider debates to come to some kind of fruition on the federal level, several cantonal governments tried to deal with these problems on their own with measures such as the sale of cantonal banks to major banks, transforming them into private companies listed on the stock exchange (though the cantons remained majority shareholders) or a financial compensation for the advantages brought about by the state guarantees.[101] Though these reforms were controversial, they managed to receive popular support in several referenda. In Zurich, however, a coalition made up of Social Democrats, the GP, and the SVP parties decided not to turn the local

---

[96] The cantonal bank in Solothurn began to experience difficulties after the takeover of a regional bank and also needed a temporary reduction of its own capital requirements (see EBK Jb 1992: 35, 1993: 39).

[97] Because of the small size of its local market, this cantonal bank found it increasingly difficult to operate profitably and was, under cantonal law, obliged to pay interest on the canton's endowment capital, a requirement it was no longer able to fulfil because of written-off loans and a write-down of its assets (see EBK Jb 1995: 33).

[98] For information on this discussion see Hirszowicz (1996: 67ff.) as well as APS (1992: 118).

[99] See EBK Jb (1994: 27f.). All these aspects are linked with one another since the state guarantee enshrined in article 3A paragraph 1 BankG was a main characteristic of the cantonal banking system and was a reason for its special status with regard to audits.

[100] The Social Democrats demanded that in return for their privileges, the cantonal banks should be legally obliged to undertake wider economic development projects. This included areas which had been a crucial part of these banks' initial role (see above) such as the maintenance of a decentral network of branches and the provision of cheap loans to small local businesses (APS 1995: 119).

[101] The first was the case in Appenzell-Ausserrhoden, with the sale to the *Schweizerischer Bankverein*, the second in St. Gallen, and the last in Berne and Aargau.

cantonal bank into a private listed company, a course of action which was also confirmed through a referendum (APS 1997: 122f.).

In 1997, a commission of experts installed by the *Bundesrat* in the previous year handed in its own report on the problems experienced by cantonal banks. Its recommendations included a proposal that cantons should in future be able to choose whether they wanted to provide their cantonal banks with state guarantees or not. A bank should only be called a "cantonal bank" if its status was enshrined in cantonal law and a minimum 33 per cent share of this bank was held by the canton (ibid.). This proposal received a largely positive response in the course of the consultation process, though the Social Democratic Party and the trade union federation registered some reservations. The resulting piece of legislation[102] was finally enacted in April 1999 and came into force in October of that year. This eventually placed all banks in Switzerland, including cantonal banks, under the supervision of the EBK.

Intriguingly, one side effect of the wide-raging debates over the difficulties experienced by the banking industry in the 1990s was an attempt to politicize the *Eidgenössische Bankenkommission*. The Berne member of the upper chamber (*Ständerat*) Zimmerli (SVP) put forward a proposal in 1993, which would have led to the creation of a body made up of both chambers of parliament to monitor and control the work of the EBK. Zimmerli tried to justify this initiative by claiming that more direct political oversight was needed over an institution with as great a significance for the functioning and reputation of the Swiss financial marketplace as the EBK. Although the legislative commission of the upper chamber of the Swiss parliament which dealt with such issues recommended that this initiative be rejected, it managed to attain a majority when it was put to a plenary vote (APS 1993: 111). In order to put this proposal in a more concrete form, the legislative commission suggested that some form of parliamentary oversight be integrated into the banking law by stipulating that the *Bundesrat* must pass on the annual report of the EBK to parliament rather than in summary form as part of its general report. A minority in this committee under Social Democratic leadership tried to push for the creation of some form of parliamentary oversight body (APS 1994: 106). After this minority initiative (if only narrowly) failed to find enough support, Zimmerli withdrew his initial bill since the resulting amendment did not match his original goals. In the end, this amendment never reached the lower chamber (*Nationalrat*) (APS 1995: 118).

---

[102] See the summary in EBK Jb (1998: 29). The only remaining privileges of the cantonal banks was the lack of any compulsory federal authorization for them (because the EBK could not revoke a cantonal bank's licence) and an asset rebate.

Another proposed amendment which resulted from this crisis failed in a similar fashion. The Social Democratic member of the lower chamber Vollmer proposed that the *Bundesrat* should be mandated to create a system of depositor protection along the lines of European Union guidelines which had been put into place in 1994. Although the *Bundesrat* admitted that there were certain gaps in the existing system which had become evident in the *Spar- und Leihkasse Thun* case, it rejected the idea that any emulation of the European Union in this respect was necessary and pointed to the crisis in the American Savings & Loans system as an example that such wide-ranging depositor protection guidelines could lead to "moral hazard" behaviour.[103]

In conclusion, the economic crisis in the first half of the 1990s had a major impact on all sub-groups within the Swiss banking system. This speeded up the concentration process of the big and regional banks (see Table 6.4) and led to partial regime changes in the cantonal banking group. But the consolidation took place in a banking system where—in international comparison—the number of banks is still high relative to the size of its market.

6.5 CHARACTERISTICS OF THE POLICY FIELD

During the period examined in the course of this study, the bank regulation system in Switzerland has largely been characterized by continuity. A liberal and codified system of some standing, it did not need to be adapted to new trends in the market. Though there emerged several political disputes in the policy field, they were usually resolved in a consensual manner. Because of the Swiss banking sector's considerable exposure to international markets, developments which took place in other major nations, particularly the trend towards liberalization in the key markets in the United States and the European Union, were bound to influence the content of domestic regulatory policy. Nevertheless, the Swiss case demonstrates that, even under these conditions, there remains substantial capacity for resistance against the supposedly irresistible surge towards more integration.

6.5.1 Consensual Approach

Already earlier studies of Swiss bank regulation as a policy field have emphasized the characteristic of the consensual approach both among the banks

---

[103] See APS (1996: 118) as well as—concerning the government's answer—AB (1996: N 1549–51). Experts also voiced the opinion that without the negative example of the United States, the problems experienced during the 1990s would have led to the establishment of a deposit insurance scheme (interview with Professor Baltensperger, 15 June 2000).

and the state (Lehner, Schubert, and Geile 1983: 374). Twenty years on, the above sections have confirmed these conclusions. The cooperation between regulatory agencies, legislators, and banking associations has remained close and continuous and regulations were only changed after extensive discussions had taken place as part of the wider consultation process. This is not just the case when it comes to the original Banking Law and the Banking By-Law, it is even so on the lowest level of state action—the EBK circulars to banks.[104]

An important reason for this approach is the relatively small administrative capacity of the Swiss state which, combined with the weak political leadership exerted by the *Bundesrat*, increases its dependence on external expertise from sources like representative associations. This also makes it easier for all sides to accept and implement compromises once they had been achieved (Busch and Merkel 1992: 210). The kind of behaviour demonstrated in this policy field fits well with the wider nature of the kind of "consensual democracy" that has always been a defining characteristic of Swiss politics:

It [consensual democracy, A.B.] neither knows the shifts in power between government and opposition nor the continuous hegemony of one party. The dualism between government and ruling party on the one hand and opposition party on the other does not exist within it. Even the dualism between government and parliament is moderated by a readiness to cooperate in a constructive and trustful manner. All major parties are represented within the government while confrontation is usually avoided. All sides attempt to reach widely supported compromises.   (Riklin and Ochsner 1984: 79)

However, as this case study has demonstrated, there still existed asymmetries in the ability of different actors in this policy field to affect the decision-making process. During the 1980s, the bank associations were much more able to organize resistance against planned changes (particularly the tightening of supervision guidelines after the "Chiasso Scandal") than the Social Democrats, whose attempts at amending the system rarely succeeded.[105] This can largely be explained through the predominance of an institutional system in which a high number of veto points puts a premium on the status quo and against change—particularly when the latter does not reflect a broad agreement. The weak position of parliament described in the section on the legislative process has been confirmed in the course of this case study, since none of the exceptions described in that section were to be found in the case study. There was neither a thematic conflict between a parliamentary majority and the government nor did the latter present proposals that were not backed by

---

[104] Interview EBK, 15 June 2000.

[105] Nevertheless, the Social Democrats had never distanced themselves from the wider consensus on banking policy by demanding the nationalization of banks in the same way that the SPD and Labour Party had done in the 1970s (see Sections 4.2.2 and 5.4.1).

a consensus on banking policy—and thus avoided the risk of a referendum being called.

6.5.2 Strong Self-Regulation

Another, and complementary, factor is the strong role played by sectoral self-regulation. This self-regulation was able to withstand attempts to expand the role of the state. The most prominent example of course was the banking initiative of the early 1980s. The institutional foundations for effective self-regulation lie in the umbrella function of the *Schweizerische Bankiervereinigung* and in the fact that the SBVg has both accepted and implemented the role of private interest government. Just like in the German case (with the *Herstatt Bank* crisis), the "Chiasso Scandal" was a key event whose consequences were dealt with promptly and efficiently by the representative banking associations.[106] The establishment of internal mechanisms by the association which created a certain level of deposit protection demonstrated a willingness to take on new self-regulatory responsibilities. With the central bank's abandonment of its role in monitoring duty of care (VSB), this aspect of regulation was also taken over by the banking associations. The resulting codes of conduct also provided the basis for much needed state legislation when the tricky issue of money laundering suddenly erupted in the late 1980s. The quick and effective setting of norms, which is the main advantage of this regulatory model (Füglister 1993: 250), is of particularly high value in a system which cannot guarantee rapid responses to new problems because of the comprehensive consultation and negotiation processes described above.

6.5.3 "Autonomous Convergence"

Although Switzerland has repeatedly rejected any form of integration into international institutions (particularly on the European level), its economic interests do necessitate a certain amount of adaptation to changes which have taken place on the international level. The rather oxymoronic term "Autonomous Convergence" has been used to name this process and is another important characteristic of this policy field during the period examined by this study. One example is the liberalization imposed by the cartel commission's dismantling of the banking cartels. This development also demonstrates that regulatory change can take place even against the interests of the banking associations as long as such change goes in the right direction—namely a

---

[106] This comparison has also been made by Winter (1977).

liberal one. Most clearly, however, this was the case during the negotiations to join the EEA, the moment when the term "Autonomous Convergence" was coined.[107] After the EEA treaty failed in a referendum, its harmonization measures were largely passed separately in order, as a legal expert observed, "not to end up standing completely outside of European legal norm development" (Lutz 1995: 478).

6.5.4 Specific Domestic Problems

A last characteristic of this Swiss case study has been the particular importance of specific domestic problems. Although this has been the case, up to a certain point, in each of the previous national case studies, the precipitate rise in the value of the Swiss Franc (in the 1970s) and the problems arising from the issues surrounding "hot money" and holocaust victims (in the 1980s and 1990s) occupy a special place. These were largely the product of Swiss particularities—a small, liberal country with the reputation of being a "safe haven" for financial investments and deposits. This stereotype has resulted in both financial benefits and economic and political costs. A large part of the problems which have consumed a great deal of public attention and legislative time and political resources would never have occurred in other countries—a clear indication of the unique nature of the Swiss case.

6.6 SUMMARY: THE SWISS CASE

In the policy field of banking regulation, there has been relatively little objective need for adaptation in Switzerland in the twenty-five years covered by this study. In contrast to the American case, this system had become liberally oriented by the 1970s and did not contain any legally imposed limits on banking services either in product, price, or geographic terms. And contrary to the British case, codification had already taken place in the 1930s. The Swiss case therefore has most in common with that of the Federal Republic of Germany where the state also plays a relatively restrained role and representative associations are comparatively important in the policy network.

A further parallel to the German case is the high level of success when it comes to policy outcome. Despite the problems described above, on balance it

---

[107] Private information from Klaus Armingeon, Berne University, July 2001.

has to be rated as quite successful.[108] Though the *Spar- und Leihkasse Thun* case was the most prominent (and damaging) example of a bank failure, Switzerland has largely been spared from comprehensive banking crises or major failures.[109] Yet Switzerland is a case in which large risks do exist, considering the important role played by the banking industry in wider economy—both with regard to employment and value added—and highly concentrated with two very large banks. If one of these two were to experience serious financial difficulties, then the consequences for the entire Swiss banking system are hard to imagine.

In institutional terms, bank regulation in Switzerland combines flexibility and continuity in the area of resource utilization. As has been described above, the use of state resources for regulatory purposes appears very low when related to the size and importance of the banking sector. If one looks at the number of people working for the EBK at the beginning of this case study's main period of focus (namely ten, see Winter 1977: 15), its staffing levels have increased substantially to over a 100 by the late 1990s. The bulk of this growth has taken place after 1990 in reaction to the crises that beset the Swiss banking system in the mid-1980s. After the "Chiasso Scandal", the number of EBK staff was doubled to twenty and then expanded to thirty-five by the early 1990s. With the "Thun case", staffing numbers grew further to about fifty as the EBK acquired new powers that led to further expansion and restructuring. As with similar agencies in the United Kingdom and Germany, the EBK also had its problems in recruiting and retaining adequate staff since private industry was able to offer much better pay and conditions. In 1999, EBK finally managed to gain permission from the Swiss government to deviate from standard civil service pay structures which, it is hoped, will improve the situation.[110] The last major change was the creation of a department directly responsible for the oversight of the two big banks in 1998. In this way, the EBK responded to the merger of the SBG and SBV as well as to wider international concerns.[111] For the banks, this marked a step away from the model of indirect oversight by auditors and towards a stronger direct role for the EBK which now employed over 100 people.

Public discussion and politicization of banking policy had, as has been described above, reached a climax in the 1980s and 1990s. The continuous controversies generated by these debates stand in marked contrast to their relatively limited effects on the legislative process. In contrast to the situation

---

[108] This opinion is also shared by other experts (interview Professor Baltensperger, 15 June 2000; interview Professor Hirszowicz, 29 June 2000; interview EBK, 15 June 2000).

[109] Twenty-one banks were closed between 1971 and 1991 (EBK Jb 1991: 26).

[110] Interview EBK, 15 June 2000 as well as EBK Jb (1999: 129).

[111] See *Financial Times*, 30 September 1998, p. 3 as well as EBK Jb (1998: 53).

in the United States, Swiss conditions did not lead to legislative deadlock. The ultimate ineffectiveness of different parliamentary initiatives in the aftermath of the banking crises of the early 1990s (which were certainly attempts to gain political capital from the initial scandals) confirms this interpretation of events. If one takes the number of referenda initiated on banking issues as an objective measure of politicization, then the indications are that with only one major plebiscitary initiative this area of policy has to be rated as not heavily politicized.[112]

The policy network in Switzerland is characterized by a relatively low number of actors on all three sides of the "iron triangle" of state administrators, interest groups, and legislators. In the context of a strong federalist system, the relatively small group of people involved in banking policy was not necessarily a given and is a major contrast to conditions in the United States, a country with a similar level of federalization. Moreover, most of the main actors in this policy network are largely focused on achieving consensus and cooperation rather than the kind of political confrontation that is so prevalent in the United States. In these circumstances, the Swiss state can intervene and take significant action without having to expend any great amount of state resources as long as it can achieve the necessary consensus.

Though the changes in the international environment led to the adaptation of the Swiss regulatory framework, these shifts were not perceived to negatively entail any kind of loss of national control. Rather, the aspects of banking in Switzerland which came to be seen in a particularly negative light during this period were some of the morally dubious consequences of the unique role played by Switzerland in the international financial system.

---

[112] Interview at the *Forschungsstelle Schweizerische Politik*, 15 June 2000.

7

State and Banking Regulation in Comparative Perspective

If one compares the four case studies in the empirical part of the present analysis, when it comes to political structures, content, and processes in the area of state regulation and oversight of the banking sector, then the differences between them are far more evident than the similarities. This is a rather intriguing conclusion to arrive at if one takes into account the parallel challenges which were faced by these four countries in the wake of the massive structural changes in world financial markets after 1974. This chapter will therefore examine the different factors which have led to these differences. It will first look at the differences between the various sectoral policy networks, then examine the impact of divergent political and constitutional variables, and finally analyse how developments were influenced by variations between economic systems.

7.1 POLICY NETWORKS IN COMPARISON

7.1.1 Industry and Interest Groups

There are great structural differences between the banking systems to be regulated in the four countries analysed in this study. Although there were strong trends towards a concentration of the banking market in Switzerland, the Federal Republic of Germany, and the United States, one cannot speak of a convergence between these different cases. Compared to the banking markets of other OECD countries (especially those in the EU), that in the United States is still characterized by a very large number of (often small- to medium-sized) banks. In stark contrast, the situation in the British banking market has been characterized by the dominance of a handful of large banks since the 1920s. What both markets do have in common, however, is that they developed a strict separation of commercial banks from investment banks (in the United States determined by strict legal regulations and in the British case through historical specialization) and the fact that there are no significant state, public-law, or cooperative banking sectors.

In Switzerland and Germany (as well as most other European countries) the banking markets do contain such segmentation of the market, though in each case the market share of the various bank groups varies considerably. Yet there are substantial differences between both cases as well. While the banking market of the Federal Republic has maintained a relatively stable balance between the market share of the commercial banking sector and that of the *Sparkassen* and cooperative banks, in Switzerland the industry has become highly concentrated with only two major banks controlling over two thirds of the market.

The differences in the prevailing market conditions of each of these four countries had significant consequences for the way in which associations representing the banking sector on a national level are organized, as the divergences between the four case studies demonstrated. In Germany and Switzerland, the heavy segmentation of the banking market has led to a system of associations in several pillars which has displayed stability over a long period of time. As a result, there was, and is, no competition for members between different banking associations. In great contrast to the relationship between banking associations in the United States, a tradition of coopera-tion between different representative associations has taken shape instead. Again, rather different structures emerged in the United Kingdom, where the consolidation of the market was fostered by geographic and business factors and big banks played a much more direct role in their representative associations.

These different associational patterns are reflected in the very different relationships that exist between banks and executive agencies. In each of these case studies, the banking sector has developed in accordance with either corporatist or pluralist patterns, thus shaping the different levels of associa-tional involvement in the formulation and implementation of policy. In the Federal Republic, the important role played by the cooperative and public-law auditing boards in monitoring the financial sector illustrates the intense engagement of the banking industry in policy implementation. In Switzer-land, the *Schweizerische Bankiervereinigung*, an umbrella association covering most of the industry, plays a key role in the self-regulation mechanisms of the sector although (unlike Germany) they are not directly involved in the auditing process. Yet the SBVg's codes of conduct fulfil a key complementary function to the legally enforceable guidelines of the state administered reg-ulation system. In both countries, deposit protection schemes are organized by the banking associations in a non-governmental fashion. In the British case there exists a strong tradition of self-regulation as well, even though it was largely conducted through informal modes of control which were largely dismantled in the course of the reforms of the 1990s. In the United States, banking associations compete for members and have been completely unable to exert any form of "private interest government" (Streeck and Schmitter 1985).

During the period examined by this study, these variables have not changed in any of the four countries. The various banking associations have been strongly shaped by historical developments and, once they had come into existence and managed to establish themselves, have remained highly stable. For example, the lack of any consolidation of the banking system in the United States in the late nineteenth and twentieth centuries led to the complex web of competing interest groups which has paradoxically stabilized the associational and banking system. Yet this link between market structures and the associational system is not an automatic one. The German case demonstrates that a highly concentrated set of associations can also exist under the conditions of a low-concentration banking system.

7.1.2 The Executive Branch

There are also great differences between the four countries when it comes to the institutionalization of state regulatory agencies. The spectrum reaches from extreme fragmentation with a multitude of agencies which even compete with one another (as in the United States) to the concentration of all regulatory powers in a single agency as in the Swiss and British cases. The executive is also heavily concentrated in Germany, where, in comparison to Switzerland, the central bank plays a more significant role.

In the United States, the division of responsibilities into the hands of a large number of different agencies—with cooperation between agencies further marred by bad coordination and unclear areas of jurisdiction—is a recipe for inefficiency and is in need of root-and-branch reform: on that, the case study showed, most experts agree. Yet the study has also shown that the existing situation is advantageous for the banks by enabling a form of "regulatory arbitrage". Taken together with the influence of state agencies afraid of losing out, these facts can well explain why repeated reform initiatives have ended in failure.

In comparison, areas of jurisdiction in Germany, Switzerland, and the United Kingdom are much more clear-cut. Yet differences also exist between these three cases. In the first two the direct auditing of banks has been subcontracted—to the banking associations in Germany and to recognized private auditors in Switzerland—leading to state agencies having little direct contact with the banks under their oversight. In the British case, the Bank of England remained convinced for a long time that an informal approach was the best way to deal with regulatory matters. By the early 1990s, the fact that the bank was preoccupied with the stabilization of fiscal policy as well as its other responsibilities increasingly convinced observers that the BoE was suffering from overstretch (*The Economist* 1993).

The level of state resources brought to bear also varies greatly. It is relatively low in Switzerland and Germany, where cooperation with the banking associations is at its most wide-ranging. That such a sectorally weak or distanced state can have its drawbacks (particularly when it comes to the lack of the expertise needed for international negotiations) has concerned many observers. Until the end of the period of investigation, however, the institutional system of banking regulation remained fairly stable in three of the cases. A major reorganization of the regulatory framework only took place in the United Kingdom with the transfer of powers from the central bank to a newly created state agency. Despite this reform, there has been little apparent convergence between the different regulatory structures. In fact, the level of variation at the end of the 1990s seems to be as great as at the beginning of the 1970s. The only area in which the different systems seem to have become increasingly similar is the introduction of greater codification, since the United Kingdom is no longer in the unique position of being a country without any legal framework for banking regulation.

7.1.3 The Legislative Branch

The third side of the "iron triangle" in the policy networks of the case studies is the legislative process. In this area, too, there are perceivable differences between the four countries.

In the United States, a considerable degree of jurisdictional fragmentation also characterizes the legislative framework dealing with banking regulation. The work of the American Congress is generally conducted through an oligarchic division of responsibility and strong specialization in independent committees, where the party loyalty of self-confident and independent Senators and Congressmen is often quite weak (Jann 1989: 485). This comes to the fore in the policy field of banking regulation since committees in the Senate are structured differently from those in the House of Representatives. The committee chairmen can act as real "veto players" because of their strong powers to guide or block legislation (Tsebelis 1995). Since congressional terms are limited to two years, there are many ways in which those who want to block change can exert pressure on legislators to maintain negative positions.

The high number of legislative initiatives that have been blocked in this field and the piecemeal nature of those that do succeed should therefore not be surprising.

In the Federal Republic of Germany, banking regulation is not subject to federal conflict since banking questions are exclusively controlled by the federal level. This not only reduces the complexity of the legislative process, it probably also reduces (because of the characteristics of the German system of intertwined federalism or *Verbundföderalismus*) the extent to which these issues are politicized and thereby strengthens the work and level of knowledge of bipartisan parliamentary committees, leading to comprehensive hearings and modifications of proposed laws.[1]

In the British system where conflict is one-dimensional between government and opposition, the strength of the government is fostered by a weak parliament which assents to laws worked out by the cabinet rather than taking an active role in amending them. This lack of independent initiative in parliament cannot be compensated for by the occasional investigations conducted at the behest of select committees. The case study demonstrated that innovative impulses tended to come from outside parliament (at times even from management consultancies hired to suggest reforms!) rather than elected representatives of the people. In Switzerland, too, parliament is not in a particularly strong position when it comes to the institutional resources available to it. Although, as in the United States, this is a policy field shaped by a federal system of government in which parliament contains symmetrical competences between both chambers, the political result is completely different from that in the United States: there is no logjam or delay, but agreement (though sometimes only after time-consuming and tough negotiations). The "militia parliamentarians" rarely have the opportunity to make substantial changes to government proposals during their short parliamentary sessions. More importantly—and in great contrast to the confrontational style of American politics—the Swiss political system is one generally oriented towards compromise and consensus.

Intriguingly, the two weakest parliaments in terms of resources and powers, the British in the 1980s and the Swiss in the 1990s, have both managed to expand their role during the thirty years under investigation. Both intend to expand their ability to take independent initiatives and control government. Yet overall it has to be said that the policy networks have remained very different from one another and have barely converged in any meaningful way. Here, too, stability and difference continue to characterize the cases.

---

[1] Interview *Deutscher Bundestag*, 21 June 2001.

7.1.4 The Need for Reform and Policy Outcomes

The differences between sectoral policy networks examined above can explain many of the differences found in the case studies. However, any analysis would not be complete without an examination of the differences in starting points and challenges with which they were confronted.

These differences were considerable. In the United States, a system with strong price, product and geographic restrictions established in the 1930s, saw itself confronted with an ideologically inspired (and therefore relatively rough) attempt at deregulation in the 1980s. Perverse incentives such as the implementation of deposit guarantees in the Savings & Loans sector helped trigger a massive and very costly wave of bank collapses. These problems can therefore be seen as a crisis of adaptation to a newly liberalized order. The consequences of the liberalization of the British credit market were quite similar in the beginning of the 1970s. The introduction of Competition and Credit Control market mechanisms in the United Kingdom which replaced existing borrowing limits was quickly followed by problems in the banking sector that culminated in the Secondary Banking Crisis.[2]

If one contrasts these experiences with developments in the Federal Republic of Germany and Switzerland, which both already possessed liberal systems when it came to controls on interest and capital movement at the beginning of the 1970s and did not experience any banking crises beyond the collapse of individual banks, and other European countries[3] then one can begin to discern a pattern. Banking crises were effectively influenced by three factors (see Busch 2001: 321f.):

1. They are more likely if the speed and extent with which the parameters of the system are changed is high.

2. They are also more likely if the state uses the banking system as a tool with which to achieve certain macroeconomic aims.

3. They vary with the number of actors in and character of the sectoral policy field: the stronger the latter is shaped by (meso-) corporatist factors and contains many actors in policy formulation and implementation, the less danger there is of a crisis.

Yet a certain level of caution is advisable when looking at these conclusions. Though they are based on case studies dealing with eight different countries,

---

[2] See Section 5.4.1 of this study.

[3] See the studies on bank regulation in several countries in Bovens, 't Hart, and Peters (2001), particularly those concerning France (Coleman 2001), the Netherlands (Eerden 2001), Spain (Pérez 2001), and Sweden (Tranøy 2001). A summary of these studies and their findings as well as the aspect of programmatic and political success or failure can be found in Busch (2001).

one should be careful to avoid generalizations. Knowledge of the exact processes and accompanying circumstances of changes in financial regulation has, with some justice, been described as still in its infancy (Quinn 1997: 531).[4]

As this comparison of the characteristics of different banking regulation systems indicates (Table 7.1 summarizes them), the four cases that have been explored in this study demonstrate serious differences when it comes to their sectoral policy network in general and their coping mechanisms for any challenges that may arise in particular. Even the nature of these challenges varied from country to country, depending on the extent to which national systems at the beginning of the period under examination were regulated or liberalized. The differences in processes and results can therefore be summarized as follows:

* In the United States, a pluralist system based on competing associations in combination with a fragmented regulatory and legislative framework led to outcome failures and reform deadlock which triggered interventionism from the courts and regulatory administrations.

* In the United Kingdom, market concentration and a tradition of preferring informal regulation led—in spite of a pluralist system of associations—a centralized regulation and legislation system to achieve high capacity for action, albeit mostly of the reactive kind after limited faliures.

* In Germany, a concerted system of associations is weakened by market segmentation and fragmentation, but—combined with centralized regulatory structures—led to outcome successes which made reforms seem unnecessary.

* In Switzerland, a segmented yet concentrated market together with a tradition of comprehensive cooperation led to flexible adaptation with a minimal use of resources and only few failures.

7.2 POLITICAL SYSTEMS IN COMPARISON

How far can the differences described above also be explained through the variables of these different political systems? Is there a relationship with the

---

[4] The study by Demirgüç-Kunt and Detragiache (1998) which claims to answer these questions is unfortunately not of any great value. It suffers from simplistic operationalization of variables and an obvious selection bias.

Table 7.1. State banking regulation: the case studies in comparison

	USA	GB	D	CH
Structure of banking market	Fragmented/homogeneous	Concentrated/homogeneous	Fragmented/segmented	Concentrated/(segmented)
Association system	Pluralist	(Pluralist)	(Corporatist)	Corporatist
Supervision (institutions)	Fragmented	Concentrated	Concentrated	Concentrated
Supervision (approach)	Heterogeneous	(Homogeneous)	(Heterogeneous)	Homogeneous
Legislative responsibility	2 Chambers, differing, powerful committees	2 Chambers, weak committees	1 Chamber, powerful committee	2 Chambers, weak committees
Position of parliament	Strong	Weak	(Strong)	(Weak)
Need for reform (regulation/codification)	High/low	Low/high	Low/low	Low/low
Banking crises	Yes	(Yes)	No	(No)
Result	Comprehensive blockade alleviated by administrative and court action	Tradition of informality and quick state action after crises	Strong sectoral self-regulation and weak state promote passivity	Comprehensive concertation and flexibility cope with high risk

type of the government system, the existence or non-existence of federalism, the character of the party system, or the dominant party in power? Does membership of the EU have a systematic impact? Drawing on the variables described at the beginning of this study (Table 1.1), these questions will be explored in the following section.

When it comes to the contrasts between presidential and parliamentary systems of government, the four case studies show no systematic differences. Rather, they have made clear that there can exist strong differences *within* both groups. Both the American and Swiss cases demonstrate that even in presidential systems, with symmetric divisions of responsibility between both chambers, the actual role played by parliament can vary greatly because of factors such as the amount of institutional resources available to legislators or the strength of parliamentary committees. The parliamentary systems of the United Kingdom and Germany also display great differences when it comes to the availability of resources or the parliamentary logic of the Westminster system as opposed to the more consensual approach which dominates the *Bundestag*. Both in terms of policy output and policy outcome, whether a country is governed along presidential or parliamentary lines, therefore, does not make much of a difference when it comes to banking regulation as a policy field.

The difference between federal and unitary states also contributes little to an understanding of the developments examined in the course of this study. This is largely because of the fact that the three federal systems in the United States, Germany, and Switzerland are as different from one another as from the unitary political system of the United Kingdom. While federalism has contributed to the administrative and legislative fragmentation of areas of jurisdiction in the United States, the cases of Switzerland and Germany demonstrate that federalism is not an *explanation*, for here—in spite of federalism—supervision and legislation are almost as strongly centralized as in the unitary United Kingdom.[5] A study written twenty years ago has already shown how federal systems could develop very different forms of regulation for the banking sector (Lehner, Schubert, and Geile 1983), conclusions which, as this study has demonstrated, are still valid today.[6]

[5] In the Federal Republic of Germany, legislation dealing with bank regulation issues is exclusively dealt with on the federal level, creating great institutional similarities with the British system.

[6] One has to refute, however, the hypothesis voiced by Lehner, Schubert, and Geile (1983: 373) that the differences between the banking systems examined by their study (Germany, Switzerland, Canada, and the United States) "can in their historical genesis be considered to be a product of state regulation". While it may be correct for the cases studied by those authors, in a generalizable sense it is not, for the British case study demonstrates that a highly segmented banking market can also develop historically in an environment *without* any banking regulation.

If one moves from the level of constitutional political variables to that of party systems and party dominance, then again we find relatively little explanation for developments in banking regulation. This is most clearly the case with the two-party systems in Britain and the United States, which despite this similarity have seen divergent legal and regulatory dynamics produce very different policy outcomes. Conversely, the predominant form of party system co-varies with the type of economic system (coordinated versus liberal market economies; see below), making it more plausible that any effects are the result of the latter variable rather than that of any party-political dynamic. For an approach towards the regulation of banking systems based upon party-political motivations has not become apparent in any of the case studies conducted in this book. This could theoretically be because variations within the group of four countries is limited with respect to these variables—with two cases dominated by conservative governments, and one each by centrist and liberal governments, a case involving a Social Democratic dominated government is missing. However, both in Germany and the United Kingdom, there have been periods during the time span under investigation in which parties of the left have been in power, and they were without any major impact on banking and banking regulation policy.[7] Further case studies also demonstrate that states dominated by Social Democratic governments (such as Sweden, or Spain in the 1980s)[8] have not developed any great programmatic alternatives to the approaches pursued in the four countries of this study.

One plausible reason for this observation is the fact that this policy field has been characterized by a relatively low level of politicization and has been primarily considered to be a "technical" matter for experts (see Busch 2001: 320f.). This is at least the case as long as massive losses incurred by certain depositor groups can be avoided, since a party could otherwise be tempted to politicize such a situation to further its electoral advantage. However, this has not taken place in any of the case studies examined here.[9] The comparatively high-level of politicization of this topic in the United States did not result in major party-political conflict, while in the Swiss case the repeated dissent displayed by the Social Democratic Party (which demanded a clear tightening of state regulations) did not lead to any policy changes because of the political weakness of the centre-left in Switzerland.

---

[7] In the case of the Federal Republic of Germany, this even included the crucial period around the *Herstatt Bank* crisis.

[8] See the studies by Tranøy (2001) and Pérez (2001).

[9] At this point, it is important to mention that even in the cited Spanish and Swedish cases in which massive losses were caused by problems in the banking system, these losses were covered by state compensation payments so that the creditors of failed banks did not have to suffer much damage. The resulting costs were therefore spread across the general public, decreasing the political damage caused by these scandals.

Finally, a last key political variable is the impact of European integration. As the case studies have shown, members of the European Union such as the United Kingdom and Germany have indeed been influenced by that factor since the growing number of European directives dealing with this policy field have had to be incorporated in national legislation.[10] Along with the resulting growth in the amount of legislation, the creation of the single European market has also fostered further liberalization. Yet this effect, though in a weaker form, has also played an important role in banking policy in the United States and Switzerland. Even in these two states which do not participate in European integration, the actions of the European Union have had an impact on policy-making on a national level. In Switzerland, the legal package known as *Swisslex* (originally *Eurolex*) was enacted despite this country's failure to join the European Economic Area (EEA) in order to make Swiss regulations more "compatible with Europe".[11] And even in the United States, directives of the European Union have forced American legislators into action when dealing with such matters as reciprocal market access.[12] Though these developments, to use Swiss terminology, represent a form of "Autonomous Convergence", European integration has had effects even on non-members, with the difference between them and "full members" of the European Union being not very large.

Towards the end of this section, two further points should be mentioned. Firstly, the case studies illustrate how several of the variables described in this section can have very different effects depending on the national, political, or economic context. Such contexts and the interaction of variables should therefore be a central element of any comparative analysis of political systems. While federalism has had no effects on Swiss regulatory bodies because of their centralized structure, when it comes to Swiss legislation the federal system of government plays a crucial role in policy-making, dealing with issues such as the abolition of the stamp duty and the transfer of regulatory powers from the cantonal to the national level. Similarly, the symmetry of competences between parliamentary chambers has in the United States led to deadlock while in Switzerland the result was consensus and compromise. This leads, secondly, to the importance of informal practices which are difficult to "capture" exactly in variables. For the last example given, the general practice of consensus and *Konkordanz* pervading Switzerland is likely to be the decisive explanatory variable—but such a "general practice" variable is hard to operationalize. A similarly illustrative case is the different attitudes concerning the acceptance of political decisions, once taken, between the United States and

---

[10] See, as an illustration, the German case study and in particular Figure 4.1.
[11] See p. 197 of this study.   [12] See p. 64 of this study.

the United Kingdom. In the United States, a tradition of conflict-oriented and legalistic political behaviour is dominant, leading opponents of change to repeatedly challenge government initiatives in the courts and Congress every step of the way. By contrast, in the United Kingdom a form of "advance compliance" is usually practiced by the main political actors, which has often led them to accept the demands of a government even if it was not (yet) backed by legislation—as exemplified by reactions to the reform initiatives of 1974 and 1997.[13]

We can conclude our consideration of the political system-level variables by saying that they do not provide a strong or relatively cogent explanation of either why or how political processes and their particular impact on banking policy have emerged differently in each of the case studies presented here. This is put in particularly stark relief when compared to the perspective on the policy networks at the beginning of this chapter.

7.3 "ANGLO-SAXON" AND "RHENISH" CAPITALISM IN COMPARISON

In light of the conclusions reached above, were the different forms of market capitalism that existed in these different countries under examination of any relevance to the explanation of banking policy? In Section 1.4, the economic systems of the United States and the United Kingdom were described as adhering to a form of "uncoordinated" or "liberal" market capitalism while the German and Swiss economies were considered to be more "coordinated" market economies. Since the differences between these two forms of market economy are strongly reflected in the financial system, one could expect the similarities *within* these two groups to be substantial and the differences *between them* marked.

Differences between the "Anglo-Saxon" and the "Rhenish" forms of capitalism[14] have already emerged in the section above dealing with policy networks in general and the structure of interest representation as well as associations' roles in policy implementation in particular. Whereas "Rhenish" economies are characterized by centralized and cooperative banking associations playing

---

[13] See Sections 5.4.1 and 5.4.3 of this study.
[14] The terms developed in Albert (1993) are used here for greater contrast and clarity. The basic differentiation remains between the term "liberal market economies" (LMEs) and "coordinated market economies" (CMEs) used by Soskice (1999). For the cases considered in this study, the two classifications produce the same groups, with the LMEs being the Anglo-Saxon and the CMEs being the Rhenish cases.

an important role in policy implementation, their counterparts in "Anglo-Saxon" economies display highly pluralist networks of associations with complex and at times antagonistic relationships with regulatory bodies. Since the structure of representative associations, as part of the wider system of industrial relations within a policy field, is a constituent component of Soskice's typology, this result is not surprising.

Yet, how great are the similarities within these groups? The similarities between the German and Swiss cases seem considerable, even beyond the characteristics of associational networks and their interaction with the executive. Both countries have had centralized and formalized regulatory systems as well as a legal framework covering all key areas relevant to the banking sector since the 1930s. From the early 1970s to the early 1990s these banking laws and directives have been adapted to changing circumstances, primarily in the form of reactive initiatives rather than fundamental alterations of the banking system. The amount of state resources used has remained relatively low—a further commonality of the "Rhenish" systems, as is the reserve ability to threaten stronger state interference should sectoral self-regulation lead to undesirable results.

A clear contrast is found, however, if we search for commonalities between the two countries with "Anglo-Saxon" capitalism. As was already pointed out in Section 1.4, the "liberal" market economies of the United Kingdom and the United States show great similarities when it comes to economic system variables,[15] yet remarkably few when it comes to their political system variables (see Table 1.1). What is more, the two countries show in fact substantial differences in the political sphere. The analysis of sectoral policy networks has also provided evidence of such substantial differences between the two "Anglo-Saxon" case studies. This is also the case when it comes to policy outputs, in which decades of legislative deadlock hindering reform in the United States have had little in common with the ability of British governments to quickly change the (particularly institutional) parameters of the sectoral regulatory system. Moreover, the great disparities between the starting positions of these two countries at the start of the 1970s are of equal importance, since the British system was largely informal and steered through clubby consultation while its American counterpart was controlled through highly detailed regulations. Though the liberalization of the American banking system and the codification of the British regulatory framework have brought both sides closer, as these case studies have demonstrated, over a quarter of a century after these changes had begun to take shape, great differences remain

---

[15] The one concrete exception to this rule is the level of concentration of the banking market, which is considerable in the United Kingdom and very low in the United States.

between the United Kingdom and the United States when it comes to banking regulation.

We can conclude that the countries which are so often lumped together as "Anglo-Saxon" are in reality very different from one another. Superficial similarities in the economic system hide significant underlying differences in political systems and sectoral mechanisms which have been shown to have far greater relevance to the analysis of the policy area examined in this study. The differentiation between "coordinated" and "uncoordinated" or "liberal" market economies must therefore be considered of limited value to the analysis conducted here.

8

Conclusion: National Institutions as Filters of Globalization

The question "what are the consequences of globalization for the nation state's capacity to act" was the cause and the starting point for the investigation presented in this book. In the concluding chapter, we shall now return to it.

As pointed out in Chapter 1, the existing literature presents us with two starkly different positions on this.[1] One—starting from considerations and modelling assumptions grounded in economic theory—expects nation state policies to largely converge. It argues that increasing economic openness results in behavioural changes in firms, interest groups, and national governments. Whoever can most credibly advance the threat of exit will increase their negotiation power. Since in the financial markets barriers against international mobility have been most comprehensively removed compared to other areas of economic activity, it will be owners of capital who assert their positions; governments, eager to offer the best possible conditions to firms, will therefore adapt their policies to the latter's demands. In the policy area of banking regulation we would, therefore, if this position were correct, expect to see a very high degree of harmonization of state regulations, and of the mechanisms for implementation. In addition, the motives outlined above should be prominently visible as guiding policy in national political debates, and substantial structural change should be taking place among national economic, but above all financial systems, towards a unitary model. Should differences between national conditions for firms continue to persist, we would expect to see exit by firms migrating to places where they can conduct business on more advantageous terms.

The counterposition to the convergence hypothesis is marked by a position which originates analytically from the differences and persistence of national policy styles and institutional arrangements. As the latter are characterized by a high degree of stability, according to this view, no fundamental unification is to be expected even through the common challenges of globalization. Rather, it is argued, the national systems will react each in their specific ways to the

---

[1] Cf. Section 1.2.

new circumstances, which means that assimilation can happen by chance but is not to be expected in principle. Thus in banking regulation we should largely see the opposite of the consequences described above: no convergence of state regulations, but system specific reactions to the challenges of globalization, and above all no assimilation of institutional rules. Domestic political discourse should focus on country-specific problems, and there should be no exit by firms for reasons of regional competition.

8.1 CONVERGENCE OR DIVERGENCE?

Financial markets have been among the sectors most exposed to globalization. In recent decades, they have been undergoing four simultaneous revolutions: the transition to flexible exchange rates; closer integration through technological innovations of telecommunications and computing; substantive innovation of new, highly sophisticated financial instruments; and the spread of deregulation (Lamfalussy 1985; Kindleberger 1987). As a consequence, state regulation in this sector has faced enormous challenges, and this—together with rather different starting positions, it was argued at the beginning of this book—makes it an excellent test case for the competing hypotheses outlined above.

So, looking back on the detailed case studies conducted in this book, the question is: Which of the two scenarios presented above describes the developments encountered best? Do national regulations converge? And if so, does this happen as a consequence of active, democratically legitimated design, or is such change—involuntarily—enforced by the functioning of international markets? Or does, alternatively, state regulation not converge, but rather remain on the tracks determined by past decisions—and if so, because of a conscious decision or rather because of an inability (for whatever reason) to adapt to new circumstances? Depending on how these questions are answered, there are four possible policy outcomes that are schematically summarized in Figure 8.1.

However, looking at these questions in the light of the results of the case studies makes a sweeping answer very difficult. None of the questions can easily be either comprehensively accepted or dismissed. In the context of empirical academic research on convergence, this should not come as a great surprise. Given the centrality of the debate about globalization and its consequences in recent years, many scholars have conducted empirical studies across a wide range of issues, but so far a homogeneous picture about the outcome has failed to emerge. As a recent survey of the field has found, there is

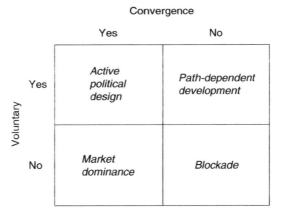

Figure 8.1. Typology of possible policy outcomes

large variation with respect to the regions, policy fields, and time periods covered, and as a consequence, there is no "convergence in convergence studies", neither concerning methodology nor results (Heichel, Pape, and Sommerer 2005: esp. 834). A study also covering banking regulation in three of the four countries considered in the present study concludes that the result is one of "convergence within national diversity" (Lütz 2004). However, this formula is not really a clear result, and the author's further distinction according to "outcome of regulatory reform", "timing of regulatory effort", and "extent of institutional change" (ibid. 184, 186) seems of little help as these three categories have no common frame tying them together. In order to improve on this, we suggest differentiating the results of the present study according to the three dimensions of *policy*, *politics*, and *polity*, thus covering the *content* of regulation, the *process* of political interaction, and the *institutional* development (if any). This should allow a more fine-grained analysis which preserves the wide range of empirical detail.

Concerning the dimension of *policy* (i.e. regulatory content), our case studies show a significant trend of convergence. Compared to the situation in the mid-1970s, countries found themselves much closer to each other in the late 1990s regarding the codification of regulations, and with respect to liberalization. But even beyond these major trends, there is assimilation in the details of supervisory regulation. These are largely owed to the standardizations introduced by the so-called *Basel process*, the cooperation of the central banks and banking regulation authorities of the G-10 countries and several additional states under the auspices of the Bank for International Settlements (BIS). This process elevated banks' own capital to be the central regulatory parameter, and it set common standards for minimum capital. But while these standards, which were agreed in 1988 after many years of detailed negotiations (and which have been updated several times since), did produce a common framework for national supervisory rules,[2] they clearly did not lead to a perfect convergence of national rules. Since the standards of the *Basel Committee* are only a voluntary accord, their compliance cannot be enforced, and individual states have considerable freedom in determining the precise definitions.[3] If, therefore, the analytical focus is not only on the agreements between states, but also on their implementation, we have to state that the situation is more aptly described as reduced but continuing heterogeneity between the countries (Bernauer 2000: 183). It is, not least, the convening of the "Basel II" round of negotiations in June 1999 that confirms the continuing regulatory dissimilarities between countries.

The big international banks are among those who most keenly feel the continuing disparities in banking regulation between countries—for they are costly to them. Former Deutsche Bank CEO Rolf Breuer, for example, criticized how the existence of inconsistent regulatory demands and the different treatment of identical facts even within the Euro zone's member states led to distortions of competition. It caused banks substantial compliance efforts, which is why in his view supervision should be shifted to the European level.[4] And the commission that prepared the "Swisslex" pack of legal changes in Switzerland (which also covered banking regulation issues) opted in 1994 for the preparation of specific Swiss solutions rather than the adoption of international rules "in view of the fact that the harmonization of international rules is still very much imperfect" (Lutz 1995: 480). Even within the European Union, expert assessments deny the existence of a "level playing field", since the directives consciously leave room for national implementations, and different "opt-out" clauses and the effects of the tax system cause further divergences (Molyneux 1996: 259–64).

Summing up this aspect, we can say that there is considerable convergence with respect to regulatory content over the period under consideration, but that it is far from perfect. Significant differences continue to exist in this area, and relevant actors agree that this is so.

---

[2] On the process leading up to the *Basel Accord* see Kapstein (1992); for an analysis of it from a game-theoretic point of view see Genschel and Plümper (1997). For a summary of the various levels required for the different categories of own capital and details about their updates over the period covered by this book see, e.g. Bernauer (2000: 175–80).

[3] Cf. Molyneux (1996: 264) and Bernauer (2000: 181).

[4] Cf. *Frankfurter Allgemeine Zeitung*, 18 Feb. 2000: 4. Bundesbank board member Edgar Meister, who was at the time in charge of banking regulation, however, spoke against such a shifting of responsibility in an interview some time later. He argued that "there are different national approaches to supervision—and they work" (*Süddeutsche Zeitung*, 17 Jan. 2002: 21).

Regarding the dimension of process (*politics*), we find practically no discernible convergence. The hypotheses stating that growing economic openness would shift the domestic power structure and lead to increased influence by capital owners due to this being the most mobile factor of production (Frieden and Rogowski 1996), which would lead to a "convergence towards an agenda set by investors" (Cohen 1996: 288) find no corroboration in the case studies. Liberalizations can fail due to resistance by parts of the capital side (as demonstrated in the case of the United States) or be pushed through against the will of the banks (as the abolishing of cartels has shown in Switzerland).[5] Assuming homogeneous interests across the financial industry must therefore seem highly questionable, and even if these stylized facts are popular and widely accepted in the literature, they should more often be "confronted with reality" (Busch 2007a). In doing so, we find that the national systems of interest intermediation work in very different ways (see on this in more detail Section 7.1) and have proven highly stable over time. If at all, we find changes only in details. Thus for Switzerland it is said that in spite of the stability of the institutions in the policy network the *handling* of domestic decision-making processes had changed as a result of pressures emanating from a changed international environment. More particularly, there was a lower degree of concertation, a changing role of the government, a more polarized parliament, and new forms of use of the referendum (Mach, Häusermann, and Papadopoulos 2001). But on the one hand, the changes described are small if compared to the difference between the case of Switzerland and, for example, the United States, so that we cannot meaningfully speak of convergence here; on the other hand, the developments described could also be caused by the institutional changes in the Swiss legislative process, especially the strengthening of the role of parliament (cf. Section 6.3.3). Since the encompassing consultation mechanisms of this country as a small, highly open economy serve above all—apart from the management of political–cultural tensions[6]—to enable adjustment to the swiftly changing circumstances of international markets,[7] a substantial change of course would seem unlikely here.

The result of a high degree of stability in the political decision-making processes can, on the one hand, be explained by the stability of the underlying

[5] Similar things can be said about Spain, where the postponement of more competition in the financial sector by many years also contradicts the hypothesis put forward by Frieden and Rogowski. They argue that liberalization in formerly interventionist states will be caused by economic and political pressure for more efficient capital markets. In Spain, however, increasing the monetary policy steering capacity of the central bank was the focus of reforms, and the banking oligopoly was consciously left intact to let banks have additional profits with which to fund the restructuring (Pérez 2001).

[6] See on this the analyses by Gerhard Lehmbruch, esp. Lehmbruch (1967).

[7] On this see the seminal work by Katzenstein (1985).

institutions (see below) and, on the other hand, by the fact that in every country there is a multitude of political issues vying for influence on the national political agenda. In this process, the "pressure" emanating from globalization—which is a comparatively slow and long-term process—proves to be relatively low. It is only in cases of acute crisis that the issue of banking regulation can claim an important place on the national political agenda, as the four case studies show. During normal times, the topic is characterized by *low politics* and largely delegated to experts—and both aspects are unlikely to make headlines.

Lastly, on the institutional dimension of the *polity*, there are no indicators for convergence. Instead, the institutional components of the national policy networks in banking regulation prove to be highly stable and resistant to change. This is particularly evident in the case of the United States, where several attempts to reduce the number of involved state authorities in this policy area (or to organize their respective responsibilities in a more logical and coherent fashion) have failed. In Germany and Switzerland, too, there were no institutional changes, and no attempts to introduce any, during the period under investigation.[8] The only exception to this emerging picture of steadiness is the case of the United Kingdom, where a new supervisory authority was created in the late 1990s that not only won the banking regulation duties from the *Bank of England*, but also took over all other financial sector supervision. This created a new institutional model completely different from all the others surveyed in this study, which is why there can be no talk of convergence towards a common model. Also, it has to be said that the British reform was triggered by the two bank crises of the 1990s (*BCCI* and *Barings Bank*) and their handling by the *Bank of England*—and not by international (market) pressure. And it took place in the country where political system parameters would most have led us to expect it.

---

[8] In early 2002, however, there was an institutional change in Germany with the introduction of a single regulator for all financial sectors, the *Bundesanstalt für Finanzdienstleistungsaufsicht* (BaFin). It took over the tasks of BAKred as well as the supervisory authorities for insurance and securities. If this, at first sight, looks like an emulation of the British model, a closer look raises doubts about such an interpretation: on the one hand, the trigger for the reform was the (failed) attempt by the Bundesbank to take over banking regulation completely—after it had largely lost its monetary policy tasks due to the introduction of European Monetary Union; on the other hand, the three predecessor institutions continue to exist in the three organizational pillars of the BaFin (supplemented by three cross-section departments, the only true innovation), and even the geographical separation between Bonn (banking and insurance) and Frankfurt (securities) is being held up. This differs considerably from the approach taken in the United Kingdom where there was a clean break (organizationally as well as geographically) when the FSA was set up (cf. Section 5.4.3). Whether Germany will manage to build a truly integrated single financial supervisor remains to be seen. The argument emphasizing the importance of nationally specific developments, however, is strengthened rather than weakened by the German reform.

Summing up this part of the analysis, we can say that there is much support for rejecting the sweeping variety, described above, of the globalization literature convergence hypothesis. While there are substantial assimilations across our cases concerning the content of regulations, there are none in the processes and institutions of banking regulation policy. In addition, the political debates in the countries covered are only to a very small degree characterized by the *frame* (Schön and Rein 1994) of international competitiveness, while the concrete debates about legislation and reform are mostly dominated by nationally specific topics.[9] And even in the case of the United States (as the most restrictively regulated case) there have been no *exit* decisions by powerful banks, as the sweeping convergence hypotheses would have led us to expect. Even though regulatory conditions would have been much more liberal in other countries, the aspect of market access obviously counted more heavily than that.

The pressure of increased economic openness therefore clearly does not lead to automatic convergence of the national policies, processes, and institutions. Instead, the concrete developments are influenced by a multitude of nationally specific contingencies that elude a common analysis and description. It seems as if this globalization literature convergence hypothesis will share the fate of its 1950s and 1960s predecessors. Back then, in the tradition of sociological theories of modernization, the cause for convergence was not seen in an opening up to foreign economic competition, but in technological development: industrial societies wishing to provide their citizens with the benefits of both increasing wealth and continued defendability, it was argued, would have to move on the same path of technological–organizational development of the production process, and thus all distinctions between systems (even between capitalist and socialist societies) would be eliminated.[10] As theoretically compelling and convincing the theoretical deduction of this argument—much like today—may have been, the 1970s and 1980s refuted them through comparative empirical research by sociologists of industry who found fundamental differences in the organization of production in similarly developed countries and thus "national diversity in industrial relations".[11] We can therefore conclude that even if countries consciously aim to achieve the same goals, this must not mean using the same paths to get there. A good recent example for that is the recent comparative case of the Central and East European countries striving to join the EU. Even though the European Union explicitly

---

[9] Examples are the issues of money laundering in Switzerland or the debates about the right to access to banking in Germany before the sixth reform of the KWG.

[10] See, e.g. the writings of Raymond Aron or the study by Kerr et al. (1960).

[11] Thus the title of the study by Dore (1973). See also the contributions to the edited volume by Goldthorpe (1984*b*), and especially Goldthorpe (1984*a*).

encouraged (and furthered) convergence, detailed studies show that complex logics of action together with institutional and strategic choices, rather unexpectedly, led to different results rather than convergence (Beyer 1999). And analyses of European Union politics show that here as well common policies are strongly influenced by factors such as national administrative traditions, leading to substantial differences in implementation (Knill 1998).

But if—as has emerged in this section so far—the convergence hypothesis in its strong, sweeping version has to be refuted, does that mean we find support for the competing hypothesis according to which nationally specific, institutional, and historical factors shape the states' reactions to globalization? Here, too, we have to enter some substantial qualifications. For countries clearly did not all try to go their own ways to solve the problems created by the new challenges—rather, a first reaction was to try to do so together through international cooperation via the *Basel Committee*. And even though the respective negotiations took fifteen years to reach an agreement, they eventually created a common regulatory framework demanding in some parts substantial changes to nationally ingrained ways of regulation.[12] In spite of the considerable (and continuing) differences in implementation described above we have to state that with respect to the content of regulation there has been a substantial assimilation of national strategies. However, regarding the two other dimensions (processes and institutions), the divergence hypothesis fares much better and seems overall better suited to explaining the events in the case studies in a comprehensive way.

8.2 HISTORY, INSTITUTIONS, AND PATH DEPENDENCE

Having established stability as the dominant feature of our case studies in the last section, we will now look at how the causes for that stability can be explained. The theoretical background of the divergence hypothesis[13] is rooted in theories of path dependence, transaction costs, and institutional economics (cf. Section 1.2). This section aims to review the case studies' findings through that lens, argue for the importance of a historical perspective, and to contrast the approach chosen here with other possible ways of analysing the impact of domestic variables in the area of banking regulation.

[12] Many of these changes, however, were implemented through the processs of Europeanization. See especially the German case, Section 4.4.2.

[13] This is a name chosen for convenience and contrast to the *convergence* hypothesis. However, it would be more apt to speak of a hypothesis expecting constant or increasing difference—for it does not necessarily imply an increase in divergence.

Growing out of studies in the areas of public administration, micro- and institutional economics as well as political science, the approach of historical institutionalism is based on a number of shared understandings:[14] historical developments are important, as are timing and sequencing;[15] institutions— "the rules of the game in a society, or, more formally, [...] the humanly devised constraints that shape human interaction" (North 1990: 3)—play a central role; they work according to established patterns; and mutually reinforce each other.[16] This mutual reinforcement is brought about by four specific factors, namely high fixed or start-up costs; learning effects; coordination effects; and adaptive expectations (Arthur 1994: 112). Originally aimed at the analysis of technological development, this insight was adapted to the analysis of institutions more generally (North 1990: 95), who argued that an "interdependent web of an institutional matrix" produces massive reinforcement effects.

Using these concepts, the high degree of institutional stability and the patterns of interaction in the policy networks found in the case studies can be explained very well. Historical developments thus led to specific institutional structures in each of the countries, and produced incentives for particular patterns of political and economic behaviour which, in turn, influenced the strategic choices of the political and economic actors. Within these national parameters, persistent strategies of action emerge which react according to the logic of the situation. Actors build routines to react to situations, and as a consequence patterns of interaction arise. This, in turn, generates stability (not least of expectations) and lowers transaction costs, but at the same time limits the room available for solutions: "The basic structure of the national state creates options that delimit solutions within society" (Zysman 1994).

John Zysman was one of the first scholars to work on the relationship between institutional features of financial markets and government policy (Zysman 1983). Much further research has been done on that relationship in the last years, and has confirmed that strong relations exist between the structure of a country's financial system, the characteristics of its industries, and the growth and investment of these industries (e.g. Carlin and Mayer 2003). Changes in the circumstances under which these financial institutions operate will therefore have a direct impact on these relationships, and with it the prospect of growth and ultimately welfare. Financial systems (and with them countries and governments) will therefore have distinct preferences about changes on the international level that impact on them. Such arguments

---

[14] See on this Waarden (1995), Zysman (1994), Thelen (1999), and Pierson (2004).

[15] The latter means that the same event at a later place in a sequence of events can unfold different consequences than at an earlier one.

[16] Economists talk of *positive returns to scale* here or of *positive feedback effects*.

and the empirical work underlying them link the abstract theories discussed above to the concrete policy area investigated in this study. They have been fruitfully expanded into theories about "comparative institutional advantage" to explain "varieties of capitalism" (Hall and Soskice 2001*a*) in recent years and point to the complex interactions that go on between the financial sector and the rest of the economy. They can both explain persistent differences between economically otherwise highly integrated countries, and they point to the importance of a historical perspective. Historical experiences inform many actors' positions, and they are ignored by scholars at their peril. An example for such a perspective disregarding the historical dimension is the study by Rosenbluth and Schaap (2003) that undertakes to explain "the domestic politics of banking regulation". Since the study includes a part that looks at three of the four countries covered here (the United States, the United Kingdom, and Germany), but arrives at rather different conclusions, a few remarks may be in place about the differences in approaches.

Rosenbluth and Schaap's study is based on regression analyses for 22 countries in which they find support for their hypothesis that financial regulatory choices are grounded in domestic politics. Specifically, they argue that the electoral system (majoritarian or proportional representation) has a significant effect (via incentives for politicians) on whether banks or consumers pay for financial system stability (ibid. 309). The core of the argument is that in majoritarian systems a smaller group of electors can bring about a change in government, and that therefore in such systems politicians will adopt policies that favour customers over banks (assuming, as the authors do, that this is the only available choice). To check their findings, Rosenbluth and Schaap also look more closely at four countries: the three mentioned above, and Japan.[17] It is here that their work really becomes questionable. A table they present (p. 326, table 7) will be rather counterintuitive to readers of the present book: it states, among other things, that interest rates and product variety in German banking are regulated, while both are classified as unregulated in the case of the United States. The authors seem to draw their knowledge on Germany from a single book chapter plus an interview with the US Federal Reserve Bank, and give no sources for their summary of the US situation. They make no use of the easily available and detailed data on most of the world's banking regulation systems assembled with the help of the World Bank (Barth, Nolle, and Rice 1997; Barth et al. 2003; Barth, Caprio, and Levine 2006); they ignore the fact that for almost all of their period of investigation (1978–98) there was banking product regulation in the United States; and they are simply wrong in their reference to a "1967 law [that] sets limits on interest rates for

[17] Both authors are Japan specialists.

deposits" (ibid. 329) in the case of Germany.[18] In conclusion, one probably has to say that the authors' ambition to provide "microfoundations" for the *varieties of capitalism* approach is a worthy one, but that they end up really making the case for empirical knowledge of countries being a good thing when engaging in comparative research. As the present study shows, the United States and the United Kingdom exhibit vastly different policy dynamics and outcomes in the field of banking regulation, even though they both have majoritarian electoral systems. And the case studies presented here show in detail why these differences exist—because a variety of political and economic actors faced the incentives they faced. To ignore this wealth of data in favour of some brave hypothesizing, and to expect a linear relationship between one institutional variable and a policy outcome that results from complex interactions cannot be the best approach to research.

Returning to the more theoretical considerations developed at the beginning of this section, we can say that an equlibrium solution, once found, can be expected to be characterized by stability through inertia as long as the benefits of stability are not outweighed by high costs of policy failures and crises (Pierson 2000: 263). Even a considerable degree of dysfunctionality does not necessarily lead to fundamental reform, as the case study about the United States has demonstrated: here inertia prevailed even in the face of considerable costs caused by the existing regulatory system.

However, the argument about path dependency should not be misconstrued as one arguing for states to move powerlessly along the tracks laid by past decisions for it is the combination of stable paths and critical junctures that is characteristic of the approach of historical institutionalism (Thelen 1999: 387). At such junctures, rather far-reaching adjustments can be made. An example would be the banking crises of the early 1930s that lead to fundamental changes (both in institutional terms as in regulatory content) in three of the four countries under examination. But such fundamental changes, of course, are ambiguous precisely because of the costs caused by having to "re-learn", which means forgoing the established increasing returns.

But crises, while heightening the probability of such change, the more the bigger they are, need not always lead to such fundamental re-orientation. The preference for stability can explain why the reaction to smaller crises is usually one of moderate measures that are consonant with the established equilibrium. It is especially interesting against the background of theories about the propelling power of international influences to note that in the four

---

[18] In fact, the law (the KWG) dates from 1961, and in 1967 the last interest rate regulations were lifted (see page 85 above). Germany was thus one of the first countries to liberalize this aspect of the financial markets, while the United States was one of the last.

case studies considered it was *exclusively* domestic banking crises that ever triggered activities in this policy area. Depending on national context, these activities then took different forms:

- In Germany, the reaction to the *Herstatt* crisis was a substantial increase in self-regulation (albeit only after the threat of state intervention in the absence of a forthcoming agreement).

- In Switzerland, the "Chiasso Scandal" also led to an increase in self-regulation, but a persistent politicization of the topic ensued because one influential political party (the Social Democrats) was not content with the solution.

- In the United Kingdom, reactions to crises came solely from the state or the *Bank of England*. Associations and the big banks did not advance their own solutions since they did not perceive that to be their business.

- In the United States, even the deep and costly S&L crisis could not break up the entrenched positions that had been blocking each other for decades about liberalization. Here as well there were no initiatives for self-regulation from the industry, even if the reason for this is more likely the competitive relationship between the associations than the perception of their role in the political system.

The arguments put forward above can now explain why national institutions play such an important role in the case studies, and why the reactions to the common challenge of globalization differed so much between these countries. National institutions, we can summarize the argument, work like *filters of globalization*. They process similar, or even the same, problems each in their specific ways, resulting in characteristic policy outcomes and dynamics in different countries.

8.3 THE CASE OF THE MISSING MODEL

So far we have argued that the absence of convergence in the institutional and process dimensions of banking regulation policy is above all owed to mechanisms of path dependence and mutual reinforcement. However, other policy areas exist which exhibit similar characteristics but have nevertheless undergone substantial change and almost complete convergence—most prominently in the case of monetary policy and the independence of the central bank from government interference in conducting it. Here, over the last decade and a half, a massive move towards a uniform model has taken place, and since this is a subject area that is in many ways very close to the subject of banking regulation, it seems important to ask why such differences exist between the two fields, and how we can explain them. This section will try to advance an explanation for this puzzle.

To anyone who has read or even only browsed through the 250 pages of the "Basel II" regulatory framework (Basel Committee on Banking Supervision 2004) it may have been surprising to find pages and pages of detailed formulae, definitions, and process descriptions, but practically no references whatsoever to the differences between national banking systems and their supervisory structures. To the parties negotiating that agreement, it would seem, all banking systems and their supervisory structures looked very much alike. Empirically this is not so, as the impressive amounts of data assembled by various authors over time demonstrate, most recently the volume by Barth, Caprio, and Levine (2006) which collects detailed information for more than 150 countries.[19] They find—among other things—that 50 per cent of all countries do not offer deposit protection schemes; that $\frac{5}{6}$ of the surveyed countries have a single banking regulator, and about $\frac{1}{6}$ has multiple regulators; that the central bank is the sole supervisor in about half of the countries (sixty-nine), one among several in twenty-one countries, and plays no role in supervision in sixty-one countries (ibid. 84–102). Given that well-functioning banking systems play an important role for economic growth, it might be expected that (with the help of economic theory) a set of "best practices" would have been established and used to guide the design of international rules such as the Basel II agreement.

However, looking into this question in more detail one finds that knowledge about what "works best" in banking regulation is severely limited. There are not many studies that empirically address the issue to find out whether best practices exist, and some which do suffer from deficiencies in the operationalization of concepts.[20] Furthermore, their approach is more of an "all-you-can-eat" nature which tries to maximize the number of observations but disregards the price that has to be paid in terms of comparability of the cases.[21] It is

---

[19] For previous such efforts, see Barth, Nolle, and Rice (1997) and Barth et al. (2003).

[20] An example would be that of "strength of supervisory regulation" in Heinemann and Schüler (2004) which simply adds together the total (normalized) budget for supervision, the number of on-site examinations of banks, the number of professional supervisors, and the supervisory power of the regulatory authority. Such an operationalization will fail to grasp adequately cases like the "delegated" supervisions described for Switzerland and Germany in the present study.

[21] Carlin and Mayer (2003: 197) make a substantive point in addition to that methodological point, but with the same result of warning against such unconsidered pooling. They argue that since capital is scarce in developing countries, monitoring costs are low relative to the cost of capital, and therefore different forms of finance will be chosen in developed and developing countries. "This suggests that developed and developing countries should not be pooled."

perhaps partially owing to that design choice that these studies produce only weak or instable results (cf. Barth et al. 2003; Heinemann and Schüler 2004). In addition to the empirical impasse, economic theory has so far not been able to agree on a theoretical "best model". Indeed, there continues to be a deep division between different camps.[22] One side advocates the view that there are significant market failures in banking which can be ameliorated through good supervision. They often argue in favour of restricting bank activities and forbidding links between banks and industry, focusing on such arguments as conflicts of interest; too much appetite for risk; complexity and the disadvantages it brings for monitoring; and the disadvantages information asymmetries may bring for customers. On the other hand, there are those who argue that regulation, above all, brings about "capture" by interested parties such as bureaucrats and politicians, and thus serves to lower efficiency of the banking system rather than protect against crises. It is private interests rather than public interests that are being served by regulation.

The situation in banking regulation is thus characterized by both empirical and theoretical ignorance: there is neither empirical knowledge about what "works best", nor is there a scholarly consensus about the approach that could be taken. If we contrast this with the situation in monetary policy, we can explain the difference between the presence of (institutional and other) convergence in that policy area, and the absence thereof in banking regulation. For in monetary policy, there are both an empirical evidence about the "ingredients" necessary to deliver low inflation and a scholarly consensus about the (institutional) mechanisms which bring it about. Economic and political science research conducted after the bout of inflation following the breakdown of the Bretton Woods system and the oil price shocks of the 1970s demonstrated that countries with independent central banks systematically produced lower rates of inflation than countries in which monetary policy was being commanded by political interests of the government of the day (Alesina 1988; Alesina and Summers 1993; Busch 1995).[23] And at the same time, economic theory was capable of producing an explanation for this phenomenon: focusing on questions of "dynamic inconsistency", it was argued that governments faced a tension between their electoral interests and those of the economy that would systematically increase inflation unless operational control over monetary policy was given to independent central bankers

---

[22] See e.g. Barth, Caprio, and Levine (2006: 21–46) for a detailed exposition of the "public interest" and "private interest" views of regulation with numerous links to the respective literatures.

[23] For a recent attempt to transfer this approach to the analysis of financial regulation agencies and analyse their political independence, see Quintyn et al. (2007).

who were free of such considerations.[24] This perspective gained the status of an orthodoxy, and central bankers across the world subscribed to it to such an extent that they served in the respective literature as prime examples of an "epistemic community" (Haas 1992).

Summing up this section we can thus add a word of caution to the above explanation of institutional inertia and increasing returns of existing networks creating stability in the policy area of banking regulation. We have seen that convergence can be brought about in spite of these variables through the influence of ideational factors–the presence of empirical and theoretical evidence of a "best practice".[25] So far, it is missing in the field of banking regulation.[26]

8.4 CONCLUSION

This study has focused on the nation state's capacity to act under conditions of globalization by analysing a specific policy area. The result is that the sweeping convergence hypothesis advanced in parts of the globalization literature has to be refuted in this case. We thus confirm results of past studies of financial market regulation which concluded that global forces contribute more to a reinforcement of national differences than their convergence (Vogel 1996) and that the underlying financial systems and their regulatory structures continue to exhibit considerable differences (Schaberg 1999; Sauvé and Scheuer 1999; Barth, Caprio, and Levine 2006).

The nation state's capacity to act, it was argued at the beginning of this book, cannot be assessed in general. Rather, this has to be done on a policy-by-policy basis. The present study in addition makes clear that such an assessment indeed needs to be made in a country-specific way. Looking at the cases considered, in the United States state capacity in banking regulation has to be classified as low.[27] On the other hand, it was undoubtedly considerable in the

---

[24] See as early examples of the respective literature Kydland and Prescott (1977), and for a later view, Walsh (1995).

[25] On the role of ideational factors and discourse in this field more generally, see Busch (2004).

[26] Kahler and Lake (2006) advance another explanation for a similar question, namely why there is "so little supranationalism" in the field of financial regulation on the global level. Indeed, this is an area where (contrary to that of trade) the influence of supranational institutions on policy has been in decline rather than increasing as theoretical considerations would lead us to believe. While we have argued here that a main reason is insufficient knowledge of what one should converge on, Kahler and Lake argue in favour of a strategic calculus of the nation states: compared to other policy areas, they had little to gain from shifting to a supranational or hierarchical mode of governance in this field, and thus continued the existing network governance approach established in this field since the 1930s.

[27] Coleman (1996: 77) also comes to that conclusion.

early 1930s when the whole sector was subjected to intense state regulation in a very short time period. The loss of said capacity, however, is not due to the influence of globalization; rather it is a prime example for a *critical juncture* followed by a high degree of stability in the path chosen. In the case of Germany, past assessments of state capacity vary between high (Coleman 1996: 75) and low (Vogel 1996: 254f.). Considering the fact that—as the case study showed—it was never really put to the test during the period under investigation, one has to warn against overestimating it. A reduction of that capacity is not evident, but a partial shift to the European level has been demonstrated in the case study. That, however, is more a pooling of capacity than a loss thereof. The British case, especially regarding the reforms of 1997, has made evident the continued high degree of state capacity in this policy field, as well as the ultimate weakness of the *Bank of England*. The fact that they could be put into place without any consultation with other actors and even surprised policy experts is testament to the utter concentration of power that is possible in a *Westminster*-type system. And lastly, in Switzerland, state capacity probably has to be rated as low if the state should attempt a *diktat*. But in cooperation with the relevant associations, the Swiss state's capacity has to be regarded as considerable. And as resources for the respective state authority have been increased substantially over the period of investigation, here as well we cannot find a reduction.

The present study also confirms the importance of the role of interest groups and the institutional structure of regulatory authorities, both of which had been recognized as playing an important role in determining sectoral policy production by previous studies of this field.[28] In addition, our findings highlight the importance of the arena of Parliament. It is most evident in the case of the United States, where Congress blocked numerous reforms proposals from various administrations over the course of several decades and has conducted "politics as a negotiation marathon".[29] There, and in Germany, parliaments also played an important role by conducting hearings; both in the United Kingdom and in Switzerland this was less the case, in part reflecting the lesser resources of both parliaments (although these have been increasing in both cases throughout the 1990s). The details of institutional structures and substructures in parliaments vary widely (see e.g. Strøm 1998), and taking them into consideration can significantly improve the understanding of the policy process and results.

---

[28] Cf. Lehner, Schubert, and Geile (1983); Coleman (1996). See also, as a plea for a better consideration of interest-group influence as a variable in globalization policy studies, Busch (2007a).

[29] This is the title of Jauß (1999), a study about immission control in the United States—but which could equally well be used to characterize the present policy field.

The globalization debate of the 1990s has initiated systematically comparative studies in a whole host of policy areas.[30] While these studies vary on
the details of their results regarding the influence of globalization, a common
thread going through most of them is the finding (echoed in this study) that
we continue to find substantial differences in the policies of the countries
under investigation: there is "persistence of national variation" (Hay 2000)
and there are "diverse responses to common challenges" (as the subtitle of
Scharpf and Schmidt (2000) states). There is also little empirical evidence of
"races to the bottom" taking place (Heichel, Pape, and Sommerer 2005: 824,
834).

But not to be misunderstood: neither the studies just quoted nor this one
deny the existence of globalization or claim that globalization has no impact.
But it has become evident that also under conditions of globalization there is
room for nationally specific political strategies. The present study has shown
that—at least in banking regulation—it is difficult to demonstrate a reduction
of state capacity compared to the past. And it is important to keep in mind that
retrospectively, past political room for manoeuvre tends to get exaggerated.
Looking at the typology of possible policy outcomes depicted in Figure 8.1, we
can say that the results vary between "active political design", "path-dependent
development", and "blockade", but that we can exclude the cell labelled "market dominance" (involuntary convergence). Not least for reasons of democratic legitimacy and accountability of (nation) state policy and politics, this
is a result to be welcomed—and comparative political scientists will not be
aggrieved either.

Like the above-mentioned convergence hypotheses of the 1950s and 1960s
that triggered a surge of research in sociology, economics, and political science,
leading to a big increase in our knowledge about the functioning of modern
industrial society, the globalization debate with its assumptions about the
impotence of national policies and the uninhibited dominance of markets has
prompted much research. The results have helped to construct a differentiated
picture about the condition of politics at the beginning of the twenty-first
century. In doing so, the globalization debate has not only fulfilled a purpose,
but it has demonstrated that unconfirmed hypotheses can decisively further
our knowledge, too.

---

[30] An overview can be found in the recent survey by Heichel, Pape, and Sommerer (2005).

Postscriptum: The 2007/8 Subprime Mortgage Crisis and Banking Regulation

In late summer 2007, the failure of two hedge funds run by US investment bank Bear Stearns marked the beginning of a crisis in the so-called subprime mortgage markets in the United States. The crisis quickly started to affect the financial markets of many other countries, and in early 2008 it looks as if it has the potential to become the biggest upset in world financial markets since the 1930s. At the time of writing this postscript (February 2008), experts are wondering whether it may spread to other sectors of the credit market (such as credit default swaps), and how deep its effects on the real economy will be in how many countries. Drastic interest cuts by central banks and violent movements on world stock markets have accompanied the crisis so far. But even more than six months after the beginning of the crisis, it is still unknown how big the losses in the financial markets will eventually be, and that uncertainty exacerbates the crisis further, making a resolution more difficult. The chairman of the US Federal Reserve, Ben Bernanke, is on record as saying that further losses may amount to several hundred billion US dollars (but short of half a trillion). The rating agency Standard & Poor put that figure at $265 billion. Many observers expect the crisis to deepen further during 2008.[1]

In such a situation, any attempt at an analysis must necessarily be incomplete and imperfect. However, in the pages that follow I will offer a summary of what is known about the manifestations of the crisis and its causes so far, and some tentative conclusions as well as some speculation about the likely consequences, informed by the analysis presented in the preceding pages.[2]

---

[1] As an example, see the interviews with noted German economists Bofinger and Franz in FTD, 16 January 2008.

[2] In addition, the analysis is informed by a close reading of several newspapers covering events, in particular *Financial Times* (FT), *The Economist*, the German dailies *Financial Times Deutschland* (FTD), *Handelsblatt* (HB), *Frankfurter Allgemeine Zeitung* (FAZ), and *Süddeutsche Zeitung* (SZ), and the Swiss daily *Neue Zürcher Zeitung* (NZZ).

THE MANIFESTATIONS OF THE CRISIS

Before the globalization of financial markets, mortgage defaults—even in large numbers—would have been an insulated problem between borrowers and banks in one domestic market. But the advent of globalization, coupled with proliferation of financial innovations such as securitization have led to the evaporation of such borders and, as a consequence, to the spread of crisis symptoms across many countries. As certain financial products are being sold and traded across the globe, the containment of crises originating in specific local financial markets thus seems to have become nearly impossible.

Initially, the financial innovations contributed considerably to growth in financial market turnover and credit availability. They made it possible for banks to extend their core business of term or maturity transformation in a new way, since the buying of packages of long-term credits could be financed by issuing short-term securities. A form that was particularly popular was mortgage-backed securities in which mortgage lenders sold the rights to future mortgage payments (and also the credit risk that mortgage holders would default on their obligations) to investors. Much of that business, however, was not done directly by the banks, but by specially set up subsidiaries, so-called conduits or structured investment vehicles or SIVs (and hence did not appear directly in banks' balance sheets). Securitization massively increased the financial system's ability for credit creation, and the expansion of credit was further facilitated by the Federal Reserve's policy of low interest rates after 2001. Low rates of return on government bonds induced investors to seek more profitable investments which many of them found in new financial instruments such as asset-backed securities.

The maturity difference between assets and liabilities of SIVs required a constant renewal of funding. But when the crisis in the US housing market led to a decline in the value of the underlying mortgages, investors were no longer prepared to buy the short-term securities that provided that funding. As the money markets dried up and became illiquid with the massive rise of interbank spreads,[3] SIVs faced a crisis. When rating agencies started to downgrade asset-backed securities and collateralized debt obligations in July 2007, the crisis was exacerbated: many institutional investors are only allowed to hold top-rated assets and had to sell the downgraded ones, putting further pressure on their valuations. Many had to turn to their owners (often banks or investment banks) to bail them out. This, in turn, caused crises in a number of banks:

---

[3] For a description of that process and detailed data, see Bank for International Settlements (2007: 6ff., 10f.).

- In Germany, *IKB Deutsche Industriebank* (IKB) had to issue a profit warning on 30 July 2007. It had previously extended a credit line of €8.1 billion to the conduit *Rhineland Funding* which with the onset of the crisis prompted several other banks (among them *Deutsche Bank*) to close their lines of credit for IKB. A joint operation of the German banking system put forward €3.5 billion guarantee fund for IKB (later raised to €6 billion), of which the lion's share was taken on by *Kreditanstalt für Wiederaufbau* (KfW), a public sector bank which holds 38 per cent of IKB. KfW also guaranteed IKB's problematic credit line. KfW's CEO Ingrid Matthäus-Maier gave the likely loss for her bank as around €5 billion (SZ, 17 December 2007).

- Two German *Landesbanken*, those of Saxony and North Rhine Westphalia, were also hit by the crisis. *Sachsen LB* very suddenly faced a liquidity crisis in August 2007 due to its involvement with Conduit Ormond Quay (located in Ireland and involved with mortgage credits in the US market). It was bailed out by a credit line of €17.3 billion advanced to it by the savings banks association under the condition that it would agree to being taken over by a financially potent investor. The latter came in the shape of *Landesbank Baden-Württemberg* (LBBW), a more powerful (and prudent) sister bank which agreed to take over *Sachsen LB* for a sum of "at least €300 million". Since the state of Saxony would have had to pay for any defaults of *Sachsen LB* in the absence of that takeover, this created a political crisis for the Land government. The takeover by LBBW sealed the fate of East Germany's only independent *Landesbank*. The importance of *Landesbanken* as a tool of regional policy prevented the takeover of *West LB*, the Landesbank of Germany's most populous state North Rhine Westphalia. Here, Minister President Rüttgers vetoed merger talks with LBBW in the autumn of 2007, because *West LB* would have become the junior partner. However, in early 2008, *West LB* needed a capital injection of €2 billion, and the state government (as one of the owners of the bank) had to provide its share (around 20 per cent directly and another 20 per cent indirectly). The crisis thus has clearly driven home to German Land governments the potential costs of bad banking.

- In the United Kingdom, the crisis triggered the first bank run in more than a century when customers of *Northern Rock* bank (a former building society) tried to withdraw their money for several days in mid-September 2007.[4] The bank had faced a liquidity crisis due to its above average

---

[4] For a detailed overview of events as well as a description of the bank's business model and an assessment of regulatory performance, see the report by the House of Commons Treasury Committee (2008).

reliance on money markets (rather than depositors) for refinancing and the growing reluctance of institutional investors to lend to mortgage banks. Thus *Northern Rock* had taken up an offer from the *Bank of England* for emergency liquidity support in the region of £3 billion. With shares in the bank plummeting and money being withdrawn at a rate of between £1 billion and £2 billion per day, the Chancellor of the Exchequer Alistair Darling announced on 17 September 2007 that the government and the *Bank of England* would guarantee all deposits held at *Northern Rock*.[5] This announcement managed to end the bank run which the government had feared might spread to other banks and get out of hand. However, this move created severe criticism of the government by some since the de facto nationalization burdened the British taxpayers with a potential liability of around £60 billion. The government also pledged to look into reforming the British deposit protection scheme which limits payouts in case of a bank defaulting to 100 per cent of the first £2,000 and 90 per cent of the next £33,000 held in any bank, thus limiting guaranteed deposits to £31,700. The queues outside *Northern Rock* branches in September 2007 can be taken as evidence that many of its customers held more than that sum in their accounts.

• In Switzerland, one of the two big banks—*UBS*—also suffered heavily: after writing off a record sFr. 12.4 billion in the fourth quarter of 2007 (due to losses in the subprime mortgage market), the bank for the first time ever had to post an annual loss of sFr. 4.4 billion (after a net profit of sFr. 11.25 billion in the previous year). UBS is thus one of the (so far) most heavily affected banks in Europe with its losses being in a similar magnitude to the worst affected American banks. As a consequence, UBS accepted a capital injection from the Government of Singapore Investment Corporation (GIC), a state-run investment fund, amounting to sFr. 11 billion, and an anonymous investor from the Middle East of sFr. 2 billion to shore up its capital base. Interestingly, UBS's main domestic competitor, Credit Suisse, has so far been far less affected by the crisis, with losses amounting to $4.7 billion.

• The United States, where the crisis started with the closing of two hedge funds by Bear Stearns in June 2007, is also the place where the biggest losses have been recorded to date. Leading the field are Citigroup and investment bank Merrill Lynch, both of which have suffered write-downs in excess of $20 billions ($24.6 billion and $23.6 billion respectively). They are followed by Morgan Stanley and Bank of America with respective

---

[5] See BBC news website at http://news.bbc.co.uk/1/hi/business/6999615.stm [17 September 2007].

losses of $9.4 billion and $5.3 billion. The mortgage financing company Freddie Mac was on record in late December 2007 as estimating losses of between $10 billion and $12 billion.

Overall write-offs by big banks amounted to $113 billion in mid-January 2008 (FTD, 16 Jan 2008), and estimates of remaining exposure to subprime loans (excluding off-balance-sheet vehicles) were put at $380 billion (*The Economist*, 10 January 2008). Consequences of the crisis could be felt in a variety of areas. One was massively increased sensitivity in the stock markets, where especially bank shares reacted feverishly to announcements or even rumours about new revelations of problems. German bank Hypo Real Estate's shares, for example, lost more than a third of their value on 15 January 2008 when unexpected further losses (although at €390 million of a comparatively modest size) were announced. Citigroup slashed its dividend by 41 per cent in a reaction to almost $10 billion losses in a single quarter (and announced 17,000 job cuts), and the CEOs of a number of banks were replaced, among them the bosses of Citigroup, Bear Stearns, and Merrill Lynch.

To balance the losses and retain the required ratio of core capital, many banks needed fresh capital injections. Since this dilutes the ownership of the previous owners, it is generally not an uncontroversial move, but for many banks there was no choice. Citigroup and Merrill Lynch raised $14.5 billion and $6.6 billion, respectively, mainly from state-run investment funds ("sovereign-wealth funds") located in places such as Singapore, China, or Abu Dhabi. This represents the biggest single transfer of capital to US banks from abroad to date. UBS's capital injection turned the Government of Singapore Investment Corporation into the bank's biggest single shareholder (SZ, 11 December 2007); Morgan Stanley received $5 billion, and Barclay's the same amount, from the China Investment Bank and China Investment Corporation, respectively. Overall, sovereign-wealth funds have invested some $69 billion to recapitalize rich Western banks (*The Economist*, 17 January 2008). While most of that investment certainly makes good sense as much of it is highly profitable (UBS, for example, has to pay 9 per cent interest on the bond part of its refinancing package, see SZ, 11 December 2007), sovereign-wealth funds are suspected to potentially follow also non-economic goals which has raised political concerns about foreign influence on the American banking system (FT, 15 January 2008). The crisis has thus already left a clear mark by changing ownership structures in the banking system to some degree.

Central banks have so far reacted in quite different ways to the crisis. There are two channels in which they have tried to help the banking system during the crisis: on the one hand, by providing liquidity help to counter the drying up of the inter-bank market, and on the other hand, by cutting interest rates to ease conditions for the banks while at the same time trying to avoid the transmission of the slowdown to the real economy. The US Federal Reserve system was most proactive in both dimensions, providing ample liquidity help to the banking system on several occasions after August 2007. In addition, a number of substantial interest rate cuts brought down the costs to banks of borrowing from the central bank repeatedly, on one occasion (30 January 2008) even outside the regular cycle of board meetings that normally decides interest rate moves. The Bank of England was cautious at the beginning of the crisis in early autumn 2007, providing no liquidity help until early September 2007, fully four weeks after both the European Central Bank (ECB) and the Fed had started doing so in their monetary areas. After the run on *Northern Rock* had acutely raised awareness of the crisis, the BoE started cutting interest rates by modest amounts in December 2007, indicating that it would follow this up by further cuts if it deemed them necessary. The ECB again followed a different mix, by being very proactive with liquidity help from an early stage in the crisis (6 August 2007), but refusing to cut interest rates until the end of January 2008 (the time of writing).

The three big central banks in the area most affected by the credit crisis have thus apparently opted not to coordinate their actions, but to follow individual and different courses of action. This can be justified with reference to the different positions in the economic cycle all three currency areas found themselves in. But in addition to this, the differences in action are also a result of differences in outlook, priorities, and strategy. It will only be possible in retrospect, after the crisis will have run its course, to assess which strategy was best. Until then, central banks will have to live with sceptical remarks about their actions—such as accusations of being too willing to bail out ailing banks and hedge funds (which may create problems of moral hazard in the future) or of trying to cure a hangover with free beer, since the original problem (some observers claim) was the excessive availability of credit in the years leading up to the crisis. This brings us to the question of the causes of the crisis.

WHAT CAUSED THE CRISIS?

The crisis is a result of past errors. Whether they are more on the side of regulatory failure or of market exuberance remains yet to be determined and will likely depend on the emergence of the full facts which will only be possible after the crisis is over. However, several mechanisms can already be determined at this stage.

It has been remarked that the banks are like the sorcerer's apprentice: they created highly complex financial instruments which earned them a lot of money in good times, but now that the crisis has unfolded, they cannot stop the dynamic unleashed by them (SZ, 16 January 2008). A once profitable line of business has turned into a loss-making one—although that assessment does not hold generally: while some banks and hedge funds have indeed been suffering huge losses (see above), some of the leading financial institutions have been able to report record profits. Examples in the latter category include *Goldman Sachs* (who recorded the best result in company history [SZ, 16 January 2008]), and *Deutsche Bank* (who, despite a fourth quarter reduction in profits and a $3.1 billion write-down in the third quarter, increased their profit by 7 per cent over the preceding year [NYT, 8 February 2008]). These institutions appear to have had much better risk management in place than their competitors.

A more general attempt at explaining the crisis, however, must go further back to both monetary policy decisions and innovations in past financial markets.[6] A loose monetary policy by the Federal Reserve in the years 2003–5 prompted low yields on (low risk) US government bonds which let investors look for higher yielding, higher risk means of investment. The expansive monetary policy also led to strong demand in the housing market as mortgages were cheap, resulting in a housing market boom. Banks and financial institutions lowered their requirements concerning creditworthiness of borrowers, and offered adjustable rate mortgages which started with very low "teaser" rates that would rise in years to come. Rising house prices induced many house buyers to take out mortgages higher than they could afford on their income, hoping that increases in the value of their home would cover the shortfall. The result was a boom in the mortgage market, especially in its low quality "subprime" sector. Once monetary policy tightened in 2006, it was clear that many debtors would not be able to service their mortgages.

But why did banks generously dish out mortgages when they must have known that their loans might become burdens once the cycle turned? In the past they would have found themselves with bad loans on their books and thus would likely have exercised some foresight when giving them out, insisting on good credit ratings of their customers. But financial innovation ("securitization") meant that they did not need to keep questionable loans on their books; instead, they could bundle them up and sell them on the international financial market. This massively increased the global potential for the creation

---

[6] For more detailed information about the issues covered in this section, see International Monetary Fund (2007), Sachverständigenrat zur Begutachtung der Gesamtwirtschaftlichen Entwicklung (2007: 89–167), and Bank for International Settlements (2007: 1–17).

of credit, and was even more attractive since no capital requirements applied to intermediation through markets. Risk could be better diversified, lowering the need to hold capital against it, further increasing the potential for credit creation. International trading of the resulting securities led to their passing on to customers in European states (most of which have relatively high savings ratios), and with them spread the risks from US mortgage loans.

But in order to be able to sell sub-prime mortgage-based securities to institutional investors (many of whom are only allowed to engage in AAA-rated investments), a process called "tranching" is applied which the German Council of Economic Advisers aptly likens to "turning table wine into vintage wine" (Sachverständigenrat zur Begutachtung der Gesamtwirtschaftlichen Entwicklung 2007: 113–15). By performing some statistical voodoo on a portfolio of loans, a large part (*senior tranche*) of a portfolio rated BBB can be turned into an AAA-grade investment, while other (smaller) tranches achieve lower ratings and the main risk is concentrated in the *equity tranche*. The latter has no rating and can thus only be sold to unregulated investors like hedge funds. Often it is being retained by the originator, thus signalling that the tranches being sold off have low risk. At the same time, it leads to an accumulation of risk with the originating banks and financial institutions.

If securitization was originally praised as a mechanism for spreading risk, the crisis of 2007/8 demonstrates an unintended opposite effect, for if creditors no longer have to deal with the consequences of taking on bad debtors, it is plausible that they will be far less cautious in choosing their customers. The instrument of securitization thus was an invitation to recklessness on the part of the banks. Rating agencies were willing accomplices: they projected confidence that they could reliably assess the risk on these securities by using historical data—from a time when these instruments had not existed and market dynamics were thus potentially quite different. And they chose to ignore the potential conflict of interest arising from the fact that they are being paid to rate bond issues or advise firms on them. But without greedy investors who did not question why such securities promised a higher yield than normal securities of the supposedly same quality and rating the financial market bonanza in that sector could not have happened. The ensuing crisis now seems to demonstrate that rather than spreading risk, these techniques have resulted in hiding risk; and once the tide on the markets turned in the summer of 2007, investors were in no mood to go searching for it. The enormous sophistication of financial innovation thus caused a stampede out of this segment, and the drying-up of the inter-bank market was the best demonstration that even the professionals no longer trusted the assurances of their colleagues. Unfortunately for the apprentices, no old sorcerer has so far materialized to bail them out.

SOME SPECULATION ABOUT CONSEQUENCES

At the end of this postscriptum, here are some conclusions and speculations about the likely consequences emanating from the crisis.

The topic of banking (and more generally, financial industry) regulation, often considered dry and technical, is back on the political agenda and, depending on circumstances and further developments, may even be put under the spotlight of public scrutiny. The latter has already happened in the United Kingdom, where the run on *Northern Rock* triggered a debate about reforms of the deposit protection system and the organizational structure of banking supervision. Given the limitations of the former in terms of amount of deposits covered and the fact that payout may take a substantial amount of time under present rules (see above), the run was more rational than was acknowledged at the time. As a result, UK Chancellor of the Exchequer Alistair Darling announced in early 2008 that he would propose new bank laws that would improve the situation in the future by raising the deposit protection threshold, clarifying responsibilities between regulatory agencies and strengthening the role of the Treasury in a crisis (FT, 4 January 2008).

One early casualty of the crisis seems to be the single financial market supervisor model pioneered by the British FSA and followed by several other countries. It had been popular in academic writing on the subject for reasons of supposed efficiency,[7] but the crisis around *Northern Rock* revealed that in fact decision-making was shared between the FSA, the Bank of England, and the Treasury, and complicated by it.[8] Given that the crisis has demonstrated the need to have ample funds for liquidity help (even if likely only for a short period) at hand—the ECB pumped almost €170 billion into money markets at one point to head off a year-end liquidity crisis (FT, 19 December 2007)—it would seem that the role of central banks has been strengthened by the events. This does not mean that general convergence on a single regulator model run by the national central bank is likely. But the role model function the UK system had for many in the last decade no longer exists after its difficulties in the *Northern Rock* episode.

Apart from this, the crisis has so far again demonstrated the tendency of national systems to react to outside stimuli each in their own ways and according to their own agendas and preferences. In Germany, the crisis was used to push the case for a rebalancing of regulatory power between BaFin and

---

[7] See Goodhart (2000) for a discussion of the pros and cons of that approach. He suggests it as the most efficient solution for developed countries. But see also Lütz (2004: 186), who notes that a substantial number of European countries have failed to do so and retained supervisory systems with subsectoral regulators.

[8] See House of Commons Treasury Committee (2008: 104f.).

the *Bundesbank*. This has been a long-standing conflict which has overtones of federal and party-political preferences.[9] Given that a 2006 study commissioned by the German Finance Ministry had resulted in criticisms of the existing system resulting in a draft bill for reforming the relationship between BaFin and *Bundesbank*, a *policy window* (Kingdon) may open up for a change in the distribution of power in sectoral regulation.

Another country-specific change could take place in the German system of *Landesbanken*. Several of them have displayed a level of incompetence in dealing with complex financial instruments that is on a par with the worst prejudices levelled against them by interested parties. As the state of Hesse did around scandals concerning its *Landesbank* Helaba in the 1970s and as the state of Berlin did around corruption in its *Landesbank* holding *Bankgesellschaft Berlin* in the early 2000s, several Minister Presidents (notably in Saxony and North Rhine Westphalia) had to learn that badly conducted banking can be very costly for their budgets—since they will have to cover any shortfalls, which in this case may run into billions of Euros. Consolidation of the German public banking sector has already been progressing over the last decade; the credit crisis is likely to further stimulate it. Those *Landesbanken* with better risk management who were not hit hard by losses from the subprime segment—like LBBW—are likely to benefit from it.

A more general consequence of the crisis, going beyond individual countries, may be a critical overall reassessment of financial markets and their existing regulation. The likelihood and severity of such a reassessment will likely depend on the eventual depth of the crisis and the number of countries affected. The deeper the crisis, and the more countries are being hit, the more likely also calls for international coordination of political measures will become, and some amount of re-regulation—either on the national or international level—may be the result. Already the finance ministers of the four biggest EU countries have issued a joint call for increased transparency in financial markets, with a particular focus on structured financial instruments and securitized mortgage loans (HB, 17 January 2008). Swiss politicians have severely criticized the conduct of the Swiss Banking Commission which was apparently unable to recognize banks' problems, especially in the case of UBS, sufficiently in advance (NZZ, 3 February 2008). And economists like the *Financial Times's* chief economics commentator Martin Wolf, have noted the high profitability of the banking sector in most countries and linked that to

[9] See Busch (2005) for the history of the conflicts around this issue. In its autumn 2007 report, the German Council of Economic Advisers also took up the issue and recommended reform in Germany along the lines of a single regulator, but one that should be integrated into the *Bundesbank*. BaFin would thus no longer be a partner but a subordinated agency (Sachverständigenrat zur Begutachtung der Gesamtwirtschaftlichen Entwicklung 2007: 150f.).

implicit government guarantees which encourage excessive risk-taking (FT, 28 November 2007). As a consequence, Wolf argues, banks should be treated as utilities and have their returns regulated. He calls for the imposition of higher capital requirements once the crisis is over.

Rating agencies may find themselves in the spotlight of criticism and attempts at altering regulation as well. It is now evident that risk has been underpriced over the last couple of years, and it may well be concluded that rating agencies have not only faced a conflict of interest that has to be corrected in the future, but also failed in their attempt to calculate risk based on historical data. If anything the crisis has so far demonstrated quite clearly that reality can deviate substantially from historical precedent, and the result has been the breakdown of certain markets. Rating agencies will have to demonstrate changes in their approach designed to avoid a repeat of this crisis if they want to convince investors in the future.

But a switch from static capital requirements to capital requirements governed by bank-based risk models on the one hand, and a reliance on rating agency classifications on the other, are at the core of the "Basel II" framework of bank regulation that is planned to be put into effect in many countries between 2008 and 2015. If calls for increasing capital requirements are being taken up, and if rating agencies come under increasing pressure, the overall result may well be a change in these plans and an increase in direct political regulation of the banking market. This could especially be so if cases like the *Société Générale* scandal of early 2008 reduce trust in banks' own risk management capabilities further.[10] It would not be the first time that a severe banking crisis leads to more regulation, and it would further strengthen the comparison of the 2007/8 crisis with that of the early 1930s. However, political calculations will also play a role in determining the course of further action as well, and it might well be that forthcoming elections in the United States (2008), Germany (2009), and the United Kingdom (2010 at the latest) will induce politicians to offer bail-outs if problems deepen or persist rather than wait for an international agreement to emerge. Usually, the losses from banking crises are being spread so that no unacceptable losses harm specific groups in the electorate which is why political fallout from such crises is mostly small (Busch 2001). But a deep recession induced by a financial crisis may well have more adverse consequences by undermining support for globalization and leading to gains for economic nationalism and protectionism. At least that was the reaction in the 1930s.

---

[10] In January 2008, a rogue trader at *Société Générale*, France's second biggest bank, ran up losses of €4.9 billion before he was discovered and arrested (FTD, 25 January 2008).

Bibliography

Adams, Willi Paul, Czempiel, Ernst-Otto, Ostendorf, Berndt, Shell, Kurt L., Spahn, P. Bernd, and Zöller, Michael (eds.) (1990). *Länderbericht USA I. Geschichte—Politische Kultur—Politisches System—Wirtschaft*. Bonn: Bundeszentrale für Politische Bildung.

Aharoni, Yair and Nachum, Lilach (2000). *Globalization of Services: Some Implications for Theory and Practice. Routledge Studies in International Business and the World Economy*. London: Routledge.

Akerlof, George A. (1970). 'The Market for "Lemons": Quality Uncertainty and the Market Mechanism', *Quarterly Journal of Economics*, 84: 488–500.

Albert, Michel (1993). *Capitalism against Capitalism*. London: Whurr.

Albisetti, Emilio, Bodmer, Daniel, Boemle, Max, Gsell, Max, and Rutschi, Ernst (1977). *Handbuch des Geld-, Bank- und Börsenwesens der Schweiz*. Thun: Ott, 3rd edn.

Alesina, Alberto (1988). 'Macroeconomics and Politics', in Stanley Fischer (ed.), *National Bureau of Economic Research Macroeconomics Annual 1988*. Cambridge, MA. MIT Press, pp. 13–52.

—— and Summers, Lawrence H. (1993). 'Central Bank Independence and Macroeconomic Performance: Some Comparative Evidence', *Journal of Money, Credit and Banking*, 25: 151–62.

Alsheimer, Constantin (1997). 'Die Entwicklung des Kreditwesengesetzes', *Die Bank* (1): 27–31.

Amable, Bruno (2003). *The Diversity of Modern Capitalism*. Oxford: Oxford University Press.

Année politique suisse (1965ff.). Année politique suisse/Schweizerische Politik, published by the Forschungszentrum für Schweizerische Politik. Berne: Institut für Politische Wissenschaft. [cited as APS 19—].

Arthur, W. Brian (1989). 'Competing Technologies, Increasing Returns, and Lock-in by Historical Events', *The Economic Journal*, 99: 116–31.

—— (1994). *Increasing Returns and Path Dependence in the Economy*. Ann Arbor, MI: University of Michigan Press.

Arthur Andersen & Co. (1996). *Findings and Recommendations of the Review of Supervision and Surveillance*. London: Arthur Andersen & Co.

Aschhoff, Gunter, Ashauer, Günter, Born, Karl Erich, Engels, Wolfram, Klein, Ernst, Kolbeck, Rosemarie, Pohl, Manfred, Treue, Wilhelm, Wolf, Herbert, and Zweig, Gerhard (eds.) (1983). *Deutsche Bankengeschichte*. Band 3: Vom Ersten Weltkrieg bis zur Gegenwart. Frankfurt am Main: Knapp.

Baecker, Dirk (1991). *Womit handeln Banken? Eine Untersuchung zur Risikoverarbeitung in der Wirtschaft*. Frankfurt am Main: Suhrkamp.

Baer, Herbert L. and Mote, Larry R. (1992). 'The United States Financial System', in Kaufman (1992), pp. 469–553.

Baltensperger, Ernst (1988). 'Die Regulierung des Bankensektors', *Wirtschaftswissenschaftliches Studium*, 17(2): 53–7.

Bank for International Settlements (2007). 'BIS Quarterly Review: International Banking and Financial Market Developments'. December 2007.

Bank of England (1996). *The Bank's Review of Supervision*. London: Bank of England.

—— (1997). *From a National to Central Bank*. London: Bank of England Museum.

Bänziger, Hugo (1985). 'Vom Sparerschutz zum Gläubigerschutz—Die Entstehung des Bankengesetzes im Jahre 1934'. *Eidgenössische Bankenkommission* (1985), pp. 3–81.

—— (1986). *Die Entwicklung der Bankenaufsicht in der Schweiz seit dem 19. Jahrhundert*. Bern, Stuttgart: Haupt.

Barth, James R., Caprio, Gerard, Jr., and Levine, Ross (2006). *Rethinking Bank Regulation. Till Angels Govern*. Cambridge, New York: Cambridge University Press.

—— Nolle, Daniel E., Phumiwasana, Triphon, and Yago, Glenn (2003). 'A Cross-Country Analysis of the Bank Supervisory Framework and Bank Performance', *Financial Markets, Institutions and Instruments*, 12(2): 67–120.

—— —— and Rice, Tara N. (1997). 'Commercial Banking Structure, Regulation, and Performance: An International Comparison', vol. 97-6, *Economics Working Papers*, Washington D.C.: Office of the Comptroller of the Currency.

Basel Committee on Banking Supervision (2004). *International Convergence of Capital Measurement and Capital Standards: A Revised Framework*. Basel: Bank for International Settlements.

Becker, Jürgen (1998). 'Banking Supervision: Who is Doing What?', in Stephen F. Frowen and Robert Pringle (eds.), *Inside the Bundesbank*. London: Macmillan, pp. 56–67.

Beisheim, Marianne, Dreher, Sabine, Walter, Gregor, Zangl, Bernhard, and Zürn, Michael (1999). *Im Zeitalter der Globalisierung? Thesen und Daten zur gesellschaftlichen und politischen Denationalisierung*. Baden-Baden: Nomos.

—— and Walter, Gregor (1997). '"Globalisierung"—Kinderkrankheiten eines Konzeptes', *Zeitschrift für Internationale Beziehungen*, 4(1): 153–80.

Benston, George J. (1995). 'The Sins of Banking Regulation in the USA', *Economic Affairs* (Spring 1995): 18–23.

—— and Kaufman, George G. (1996). 'The Appropriate Role of Bank Regulation', *The Economic Journal*, 106: 688–97.

Berger, Allen N., Kashyap, Anil K., and Scalise, Joseph M. (1995). 'The Transformation of the U.S. Banking Industry: What a Long, Strange Trip It's Been', *Brookings Papers on Economic Activity*, 2: 55–218.

Berger, Suzanne (2000). 'Globalization and Politics', *Annual Review of Political Science*, 3: 43–62.

—— and Dore, Ronald (eds.) (1996). *National Diversity and Global Capitalism*. Ithaca, NY: Cornell University Press.

Bernauer, Thomas (2000). *Staaten im Weltmarkt. Zur Handlungsfähigkeit von Staaten trotz wirtschaftlicher Globalisierung*. Opladen: Leske + Budrich.

Beyer, Jürgen (1999). 'Integration und Transformation: Das Divergenz-Paradoxon des Beitrittswettbewerbs', *Politische Vierteljahresschrift*, 40(4): 537–64.

Beyme, Klaus von (1997). *Der Gesetzgeber: Der Bundestag als Entscheidungszentrum*. Opladen: Westdeutscher Verlag.

——(1998). *The Legislator. German Parliament as a Centre of Political Decision-making*. Aldershot, Brookfield (VT), Singapore, Sydney: Ashgate.

——(1999). *Die Parlamentarische Demokratie. Entstehung und Funktionsweise 1789–1999*. Opladen: Westdeutscher Verlag, 3., völlig neubearbeitete ed.

Bingham, Lord Justice (1992). *Inquiry into the Supervision of The Bank of Credit and Commerce International*. London: HMSO.

Birchler, Urs W. and Rich, George (1992). 'Bank Structure in Switzerland', in Kaufman (1992), pp. 389–427.

Blunden, Sir George (1987). 'Supervision and Central Banking', *Bank of England Quarterly Bulletin*, 27: 380–5.

Board of Banking Supervision (1996). *Report of the Board of Banking Supervision Inquiry into the Circumstances of the collapse of Barings*. London: HMSO.

Bodmer, Daniel, Kleiner, Beat, and Lutz, Benno (2000). *Kommentar zum schweizerischen Bankengesetz*. Zürich: Schulthess. [Stand 11. Lieferung, Februar 2000].

Bonn, Joachim K. (1998). *Bankenkrisen und Bankenregulierung*. Wiesbaden: Gabler.

Boos, Karl-Heinz, Fischer, Reinfrid, and Schulte-Matler, Hermann (eds.) (2000). *Kreditwesengesetz. Kommentar zu KWG und Ausführungsvorschriften*. München: Beck.

Born, Karl Erich (1977). *Geld und Banken im 19. und 20. Jahrhundert*. Stuttgart: Kröner.

——(1983). 'Vom Beginn des Ersten Weltkrieges bis zum Ende der Weimarer Republik (1914–1933)', in Aschhoff et al. (1983), pp. 17–146.

Bovens, Mark, 't Hart, Paul, and Peters, B. Guy (eds.) (2001). *Success and Failure in Public Governance: A Comparative Analysis*. Cheltenham: Edward Elgar.

Boyer, Robert and Drache, Daniel (eds.) (1996). *States Against Markets. The Limits of Globalization*. London, New York: Routledge.

Brash, Donald T. (1995). 'Banking Supervision in New Zealand', *Economic Affairs* (Spring 1995), pp. 28–33.

Braun, Dietmar and Busch, Andreas (eds.) (1999). *Public Policy and Political Ideas*. Aldershot: Edward Elgar.

Brittan, Samuel (1996). 'Keynes and Globalisation', *Financial Times* (European edn.), 6 June 1996, p. 12.

Broz, J. Lawrence (1999). 'Origins of the Federal Reserve System: International Incentives and the Domestic Free-rider Problem', *International Organization*, 53(1): 39–70.

Bundesaufsichtsamt für das Kreditwesen (1999). *Jahresbericht 1998*. Berlin: Bundesaufsichtsamt für das Kreditwesen.

Bundesverband Deutscher Banken (1974). *Jahresbericht 1973/74*, Köln: Bundesverband, chapter Banken in der Bewährung, pp. 14–17.

——(1975). Jahresbericht 1974/75, Köln: Bundesverband, chapter Stabilisierungsfaktor Einlagensicherung, pp. 17–19.

Burghof, Hans-Peter and Rudolph, Bernd (1996). *Bankenaufsicht. Theorie und Praxis der Regulierung.* Wiesbaden: Gabler.

Busch, Andreas (1989). *Neokonservative Wirtschaftspolitik in Großbritannien: Vorgeschichte, Problemdiagnose, Ziele und Ergebnisse des 'Thatcherismus'.* Mit einem Vorwort von Klaus von Beyme. Frankfurt am Main, Berne, New York, Paris: Peter Lang.

—— (1995). 'Preisstabilitätspolitik. Politik und Inflationsraten im internationalen Vergleich, vol. 8 of *Gesellschaftspolitik und Staatstätigkeit.* Opladen: Leske + Budrich.

—— (2000). 'Unpacking the Globalization Debate: Approaches, Evidence and Data', in Colin Hay and David Marsh (eds.), *Demystifying Globalization.* Basingstoke: Macmillan, pp. 21–48.

—— (2001). 'Managing Innovation: Regulating the Banking Sector in a Rapidly Changing Environment', in Bovens et al. (2001), pp. 311–25.

—— (2004). 'National Filters: Europeanisation, Institutions, and Discourse in the Case of Banking Regulation', *West European Politics*, 27 (2): 310–33. [= Special issue on "Policy Change and Discourse in Europe", ed. by Claudio M. Radaelli and Vivien A. Schmidt].

—— (2005). 'Shock-absorbers Under Stress: Parapublic Institutions and the Double Challenges of German Unification and European Integration', in Simon Green and William E. Paterson (eds.), *Governance in Contemporary Germany: The Semisovereign State Revisited.* Cambridge: Cambridge University Press, pp. 94–114.

—— (2007*a*). 'Confronting Stylized Facts with Reality: The Role of Interest Groups in Banking Regulation Policy', *Economics of Governance*, 8(3): 219–32.

—— (2007*b*). 'The Development of the Debate: Intellectual Precursors and Selected Aspects', in Stefan A. Schirm (ed.), *Globalization. State of the Art and Perspectives.* London, New York: Routledge, pp. 22–39.

—— and Merkel, Wolfgang (1992). 'Staatshandeln in kleinen Staaten: Schweiz und Österreich', in Heidrun Abromeit and Werner W. Pommerehne (eds.), *Staatstätigkeit in der Schweiz.* Bern, Stuttgart, Wien: Haupt, pp. 193–219.

—— and Plümper, Thomas (eds.) (1999). *Nationaler Staat und Internationale Wirtschaft. Anmerkungen zum Thema Globalisierung.* Baden-Baden: Nomos.

Büschgen, Hans E. (1983). 'Zeitgeschichtliche Problemfelder des Bankwesens in der Bundesrepublik Deutschland', in Aschhoff et al. (1983), pp. 349–409.

Cable, John R. (1985). 'Capital Market Information and Industrial Performance: The Role of West German Banks', *Economic Journal*, 95(1): 118–32.

Campbell, Mary (1974). 'Das Bankwesen in Großbritannien', in Regul and Wolf (1974), pp. 297–336.

Canals, Jordi (1997). *Universal Banking: International Comparisons and Theoretical Perspectives.* Oxford: Clarendon Press.

Caprio, Jr., Gerard and Klingebiel, Daniela (1996). *Bank Insolvencies: Cross-country Experience*, vol. 1620, *Policy Research Working Papers.* Washington D.C.: The World Bank.

Carlin, Wendy and Mayer, Colin (2003). 'Finance, Investment, and Growth', in *Journal of Financial Economics*, 69(1): 191–226.

Cassis, Youssef (1994). 'Banks and Banking in Switzerland in the Nineteenth and Twentieth Centuries', in Pohl (1994), pp. 1015–36.

Castles, Francis G. (ed.) (1993). *Families of Nations: Patterns of Public Policy in Western Democracies*. Aldershot: Gower.

—— and Obinger, Herbert (2008). 'Worlds, Families, Regimes: Country Clusters in European and OECD Area Public Policy', *West European Politics*, 31(1–2): 321–45.

Cerny, Philip G. (ed.) (1993). *Finance and World Politics. Markets, Regimes and States in the Post-Hegemonic Era*. Aldershot: Elgar.

—— (1994). 'Money and Power: The American Financial System From Free Banking to Global Competition', in Grahame Thompson (ed.), *Markets*. London: Hodder & Stoughton in association with the Open University, vol. 2 of *The United States in the Twentieth Century*, pp. 175–213.

Chandler, Lester V. and Jaffee, Dwight M. (1977). 'Regulating the Regulators: A Review of the FINE Regulatory Reforms', *Journal of Money, Credit and Banking*, 9(4): 619–35.

Chew, Lillian [n.d.]. 'Not Just One Man—Barings'. [Case Study, International Financial Risk Institute]. URL http://riskinstitute. ch/137550.htm

Christen, Heinrich (1999). 'Schweiz', in Werner Weidenfeld (ed.), *Europa-Handbuch*. Gütersloh: Bertelsmann-Stiftung, pp. 208–20.

Clark, Ian (1999). *Globalization and International Relations Theory*. Oxford: Oxford University Press.

C&N (1981). *Congress and the Nation: A Review of Government and Politics. Volume V: 1977–1980*. Washington D.C.: Congressional Quarterly.

—— (1985). *Congress and the Nation: A Review of Government and Politics. Volume VI: 1981–1984*. Washington D.C.: Congressional Quarterly.

—— (1990). *Congress and the Nation: A Review of Government and Politics. Volume VII: 1985–1988*. Washington D.C.: Congressional Quarterly.

—— (1993). *Congress and the Nation: A Review of Government and Politics. Volume VIII: 1989–1992*. Washington D.C.: Congressional Quarterly.

—— (1998). *Congress and the Nation: A Review of Government and Politics. Volume IX: 1993–1996*. Washington D.C.: Congressional Quarterly.

Cohen, Benjamin J. (1996). 'Phoenix Risen: The Resurrection of Global Finance', *World Politics*, 48(1): 268–96.

Coleman, William D. (1994). 'Banking, Interest Intermediation and Political Power. A Framework for Comparative Analysis', *European Journal for Political Research*, 26(2): 31–58.

—— (1996). *Financial Services, Globalization and Domestic Policy Change: A Comparison of North America and the European Union*. London: Macmillan.

—— (2001). 'Governing French Banking: Regulatory Reform and the Crédit Lyonnais Fiasco', in Bovens et al. (2001), pp. 326–42.

Committee Set up to Consider the System of Banking Supervision (Chairman: Robin Leigh-Pemberton) (1985). Report. London: HMSO. [Cmnd. 9550].

Committee to Review the Functioning of Financial Institutions (Chairman: Sir Harold Wilson) (1980). Report and Appendices. London: HMSO. [Cmnd. 7937].

Cooke, Peter (1985). 'Some Reflections Arising From Comparisons Between the Swiss and Other Banking Supervisory Systems', *Eidgenössische Bankenkommission* (1985), pp. 139–50.

Cooper, Richard (1968). *The Economics of Interdependence*. New York: McGraw-Hill for the Council on Foreign Relations.

Cottrell, Philip L. (1994). 'The Historical Development of Modern Banking Within the United Kingdom', in Pohl (1994), pp. 1137–61.

Cox, Andrew (1986). *State, Finance and Industry. A Comparative Analysis of Post-War Trends in Six Advanced Industrial Economies*. Brighton: Wheatsheaf.

Dale, Richard (1992). *International Banking Deregulation. The Great Banking Experiment*. Oxford: Blackwell.

De Jong, H. W. (1995). 'European Capitalism: Between Freedom and Social Justice', *Review of Industrial Organization*, 10: 399–419.

Deeg, Richard (1999). *Finance Capitalism Unveiled. Banks and the German Political Economy*. Ann Arbor, MI: University of Michigan Press.

Demirgüç-Kunt, Asli and Detragiache, Enrica (1998). 'The Determinants of Banking Crises in Developing and Developed Countries', *IMF Staff Papers*, 45(1): 81–109.

Dettling, Warnfried (1999). 'Rettet den Rheinischen Kapitalismus!', in Karl Rohe and Klaus Dicke (eds.), *Die Integration politischer Gemeinwesen in der Krise?*, Baden-Baden: Nomos, pp. 54–65.

Deutsche Bundesbank (1976). 'Die Sofortnovelle zum Kreditwesengesetz', *Monatsberichte der Deutschen Bundesbank*, 28(7): 18–23.

—— (1985). 'Die Novellierung des Kreditwesengesetzes', *Monatsberichte der Deutschen Bundesbank*, 37(3): 37–43.

—— (ed.) (1988). *40 Jahre Deutsche Mark. Monetäre Statistiken 1948–1987*. Frankfurt am Main: Fritz Knapp.

—— (1992). *Internationale Organisationen und Abkommen im Bereich von Währung und Wirtschaft*, vol. 3 of *Sonderdrucke der Deutschen Bundesbank*. Frankfurt am Main: Deutsche Bundesbank.

—— (1993). 'Die Vierte Novelle des Kreditwesengesetzes—ein Schritt weiter zum europäischen Bankenmarkt', in *Monatsberichte der Deutschen Bundesbank*, 45(1): 35–42.

—— (1994). 'Die Fünfte Novelle des Kreditwesengesetzes. Ein weiterer Schritt zur Harmonisierung der europäischen Bankaufsichtsregelungen', *Monatsberichte der Deutschen Bundesbank*, 46(11): 59–67.

—— (1998). 'Bankinterne Risikosteuerungsmodelle und deren bankaufsichtliche Eignung', *Monatsberichte der Deutsche Bundesbank*, 50(10): 69–84.

—— (1999). *Bankenstatistik Februar 1999. Statistisches Beiheft zum Monatsbericht 1*. Frankfurt am Main: Deutsche Bundesbank.

—— (2000). 'Die Mitwirkung der Deutschen Bundesbank an der Bankenaufsicht', in *Monatsberichte der Deutschen Bundesbank*, 52(9): 33–45.

Dewatripont, Mathias and Tirole, Jean (1994). *The Prudential Regulation of Banks.* Cambridge (MA), London: MIT Press.

Dore, Ronald (1973). *British Factory—Japanese Factory: The Origins of National Diversity in Industrial Relations.* Berkeley, CA: University of California Press.

Dow, J. C. R. (1970). *The Management of the British Economy 1945–60.* London: Cambridge University Press.

Dowd, Kevin (1996). 'The Case for Financial *Laissez-faire*', *The Economic Journal*, 106: 679–87.

Dziobek, Claudia and Pazarbaşioğlu, Ceyla (1998). 'Lessons from Systemic Bank Restructuring', vol. 14 of *Economic Issues*, Washington D.C.: International Monetary Fund.

Eckstein, Wolfgang (1980). 'The Role of the Banks in Corporate Concentration in West Germany', *Zeitschrift für die gesamte Staatswissenschaft*, 136(3): 465–82.

Eerden, Leo A. van (2001). 'Structural Regulation of the Banking Industry in the Netherlands: A Shift of Power', in Bovens et al. (2001), pp. 363–82.

Eichengreen, Barry (1997). 'The Tyranny of the Financial Markets', *Current History*, 96(613): 377–82.

Eidgenössische Bankenkommission (ed.) (1985). *50 Jahre eidgenössische Bankenaufsicht. Jubiläumsschrift.* Zürich: Schulthess.

—— (1974ff.). Jahresbericht. Bern: Eidgenössische Bankenkommission. [cited as EBK Jb 19—].

Engenhardt, Gerold F. (1995). *Die Macht der Banken. Politische Positionen zur Neuregelung der gesetzlichen Grundlagen.* Wiesbaden: Deutscher Universitätsverlag.

FDIC (1997). *History of the Eighties—Lessons for the Future.* Washington D.C.: Federal Deposit Insurance Corporation. 2 Vols.

Fischer, Reinfrid (1997a). 'Das Recht der Bankenaufsicht', in Schimansky et al. (1997), pp. 3715–24.

—— (1997b). 'Die Aufsichtsbehörden und ihre Instrumente', in Schimansky et al. (1997), pp. 3725–32.

—— (1999). 'Nachtrag zu §§125–133: Das Recht der Bankenaufsicht', in Schimansky et al. (1997), pp. 1–35. (Ergänzungsband. 1. Ergänzung: Januar 1999).

Foot, Michael (1996). 'Managing Change in Banking Supervision', in *Butterworths Journal of International Banking and Financial Law*, 11(8): 359–60.

Franke, Günter (1998). 'Notenbank und Finanzmärkte', in Deutsche Bundesbank (ed.), *Fünfzig Jahre Deutsche Mark. Notenbank und Währung in Deutschland seit 1948*. München: Beck, pp. 257–306.

Freitag, Markus (1999). 'Globalisierung und Währung: Politisch-institutionelle Grundlagen unterschiedlicher Wechselkursentwicklungen in integrierten Finanzmärkten', in Busch and Plümper (1999), pp. 143–66.

Frieden, Jeffry A. and Rogowski, Ronald (1996). 'The Impact of the International Economy on National Policies: An Analytical Overview', in Robert O. Keohane and Helen V. Milner (eds.), *Internationalization and Domestic Politics*. New York, Cambridge: Cambridge University Press, pp. 25–47.

FRS (1997). 84th Annual Report. Washington D.C.: Board of Governors of the Federal Reserve System.

Füglister, Viktor (1993). 'Die Standesregeln der Schweizer Banken', in Gehrig and Schwander (1993), pp. 229–50.

Gail, Daniel and Norton, Joseph (1990). 'A Decade's Journey from "Deregulation" to "Supervisory Regulation": The Financial Insitutions Reform, Recovery, and Enforcement Act of 1989', *Business Lawyer*, 45(3): 1103–228.

Gall, Lothar (1995). 'Die Deutsche Bank von ihrer Gründung bis zum Ersten Weltkrieg', in Gall et al. (1995), pp. 1–135.

——Feldman, Gerald D., James, Harold, Holtfrerich, Carl-Ludwig, and Büschgen, Hans E. (1995). *Die Deutsche Bank 1870–1995*. München: Beck.

Gardener, Edward P. M. (1986*a*). 'Supervision in the United Kingdom', in Gardener (1986*b*), pp. 70–81.

——(ed.) (1986*b*). *UK Banking Supervision: Evolution, Practice and Issues*. London: Allen & Unwin.

——(1992). 'Banking Supervision', in Newman et al. (1992), pp. 156–8.

Garrett, Geoffrey (1998). *Partisan Politics in the Global Economy*. Cambridge: Cambridge University Press.

Gehrig, Bruno and Schwander, Ivo (eds.) (1993). *Banken und Bankrecht im Wandel. Festschrift für Beat Kleiner*. Zürich: Schulthess.

General Accounting Office (1994*a*). Bank Regulatory Structure: The Federal Republic of Germany. Washington D.C.: U.S. General Accounting Office. [GAO/GGD-94-134BR].

——(1994*b*). Bank Regulatory Structure: The United Kingdom. Washington D.C.: U.S. General Accounting Office. [GAO/GGD-95-38].

Genschel, Philipp and Plümper, Thomas (1997). 'Regulatory Competition and International Co-operation', *Journal of European Public Policy*, 4(4): 626–42.

—— ——(1999). 'Wettbewerb und Kooperation in der internationalen Finanzmarktregulierung', in Busch and Plümper (1999), pp. 251–75.

George, Eddie (2000). 'Financial Stability and the City: The Evolving Role of the Bank of England [Speech at the London Chamber of Commerce Conference, 13 June 2000]'. URL http://www.bankofengland.co.uk/publications/speeches/2000/speech89.htm

Gerschenkron, Alexander (1966). *Economic Backwardness in Historical Perspective. A Book of Essays*. Cambridge, MA: Harvard University Press, 2nd. edn., pp. 5–30.

Giddens, Anthony (1994). *Beyond Left and Right: The Future of Radical Politics*. Cambridge: Polity.

Gilbert, R. Alton (1986). 'Requiem for Regulation Q: What It Did and Why It Passed Away', *Federal Reserve Bank of St. Louis Review*, 68(2): 22–37.

Ginsberg, Benjamin, Lowi, Theodore J., and Weir, Margaret (1997). *We the People. An Introduction to American Politics*. New York, London: W. W. Norton.

Gläser, Anja (1999). 'Prudential Supervision of Banks in Germany and in the European Economic Area', in Norbert Horn (ed.), *German Banking Law and Practice in International Perspective*. Berlin, New York: de Gruyter, pp. 39–58.

Glauber, Robert R. (1993). 'FDICIA: The Wheels Came Off on the Road through Congress', in Kaufman and Litan (1993), pp. 33–41.

Glyn, Andrew (2006). *Capitalism Unleashed: Finance, Globalization, and Welfare.* Oxford: Oxford University Press.

Goldthorpe, John (2002). 'Globalisation and Social Class', in *West European Politics*, 25(3): 1–28.

Goldthorpe, John H. (1984a). 'The End of Convergence: Corporatist and Dualist Tendencies in Modern Western Societies', in Goldthorpe (1984b), pp. 315–43.

——(ed.) (1984b). *Order and Conflict in Contemporary Capitalism. Studies in the Political Economy of Western European Nations.* Oxford: Clarendon Press.

Goodhart, Charles (2000). *The Organisational Structure of Banking Supervision,* vol. 127 of *LSE Financial Markets Group Special Paper Series.* London: LSE Financial Markets Group.

——Hartmann, Philipp, Llewellyn, David, Rojas-Suárez, Liliana, and Weisbrod, Steven (1998). *Financial Regulation. Why, How and Where Now?* London, New York: Routledge.

——Hofmann, Boris, and Segoviano, Miguel (2004). 'Bank Regulation and Macroeconomic Fluctuations', in *Oxford Review of Economic Policy*, 20(4): 591–615.

Gourevitch, Peter (2002). 'Domestic Politics and International Relations', in Walter Carlsnaes, Thomas Risse, and Beth A. Simmons (eds.), *Handbook of International Relations.* London, Thousand Oaks, New Delhi: Sage, pp. 309–28.

Gourevitch, Peter A. (1978). 'The Second Image Reversed: The International Sources of Domestic Politics', in *International Organization*, 32(4): 881–912.

Gray, John (1998). *False Dawn. The Delusions of Global Capitalism.* London: Granta.

Grimm, Dieter (1990). 'Der Wandel der Staatsaufgaben und die Krise des Rechtsstaats', in Dieter Grimm (ed.), *Wachsende Staatsaufgaben—sinkende Steuerungsfähigkeit des Rechts.* Baden-Baden: Nomos, pp. 291–307.

Haas, Peter M. (1992). 'Introduction: Epistemic Communities and International Policy Coordination', in *International Organization*, 46(1): 1–35.

Hadjiemmanuil, Christos (1996). *Banking Regulation and the Bank of England.* London: LLP.

Hall, Maximilian J. B. (1983). *Monetary Policy since 1971: Conduct and Performance.* London: Macmillan.

——(1996a). 'Barings: The Bank of England's First Report to the Board of Banking Supervision', *Butterworths Journal of International Banking and Financial Law*, 11(3): 128–30.

——(1996b). 'UK Banking Supervision after the Anthur Andersen Report', *Butterworths Journal of International Banking and Financial Law*, 11(11): 525–9.

Hall, Peter A. (1986). *Governing the Economy. The Politics of State Intervention in Britain and France.* Cambridge: Polity.

——(1999). 'The Political Economy of Europe in an Era of Interdependence', in Kitschelt et al. (1999), pp. 135–63.

Hall, Peter A. and Soskice, David (2001*a*). 'An Introduction to Varieties of Capitalism', in Hall and Soskice (2001*b*), pp. 1–68.

———— (eds.) (2001*b*). *Varieties of Capitalism. The Institutional Foundations of Comparative Advantage*. Oxford, New York: Oxford University Press.

Hay, Colin (2000). 'Contemporary Capitalism, Globalization, Regionalization and the Persistence of National Variation', *Review of International Studies*, 26(4): 509–31.

—— and Rosamond, Ben (2002). 'Globalisation, European Integration and the Discursive Construction of Economic Imperatives', *Journal of European Public Policy*, 9(2): 147–67.

Hays, Jude C. (2003). 'Globalization and Capital Taxation in Consensus and Majoritarian Democracies', *World Politics*, 56(1): 79–113.

Heichel, Stephan, Pape, Jessica, and Sommerer, Thomas (2005). 'Is There Convergence in Convergence Research? An Overview of Empirical Studies on Policy Convergence', *Journal of European Public Policy*, 12(5): 817–40.

Heinemann, Friedrich and Schüler, Martin (2004). 'A Stiglerian View on Banking Supervision', *Public Choice*, 121(1–2): 99–130.

Held, David and McGrew, Anthony (eds.) (2000). *The Global Transformations Reader. An Introduction to the Globalization Debate*. Cambridge, Oxford: Polity.

———— Goldblatt, David, and Perraton, Jonathan (1999). *Global Transformations. Politics, Economics and Culture*. Cambridge, Oxford: Polity.

—— and McGrew, Anthony G. (2002). *Globalization/Anti-globalization*. Cambridge: Polity.

Helleiner, Eric (1994). *States and the Reemergence of Global Finance: From Bretton Woods to the 1990s*. Ithaca, NY: Cornell University Press.

Helms, Ludger (2001). 'Der parlamentarische Gesetzgebungsprozeß in Großbritannien. Ein Vergleich mit den Verfahrensregeln im Deutschen Bundestag und Bundesrat', *Der Staat*, 40(3): 405–19.

Herring, Richard J. (1993). 'BCCI: Lessons for International Bank Supervision', *Contemporary Policy Issues*, 11(2): 76–86.

—— and Litan, Robert E. (1995). *Financial Regulation in the Global Economy*. Washington D.C.: The Brookings Institution.

Hilpert, Ulrich (1994). 'Das politische Risiko erfolgreicher Partizipation an neuen Weltmärkten. Zum Problem tendenzieller Erosion staatlicher Steuerungskompetenz bei erfolgreicher Integration in die internationale Arbeitsteilung', in Ulrich Hilpert (ed.), *Zwischen Scylla und Charybdis? Zum Problem staatlicher Politik und nicht-intendierter Konsequenzen*. Opladen: Westdeutscher Verlag, pp. 87–106.

Hintze, Otto (1970). 'Wesen und Wandlung des modernen Staats', in Otto Hintze, *Staat und Verfassung. Gesammelte Abhandlungen zur allgemeinen Verfassungsgeschichte*. Göttingen: Vandenhoeck & Ruprecht, 3rd edn., pp. 470–96.

Hirst, Paul and Thompson, Grahame (1996). *Globalization in Question. The International Economy and the Possibilities of Governance*. Cambridge: Polity.

Hirszowicz, Christine (1996). *Schweizerische Bankpolitik*. Berne, Stuttgart, Wien: Haupt, 4th edn.

His, Eduard (1938). *Geschichte des neuern Schweizerischen Staatsrechts. Dritter Band: Der Bundesstaat von 1848 bis 1914.* Basel: Helbing & Lichtenhahn.

H. M. Treasury (United Kingdom) (1976). *The Licensing and Supervision of Deposit-Taking Institutions.* London: HMSO. [Cmnd. 6584].

—— (1985). *Banking Supervision.* London: HMSO. [Cmnd. 9695].

Hollingsworth, J. Rogers, Schmitter, Philippe C., and Streeck, Wolfgang (1994). 'Capitalism, Sectors, Institutions, and Performance', in J. Rogers Hollingsworth, Philippe C. Schmitter, and Wolfgang Streeck (eds.), *Governing Capitalist Economies.* New York, Oxford: Oxford University Press, pp. 3–16.

Holm, Hans-Henrik and Sorensen, Georg (eds.) (1995). *Whose World Order? Uneven Globalization and the End of the Cold War.* Boulder, CO, San Francisco, Oxford: Westview.

House of Commons Treasury Committee (2008). The Run On the Rock. vol. 56-I, *HC 2007–08,* London: Stationery Office.

Hurrelmann, Achim, Leibfried, Stephan, Martens, Kerstin, and Mayer, Peter (eds.) (2007). *Transforming the Golden-age Nation State, Transformations of the State.* Basingstoke: Palgrave Macmillan.

Höpflinger, François (1984). 'Verbände', in Klöti (1984), pp. 163–88.

International Monetary Fund (2007). *Global Financial Stability Report: Market Developments and Issues.* Washington, D.C.: International Monetary Fund.

Jann, Werner (1989). 'Parlamente und Gesetzgebung. Akteure und Ressourcen der parlamentarischen Gesetzgebung im internationalen Vergleich'. Ph.D. thesis, Habilitationsschrift, Hochschule für Verwaltungswissenschaften, Speyer.

Jauß, Claudia (1999). *Politik als Verhandlungsmarathon. Immissionsschutz in der amerikanischen Wettbewerbsdemokratie.* Baden-Baden: Nomos.

Jegher, Annina (1999). *Bundesversammlung und Gesetzgebung. Der Einfluß von institutionellen, politischen und inhaltlichen Faktoren auf die Gesetzgebungstätigkeit der Eidgenössischen Räte.* Berne, Stuttgart, Wien: Haupt.

Jung, Joseph (2000). *Von der Schweizerischen Kreditanstalt zur Credit Suisse Group. Eine Bankengeschichte.* Zürich: NZZ Verlag.

Kagarlitsky, Boris and Clarke, Renfrey (1999). *New Realism, New Barbarism: Socialist Theory in the Era of Globalization. Recasting Marxism.* London: Pluto Press.

Kahler, Miles and Lake, David A. (eds.) (2006). Economic Integration and Global Governance: Why So Little Supranationalism?, Workshop on Explaining Global Regulation, University of Oxford, 20–21 October 2006.

Kalkstein, Heinz (1962). Die Arbeit des neuen Bundesaufsichtsamts für das Kreditwesen, in Mayschosser Gespräche 1962. Fachtagung für Leiter von Kreditgenossenschaften, Mayschoss, pp. 125–35.

Kapstein, Ethan B. (1992). 'Between Power and Purpose: Central Bankers and the Politics of Regulatory Convergence', *International Organization,* 46(1): 265–87.

—— (1994). *Governing the Global Economy. International Finance and the State.* Cambridge (MA), London: Harvard University Press.

Kareken, John H. (1992). 'Regulation of Commercial Banking in the United States', in Newman et al. (1992), pp. 315–20.

Katzenstein, Peter J. (1985). *Small States in World Markets. Industrial Policy in Europe.* Ithaca, NY: Cornell University Press.

Kaufman, George G. (ed.) (1992). *Banking Structures in Major Countries.* Boston, MA, Dordrecht, London: Kluwer Academic Publishers.

——and Litan, Robert E. (1993). *Assessing Bank Reform: FDICIA One Year Later.* Washington D.C.: The Brookings Institution.

Kenyon, Daphne A. (1997). 'Theories of Interjurisdictional Competition', *New England Economic Review*, March/April 1997(2): 13–28.

Keohane, Robert O. and Nye, Joseph S. (1977). *Power and Interdependence: World Politics in Transition.* Boston, MA: Little Brown.

Kerr, Clark, Dunlop, J. T., Harbison, F., and Myers, C. A. (1960). *Industrialism and Industrial Man: The Problems of Labor and Management in Economic Growth.* Cambridge, MA: Harvard University Press.

Khademian, Anne M. (1996). *Checking On Banks. Autonomy and Accountability in Three Federal Agencies.* Washington D.C.: Brookings Institution Press.

Khoury, Sarkis Joseph (1997). *U.S. Banking and its Regulation in the Political Context.* Lanham, MD, New York, Oxford: University Press of America.

Kindleberger, Charles Poor (1987). *International Capital Movements: Based on the Marshall Lectures Given at the University of Cambridge 1985.* Cambridge: Cambridge University Press.

Kitschelt, Herbert, Lange, Peter, Marks, Gary, and Stephens, John D. (eds.) (1999). *Continuity and Change in Contemporary Capitalism.* Cambridge: Cambridge University Press.

Klein, Dietmar K. R. (1991). Die Bankensysteme der EG-Länder, vol. 99 of *Taschenbücher für Geld · Bank · Börse.* Frankfurt am Main: Knapp.

Kloten, Norbert and Stein, Johann Heinrich von (eds.) (1993). *Geld-, Bank- und Börsenwesen. Ein Handbuch.* Stuttgart: Schäffer-Poeschel, 39th edn.

Klöti, Ulrich (eds.) (1984). *Handbuch Politisches System der Schweiz. Band 2: Strukturen und Prozesse.* Berne, Stuttgart: Haupt.

Knapp, Joachim (1976). 'Die Novelle zum Kreditwesengesetz', *Neue Juristische Wochenschrift*, 29(20): 873–7.

Knill, Christoph (1998). 'European Policies: The Impact of National Administrative Traditions', *Journal of Public Policy*, 18(1): 1–28.

Knorr, Andreas (1999). 'Staatliche Bankenaufsicht—eine effiziente Institution?', *ORDO. Jahrbuch für die Ordnung von Wirtschaft und Gesellschaft*, 50: 345–69.

Kriesi, Hanspeter (2001). 'The Federal Parliament: The Limits of Institutional Reform', *West European Politics*, 24(2): 59–76. [= Special Issue on "The Swiss Labyrinth. Institutions, Outcomes and Redesign", editor Jan-Erik Lane].

Krugman, Paul (1991). 'History and Industry Location: The Case of the Manufacturing Belt', *American Economic Review*, 81: 80–3.

Kydland, Fin E. and Prescott, Edward C. (1977). 'Rules Rather than Discretion: The Inconsistency of Optimal Plans', *Journal of Political Economy*, 85(3): 472–91.

Lamfalussy, Alexandre (1985). 'The Changing Environment of Central Bank Policy', *American Economic Review*, 75(2): 409–13.

Landesbank Rheinland-Pfalz (ed.) (1983). *Banken. Erfahrungen und Lehren aus einem Vierteljahrhundert 1958–1983*. Frankfurt am Main: Knapp.

Lawson, Nigel (1992). *The View From No. 11. Memories of a Tory Radical*. London: Bantam.

Lawson, Stephanie (ed.) (2002). *The New Agenda for International Relations: From Polarization to Globalization in World Politics?* Cambridge: Polity.

Lehmbruch, Gerhard (1967). *Proporzdemokratie. Politisches System und politische Kultur in der Schweiz und Österreich*. Tübingen: J. C. B. Mohr (Paul Siebeck).

Lehner, Franz, Schubert, Klaus, and Geile, Brigitte (1983). 'Die strukturelle Rationalität regulativer Wirtschaftspolitik: Theoretische Überlegungen am Beispiel der Bankenpolitik in Kanada, der Bundesrepublik Deutschland, der Schweiz und den Vereinigten Staaten von Amerika', *Politische Vierteljahresschrift*, 24(4): 361–84.

Leibfried, Stephan and Zürn, Michael (eds.) (2005). *Transformations of the State?* Cambridge: Cambridge University Press.

Lijphart, Arend (1971). 'Comparative Politics and the Comparative Method', *American Political Science Review*, 65: 682–93.

—— (1999). *Patterns of Democracy. Government Forms and Performance in Thirty-Six Countries*. New Haven, CT, London: Yale University Press.

Linder, Wolf (1999). *Schweizerische Demokratie. Institutionen—Prozesse—Perspektiven*. Berne, Stuttgart, Wien: Haupt.

Lindgren, Carl-Johan, Garcia, Gillian, and Saal, Matthew I. (1996). *Bank Soundness and Macroeconomic Policy*. Washington D.C.: International Monetary Fund.

Lipset, Seymour Martin and Rokkan, Stein (1967). 'Cleavage Structures, Party Systems and Voter Alignments: An Introduction', in Seymour Martin Lipset and Stein Rokkan (eds.), *Party Systems and Voter Alignments*. New York: Free Press, pp. 1–64.

Llewellyn, David T. (1992). 'Competition, Diversification, and Structural Change in the British Financial System', in Kaufman (1992), pp. 429–68.

Longley, Lawrence D. and Davidson, Roger H. (eds.) (1998). *The New Roles of Parliamentary Committees*. London: Frank Cass. [= Special issue of *Journal of Legislative Studies*, Spring 1998].

Lowi, Theodore J. (1964). 'American Business, Public Policy, Case Studies, and Political Theory', *World Politics*, 16(4): 677–715.

Lüthi, Ruth (1997). *Die Legislativkommissionen der Schweizerischen Bundesversammlung. Institutionelle Veränderungen und das Verhalten von Parlamentsmitgliedern*. Berne, Stuttgart, Wien: Haupt.

—— (1999). 'Parlament', in Ulrich Klöti, Peter Knoepfel, Hanspeter Kriesi, Wolf Linder, and Yannis Papadopoulos (eds.), *Handbuch der Schweizer Politik. Manuel de la politique suisse*. Zürich: NZZ Verlag, 131–57.

Lutz, Benno (1995). 'Bankenaufsicht und Standort unter besonderer Berücksichtigung der Entwicklung in der Schweiz', in Volker H. Peemöller and Peter Uecker (eds.) *Standort Deutschland. Grundsatzfragen und aktuelle Perspektiven für die Besteuerung, die Prüfung und das Controlling*. Anton Heigl zum 65. Geburtstag Berlin: Erich Schmidt, pp. 471–82.

Lütz, Susanne (1999). 'Globalisierung und der regulative Umbau des "Modells Deutschland"—das Beispiel der Bankenregulierung', in Hans-Georg Brose and Helmut Voelzkow (eds.), *Globalisierung und institutioneller Wandel*. Metropolis, Marburg, pp. 205–30.

—— (2004). 'Convergence Within National Diversity: The Regulatory State in Finance', *Journal of Public Policy*, 24(2): 169–98.

Mach, André, Häusermann, Silja, and Papadopoulos, Yannis (2001). 'Changes in Decision-Making Processes and State Interventionism under External Pressure: Patterns of Liberalisation and Re-regulation in two sectors – the Case of Switzerland'. IEPI, Université de Lausanne. [= Paper presented for the 29th ECPR Joint Sessions of Workshops, 6–11 April 2001 in Grenoble, Workshop 20: *National Regulatory Reform in an Internationalised Environment*].

Majone, Giandomenico (1996). *Regulating Europe*. London, New York: Routledge.

March, James G., and Olsen, Johan P. (1989). *Rediscovering Institutions. The Organizational Basis of Politics*. New York: Free Press.

Mast, Hans J. (1974). 'Das schweizerische Bankwesen', in Regul and Wolf (1974), pp. 484–515.

Mayer, Helmut (1981). *Das Bundesaufsichtsamt für das Kreditwesen*. Düsseldorf: Droste.

McKenzie, George and Khalidi, Manzoor (1996). 'The Globalization of Banking and Financial Markets: The Challenge for European Regulators', *Journal of European Public Policy*, 3(4): 629–46.

Metcalfe, J. L. (1986). 'Self-Regulation, Crisis Management and Preventive Medicine: the Evolution of UK Bank Supervision', in Gardener (1986*b*), pp. 126–41.

Miller, Richard B. (1982). 'Conversations with the Reagan Regulators', *The Bankers Magazine*, 165(2): 34–49.

Moerland, Pieter W. (1995). 'Alternative Disciplinary Mechanisms in Different Corporate Systems', *Journal of Economic Behavior and Organization*, 26: 17–34.

Molyneux, Phil (1996). 'Banking and Financial Services', in Hussein Kassim and Anand Menon (eds.), *The European Union and National Industrial Policy*. London, New York: Routledge, pp. 247–66.

Monopolkommission (1976). *Mehr Wettbewerb ist möglich. Hauptgutachten 1973/1975*. Baden-Baden: Nomos.

Moran, Michael (1991). *The Politics of the Financial Services Revolution: The USA, UK and Japan*. Basingstoke: Macmillan.

Neely, Michelle Clark and Wheelock, David C. (1997). 'Why Does Bank Performance Vary Across States?', *Federal Reserve Bank of St. Louis Review*, 79: 27–40.

Newman, Peter, Milgate, Murray, and Eatwell, John (eds.) (1992). *The New Palgrave Dictionary of Money & Finance*. London: Macmillan.

Niethammer, Thomas (1990). *Die Ziele der Bankenaufsicht in der Bundesrepublik Deutschland. Das Verhältnis zwischen 'Gläubigerschutz' und 'Sicherung der Funktionsfähigkeit des Kreditwesens'*. Berlin: Duncker & Humblot.

Nolle, Daniel E. (1995). 'Banking Industry Consolidation: Past Changes and Implications for the Future', vol. 95-1 of *Economic & Policy Analysis Working Papers*, Washington D.C.: Office of the Comptroller of the Currency.

North, Douglass C. (1990). *Institutions, Institutional Change and Economic Performance*. Cambridge, New York: Cambridge University Press.

Norton, Philip (1998). 'Nascent Institutionalisation: Committees in the British Parliament', in Longley and Davidson (1998), pp. 143–62. [= Special issue of *Journal of Legislative Studies*, Spring 1998].

OCC [n.d.]. *Bank Regulation and Supervision*. Washington D.C.: Office of the Comptroller of the Currency.

OECD (1992). *Banks Under Stress*. Paris: Organisation for Economic Cooperation and Development.

—— (1996). *Globalisation of Industry*. Overview and Sector Reports. Paris: OECD.

Oertzen, Peter von, Ehmke, Horst, and Ehrenberg, Herbert (eds.) (1976). *Orientierungsrahmen '85*. Text und Diskussion. Bonn-Bad Godesberg: Neue Gesellschaft. Bearbeitet von Heiner Lindner.

Ohmae, Kenichi (1990). *The Borderless World. Power and Strategy in the Interlinked Economy*. London: Collins.

—— (1995). *The End of the Nation State: The Rise of Regional Economics*. London: HarperCollins.

Oleszek, Walter J. (1989). *Congressional Procedures and the Policy Process*. Washington D.C.: CQ Press, 3rd edn.

Pauly, Louis W. (1988). *Opening Financial Markets: Banking Politics on the Pacific Rim*. Ithaca, NY: Cornell University Press.

Pecchioli, Rinaldo M. (1987). *Prudential Supervision in Banking*. Paris: Organisation for Economic Co-operation and Development.

—— (1989). *Bankenaufsicht in den OECD-Ländern. Entwicklungen und Probleme*. Baden-Baden: Nomos.

Peek, Joe, Rosengren, Eric S., and Tootell, Geoffrey M. B. (1999). 'Is Bank Supervision Central to Central Banking?', vol. 99-7 of *Working Papers*. Boston, MA: Federal Reserve Bank of Boston.

Peele, Gillian (1995). *Governing the UK*. Oxford: Blackwell, 3rd edn.

Pensky, Max (2005). *Globalizing Critical Theory*. New Critical Theory. Lanham, MD, Oxford: Rowman & Littlefield.

Pérez, Sofía A. (2001). 'The Liberalization of Finance in Spain: From Interventionism to the Market', in Bovens et al. (2001), pp. 383–400.

Peters, B. Guy (1999). *American Public Policy: Promise and Performance*. New York, London: Chatham House Publishers, 5th edn.

Pierce, James L. (1977). 'The FINE Study', in *Journal of Money, Credit and Banking*, 9(4): 605–18.

Pierson, Paul (2000). 'Increasing Returns, Path Dependence, and the Study of Politics', *American Political Science Review*, 94(2): 251–67.

—— (2004). *Politics in Time: History, Institutions, and Social Analysis*. Princeton, NJ, Oxford: Princeton University Press.

Pohl, Manfred (1983). 'Die Entwicklung des privaten Bankwesens nach 1945. Die Kreditgenossenschaften nach 1945', in Aschhoff et al. (1983), pp. 205–76.

—— (1993). 'Die Entstehung und Entwicklung des Universalbankensystems seit der Mitte des 19. Jahrhunderts', in Kloten and Stein (1993), pp. 187–93.

Pierson, Paul (ed.) (1994). *Handbook on the History of European Banks*. Aldershot: Elgar.

Porter, Michael E. (1990). *The Competitive Advantage of Nations*. New York: Free Press.

—— (1992). 'Capital Disadvantage: America's Failing Capital Investment System', in *Harvard Business Review*, September–October 1992: 65–82.

Przeworski, Adam and Teune, Henry (1970). *The Logic of Comparative Social Inquiry*. New York, London, Toronto, Sidney: Wiley-Interscience.

Putnam, Robert D. (1993). *Making Democracy Work: Civic Traditions in Modern Italy*. Princeton: Princeton University Press.

Quinn, Brian (1993). 'The Bank of England's Role in Prudential Supervision', Bank of *England Quarterly Bulletin*, 33(May): 260–64.

Quinn, Dennis (1997). 'The Correlates of Change in International Financial Regulation', *American Political Science Review*, 91(3): 531–51.

Quintyn, Marc, Ramirez, Silvia, and Taylor, Michael (2007). 'The Fear of Freedom: Politicians and the Independence and Accountability of Financial Sector Supervisors', vol. 07/25 of *Working Papers*. Washington, D.C.: International Monetary Fund.

Regul, Rudolf and Wolf, Herbert (eds.) (1974). 'Das Bankwesen im größeren Europa', vol. 67 of *Schriftenreihe Europäische Wirtschaft*. Baden-Baden: Nomos.

Reid, Margaret (1982). *The Secondary Banking Crisis, 1973–75. Its Causes and Course*. London, Basingstoke: Macmillan.

—— (1986). 'Lessons for Bank Supervision from the Secondary-Banking Crises', in Gardener (1986*b*), pp. 99–108.

—— (1988). *All-Change in the City: The Revolution in Britain's Financial Sector*. Basingstoke: Macmillan.

Rein, Martin and Schön, Donald A. (1993). 'Reframing Policy Discourse', in Frank Fischer and John Forester (eds.), *The Argumentative Turn in Policy Analysis and Planning*. Durham, London: Duke University Press, pp. 145–66.

Reinhard, Wolfgang (1999). *Geschichte der Staatsgewalt. Eine vergleichende Verfassungsgeschichte Europas von den Anfängen bis zur Gegenwart*. München: Beck.

Reinicke, Wolfgang (1995). *Banking, Politics and Global Finance. American Commercial Banks and Regulatory Change 1980–1990*. Aldershot: Elgar.

Rhodes, Martin and Apeldoorn, Bastiaan van (1997). 'Capitalism versus Capitalism in Western Europe', in Martin Rhodes, Paul Heywood, and Vincent Wright (ed.), *Developments in West European Politics*. Houndmills, Basingstoke, London: Macmillan, pp. 171–89.

Richardson, Jeremy J. (ed.) (1982). *Policy Styles in Western Europe*. Boston, MA: Allen & Unwin.

—— Gustafsson, Gunnel, and Jordan, Grant (1982). 'The Concept of Policy Style', in Richardson (1982), pp. 1–16.

Rieselbach, Leroy N. (1986). 'Congress and Policy Change: Issues, Answers, and Prospects', in Gerald C. Wright, Jr., Lervoy N. Rieselbach, and Lawrence C. Dodd (eds.), *Congress and Policy Change*. New York: Agathon Press, pp. 257–89.

Riklin, Alois and Möckli, Silvano (1991). 'Milizparlament?', in Parlamentsdienste ⟨Schweiz⟩ (ed.), *Das Parlament—Oberste Gewalt des Bundes?* Berne: Haupt, pp. 145–63.

—— and Ochsner, Alois (1984). 'Parlament', in Klöti (1984), pp. 77–115.

Ritzmann, Franz (1973). *Die Schweizer Banken. Geschichte—Theorie—Statistik.* Berne: Haupt.

Robertson, Ross M. (1995). *The Comptroller and Bank Supervision. A Historical Appraisal.* Washington D.C.: Office of the Comptroller of the Currency.

Rodrik, Dani (1997). *Has Globalization Gone Too Far?* Washington D.C.: Institute for International Economics.

Rogowski, Ronald (1987). 'Political Cleavages and Changing Exposure to Trade', *American Political Science Review*, 81(4): 1121–37.

—— (1989). *Commerce and Coalitions: How Trade Affects Domestic Political Alignments.* Princeton, NJ: Princeton University Press.

Rokkan, Stein (2000). *Staat, Nation und Demokratie in Europa.* Die Theorie Stein Rokkans aus seinen gesammelten Werken rekonstruiert und eingeleitet von Peter Flora. Frankfurt am Main: Suhrkamp.

Ronge, Volker (1979). *Bankpolitik im Spätkapitalismus: Politische Selbstverwaltung des Kapitals?* Frankfurt am Main: Suhrkamp.

Rosenau, James N. (ed.) (1967). *Domestic Sources of Foreign Policy.* New York: Free Press.

—— (1990). *Turbulence in World Politics. A Theory of Change and Continuity.* Princeton, NJ: Princeton University Press.

Rosenbluth, Frances and Schaap, Ross (2003). 'The Domestic Politics of Banking Regulation', *International Organization*, 57(2): 307–36.

Rupert, Mark and Solomon, M. Scott (2006). *Globalization and International Political Economy: The Politics of Alternative Futures.* Lanham: Rowman & Littlefield.

Sachverständigenrat zur Begutachtung der Gesamtwirtschaftlichen Entwicklung (2007). *Das Erreichte nicht verspielen.* Vol. 44 of *Jahresgutachten*, Wiesbaden: Statistisches Bundesamt.

Sally, Razeen (2000). 'Globalization and Policy Response: Three Perspectives', *Government & Opposition*, 35(2): 237–53.

Sassen, Saskia (1998). 'Zur Einbettung des Globalisierungsprozesses: Der Nationalstaat vor neuen Aufgaben', *Berliner Journal für Soziologie*, 8(3): 345–57.

Saunders, Anthony and Walter, Ingo (1994). *Universal Banking in the United States: What Could We Gain? What Could We Lose?* New York, Oxford: Oxford University Press.

Sauvé, Annie and Scheuer, Manfred (eds.) (1999). *Corporate Finance in Germany and France.* A Joint Research Project of the Deutsche Bundesbank and the Banque de France, Deutsche Bundesbank.

Savage, Michael, Bagnall, Gaynor, and Longhurst, Brian (2005). 'Globalization and Belonging', *Theory, Culture & Society*, London: Sage.

Schaberg, Marc (1999). *Globalization and the Erosion of National Financial Systems. Is Declining Autonomy Inevitable?* Cheltenham: Elgar.

Scharpf, Fritz W. (1996). 'Föderalismus und Demokratie in der Transnationalen Ökonomie'. in Klaus von Beyme and Claus Offe (eds.), *Politische Theorien in der Ära der Transformation*. Opladen: Westdeutscher Verlag, pp. 211–35. [= PVS Sonderheft 26].

——and Schmidt, Vivien A. (eds.) (2000). *Welfare and Work in the Open Economy. Volume II: Diverse Responses to Common Challenges*. Oxford: Oxford University Press.

Scheidl, Karl (1993). 'Die Geschäftsbanken', in Kloten and Stein (1993), pp. 216–58.

Schimansky, Herbert, Bunte, Hermann-Josef, and Lwowski, Hans-Jürgen (eds.) (1997). *Bankrechts-Handbuch*. München: Beck.

Schirm, Stefan A. (2002). *Globalization and the New Regionalism: Global Markets, Domestic Politics and Regional Co-operation*. Cambridge: Polity.

Schmidt, Manfred G. (1996). 'When Parties Matter: A Review of the Possibilities and Limits of Partisan Influence on Public Policy', *European Journal of Political Research*, 30: 155–83.

——(1978). *Praxis der Bankenaufsicht*. vol. 57 of *Taschenbücher für Geld · Bank · Börse*. Frankfurt am Main: Knapp.

Schneider, Uwe H., Böttger, Günter, and Uebe, Klaus (1980). *Das englische Bankgesetz 1979* (Banking Act 1979). Berlin: Duncker & Humblot.

Schön, Donald A. and Rein, Martin (1994). *Frame Reflection: Resolving Intractable Policy Issues*. New York: Basic Books.

Schultze-Kimmele, Horst-Dieter (1978). 'Von der informellen Beaufsichtigung zur gesetzlichen Reglementierung des britischen Kreditwesens', in *Österreichisches Bank Archiv*, 26(1): 22–31.

Schulze, Günther G. and Ursprung, Heinrich W. (1999). 'Globalisierung contra Nationalstaat? Ein Überblick über die empirische Evidenz', in Busch and Plümper (1999), pp. 41–89.

Schuppert, Gunnar Folke (1999). 'Zur notwendigen Neubestimmung der Staatsaufsicht im verantwortungsteilenden Verwaltungsstaat', in Gunnar Folke Schuppert (ed.), *Jenseits von Privatisierung und 'schlankem' Staat*. Verantwortungsteilung als Schlüsselbegriff eines sich verändernden Verhältnisses von öffentlichem und privatem Sektor. Baden-Baden: Nomos, pp. 299–329.

Schuster, Leo (1988). 'Deregulierung im schweizerischen Bankwesen', *Die Bank* (2): 75–7.

Schweizerische Bankiervereinigung (1983). 'Vernehmlassung zur Revision des Bankengesetzes'. Basel: Schweizerische Bankiervereinigung.

——(1993). Vereinbarung über den Einlegerschutz bei zwangsvollstreckungsrechtlicher Liquidation einer Bank vom 1. Juli 1993.

——(1998). Vereinbarung über die Standesregeln zur Sorgfaltspflicht der Banken (VSB 98) vom 28. Januar 1998.

——(1999). 87. Jahresbericht der Schweizerischen Bankiervereinigung über das Geschäftsjahr vom 1. April 1998 bis 31. März 1999, Basel: Schweizerische Bankiervereinigung.

—— (2000*a*). Der schweizerische Bankensektor: Entwicklung, Struktur und internationale Position, Basel: Schweizerische Bankiervereinigung.

—— (2000*b*). Der schweizerische Bankensektor in Zahlen, Basel: Schweizerische Bankiervereinigung.

Schweizerische Nationalbank (1999). 92. Geschäftsbericht 1999, Zürich und Bern: Schweizerische Nationalbank.

Schwintowski, Hans-Peter and Schäfer, Frank (1997). *Bankrecht. Commercial Banking—Investment Banking.* München: Heymanns.

Scott, Kenneth E. and Weingast, Barry R. (1992). *Banking reform: Economic Propellants, Political Impediments,* vol. 34, *Essays in Public Policy,* Stanford, CA: Hoover Institution.

Shell, Kurt L. (1990). 'Kongreß und Präsident', in Adams et al. (1990), pp. 303–38.

Shonfield, Andrew (1965). *Modern Capitalism. The Changing Balance of Public and Private Power.* London, New York, Toronto: Oxford University Press.

Simmons, Beth (1999). 'The Internationalization of Capital', in Kitschelt et al. (1999), pp. 36–69.

Soskice, David (1999). 'Divergent Production Regimes: Coordinated and Uncoordinated Market Economies in the 1980s and 1990s', in Kitschelt et al. (1999), pp. 101–34.

Spahn, P. Bernd (1990). 'Verfassung der Geld- und Kapitalmärkte', in Adams et al. (1990), pp. 590–601.

Spong, Kenneth (1994). *Banking Regulation. Its Purposes, Implementation, and Effects.* Kansas City: Federal Reserve Bank of Kansas City, 4th edn.

Steffani, Winfried (1983). 'Zur Unterscheidung parlamentarischer und präsidentieller Regierungssysteme', *Zeitschrift für Parlamentsfragen,* 14(3): 390–401.

—— (1992). 'Parlamentarisches und präsidentielles Regierungssystem', in Manfred G. Schmidt (ed.), *Die westlichen Länder* [= *Lexikon der Politik,* edited by Dieter Nohlen, Vol. 3]. München: Beck, pp. 288–95.

Story, Jonathan and Walter, Ingo (1997). *Political Economy of Financial Integration in Europe: The Battle of the Systems.* Manchester: Manchester University Press.

Strange, Susan (1986). *Casino Capitalism.* Oxford: Blackwell.

—— (1995). 'The Limits of Politics', *Government and Opposition,* 30(3): 291–311.

—— (1996). *The Retreat of the State: The Diffusion of Power in the World Economy.* Cambridge: Cambridge University Press.

Streeck, Wolfgang (1995). *German Capitalism: Does It Exist? Can It Survive?* Vol. 95/5 of MPIfG Discussion Papers. Köln: Max-Planck-Institut für Gesellschaftsforschung.

—— and Schmitter, Philippe C. (eds.) (1985). *Private Interest Government.* London: Sage.

Strøm, Kaare (1998). 'Parliamentary Committees in European Democracies', in Longley and Davidson (1998), pp. 21–59. [= Special issue of *Journal of Legislative Studies,* Spring 1998].

Studienkommission Grundsatzfragen der Kreditwirtschaft (1979). 'Bericht der Studienkommission "Grundsatzfragen der Kreditwirtschaft" ', vol. 28 of *Schriftenreihe des Bundesministeriums der Finanzen.* Bonn: Bundesministerium der Finanzen.

Swank, Duane (2002). *Global Capital, Political Institutions, and Policy Change in Developed Welfare States*, Cambridge Studies in Comparative Politics. Cambridge: Cambridge University Press.

Swary, Itzhak and Topf, Barry (1992). *Global Financial Deregulation: Commercial Banking at the Crossroads*. Cambridge, MA, Oxford: Blackwell.

Task Group on Regulation of Financial Services (1984). *Report: Blueprint for Reform*. Washington D.C.: U.S. Government Printing Office.

Terberger-Stoy, Eva (2000). 'Bankenaufsicht und Asienkrise', in Renate Schubert (ed.), *Ursachen und Therapien regionaler Entwicklungskrisen—Das Beispiel der Asienkrise*. Duncker & Humblot, pp. 91–115.

Teune, Henry (1990). 'Comparing Countries: Lessons Learned', in Else Øyen (ed.), *Comparative Methodology. Theory and Practice in International Social Research*. London: Sage, pp. 38–62.

Thatcher, Mark (1998). 'The Development of Policy Network Analyses. From Modest Origins to Overarching Frameworks', in *Journal of Theoretical Politics*, 10(4): 389–416.

The Economist (1993). 'Too many pies for the Old Lady', *The Economist*, 28th August 1993, pp. 67–8.

Thelen, Kathleen (1999). 'Historical Institutionalism in Comparative Perspective', *Annual Review of Political Science*, 2, pp. 369–404.

Thelen, Kathleen Ann (2004). *How Institutions Evolve: The Political Economy of Skills in Germany, Britain, the United States, and Japan*, Cambridge studies in Comparative Politics. Cambridge: Cambridge University Press.

Tickell, Adam (1996). 'Making a Melodrama Out of a Crisis: Reinterpreting the Collapse of Barings Bank', *Environment and Planning D: Society and Space*, 14(1): 5–33.

—— (2001). 'The Transformation of Financial Regulation in the United Kingdom: the Barings Case', in Bovens et al. (2001): 419–36.

Tilly, Richard H. (1990). *Vom Zollverein zum Industriestaat. Die wirtschaftlich-soziale Entwicklung Deutschlands 1834 bis 1914*. München: dtv.

—— (1994). 'A Short History of the German Banking System', in Pohl (1994), pp. 299–312.

Tranøy, Bent Sofus (2001). 'The Swedish Financial Sector, 1985–92: Policy-Assisted Boom, Bust and Rescue', in Bovens et al. (2001), pp. 401–18.

Treasury Select Committee (1996). *Barings Bank and International Regulation*. London: HMSO. [HC 65-I und II].

Tsebelis, George (1995). 'Decision Making in Political Systems: Veto Players in Presidentialism, Parliamentarism, Multicameralism and Multipartyism', *British Journal of Political Science*, 25(3): 289–325.

Underhill, Geoffrey R.D. (1991). 'Markets Beyond Politics? The State and the Internationalisation of Financial Markets', *European Journal of Political Research*, 19(2–3): 197–225.

United States Department of the Treasury (1991). *Modernizing the Financial System: Recommendations for Safer, More Competitive Banks*. Washington D.C.: Department of the Treasury.

Valdez, Stephen (1993). *An Introduction to Western Financial Markets*. Houndsmill, Basingstoke, London: Macmillan.

Vernon, Raymond, Spar, Deborah L., and Tobin, Glen (1991). *Iron Triangles and Revolving Doors: Cases in U.S. Foreign Economic Policymaking*. New York, Westport, CT, London: Praeger.

Vogel, David (1986). *National Styles of Regulation: Environmental Policy in Great Britain and the United States*. Ithaca, NY: Cornell University Press.

——(1995). *Trading Up: Consumer and Environmental Regulation in a Global Economy*. Cambridge, MA: Harvard University Press.

Vogel, Steven K. (1996). *Freer markets, More rules. Regulatory Reform in Advanced Industrial Countries*. Ithaca, NY: Cornell University Press.

Vogler, Robert Urs (2000). 'Das Bankgeheimnis—seine Genese im politisch-wirtschaftlichen Umfeld', *Schweizer Monatshefte*, 80(3): 37–43.

Waarden, Frans van (1993). 'Über die Beständigkeit nationaler Politikstile und Politiknetzwerke. Eine Studie über die Genese ihrer institutionellen Verankerung', in Roland Czada and Manfred G. Schmidt (eds.), *Verhandlungsdemokratie, Interessenvermittlung, Regierbarkeit*. Festschrift für Gerhard Lehmbruch. Opladen: Westdeutscher Verlag, pp. 191–212.

——(1995). 'Persistence of National Policy Styles: A Study of Their Institutional Foundations', in Brigitte Unger and Frans van Waarden (eds.), *Convergence or Diversity? Internationalization and Economic Policy Response*. Aldershot: Ashgate, pp. 333–72.

Wagner, Kurt (1976). *Stationen deutscher Bankgeschichte: 75 Jahre Bankenverband*, Köln: Bank-Verlag.

Walsh, Carl E. (1995). 'Optimal Contracts for Central Bankers', *The American Economic Review*, 85(1): 150–67.

Waschbusch, Gerd (2000). *Bankenaufsicht. Die Überwachung der Kreditinstitute und Finanzdienstleistungsinstitute nach dem Gesetz über das Kreditwesen*. München, Wien: Oldenbourg.

Waters, Malcolm (1995). *Globalization*. London: Routledge.

Wehler, Hans-Ulrich (1995). *Deutsche Gesellschaftsgeschichte. Band 3: Von der 'Deutschen Doppelrevolution' bis zum Beginn des Ersten Weltkrieges: 1849–1914*, München: Beck.

Weiss, Linda (1998). *The Myth of the Powerless State*. Ithaca, NY: Cornell University Press.

Williamson, Oliver E. (1994). 'Transaction Cost Economics and Organization Theory', in Neil J. Smelser and Richard Swedberg (eds.), *The Handbook of Economic Sociology*. Princeton: Princeton University Press, pp. 76–107.

Winter, Wolfgang (1977). 'Im Jahr 1 nach Chiasso', *Die Bank* (7–8): 13–16.

World Bank (2007). *Global Economic Prospects: Managing the Next Wave of Globalization*. Washington, D.C.: World Bank.

Worsham, Jeffrey (1997). *Other People's Money: Policy Change, Congress, and Bank Regulation*. Boulder, CO: Westview Press.

Zimmer, Klaus (1993). *Bankenregulierung: Zur Begründung und Ausgestaltung der Einlagensicherung. Eine ordnungstheoretische Analyse auf der Grundlage der Modernen*

Institutionenökonomie, vol. 26 of *Studien zum Bank- und Börsenrecht*. Baden-Baden: Nomos.

Zimmermann, Heinz and Barbrock, Vera (1993). 'Einlagenversicherung—aus ökonomischer Sicht', in Gehrig and Schwander (1993), pp. 261–302.

Zimmermann, Rolf (1987). *Volksbank oder Aktienbank? Parlamentsdebatten, Referendum und zunehmende Verbandsmacht beim Streit um die Nationalbankgründung, 1891–1905*. Zürich: Chronos.

Zysman, John (1983). *Governments, Markets and Growth: Financial Systems and the Politics of Industrial Change*. Ithaca, NY: Cornell University Press.

—— (1994). 'How Institutions Create Historically Rooted Trajectories of Growth', in *Industrial and Corporate Change*, 3(1): 243–83.

Zürn, Michael (2002). 'From Interdependence to Globalization', in Walter Carlsnaes, Thomas Risse and Beth A. Simmons (eds.), *Handbook of International Relations*. London: Sage, pp. 235–54.

Index

A. Schaafhausenscher Bankverein 77
American Bankers Association (ABA) 47
America's Community Bankers (ACB) 48
Anglo-Saxon capitalism 224–6
Apel, Hans 102, 106
Arthur Andersen & Co. 152, 160
Association of Bank Holding Companies 48
Association of Reserve City Bankers 48

BAKred 85, 95–7, 102, 105–6, 108, 114–15,
    119–20, 122, 232
BaFin 232, 253–4
Bank für Handel und Industrie 77
Bank Holding Company Act of 1956 41
Bank Leu 166, 178
Bank of England 124, 128–30, 132, 136–9,
    142–5, 147, 150, 153, 158, 161, 216,
    232, 250
Bank of Credit and Commerce International
    (BCCI) 149–50
Bank of the United States 37
Bankengesetz 174, 185–6, 196–7
Bankers Association of Foreign Trade 48
Banking Act (1979) 145
Banking Act (1987) 149
banking crises 30–1, 218
    Germany 79, 81, 83, 100, 120–1
    Switzerland 168–9, 202–5
    United Kingdom 129, 141–4, 146–7,
        149–50, 151–2
    USA 36, 38, 40, 44, 65
banking regulation as a policy field 13–15
banking regulation 26–31
    asymmetric information 24–5
    goals 26
    instruments 26–7
    new challenges 29–31
    theoretical justification 25–6
banking sector characteristics 23–8
Banque Cantonale Vaudoise 166
Banque Générale Suisse 166
Barclays Bank 127, 128, 249
Barings Bank 126, 129, 151–2
Baring Futures Singapore 151
Basel Committee 19, 196, 229–30, 239, 255
Basel II (see Basel Committee)

Bear Stearns 245, 248, 249
Bingham, Lord Justice 150
Bingham Report 150
Board of Banking Supervision (BoBS) 148,
    150, 152
Bretton Woods System 28, 37, 240
British Bankers Association (BBA) 134
British Merchant Banking and Securities
    Houses Association 134
Building Societies Association (BSA) 134
Bundesanstalt für
    Finanzdienstleistungsaufsicht
    (see BaFin)
Bundesaufsichtsamt für das Kreditwesen
    (see BAKred)
Bundesbank 96–7, 100, 102, 105, 108, 122
Bundesverband der Deutschen Volksbanken
    und Raiffeisenbanken (BVR) 93, 102
Bundesverband deutscher Banken (BdB) 88,
    93, 101, 102, 104, 108
Bundesverband Öffentlicher Banken
    Deutschlands (VÖB) 93

Capital controls 28–9
Chiasso Scandal 208
Citigroup 248–9
Coalition of Regional Banking and Economic
    Development 48
Commercial Bank of Scotland 125
Commerzbank 81
Committee of London and Scottish Bankers
    (CLSB) 134
Community Reinvestment Act 41, 69
Competition and Credit Control (CCC) 132,
    142–3
Conference of State Bank Supervisors
    (CSBS) 51
Consumer Bankers' Association 48
Continental Illinois National Bank 61
convergence (see policy convergence)
Coordinated Market Economies 224–6
Crédit Mobilier 77, 166

D'Amato, Alfonse 199–200
Darling, Alistair 253
Darmstädter und Nationalbank 81

deposit protection 25
Depository Institutions Deregulation
    Committee 70
Depository Institutions Deregulation and
    Monetary Control Act (DIDMCA) 58
Deutsche Bank 81, 251
Deutscher Sparkassen- und Giroverband
    (DSGV) 93, 102
Dingell, John 64, 71
divergence (*see* policy divergence)
Dresdner Bank 81
dynamic inconsistency 240

Eidgenössische Bankenkommission
    (EBK) 174, 185–8, 191, 202, 205,
    210, 254
Euromarkets 132, 138, 191
European Central Bank (ECB) 250
European Economic Area 209
European integration 223

FDIC 41, 51, 52, 56, 60, 65
Federal Deposit Insurance Corporation
    (*see* FDIC)
Federal Finance Ministry (BMF) 97, 114
Federal Financial Institutions Examination
    Council (FFIEC) 51, 70
Federal Reserve Bank (*see* Federal Reserve
    System)
Federal Reserve System 39, 41, 50, 52, 60, 63,
    250, 251
    reinterpretation of Glass–Steagall
    Act 63–4, 66
federalism 221
Financial Institutions Reform, Recovery and
    Enforcement Act (FIRREA) 65
Financial Services and Markets Act 2000
    155
Financial Services Authority (FSA) 155–6
Financial Services Modernization Act 67
Financial Services Roundtable 48
FINE report 56
Franklin National Bank 100
free banking 35, 37, 38

George, Eddy 137
Germany
    banking enquiry 1908/9 82
    banking regulation
        influence of associations 84, 98–9,
        108–9, 114–15
        interest rate liberalization 85, 88
        legislative responsibility 97–9

politicisation 117–18
    state capacity 121
    banking system 76–8, 91–3
        associations 80, 93–4
        credit unions 79
        Sparkassen 78–9
    banks and industry 80, 86–7, 90–1
        deposit protection 82, 88–9, 101, 103–6
Glauber, Robert 66
globalization 2–4
    academic debate 4–5, 241–3
    consequences 6–11, 227–8
    definitions 3
Goldman Sachs 251

Heckscher–Ohlin theorem 8
Herstatt Bank 100–1, 116, 118, 238
Hessische Landesbank (HeLaBa) 101
Hilferding, Rudolf 80
Hintze, Otto 1
historical institutionalism 235–8
HSBC 157

IKB Deutsche Industriebank 247
Independent Bankers' Association of America
    (IBAA) 47, 65
Independent Community Bankers of America
    (ICBA) 47
interstate banking ban 36

Johnson Matthey Bankers (JMB) 146–7

Kantonalbank Bern 166, 170, 203
Kreditwesengesetz (KWG) 75, 84, 85, 88,
    94, 97–8, 102, 106, 110, 111–19,
    121–2

Lawson, Nigel 147, 152
Lazard's 136
Leeson, Nick 151
Leigh-Pemberton, Robin 137, 147
lender of last resort 38, 100, 187
Liberal Market Economies 224–6
Liquiditäts-Konsortialbank GmbH
    (LiKo-Bank) 101–2
Lloyds Bank 127
London & Westminster Bank 125

market economy
    typologies 16
Matthöfer, Hans 110
Merrill Lynch 248–9
Midland Bank 127

Monopolkommission 90
moral hazard 25, 69, 103–4, 204, 206
mortgage-backed securities 246

National Currency Act of 1863 35, 38
National Bank Act of 1864 35, 38, 39
National Bankers' Association 48
National Provincial Bank 127
National Westminster Bank 127
Northern Rock 247–8, 253

OCC 35, 38, 39, 41, 49–50, 52, 56, 60
Office of the Controller of the Currency
    (*see* OCC)
Offshore markets (*see* Euromarkets)
Online Banking Association (OBA) 48
Orientierungsrahmen '85 90

parliamentarism vs. presidentialism 221
party systems 222
path dependence 10–11, 72, 234–8,
    242
Peel Banking Act (1844) 128–9, 136
Pfalz-Kredit-Bank 107
policy convergence 7–9, 227–34
policy divergence 9–11, 227–34
policy style 10, 223–4
    Germany 113–15
    Switzerland 206–8
    United Kingdom 158–9, 160
    USA 68–9
policy network 10, 45, 217–19, 235
power of the banks 109, 117–18
private interest government 215
Price Waterhouse 149
Proxmire, Senator William 62, 63

Radcliffe Committee 137
RATE system 153
rating agencies 246, 252, 255
Regulation Q 59
regulatory arbitrage 215
regulatory capture 153
regulatory policy 13
Reichsbank 81
Reichsgesetz über das Kreditwesen
    (*see* Kreditwesengesetz)
Resolution Trust Corporation (RTC) 70
Rhenish capitalism 224–6
Riegle-Neal Interstate Banking and Branching
    Efficiency Act 67
Riksbank 124
Rogowski, Ronald 8

Sanio, Jochen 116–17
Savings & Loans 57–9, 62, 65
Schweizer Verband der Raiffeisenkassen 182
Schweizerische Bankgesellschaft 166, 178,
    200
Schweizerische Kreditanstalt 166, 178, 199
Schweizerische Nationalbank 171, 173, 181,
    187–8, 191, 201
Schweizerische Volksbank 166, 178
Schweizerischer Bankverein 166, 178, 200
Schweizerische Bankiervereinigung (SBVg)
    173, 179–83, 183–5, 187, 192, 201,
    208
Securities and Investment Board (SIB) 155
securitisation 252
Spar- und Leihkasse Thun 202–3, 210
self-regulation 214
state
    capacity 6–7, 241–3
    classical definition 1
Stolper–Samuelson theorem 8
Studienkommission Grundsatzfragen der
    Kreditwirtschaft 108–10
    report 109
subprime mortgage crisis 245–52
Swisslex 223, 230
Switzerland
    Autonomous Convergence 208–9
    banking confidentiality 177, 193–5,
        198–200
    banking initiative 193–5
    banking regulation 169, 172–6, 195
        influence of associations 184–5, 187
        legislative responsibility 189
        politicization 167, 192–4, 197, 205,
            210–11
        role of auditors 187
        self regulation 183–4, 192, 196, 208
        special state of cantonal banks 186
        state capacity 211
    banking system 164–9, 177
        associations 179
        banks and industry 166
        cartel of conditions 200–2
        consolidation 178
        liberalization 201
        Sparkassen 165–6
    Chiasso Scandal 191–3, 238
    deposit protection 174, 202–3, 206
    European Economic Area (EEA) 197–8,
        201, 209
    revaluation 176
    Swisslex 197

Theories of interjurisdictional
    competition 8–9
Theory of international trade 7–8
Treasury 139
    relationship with Bank of England 147,
        148
Treasury and Civil Service Select
    Committee 150, 153

United Banks of Switzerland (UBS) 178, 248,
    254
United Kingdom
    banking regulation 128, 141–2, 144–5, 155
        influence of associations 135
        legislative responsibility 140–1, 159–60
        state capacity 160
    banking system 124–8, 133–4
        associations 134, 135
        building societies 133
        interest rate cartel 131, 143
        joint-stock banks 125
        savings banks 126
        secondary banks 143–5
        separation of commercial and
            investment banking 126–7, 130–1
    banks and industry 126–7
    City 123, 132, 137, 138, 139, 146, 147,
        151, 157
    credit allocation 131
    deposit protection 146
    interest rate liberalisation 132, 143
    secondary banking crisis 144
universal banking 77, 109, 127, 128, 168
USA
    banking regulation
        Brady Plan 65
        Glass–Steagall Act 40, 59, 60, 63, 64,
            66, 67
        legal framework 55

legislative process 70–1
policy goals 68
politicization 42, 67–8
regulatory competition 52–4, 69–70
reform proposals 55–6
Savings & Loans deregulation 57–9, 238
state capacity 73
banking system 34–7, 45–7
    challenges 43, 62
deposit protection (*see* FDIC)
New Deal Legislation (*see* Glass–Steagall
    Act)

varieties of capitalism 21, 236, 237
Verband der Auslandsbanken in der
    Schweiz 182
Verband Deutscher Hypothekenbanken
    (VDH) 93
Verband Schweizer Regionalbanken 181–2
Verband Schweizerischer Kantonalbanken
    180–1
Verband Schweizerischer Kreditbanken und
    Finanzierungsinstitute 182
Vereinigung schweizerischer Handels- und
    Verwaltungsbanken 182
Vereinigung schweizerischer Privatbankiers
    182
veto players 216
Volcker, Paul 63
Vollmer, Peter 206

Wagner, Adolph 82
Weber, Max 1
Westminster Bank 127

Zentraler Kreditausschuß (ZKA) 93, 98, 114,
    120
Zimmerli, Ulrich 205
Zürcher Kantonalbank 167